HOW TO PUBLISH
YOUR ARTICLES

SHIRLEY
KAWA-JUMP

SQUAREONE
WRITERS GUIDES

Cover Designer: Phaedra Mastrocola
Typesetter: Gary A. Rosenberg
In-House Editor: Joanne Abrams
Printer: Paragon Press, Honesdale, PA

Square One Publishers
Garden City Park, NY 11040
(516) 535-2010
www.squareonepublishers.com

The article on pages 260 to 261 originally appeared in the Nov. 15, 1999, issue of the Cincinnati *Business Courier.* Reprinted by permission.

Library of Congress Cataloging-in-Publication Data

Kawa-Jump, Shirley.
    How to publish your articles : a complete guide to making the right publication say yes / Shirley Kawa-Jump.
        p.cm — (Square One writers guide)
Includes index.
    ISBN 0-7570-0016-9 (Paperback)
    1. Journalism—Authorship—Marketing. I. Title. II. Series.
    PN147.K38 2002
    808'.06607—dc21
                                              2001003489

Printed in the United States of America

10   9   8   7   6   5   4   3   2   1

CONTENTS

ACKNOWLEDGMENTS

Many people made this book possible, simply by teaching me what they knew and helping me along my own career path. Countless editors, writers, and friends provided support and feedback when I needed it most. My parents provided the initial encouragement for my writing dream and set me on the path that brought me here today. For that, I thank them.

In addition, I'd like to thank the people who provided information for this book, voicing the advice writers need to hear.

I would also like to thank my support group of writer friends, both online and in person, who are there in an instant to cheer a success and cry over a setback.

And finally, a tremendous thank-you to my family—particularly my children and my husband, Jeff, who are the backbone of my life—for providing me with the strength and encouragement to pursue my dreams.

A NOTE ON GENDER

To avoid long and awkward phrasing within sentences, the publisher has chosen to alternate the use of male and female pronouns according to chapter. Therefore, when referring to the third-person writer, editor, or interview subject, odd-numbered chapters use male pronouns, while even-numbered chapters employ female pronouns, to give acknowledgment to writers, editors, and interviewees of both genders. Please realize that no offense or slight is intended.

$\mathcal{J}$NTRODUCTION

Get ready to achieve your goal, because you've already taken a big step toward it. Simply by picking up this book, you've moved closer to being published.

Whether you are a writer who is composing articles out of love for the written word or an academic striving to publish your research and conclusions, your objective is the same—to see your work in print and receive confirmation that you are an accomplished writer and/or an expert in your field. However, if you aren't already a part of the world of publishing, publication may seem like a dream that will never come true. You may be at a loss as to where your idea or already-written piece would fit. The quandary lies not so much in creating, but in knowing how to get from having written to having published.

It's not as hard as it may seem to realize your dream. Richard Bach, author of *Jonathan Livingston Seagull*, once said, "A professional writer is an amateur who didn't quit." Replace the word "professional" with "published," and you have the truth about the publishing industry in your hands. You can and will be published—if you don't give up at the first setback, and if you apply yourself to the task in a sensible, informed manner.

Whatever your goal is—publication in commercial magazines, academic journals, newspapers, or e-zines—*How to Publish Your Articles* provides the comprehensive, practical information you need to break into the world of print or online publication. The information

This book is designed to be the map that guides you through the publishing maze so that you can successfully reach your objective.

and advice presented in this book are the result of years of experience, as well as research into current industry data. As a freelancer for twenty-plus years, I have written and published more than 2,500 articles, working for more than 100 magazines, newspapers, and journals. I have been rejected (more times than I'd like to remember), and I have felt the joy of acceptance. I have been where you are now, and I know that it is possible to get your work into print.

The world of publishing is like a maze. It's easy to get lost or be confused by all the different terms and "rules" you encounter along the way. You could get bad directions or take a wrong turn and end up hitting a wall. This book is designed to be the map that guides you through that maze, arming you with the knowledge, skills, and confidence you need to reach your objective successfully.

How to Publish Your Articles is divided into three parts, each of which is designed to address the needs of writers at various stages in their publishing career, as well as the needs of people who are not working toward a writing career, but would simply like to get an article or two into print.

By covering the basics of the world of print publication, Part One provides important material for all writers, regardless of their specific objectives. Chapter 1 gives you a realistic view of the article market, helps you understand and define your goals, and directs your initial steps toward those goals. Then Chapter 2 breaks down the different markets and periodicals, and discusses how each works, as well as the kinds of material that each publishes. By the end of Part One, you should have a clearer idea of where you want to go and how you can best get there.

If you have already written an article and need to find a place to publish it, Part Two was designed specifically for you. Putting first things first, Chapter 3 guides you in defining your article's topic, approach, and audience. Once you have a full understanding of what your piece is and whom it addresses, you're ready for Chapter 4, which helps you use the many available resource materials to zone in on those publications that are the best match for your article. Chapter 5 assists you in the preparation of an effective submission package, and Chapter 6 guides you in using the Square One System, a step-by-step strategy for sending out your submissions in the most effective way possible. Finally, when the responses start rolling in, Chapter 7 helps you deal with them—whether the results are a much-longed-for contract, multiple acceptance letters, or a disappointing stack of rejection letters.

If you already have a few publishing credits under your belt, and want to move up the ladder into freelancing part- or full-time—or even if you have not made your first foray into print or online publishing, but feel that your talents are well suited to the profession—you will find that Part Three provides invaluable guidance. Chapter 8 teaches you how to develop great article ideas, tailor them to fit specific markets, and spin several ideas off of one to increase your potential for sales. Then Chapter 9 helps you write an effective query package—a package that will convince the editor not only that your idea is a good one, but that you're the right person to write the article. If you need a hand with the article-writing process, Chapter 10 is the place to go. It guides you from the lead to the conclusion, and enables you to recognize article elements that make editors happy. To help you make the most of every sale, Chapter 11 explains contract issues and discusses how you can preserve your rights throughout the negotiation process. And finally, Chapter 12 assists you in building your career. Should you choose part-time work or go full-time? Should you specialize in one area or write on a broad range of topics? How can you get your work into bigger publications? Chapter 12 will help you answer all of these questions, and will also look at other ways in which you can put your writing ability to use in order to maintain a steady income and gain valuable experience.

This book is filled with information, but you'll find that it's presented in an easy-to-read format that is designed to inform, not overwhelm you. Whether you are an academic looking for entry into respected journals, a writer who is serious about building a full-time career, or just someone with a love of writing who wants to get that occasional article into print, when you are finished reading *How to Publish Your Articles*, you will be well on your way to publication, strengthened by a solid understanding of how the markets work—an understanding that is essential for success.

When you see your words take shape beneath your pen or on your computer screen, it's an exciting process. But when you see those same words in a magazine, a newspaper, a journal, or an e-zine, the thrill is compounded. You're published!

To take yet another step toward your goal, just turn the page.

PART ONE

THE BASICS

Every writer—whether he dreams of getting a single article into print, launching a freelance career, or establishing himself in the world of academic journals—has to know certain basics or he'll waste his time channeling his efforts in the wrong direction. First, he has to acquire an understanding of his own goals. Then, he has to attain a grasp of the article market and how it works. That's what Part One is all about. Chapter 1 will help you understand and define your goals, and will direct your initial steps toward those goals. Then Chapter 2 will break down the different markets—including consumer magazines, trade journals, newspapers, e-outlets, academic publications, and more—and discuss how each works, as well as the kinds of material that each publishes.

In the following pages, you will:

■ Gain a practical understanding of the article marketplace and the world of freelance writing.

■ Examine what you want out of your writing so you can set realistic long-term and short-term goals.

■ Find out how several different writers realized their own goals.

■ Discover how to arrange a functional workspace.

■ Learn how to efficiently use your time.

■ Explore the many different article markets, including consumer magazines, trade journals, newspapers, academic publications, and e-outlets.

■ Pinpoint the markets that are the best match for your writing and your level of experience.

Whatever your dreams, whatever your goals, Part One will help you lay the necessary groundwork for your writing success.

CHAPTER 1

UNDERSTANDING YOUR GOALS

There's a simple fact in life: You can't get where you want to go if you don't have a destination clearly in mind, and you don't take the steps necessary to reach it. It would be senseless to get in your car and drive aimlessly for hours, only *hoping* that you'll end up in a place you'd like to be. And the same goes for your dream of publication. It would be a waste of time—yours and an editor's—to send pieces out here, there, and everywhere without first doing some homework. A talent for communicating with the written word is vital, yes, but it isn't all you need to be published. There are plenty of talented writers who have articles sitting in a drawer because they failed to prepare themselves for the journey ahead.

What does it mean to prepare yourself for the work ahead? First, it means being realistic about the marketplace. This will allow you to set goals that are truly achievable. Second, it means being realistic about what you want out of publication. This, too, will help you set reasonable goals, both for the short-term and for the long-term. It will also keep you from spinning in several different directions without much result. Finally, it means carving out the time and space needed to work toward your goals. In short, it means treating publishing like a job. By doing so, and by following the Square One System, you should soon see your words in print.

BE REALISTIC ABOUT THE MARKET

To be blunt, writing and selling articles is not a pursuit for the lazy or for those who see it as a road to fortune or fame. Competition is fierce, pay is low, and the chances of fame are slim.

Recently, Nancy DuVergne Smith conducted an interesting study for the National Writers Union (NWU). Called "The Freelance Writer's Lot," the survey found that 61 percent of writers worked full-time, but only 16 percent of them earned more than $30,000 a year from their writing. More than half worked outside the writing industry for additional income. Smith concluded that despite demand for their product, writers aren't treated very well economically. Even though this survey was completed several years ago, many of the facts uncovered in Smith's research still hold true, unfortunately.

If only the top freelancers earn more than $30,000 a year, what can the average writer expect to make? According to the NWU, the typical freelance writer makes $7,500 per year, working twenty-six hours a week on magazine articles and twelve hours per week on newspaper feature stories. Calculating the hourly wage on that much work would send most people scrambling for a job flipping hamburgers. Clearly, reasons other than money drive people to write and publish.

In the academic arena, pay for articles is almost nonexistent, and at some journals, it's the *writer* who pays to have his work published. The money goes to support the high cost of running and printing the journal. Only 5 percent of the academics surveyed by the NWU made more than $30,000 per year from their writing endeavors, and the average income drawn from publishing articles was around $4,000 per year.

As more and more websites pop up, the need for well-written content will also rise. Writers can expect the future of publishing to improve with this increasing demand.

However, there is some good news for the aspiring freelance writer. While recognizing that competition for writing jobs would continue to be great, the Bureau of Labor Statistics (BLS) predicted that the increased need for online content would spur demand for writers. "Employment of writers and editors is expected to increase faster than the average of all occupations through the year 2006," says the BLS.

You may not be looking for a career as a writer, but when the overall job picture is strong and healthy, that translates into better publishing opportunities for everyone. Higher demand for written products benefits writers across the board.

I haven't met anyone who makes a phenomenal living writing articles, but it is possible to slowly build a career in writing. While you are working your way through the ranks of publishing, however, it's probably wise to keep your day job so you can have the benefits of steady income and health insurance. Then achieve your writing successes one step at a time, building a solid reputation as you go. The fact is that many people *do* enjoy publishing success—although not all define success as a full-time career in freelance writing. While some writers seek to make their livelihood from writing, others aim for occasional publication in local newspapers, and still others hope to build a reputation in academia. Let's look at a few of their stories.

From Sunday School to *Woman's Day*

Kathryn Lay's career, which began in 1989, is a perfect example of how writers can work their way to the top. Kathryn started writing for religious publications, with her first sales coming from Sunday school take-home papers and a religious literary journal that a friend's mother had started. In the beginning, she worked full-time at another job and wrote only during her spare time.

Take publishing one step at a time. It is fine to set high goals, but realize that the course to achieving them is completed one writing credential at a time.

Since then, Kathryn has written for a wide variety of publications, including *Woman's Day*—one of the top markets. "It wasn't until I really started studying the larger magazines that I began seeing my bylines in those publications," she says. By researching each of the publications, Kathryn learned the style and tone of each one, and discovered which topics had been covered in the recent past, and which had not. She then created queries designed to meet the specific needs of the various markets.

Throughout her career, Kathryn has kept a constant round of articles and queries in the mail, and says she has never been afraid to query the top magazines. "My break with *Woman's Day* came through a query for one of their smaller sections. I developed a relationship with the editor and was then able to suggest bigger pieces."

"If you truly believe in an idea or piece, don't give up after one rejection," she advises. "I've had pieces sell on their first time out, others on their eighteenth or more. I've had pieces rejected from small magazines and later accepted by a much bigger magazine."

A work-at-home mother in Arlington, Texas, Kathryn home schools her daughter and writes part-time. She says that the Internet made the biggest impact on her career because of the vast amount of market information available and the speed of responses from editors.

From Term Papers to Academic Journals

When she became a teacher in the Department of Earth and Atmospheric Sciences at a state university, Karen Mohr was faced with making the transition from writing student term papers to writing for academic journals. Karen feels that the most important thing she learned was how to narrow her ideas and construct an article that would appeal to fellow scientists in her field, but still be readable by the entire audience of the targeted journal. "I had to learn to be selective in choosing the most important results to report, providing unambiguous graphs and diagrams to illustrate them, and making sure that any statements I made were clearly labeled as assumptions, speculation, or findings," she says.

Published in such notable publications as the *Journal of Applied Meteorology, Monthly Weather Review,* and the *Journal of Geophysical Research,* Karen uses non-refereed forums, such as conference preprints, to put together a first draft of her ideas and receive peer input. "They provide the criticism I need to improve my work and get it ready for formal (i.e., refereed) publication."

Over the years, Karen has built up a network of academic friends who offer criticism of her work at all stages of the project, providing valuable insight that helps her send thoroughly polished pieces out to journals. She says that rushing any step of the submission process can lead to an automatic rejection. "It takes time to understand the implications of your work, write a clear, concise manuscript, and have your peers comment on the first draft. If any of these steps is cut short, the possibility of rejection and the amount of time for revision go up astronomically."

A network of colleagues who provide feedback at all stages of the writing process can help you polish your academic article before you submit it to your target journals.

Grabbing the Editor With Humor

Bob Love, who lives in Long Island, New York, didn't start out to be a writer. In fact, he was first a caterer by trade. But when he retired from catering, he found himself with some time on his hands. He'd been friends with a publisher for more than twenty years, and had told his friend that he wanted to write. "Go to school, learn the vernacular, know the industry," Bob was told. He did. He took a few English and creative writing courses and then began writing.

"I started out just trying to string a thousand to two thousand words together, to see where I got with that," Bob recalls. He wrote a series of humorous essays that captured his own sardonic views on life, and sent them out to a number of different publications. "Finally, I found a niche with the local newspaper. The editor there found my sort of humor entertaining," says Bob.

All in all, he sold ten humorous essays to the newspaper and two to a Long Island magazine, on topics ranging from memories of a favorite greasy spoon to a remarkable Halloween night. "I was never looking for a career in writing. What I wanted was to see something I'd created in print, with my name on it."

Since then, Bob has dabbled in screenplay writing and been rejected once. He now works for his publisher friend, but as a job, not as a way to get further along in his writing venture. For Bob, the goal was always to have fun, not to become the next John Grisham. "I tell people who ask me about writing that they should go back to school, take some classes, and then sit down to write. They should start out writing just a couple thousand words with a beginning, middle, and an end, and then grow from there."

Breaking Into Health and Fitness Publications

Karen Asp was writing about paint chips and plastic bottles—and hating her job. A copywriter for an advertising agency, she kept imagining the day she'd be out on her own, writing what she wanted to.

Finally, one day in 1995, Karen decided she'd had enough, and walked away from her job to make the leap into freelance writing. "I didn't even know if I'd make it in this business," she says. "My dream was to write for magazines like *Shape* and *Fitness*. I wanted to combine my passion for writing with my passion for fitness."

In her first year, Karen studied resource books, wrote away for guidelines and sample copies of magazines, and subscribed to writers' magazines for market information. Then she started querying. "Stupidly, though, I sent to big magazines from the start. I didn't have the right clips and I certainly didn't have the experience. But I kept at it."

Working her way up through trade magazines for the fitness industry, she eventually broke into small consumer health and fitness

Freelancing offers many writers an opportunity to write about subjects that interest them for publications they love.

publications, both print and online editions. Her big break finally came, and she landed an assignment with *Shape* magazine. "Today, I bill myself as a health and fitness writer and no longer do I write about plastic bottles and paint chip cards. Instead, I write about all sorts of health and fitness issues for leading magazines like *Shape, Fitness, McCall's, Cooking Light, Walking,* and *Fit Pregnancy.* I also write about health and fitness for a slew of online magazines and contribute to health books."

Karen continues to work full-time at freelancing, and says that goal setting has gotten her to the point she is at today. "Three years ago, I made it a priority to send out three new queries a week, and I've never missed that goal. That means I have to spend lots of time thinking of new ideas and rehashing old ideas. But, it's paid off. I wouldn't be where I am today without having set that goal. That goal keeps me focused and forward-looking."

Writing About Children

From the start of her career, Jennifer Galvin, a Boston writer, has specialized in articles for and about children. Her first writing job was as a reporter for a local newspaper, covering school events. Taking a chance, she called the editor and pitched herself, offering to write her first article for free. Her first paid assignment was to go to the Upside Down Store in Boston and write, from a personal perspective, about the health effects of hanging upside down.

In addition, Jennifer joined an online critique/support group that offered feedback, hints, and tips on advancing her career. She says that the group provided the push she needed to keep going through the rejections.

Jennifer now writes a column for *The Boston Herald* called "Read and Play," which is featured in the print and online versions of the paper. Directed to parents, the column offers lessons and games designed to inspire fun and creativity. "I believe perseverance is the key to getting published. Start small, collect clips, and keep trying," she says.

The *Herald* column came about as a result of several past columns on similar subjects for online portals like *Moms Online.* The wait for the *Herald* editor to make the decision to carry the column was several months long, but was worth every ounce of Jennifer's patience.

"Aspiring writers need to have the ability to believe in themselves even when rejections start rolling in," she adds.

With three children at home, Jennifer writes part-time and says she is driven to write by passion, not financial reward. "The worst mistake a writer can make is not writing. If writing is in your heart, you need to write."

Establishing a Reputation in Academia

Soon after Lawrence K. Cormack landed a teaching position in the University of Texas' Department of Psychology, he realized that "publish or perish" was alive and well in his field, as in many other academic areas. He chose to specialize in one arena of his field to establish himself as an expert in that type of research, a necessity for advancement. "With rare exception, what universities want to see from a young person going up for tenure is a solid, coherent research program, and that means that the research should be fairly tightly focused," he says.

The biggest early hurdle for Lawrence was learning to master English and writing. "I spent most of my student life sleeping through English classes. Suddenly, it became clear that I should have been paying attention. Now, I always have a dictionary, a thesaurus, a basic English handbook covering grammar, punctuation, etc., and my beloved copy of *The Elements of Style* by Strunk and White."

Lawrence's work on depth perception, motion perception, and computational vision has been published entirely as chapters in edited scientific books or in refereed journals, including *Vision Research, Vision Neuroscience*, and the *Journal of the Optical Society of America*. He says that fear is the biggest obstacle in an academic's publishing career. "The cause of this [failure to get published] is almost always procrastination or fear of failure/criticism. It's very rare that an Assistant Professor who writes and submits a lot of papers, responds to reviewers' comments, and re-submits if necessary, doesn't get published. Usually, if they weren't good enough or bright enough, they wouldn't have gotten to an Assistant Professorship in the first place, so it is generally a matter of hard work."

Academic journals look for strong research and good writing. Be sure that both are demonstrated in all your submissions.

Each of the people profiled above worked hard to achieve their success. In addition, from the start, they all knew what they wanted and, for the most part, took appropriate steps to reach their objectives. The next section will help you understand the importance of examining your own goals and keeping them in mind as you chart your course toward publication.

BE REALISTIC ABOUT YOURSELF

Now you have a clearer picture of what the industry is really like, and you have some idea of what it takes to get articles into print. At this point, you need to take a good, hard look at yourself and understand your own motivations. Why do you want to be published? By answering this question, you will be able to set realistic long- and short-term goals, and to choose the right path toward publication—the one that will work best for you.

Why Do You Want to Be Published?

People write articles for a variety of reasons. Some want to share information. Some hope to build a reputation in their field. Some seek additional income. And some desire the validation that comes from seeing their work in print. By knowing your reason for seeking publication, you will be better able to set realistic goals.

Ask different writers why they want to be published, and you'll find that the answers are almost as varied as jellybean flavors. Some want to share information, possibly as a means of establishing a reputation in their field; some view writing as a source of income; and some simply want to receive validation that they are writers. Let's take a closer look at these aspirations.

You Want to Share Information

You may write because you have important things to say or teach others. Physicians, for example, write articles to inform their peers about advances in the medical field and, ultimately, benefit patients with new treatments. Academics, too, seek to share knowledge through publication, usually as a means of solidifying their tenure. And still others write not for their peers, but for people outside their field who may benefit from what they have learned. A teacher, for instance, may want to tell parents how they can motivate kids who have a lack of interest in their school work.

If your goal is to share information with others, you'll want to look for publications that deal with your subject and are able to reach your target audience. Are you addressing a general audience best reached through consumer publications, are you speaking to the readers of an academic journal, or is your audience comprised of professionals who read specific trade journals? An understanding of your reason for publishing will help you not only find the best publications for your work, but also tailor your article for your audience.

You Want to Make Money

You may seek to publish because you want the income that can come from selling articles. As discussed earlier in the chapter, if your motivation for selling articles is to get rich, it's time for a reality check. Few, if any, freelance writers make a fabulous living from selling articles. However, it is possible to supplement your current income with money earned from your writing, and to gradually build a career. Notice, though, that I said "gradually"; writing careers cannot be established overnight. Whether your goal is to generate supplementary income or to develop a full-time business, you have to be ready to start with smaller publications—or with smaller pieces in larger publications—and to work your way up through the ranks.

You Want Validation That You Are a Writer

Some writers simply want the validation that comes from seeing their work in print. They are not writing to build a reputation in their field or to generate income, but because they want to express their thoughts in the written word. When they see their work in print, it reaffirms their belief that they write well, and that their words have the power to provoke thought, to entertain, or to reach the heart of another person.

If you simply want to see your work in print, your search for a likely publication will be easier than it would be if your aim was to make money or to make a mark in the academic community. Local newspapers, small magazines, and electronic magazines may give you the ready forum for which you're looking. Chapter 2, which explores the article market, will guide you to the types of publications that are your best bet.

No matter which of the above profiles describes you, the end result of your efforts—a published article—will provide tangible proof that your work is valuable. Yes, rejection is an inevitable part of publishing, but acceptance is just as common. In the following

Understand and know your goals before you start so you aren't running in the wrong direction with no idea of your destination.

discussion, you'll see how the setting of realistic goals can help you bring about the results you seek.

What Are Your Goals?

The fact that you picked up this book shows that you dream of seeing your work in print—of seeing it published. While this dream can be enjoyable and even motivating, in order to make it come true, you have to establish specific goals, both long-term and short-term. By choosing long-term goals that are in line with your reason for seeking publication, and then setting and meeting realistic short-term goals, you will be able to maintain your motivation and realize your dream of seeing your work in print.

For example, if you are trying to build a career by writing articles for commercial business magazines—those available on newsstands—you might establish the long-term goal of selling an article to *Success* magazine. But to reach that level, you need to set several smaller goals that will take you sale by sale toward *Success*. Your first endeavors should be directed toward local business publications and smaller business-related journals.

That's not to say that you can't start submitting ideas and articles to *Success* from the start. It's fine to set lofty goals and to work toward them. Just be sure to temper those goals with a realistic understanding of the industry. Editors at high-level magazines tend to work with established writers who have a proven record of accomplishment. You can create one for yourself by starting at the lower levels and working your way up, article by article.

Don't give up at the first setback. There will be days when it seems that your long-term goals are unattainable. Slow down, and take it one step at a time. Small steps add up gradually to big leaps.

If you are an unpublished academic who is seeking to build a reputation, you probably have the long-term goal of seeing your articles printed in serious, respected journals that reach your desired audience—especially refereed journals, which accept only those articles that meet rigorous standards. In the short term, though, it would be wise to submit material to smaller journals and magazines, and maybe even online journals. This will both familiarize you with the editing and submissions process, and send the message to other editors that you are an accomplished writer.

Above all, don't expect anything to happen overnight. The publishing industry, both commercial and academic, doesn't move quickly. Newspapers and online e-zines are the only media that provide fast turnarounds and printing. When you are setting your short-term goals, remember that it can sometimes take weeks, even months, to get a response to a submission. While this is frustrating, it is the nature of the industry. Professional writers make room for these delays in their goal plans.

As with any job or skill, you work your way up to the top a little at a time. By breaking your goals into small, achievable steps, you can measure and track your progress. Once you have set your goals, Chapter 2 will help you find the direction in which you should target your efforts, and Parts Two and Three will assist you in putting that plan into motion.

THE WRITE STUFF

Mentally, you're prepared. You know where you want to go with your writing, and you have a basic idea of how you will get there. The road map, essentially, is laid. Now all you need is the vehicle to get you there. In other words, you have to provide both the physical space and the time needed to do your job.

If you're like most writers, you have a regular job and/or a family, both of which consume a great deal of time and energy. I freelance full-time out of my home office, and have two small children. Without a doubt, it is a challenge to write forty-plus hours a week, but I find that by being organized, dedicated, and creative, I can dig up hours I didn't realize I had. This section is designed to help you find the space and time you need to work toward *your* goals.

Where Will You Work?

Whether you are establishing a freelance writing career or simply trying to find a home for the article you have so painstakingly written, a functional workspace is a basic necessity. If you can't find your research, haven't seen a pen in days, and have lost your word processing software disks, it's going to be nearly impossible for you to do what needs to be done. A well-organized space is essential to success.

Fortunately, you don't need a whole room or an office suite to tend to the publication process, or even to take the first steps toward launching a new career. But you do need an area that has room for the basics—a desk, pens, paper, and a computer. There are several computer desks on the market that are small enough to fit in a closet or to

There are four time zones in the continental United States and then a fifth one, reserved especially for the publishing industry. Things move at a snail's pace in editorial offices because of the slew of submissions. Be patient, and take no news as good news.

Consider creating a mini-post office in a drawer or on a shelf. Buy a scale, a supply of stamps, different-sized envelopes, and return address labels. You can get a free postal rate card from the post office or check rates online at www.usps.gov. By having a post office at your fingertips, you can mail out queries and articles without leaving your office, saving time and reducing excuses for procrastination.

close up at the end of the day like an armoire. Add a few bookshelves and, if appropriate, a bulletin board for keeping track of assignments, and you've created a great workspace.

In addition to a place for writing, you'll need to establish a filing system to keep track of submissions and, perhaps, notes and interviews. Writers are said to be right-brained people who have trouble with left-brained activities like organization and accounting. If this describes you, and if you are interested in building a writing career, consider finding someone who is skilled in your weak areas. If you have a friend who has good administrative assistant skills, offer to baby-sit his children or treat him to dinner in exchange for a few hours of organizational help.

If you are simply trying to publish an article or two, you can get away with a small filing cabinet; a rollaway filing system; or, in a pinch, even a deep cardboard box and a stack of manila folders. But if you decide to build your writing into a business, you will want to archive your files after a year or so, keeping them for future reference or for the (very unlikely) chance of a libel suit. This will also protect you when you negotiate contracts and dispute copyright issues. (More on that in Chapter 11.) Besides your research information, you should save copies of all business and tax-related information, contracts, and response letters.

If and when you become serious about writing, you should have one large hanging file folder labeled with the title of each article and idea. Subdivide that with individual manila folders for notes, data, potential market information, and when it's done, a printed copy of the piece. Also save a version of your article on your computer or on a floppy disk, but don't rely solely on technology. While electronic records are easy to keep, paper records provide a reliable and tangible resource. If your computer goes down or you just need a quick piece of information, paper files are the easiest to access.

Keep a shelf of good resource books, both those that cover writing markets and those that deal with grammar and style issues. *The Chicago Manual of Style*, Strunk and White's *The Elements of Style*, and *The Associated Press Stylebook and Libel Manual* are valuable additions to any writer's shelf. And if you wish to pursue publication on a regular basis, you'll also want to have on hand several market resource books, like *Writer's Market*. These books, along with a dictionary and thesaurus, provide a great resource library. By looking in the Associated Press book, for example, you'll be able to find the proper spelling for "cha-cha" and whether to capitalize a title when it's used after a person's name. Most magazines and newspapers subscribe to either the Chicago or Associated Press style guidelines. Having these in front of you will ensure that your submission is in the proper format.

Be sure that your computer is ready, too. Although Internet access is not a must, it certainly is useful both for research and for sending articles to editors. While the traditional methods of library visits and post office mailings work, the Internet is fast becoming the best way to find and distribute information. You should also have a good word processing program that provides spelling and grammar checks as a fail-safe against your own mistakes.

If you are interested in beginning a writing career, and you have yet to buy a computer, consider a laptop. This will allow you to take your work anywhere you need to go, and to write in almost any size space. Set up a small portable office in your car by filling a plastic container with a little of everything you have in your regular office—pencils, pens, paper clips, and the like. When you are stuck in traffic or waiting for an appointment, you can use those few minutes to carve out an outline, jot down some ideas, or edit a piece. By setting up a good mobile space that is conducive to writing, you will make it that much easier to be productive and successful.

In addition, a printer with a built-in fax machine can save you a great deal of time and money. While it isn't essential, consider an all-in-one model. These machines offer printing, scanning, copying, and faxing, for not much more money than a print-only model.

Finally, have plenty of pens, printer paper, sticky notes, lined pads, and paperclips on hand. If you are prepared before you start the submission process, you will avoid wasting time as you run out to buy another ream of paper or another box of pens.

When Will You Work?

You have a goal in mind, and you have a space to work. Now all you need is a thirty-hour day that will let you meet all your usual commitments *and* pursue publication. Since that isn't possible, you need to carve time out of the twenty-four hours you already have.

Let's start by reviewing the basic steps you'll need to take to get published—essentially an overview of the Square One System for get-

If you're a paper-holic, there's a great book that can help you tackle your mountain of notes and get them organized. *File . . . Don't Pile!: For People Who Write: Handling the Paper Flow in the Workplace or Home Office,* by Pat Dorff, Edith Fine, and Judith Josephson, has tips on filing and organizing designed specifically for writers. The authors describe methods of attacking paperwork, and provide a system for storing research material, work in progress, ideas, business and tax information, and marketing suggestions. (See the Resource Directory on page 324.)

Are you a procrastinator? If you dream of getting your articles into print, but can never make yourself sit down and do the necessary work, you might find some much-needed help in *The Procrastinator's Handbook: Mastering the Art of Doing It Now*. (See the Resource Directory on page 326.) Written by Rita Emmett, this book is filled with tips for writers—and other people, too—who would rather do everything tomorrow. Plus, you'll find loads of inspirational quotes to get you back on track.

ting your articles into publication. First, you should read through this book, paying special attention to the sections that focus on your level of experience and your specific goals. Even if you don't feel that you want to make a career out of writing, it's advisable to read everything in this book so that you'll be familiar with different situations as they arise.

Then, you will need to decide who your target audience is—the group of people whom you believe will read your work. This, in turn, will enable you to choose the type of publication on which you should concentrate your efforts. You will need to spend a great deal of time studying publications and their competitors so you can thoroughly understand your potential market. Use resource books, the library, and the Internet to gather this information. Then, read the publications to which you would like to submit your articles to discover if your style and voice will complement what is already in the publications. Contact the publication for their submission guidelines, and study these to determine which doors are open to you as an outside submitter.

Next, you will put together your submission package. This should be done with great care, as the package will be your salesperson, traveling out into the world to sell your article to the targeted publications.

Finally, you will have to wait for the responses to your mailings. After sending out each batch of submissions, you can work on preparing the next batch. And, of course, if you are interested in a freelance writing career, you should be continuously developing new articles or ideas.

As you can see from this sketch of the Square One process, it takes time to work toward the goal of publication. Therefore, you should commit a few hours every week to your publishing endeavor. While you can do some work in little snippets, it's best to carve out two or three hours of uninterrupted time so you can concentrate on your goals. This will lead to steadier research and more consistent editing of your submission package.

If your life is so full of "musts" that it seems impossible to find time for your publishing efforts, try prioritizing all the various events and commitments on your schedule. If publishing articles is high on that list, then the time to pursue that goal must be, too. Find your most productive time of the day or week—whether it's early in the morning, late at night, or on the weekends—and commit that time to the submission process.

Getting published is mostly a matter of setting goals and devising ways to meet those goals in the midst of the other demands on your time. After you've carved out an office and some time, you'll be ready to actually get down to work.

CONCLUSION

You should now have a realistic view of the article publishing industry, and a firm grip on your goals and expectations. If you've made the time and space you need to pursue publication, you have set yourself up to be productive and efficient. Chapter 2 discusses the various types of publications open to you and the best ones to target. To begin working toward your goal, turn the page and start your research.

CHAPTER 2

UNDERSTANDING THE ARTICLE MARKET AND HOW IT WORKS

Look around you. There are publications everywhere you turn—at the newsstand, in the bookstore, in your mailbox, by the grocery checkout, and now at thousands of online portals. For every field, every interest, there is some type of publication, and possibly more than one. For the writer, that means there are many potential homes for her work.

The key is to understand each of these markets so you can direct your efforts toward publication efficiently. If you have previous writing credits, you can start at some of the higher-paying and more selective publications. If you are a new writer and you don't have any clips (copies) of published works to show to an editor, thus proving your writing abilities, you should look at smaller publications for entry into the market.

This chapter examines a wide range of publications, from consumer magazines, trade journals, newspapers, and newsletters, to electronic outlets and academic journals. In each case, you'll learn about the publication's general editorial structure, about the basic criteria it uses to review and determine the acceptability of each submission or query, and about the advantages and disadvantages of submitting material to that market. Thus, this chapter serves as a guide, steering you toward the most appropriate outlets for your articles—the outlets that will enable you to reach your goal of publication.

CONSUMER AND TRADE PUBLICATIONS

The broad category of consumer and trade publications includes consumer magazines, trade journals, newspapers, newsletters, and electronic outlets, sometimes referred to as e-outlets. In some cases, you'll find that a particular market—consumer magazines, for instance—can be further categorized as large, medium-sized, or small. As you'll see, the size of a publication does, to a large extent, determine the way it operates, and therefore the way it views and handles submissions and queries from new authors. By understanding the differences between these publications and targeting those that are the best match for you and your article, you can maximize your chance of getting your article into publication.

Consumer Magazines

The term *consumer magazine* is used to describe magazines that are available to readers on newsstands or through subscriptions. Some magazines address a broad audience, such as women, while others address a niche market, such as people interested in the history of a certain region. Thus, the magazine's focus generally affects its size and circulation, placing it in a specific category. As a new writer, your chances of getting your work published are better at the smaller magazines.

Large Consumer Magazines

These magazines are impossible to miss. Their shiny covers and blaring headlines can be seen in every supermarket, bookstore, and newsstand in the country. They are characterized by slick paper stock, a strong ratio of editorial content to advertising, and generally decent pay rates for writers.

Large consumer magazines, which are also referred to as *mass-market magazines,* are defined mainly by their circulation and the advertisers who support them. Any magazine with a circulation of over a half million would be considered large. Publications that fit into this category include *Cosmopolitan, Working Woman, Sports Illustrated, Vogue,* and *McCall's.* Because these publications reach such an enormous audience, major advertisers are always vying for their pages. These magazines can afford to be choosy about everything—

who works for them, who is given the coveted back cover for advertising space, and who writes for them.

As in other parts of the publishing industry, a few big players control a large portion of the consumer magazine market. The Hearst Corporation, for instance, publishes *Harper's Bazaar, Good Housekeeping, Popular Mechanics, Esquire,* and *O: The Oprah Magazine.* Hearst is the world's largest publisher of monthly magazines, with sixteen magazines published for United States audiences and ninety-eight international editions distributed in more than a hundred countries. Each magazine is headed by different editors. Hearst magazines are considered among the best in the nation and offer some of the highest circulations and payment rates. Gruner & Jahr, owned by Bertelsmann AG, produces ninety magazines and newspapers in thirteen different countries. They own *Child, Family Circle,* and *National Geographic,* to name just a few. There are several other biggies in the market you should be aware of: Meredith Corporation, which owns *Better Homes & Gardens;* Hachette Filipacchi, publisher of *Woman's Day* and *Elle;* Primedia Company, which publishes *American Baby;* and the Washington Post Company, which owns the newspaper of the same name, as well as a number of magazines. These companies hold the reins in the consumer market.

How They Work

If you look at the masthead of a large consumer magazine, you'll see a dizzying array of names and titles. Each acquiring editor is given a section of the magazine to oversee, and several assistants to help her accomplish that task. All of these editors are supervised by the managing editor, who makes preliminary decisions on what will be bought and what won't. Once the managing editor gives her okay, the editor-in-chief, whose job is to ensure that everything which runs in the magazine fits its intended tone and purpose, makes the final decision.

There are two main questions an editor asks to determine if an article fits her magazine: will the article help sell copies at the newsstand, and does the article suit the magazine's needs?

Let's consider the first criterion: selling copies. Virtually every aspect of publishing is driven by money. Magazines that don't sell copies don't make money, not just because readers aren't buying, but also because advertisers pull their ads. The bottom line is always a consideration for large magazines. Articles that attract readers or give

Editors at large magazines are always on the lookout for articles that will boost newsstand sales. Exclusive interviews, groundbreaking information, and innovative ideas do well here. If you can offer something of value that will give the magazine an edge over its competition, you stand a better chance of selling your article.

the magazine an edge over its competition are, of course, welcome. If you can land a heart-to-heart interview with Barbra Streisand, or if you have the scoop on a revolutionary new weight-loss drug, you'll be offering something valuable to the magazine.

Second, the editor needs to determine if your article matches what the magazine needs. Initially, it has to match the publication's tone and approach. No matter how exclusive that interview with Barbra might be, it won't work in *Outdoor Life* unless the singer is talking about her camping adventures. Then, your writing abilities and credentials have to be a good fit. An editor at a busy magazine doesn't have time to do significant editing on a piece. She wants it to be right the first time out, and to know that the writer is someone who has the expertise needed to handle the more complicated articles that larger magazines assign. The writer also has to have a clearly demonstrated ability to find national sources and reach experts and/or celebrities. A small-town writer who has published only in the local newspaper is unlikely to land an exclusive interview with Barbra. These are the kinds of points editors at large magazines take into account when making decisions.

HOW AN ARTICLE REACHES AN EDITOR'S DESK

When you send off your article or query to a large magazine, you are entering a maze of different levels. Depending on whether the article was requested *(solicited)* or not *(unsolicited)*, the path it takes through the magazine's offices differs. Unsolicited articles are at the bottom of the priority pile. Editors at monthly magazines are focused on the work they have at hand—on getting this month's issue out the door and planning for the issues ahead. They have a steady stream of work from regular writers and contributing editors who are usually experts in their fields, and whose credentials help sell issues.

If your article is unsolicited, it is sent to an editorial assistant's desk no matter whose name you put on the cover letter. In order to speed up the process of reaching the right editor, be sure to study the masthead and address your article to the right acquiring editor. That way, you'll wind up with an editorial assistant or assistant editor who works in that department, putting you one step closer to the editor who actually makes decisions regarding acquisitions. Sending a piece on cancer drugs to the book editor will only throw a wrench into the already slow process.

An unsolicited article is one that an editor did not request. These are the last ones on the editor's priority list, and wait the longest to be read and reviewed.

Managing editors and editors-in-chief are busy throughout the day in meetings, discussing the magazine's focus and planning future issues and themes. They don't have time to review every package that comes through the door, which is why unsolicited material is given to an assistant. Even solicited articles are sometimes handed over to editors lower on the ladder for a first look.

The editorial assistant initially looks at your submission to determine if the article's topic is even something that the magazine covers. Some writers do so little research that they might, for instance, send an article on the process of obtaining American citizenship to *American Baby*, a parenting publication. All such queries and submissions are automatically rejected.

If your article or idea makes it past this first review, it is then sent on to a section editor, who reads each of the submissions in order of receipt. The pile is often very high and the editor's time extremely limited, so the decision on buying or passing is made in a few seconds. This is why your cover letter and the opening of your submitted article need to be strong and well written. I have heard some editors say they read no more than three sentences of a submission before making a decision. While that's a scary thought, it's the likely reality in a fast-paced industry.

If the section editor likes the article, she passes it on for approval to the articles editor or managing editor. Finally, the editor-in-chief has the last say as to whether the article will make it into the magazine's pages. All of these steps take a great deal of time, which is why responses from large magazines are so slow in coming.

THINGS TO CONSIDER WHEN WORKING WITH A LARGE MAGAZINE

The benefits of publishing an article in a large consumer magazine are many. If you sell an article to a magazine such as *Cosmopolitan*, for instance, you will get paid relatively well—about $1,000 and up per article, or $1 and up per word. In addition, you will be rewarded with an impressive byline, and you'll find that a number of other doors open up more easily for you. Although it looks enormous, publishing is actually a very small industry. Editors move from place to place, network with other editors, and pass on information about good and bad writers. Your single credit in *Cosmopolitan* may make it ten times easier to sell an article to *Glamour* next month.

Editorial assistants want to be promoted to the editor level. The best way for them to do this is by consistently "finding" good submissions in the *slush pile*—the term used to describe the stack of unsolicited articles. If your work is good and is targeted correctly, rest assured that it will get passed up the chain of command.

One of the benefits of publishing a piece in a large consumer magazine is an impressive *byline*—your name printed at the head of an article in a major publication.

Editors at large magazines don't have the time to develop relationships with their writers or to provide large amounts of feedback. Don't expect the same degree of personal attention that you would receive at a smaller publication.

However, there are also disadvantages to working with a large publication. For instance, you can't expect a great deal of handholding or personal attention from a large magazine. These publications are on tight schedules, and the editors there are always busy. Unlike small publications, where a more personal relationship is forged between writers and editors, large magazines are always looking ahead to tomorrow. They won't spend as much time on you or your article as a smaller place might.

As a new writer for a large magazine, you also can't expect to land the cover article or to receive one of the coveted spots on that month's list of contributors. Those spaces are reserved for the writers and articles that will sell the most copies. A first-person essay written by the First Lady will probably attract more readers than yours will, and it is this economic factor that determines cover placement.

In addition, keep in mind that most writers do not successfully submit to large magazines without first paying their dues at smaller ones. Only about 25 percent of the content in magazines like *Cosmopolitan* is written by freelancers, and those outside writers that are used tend to be recognized, experienced freelancers who have already built up a reputation and an excellent file of clips. Editors at magazines with high visibility and millions of subscribers aren't willing to take a chance on an unproven writer. They can't afford to, both financially and deadline-wise. A new writer is essentially an unknown who could throw off an entire editorial schedule by missing a deadline or turning in substandard work.

Nothing can take the place of a good clips file. By having tangible proof of your experience and skill, you show the editor you are up to the job.

If you are interested in pursuing a career in writing, it's vitally important that you build up a solid list of publication credits before attempting a large consumer magazine. A magazine like *Complete Woman*, for example, pays less than *Cosmopolitan*—only about $160 to $400 per article—but the magazine is 90 percent freelance written, which greatly increases your chances of landing an assignment. You could sell the article to *Complete Woman*, be rewarded with a clip and a check, and then use that experience to sell another article to the same magazine or move on to other publications. This will provide a guarantee to an editor that you can do the job, and do it well.

Do new, unproven writers have *any* chance of getting articles into large consumer magazines? Yes, but for a new writer, the best opportunities at a publication like *Cosmopolitan* are in shorter pieces such as reviews or quick information and tips articles. In an article called

"Advice on How to Get Published in Magazines" in the *Writer's Digest* special edition "Start Writing Now," editor and writer David Fryxell advises writers to start at the bottom by submitting ideas for the smaller stories in a magazine. "Just as you should not try to break into a market with a complex proposal, you should not start out competing with a magazine's regular writers for the top-flight assignments. Find the stories nobody else wants to do, and offer to write them. Editors will love you." These can be anything from filler articles that are packed with resource information to annual pieces on holiday traditions that the regular writers are tired of covering. Keep in mind that your best weapon here is tenacity. Querying again and again, with excellent ideas and with consistently improving clips, will show the editor that you are determined and persistent.

> The best way to break into magazines is to pitch small, filler stories or new slants on topics covered annually in the publication.

If you want to get an article or two into publication, but have no intention of building a writing career, you might be better off skipping the top magazines, unless you have outstanding credentials. Remember that most editorial decisions at top magazines are driven by economics and expertise. If you can't help the magazine sell more copies, the editor will assign the piece to a writer who can. Try your hand at the smaller magazines, being sure to match your piece with the publication's mission and audience. (More on this in Chapter 4.)

Medium-Sized Consumer Magazines

Medium-sized magazines usually have circulations between 100,000 and 500,000. This is not the only characteristic, however, that defines the magazines which fall into this category. Reputation and coverage of topics also help differentiate these magazines from their smaller and larger counterparts. Like the large mass-market magazines, medium-sized magazines are available on newsstands. They may also address the same subjects as the larger publications. However, mid-sized magazines often have a regional or niche focus that directs them toward audiences with specialized interests. They therefore cover the secondary market, picking up readers who want more information on a given topic than a larger, general interest magazine might offer. As a result, these publications are often referred to as *secondary magazines.*

Consider, for example, the magazines *Entrepreneur* and *Indiana Business Magazine.* Both cover the world of business. However, *Entre-*

Medium-sized magazines tend to focus on specific niches in order to carve out their own spot on newsstands. They usually fill in the gaps left by large magazines, which try to address the needs of many different kinds of readers.

preneur, a mass-market (large) magazine, focuses on a wide variety of companies and issues in order to address a national audience. *Indiana Business*, a secondary magazine, focuses solely on businesses in the state of Indiana.

How They Work

Understandably, medium-sized magazines have smaller staffs than larger publications. A handful of section editors oversee different departments, and one editor-in-chief makes the final decision regarding the acquisition of any article. Usually, each editor has one assistant—not several—who screens incoming material and determines its suitability before passing it on to the section editor. Often, one editor does double duty, heading both the health and parenting sections, for example.

Like larger magazines, when selecting manuscripts, medium-sized publications are driven by economics, and are often just as hungry for exclusive articles as bigger magazines are. Getting Barbra Streisand on the cover of a medium-sized magazine is a far bigger coup than it would be for a large magazine.

Also like larger magazines, these secondary publications need articles that fit the magazine's needs. In this case, the magazine wants pieces that focus on its one area or specialty. Its readers expect the publication to provide the very specific information for which they are looking, and it's imperative that all articles meet those expectations.

Finally, editors at moderate-sized magazines are eager for articles that take an original approach. Unlike editors of mass-market magazines, which have perennial article slants, editors of secondary magazines rarely run the same type of piece twice. Readers of these secondary magazines tend to be loyal and subscribe year after year. They don't want to read the same basic article over and over again. They want unique twists on interesting topics, and so do the editors.

How an Article Reaches an Editor's Desk

Like large magazines, medium-sized magazines are inundated with unsolicited articles. Many writers see mid-sized magazines as a means of building up a portfolio of clips before approaching larger publications. Although material in medium-sized magazines is more likely to be freelance written—on the average, about 50 percent of the material comes from outside sources—there are also more writers vying for those spots.

Here, your unsolicited submission will usually be routed first through an editorial assistant, who spends her days weeding through the volume of mail that comes into the office. If your submission is totally inappropriate for that publication—if , for instance, it is on a subject that the magazine doesn't cover—it will be automatically rejected at this point. If the submission seems viable, though, it will be passed on to the section editor and then to the editor-in-chief, who makes the final decisions on content.

THINGS TO CONSIDER WHEN WORKING WITH A MEDIUM-SIZED MAGAZINE

Like their larger counterparts, medium-sized magazines offer many advantages to the writer. Writing credits from mid-sized magazines are valued by editors in the industry, and can help you move up to large magazines, if that's what you want to do. Moreover, as a new writer, you have a better chance of selling an article to a medium-sized magazine than you would at a larger publication. These magazines are far more approachable than are the top consumer publications. Editors respect persistent writers who put time into their submissions and grow in skill with each piece. And they are always hoping to find that great article that will increase their sales and revenue. So if you continue to submit good ideas, you will eventually make a sale.

Editors at moderate-sized magazines are also hungry for writers with the credentials or expertise in the publication's area of focus. For instance, the secondary publication *Spare Time Magazine* is targeted to people who want to start businesses in their spare time. Thus, *Spare Time* frequently uses freelancers—in fact, it was one of the first magazines I sold a piece to—and is especially open to people who are writing about a business they run on a part-time basis. If you fit that description, you have a better shot of selling a piece to *Spare Time* than would someone who is unfamiliar with the challenges faced by part-time business owners.

Although you may start off doing occasional freelancing for medium-sized magazines, if your work is consistently good, you may find it quite easy to move into contributing writer positions. Editors at

To learn which sections of a magazine accept freelance-written material, compare the *masthead*—the list of staff members, usually printed in the beginning pages of the magazine—to the article bylines in different portions of the publication. Many times, the smaller articles are written by freelancers, while the main article and filler columns are handled by the staff.

these publications are as busy as those at larger magazines, and appreciate a writer who meets deadlines and submits polished material. It's not unusual for a skilled writer to start with a tiny filler piece and move up to a cover article within a few months' time.

However, like large magazines, moderate-sized publications also have their drawbacks. Payment at these magazines is generally not as good as that at larger publications. Per article, fees range between $100 and $1,000. In other cases, publications offer from about 20 cents to under a dollar per word.

In addition, even at this level, you can't hope for much hand-holding. Most editors expect you to have some experience and familiarity with the publishing process before you submit a piece to a mid-sized magazine. So if you are a new writer just breaking into the business, try not to show your newness. Research a publication—its needs, its style, and its submission guidelines—before you approach its editors so that you can be as informed and professional as possible in all of your dealings.

Small Consumer Magazines

Small magazines can loosely be defined as publications with circulations of less than 100,000. These magazines can also be defined by their topic focus, which is even tighter than that of moderate-sized publications. Therefore, smaller magazines are usually directed toward a smaller audience. Publications like *Chicago History* and *Tuscon Lifestyle*, for instance, have circulations of less than 50,000.

Small magazines offer some of the best opportunities for new writers trying to break into the market or just to place a couple of articles. The exception is literary magazines, which have small circulations but tend to be very selective about the material they accept.

Be aware that the category of small magazines includes the local and "throwaway" magazines you find on stand-alone shelves at shopping centers, video stores, and supermarkets. Like other magazines in this category, these publications aim to reach specific markets such as seniors, golfers, or homebuyers. A number of alternative publications that use literary, social, and political commentaries also fall within this category. (See page 61 for more information on these types of magazines.)

How They Work

At small publications, everyone in the office wears several hats, and one or two people make all the decisions. The editor-in-chief might also serve as the marketing director and as a salesperson, depending on the budget of the publication. Similarly, the acquiring editor is also very likely to be the owner and the publisher.

Because of the small staff, the acquiring editor doesn't have to consult with other editors before making the decision to buy an article. She has a specific vision for her magazine, as well as an understanding of the financial needs of the business, and evaluates submissions based on these needs.

Although small magazines rely on advertising and subscription dollars to remain afloat, these publications rarely even try to compete for big-name writers or celebrity interviews. They generally look for articles that are well written, hit the specific niche of the magazine, and offer value to the reader. They are the most likely to try new approaches and be open to unique ideas, because the flexibility of a small staff means that these kinds of decisions are easier to make.

At a small magazine, staff members normally perform double duty. The editor may also be the owner, publisher, and bookkeeper. A salesperson might also take care of the marketing and distribution.

How an Article Reaches an Editor's Desk

At a small magazine, it's highly likely that the person collecting the mail from the mailbox every day is the same one who determines the content of the magazine. And that mail is not likely to be the flood of envelopes sent to larger publications, because the pay rates and prestige value of these publications are lower, making them less appealing to career-oriented writers. That's why these magazines offer the best opportunity to new writers. If the article is a good match for the acquiring editor's tastes, a sale will be made.

It's important to note that at small magazines, submissions don't always reach an editor's desk via the mail. These publications tend to be more informal, and are often open to phone call or e-mail queries. If you are a local writer who wants to pick up a few extra writing jobs, sometimes all you have to do is arrange a meeting with the editor to show her some of your previous work and present your article ideas.

Things to Consider When Working With a Small Magazine

There is no doubt that there are some drawbacks to working with a small magazine. Because their budgets are so small, the payment for articles is low—from $10 to $200 per article—and is usually calculated after that issue of the magazine has been published and the advertising revenue has been received. Another problem is that a byline in a small magazine is not as impressive as one from a larger publication.

Despite these disadvantages, small magazines have much to offer the new writer. Their editors value good writers and are more likely to work with a new freelancer and help her develop the skills she needs—especially if the writer lives in that area and can offer an insider's perspective. Many of the people who start small magazines were once writers themselves. They understand that their contributors need feedback, and tend to work with writers on a one-to-one basis, providing constructive criticism and praise. Many of these magazines are published bimonthly or quarterly, giving the editor more time between issues to work with writers. Therefore, the small magazine can offer the budding writer a wonderful opportunity for learning and developing her craft.

Nevertheless, don't expect a small magazine to accept any article, regardless of its topic and its approach. It is in your best interests to study each magazine and gain a firm grasp of the type of material it regularly carries, as well as the material that does not make it into the magazine's pages. This will help you find the best home for your piece.

Small magazines are more willing to work with writers and help them cultivate their talent. At these publications, writers are usually partners in the editorial process, and receive helpful feedback and encouragement from the editor.

Trade Journals

Trade journals are magazines and small newspapers published specifically for people in certain businesses or professions. Magazines like *Writer's Digest, Real Estate Forum*, and *Human Resource Executive* all fall into this category. The content of these journals includes articles on new technologies or products, articles that present tips and ideas, and how-to articles. If the journal is published by a certain group—*Distribution Channels*, for instance, is published by the American Wholesale Marketers Association—there is often news about upcoming conventions and member achievements.

Note that while trade journals sometimes address the same audience targeted by academic journals—physicians, for instance—the trade journals' articles differ from those in academic journals in both subject and format. Trade journals are designed specifically to help readers better run their business or better perform their job. Thus, a trade article geared for physicians might contain helpful information on setting up a private practice or dealing with HMOs. Academic journals, on the other hand, deal more with theories, breakthroughs, and research, and often include the graphs, tables, and bibliographies that are so important in scholarly papers. An academic journal geared for physicians, then, might present the findings of the latest skin cancer studies or discuss the newest techniques used in gallbladder surgery. If you think your article more closely fits the description of academic articles, please turn to the information on page 51.

Although you will find size variations in trade journals, very few reach the mass circulations of consumer magazines. The majority of trade journals fit in the small to medium-sized magazine market, and work in the same manner.

Trade journals cover the gamut of subject areas. They are produced by companies, publishers, and organizations, and are usually distributed to industry professionals, employees, members, or stockholders. From *Advertising Age* to *Veterinary Economics,* there's a magazine available for everyone.

The good news is that these types of journals are among the most likely to accept articles from unknown freelancers. They rarely have many staff writers, usually face little competition, and are often hungry for content. Many editors at these magazines wear a number of hats, which means that fewer people have to okay a submission before it is accepted. Plus, editors at these types of magazines are especially interested in articles composed by their readers. If you are an electrician by trade, for instance, take a look at the industry magazines you subscribe to—*Electrical Apparatus* and *Home Energy,* for example. Your credentials will be a bonus when you approach the editor with an article idea.

In the case of some journals, however, a number of writers do vie for the same space. Publications geared toward industries that employ people with writing skills—journals that address people in advertising, for instance—receive just as many submissions as some consumer magazines. If you are considering publications such as these, you would do better to offer your skills to a magazine in another field. An article on promoting your business can be applied to virtually any trade journal. Tips on increasing sales also work well in a variety of professional publications.

The pay at trade magazines is not as high as that of commercial magazines; sometimes, there is no pay besides a byline credit. However, if you are just starting out, these publications offer a great opportunity and generally provide a good credential for your writing resumé.

You can look up associations and their publications in the *Encyclopedia of Associations,* published by The Gale Group and available in the reference collection of most libraries.

There are a number of different classifications within the world of trade journals. *Vertical trades* are directed toward everyone in one particular industry, such as veterinarians. *Horizontal trades* are targeted toward people in the same type of job—human resource managers, for instance— though not necessarily in the same industry.

Newspapers

Editor and Publisher magazine annually ranks the top ten newspapers in the country. From year to year, the list varies little: *The Wall Street Journal, USA Today, The New York Times, Los Angeles Times, The Washington Post, New York Daily News, Chicago Tribune, Newsday, Houston Chronicle,* and *The Dallas Morning News.* Because of their stature, these newspapers are the least likely to accept articles from unknown writers.

The newspaper industry is gigantic. There are more than 2,000 daily and 8,000 weekly newspapers in the United States and Canada, generating $57 billion a year in revenue. According to the *Competitive Media Index,* 60 percent of all adults read a daily newspaper and another 10 percent read one on Sunday.

While most magazines are published on a monthly basis, newspapers come out much more often and are sometimes categorized based on frequency of publication. Daily papers come in morning or evening editions and are distributed locally, like the *Brockton Enterprise,* or nationally, like *The New York Times.* Weekly papers—*The Village Voice,* for instance—also come in small, local versions and larger national releases. There are also papers generated for specific areas of a city.

Like magazines, newspapers can be large, medium, or small in size. Newspapers of all sizes need a great deal of well-written content on a continuous basis. In fact, newspapers are the number-one way for an unpublished or new writer to get a foot in the door of the article market. But when you don't have a list of writing credits under your belt, it's best to start locally, particularly with the smaller weekly newspapers.

Large Newspapers

Large metropolitan and national newspapers—papers like *The New York Times*—range in circulation from 750,000 to nearly 2 million. These papers not only have a large local reach, but are also generally distributed on a national basis. Instead of serving a particular region, some of these publications establish a specific niche by concentrating on one issue. *The Wall Street Journal,* for instance, focuses on the world of business.

Larger papers generally have the budgets necessary to produce more sections on special areas of interest—book review, entertainment, and travel sections, for instance—and more material within those sections. Many large papers also put out different editions designed for different regions. The main section of the paper containing national news, sports, and business reports remains the same, but the Living and Metro sections are customized to fit each particular area. If you have a story with a local slant, these area-specific

Know Which Doors Are Open

There are four sections of the newspaper that offer good opportunities for outside contributors. The first is the Lifestyle section, which deals with gardening, books, home interiors, food, and other topics that are not hard news. The editors of these sections are always on the lookout for stories on new trends. The second section that holds promise is the Op-Ed section, which is formally called the Opinion-Editorial section. This is good for people who want to submit completed essays on hot topics. Third, the specialty inserts created by the newspaper for both informational and advertising purposes often supplement the space with freelanced tips articles or reports written by business owners. Finally, the inserts that deal with particular areas of the community are perfect for writers who can compose a profile on an interesting resident or business. If you're a history buff, inquire about writing a piece on the history of the area in which the newspaper circulates. You can also offer to do a "Best of" article, compiling information on the top restaurants, golf courses, or entertainment venues in the area. The key to getting your work into any of these sections is to be trendy and timely with your ideas.

editions represent the best opportunity for entry into the large-newspaper market.

HOW THEY WORK

Large newspapers are structured much like large magazines. Each section of the paper is headed by an editor who has several assistant editors and reporters working beneath her. A managing editor oversees the different departments, and an editor-in-chief makes the final decisions on content.

Most large newspapers hold weekly editorial meetings at which they discuss ideas and brainstorm approaches to stories. Breaking news is the priority at these newspapers, which have big budgets for reporter travel. The pressure to get there first and have the best coverage is intense. Rival editors do not share reporters and generally aren't interested in freelancers who are also subcontracting for a competing paper. Most newspapers, especially ones in this size category, are very proprietary about both their information and their in-house and freelance writers.

Newspaper editors are always looking for a local slant, although the term "local" covers a wider swath at a large paper than at a small

Newspaper articles are frequently bumped in favor of breaking news. When submitting work, be ready to adapt and react to trends and current events.

publication. An article on lobster preparation for the cooking section should feature tips from area chefs; a story on preparing for the SATs should include quotes from students and teachers who live in the paper's circulation area. Newspapers set themselves apart from national magazines by covering issues of interest to local readers, and always need writers who are in tune with local concerns and events.

Editors also look for articles that fit their paper's particular focus and style. *The New York Times,* for instance, carries material far different from that found in *The New York Post.* The former is more sophisticated in its approach, and meets the needs of a better educated audience by providing detailed stories on hard news. The *Post,* on the other hand, is more sound-bite oriented, and focuses less on hard news and more on pop culture. Judge a paper's approach to news. Does it offer serious stories that explore the economy, education, and politics, for instance; or does it take a lighter approach, dealing primarily with celebrities and lifestyle issues? Editors want pieces that will give their readers what they have come to expect from that paper.

HOW AN ARTICLE REACHES AN EDITOR'S DESK

At large newspapers, the process is much the same as it is at large magazines. Queries and article submissions are sent in either solicited or unsolicited. Requested material is reviewed first, and bought if it fits what the newspaper needs at the time. Unsolicited articles are left at the bottom of the pile on an editorial assistant's desk, and may not be looked at for weeks, maybe even months.

Once an editorial assistant has a chance to screen out the truly unsuitable submissions, she either passes the remaining ones on to her section editor or presents them at an editorial meeting, depending on whether the pieces fit the section in which she works or address another area of interest. When the appropriate section editor receives an unsolicited article, she may or may not act right away. Often, an editor keeps an article or query on hand for an indefinite period of time, waiting for an appropriate slot to open up.

THINGS TO CONSIDER WHEN WORKING
WITH A LARGE NEWSPAPER

One of the biggest drawbacks to working for newspapers of any size is the relatively low pay. The pay structure at newspapers is different from that at magazines, with fees being determined by column inch rather than word. At large newspapers, payment per article is comparable to that at medium-sized magazines—from about $100 to $1,000.

Another drawback is the extremely short lead time. In certain instances, freelance writers are given as little as two hours to research, write, and turn in a piece. Moreover, because newspapers react lightning fast to area news, your article may get bumped and possibly never get used, especially at bigger newspapers. For an extreme example, look at the presidential election of 2000. The drawn-out results process bumped untold numbers of good stories from newspaper pages and airwaves, in favor of more election coverage. Timeliness is key here.

Yet another problem is that editors at big newspapers don't have the time to work with writers or show them the ropes. The editor expects you to know how to construct a newspaper article, assumes that you have leads on interview sources, and counts on your handling the assignment with a minimum of input. Like large magazine editors, the editorial staff of large newspapers has little time to cultivate or praise writers. If the editor likes your work, chances are she won't call you to rave about it. A check in the mail and a call to write another article are all the encouragement you're likely to receive, and are a sure sign that your work is up to snuff.

Also keep in mind that like large magazines, the larger newspapers do use freelance material, but only on a limited basis. The chances of breaking in as a new writer are slim unless you are providing something that is innovative or unique. Even then, unless you can demonstrate a clear ability to write the article as well as a staff reporter, the editor may elect to use you as a source for the piece rather than assign you as the writer. Editors at these major publications are under tremendous pressure to deliver up-to-the-minute, accurate news. They rarely take a chance on an unproven writer who doesn't have a background in journalism. It's simply not good economics, because one bad story filled with inaccuracies can haunt a newspaper for many decades.

However, clearly, there are also benefits to working for newspapers in general, and for large newspapers in particular. Exposure can be good, and there's always a chance that your article will be picked up by a syndicate and run in other newspapers. (See page 45 for further information about syndicates.) And writing for news-

Although new writers stand a better chance of getting their articles into a small or medium-sized newspaper, be aware that if your idea is unique—and especially if you can offer the paper something that it wouldn't otherwise be able to obtain—you may be able to get your article printed in a large metropolitan paper.

papers can open doors to publications in other media. Overall, editors at magazines value newspaper experience because they see these writers as fast, professional, and experienced.

Despite these pluses, though, don't try to start at the top unless you have a nationally recognized name or an exclusive interview that no one else would be able to get. The reporters at major newspapers have strong networks and rarely hit many roadblocks in developing stories. Unless you can offer something that the paper wouldn't otherwise be able to obtain, it would be best to start with the smaller papers.

Medium-Sized Newspapers

Medium-sized newspapers generally have a large local reach, covering major cities like Pittsburgh and Detroit, and enjoying circulations that range from 100,000 to 750,000. However, they are not distributed on a national basis. In some cities, there are two or more newspapers competing for the same group of readers so any story that can help that paper sell more copies is welcome.

How They Work

There is very little difference between the internal staff makeup of a medium-sized newspaper and that of a large newspaper. Each section of the paper is headed by an editor, who has assistant editors and reporters working for her. A managing editor is in charge of making things run smoothly, and an editor-in-chief makes the final decisions on what goes into the paper.

Like large newspapers, moderate-sized ones have weekly editorial meetings to discuss ideas and stories. And like any newspaper, these publications want stories on breaking news. However, because of their smaller budgets, medium-sized papers can't send reporters across the country or overseas to cover the big national and international stories. Instead, they buy these articles from freelancers in those areas or purchase them from wire services like the Associated Press.

Because it is far cheaper for a newspaper to purchase a story from a wire service than it is to buy a piece from a freelancer, editors at moderate-sized papers need a strong reason to use a new writer. Generally, the better the local slant, the more attractive the story. A child prodigy who has a special skill in chess would make a great Lifestyle feature. A neighborhood that's undergoing a revitalization would also be of interest.

An exclusive is also a big draw to newspaper editors. Even at the middle levels, there is a great deal of competition to get there and get there first. If a story has not been covered by a competitor, even if it's one as simple as how to construct a water garden, the editor will be more interested.

Finally, editors look for stories that will interest a large number of their readers, rather than just a few. In a predominantly agricultural area comprised of middle-class families, for instance, a newspaper would want articles that deal with issues like harvesting crops and animal care. An article on an online singles club run by a woman in the next town, on the other hand, would be a hard sell.

At all publications, editors look for articles that will appeal to the majority of their readers. Be sure that your piece will be of interest to the bulk of the publication's audience—not to just a few of its readers.

HOW AN ARTICLE REACHES AN EDITOR'S DESK

When an unsolicited submission arrives at a medium-sized newspaper, it is usually reviewed by an assistant editor, who then passes it on to a section editor if she thinks it fits the paper. If the section editor agrees that the article would be of value to the publication's readers, she pitches the idea in an editorial meeting or proposes it directly to the managing editor. The editor-in-chief makes all final decisions to ensure that every article reflects the tone and style of the newspaper. This process may take weeks because newspaper editors are so frequently interrupted by new stories.

THINGS TO CONSIDER WHEN WORKING WITH A MEDIUM-SIZED NEWSPAPER

Working with medium-sized newspapers has some of the same drawbacks as working for large newspapers. The payment for articles is not great—usually from about $75 to $400 per piece. And, of course, the lead time is short, as it is with all newspapers.

Much like the staff of larger papers, editors at this level expect writers to have some experience and familiarity with the editorial process. It is unusual for an editor to spend time working with a new writer to help her develop her skills. Deadlines are often too tight, and editors are frequently overworked, so a needy writer is an annoyance. That's why it's so important for you to study the way newspapers work and to understand the style and specific needs of a publication before you submit a piece to it.

On the other hand, medium-sized newspapers are the biggest consumers of freelanced material, and so present great opportunities to freelancers in general. These publications welcome outside articles and are apt to publish well-written pieces composed by members of the community served by the paper. Life experience, too, can be an asset here. For example, a teacher can write articles about education issues, and a contractor can provide information on new building trends. Coupled with a good idea or unusual slant, you stand a good chance if you have the right area of expertise. However, keep in mind that even at mid-sized papers, editors prefer writers with a background in journalism and familiarity with the tight, exacting writing that newspapers demand. So despite your knowledge in a given field, your article may be rejected if the editor prefers to work with more experienced writers.

The best way of approaching the paper is to call the editorial department first, and ask an assistant if the publication accepts outside submissions and, if it does, how such material should be sent to the paper. Follow this approach to the T, because an editor looks for writers who can follow directions.

At medium-sized papers, you will best succeed by targeting the Lifestyle section, Opinion-Editorial section, specialty inserts, and community inserts, which are the areas most often covered by outside contributors. (See the inset on page 37 for more information on these sections.) "My freelancing career started with an opinion/editorial piece in the Albany *Times-Union* about a pet peeve of mine," says Shannon Riggs, a freelance writer in Virginia. "It paid $50, and I was hooked. I soon moved on to local 'free' parenting publications. Now, two years later, I write for local and national publications both online and off. I write travel articles, a sewing column, informational parenting articles, and humorous essays about raising children."

Small Newspapers

Small newspapers range in circulation from 500 to 100,000, depending on the area. In Boston, a paper with a circulation of 100,000 is considered small because the population is so large. But in a tiny town, a paper with a circulation of 500 might be the biggest publication around, but still fall into the classification of small in the broad category of newspapers. These papers generally have an extremely localized reach, and work very hard to address the needs of everyone in their readership. They are neighborhood papers in every sense of the word, and are filled with community news, from events at the local library to family gatherings to local 4-H fair winners.

Another category of small newspapers is directed toward specialty groups or organizations. These publications are generally distributed on a weekly basis and are targeted to particular groups, like parents, golf enthusiasts, or retirees. Everything within the papers' pages is on a topic of interest to those readers.

How They Work

Some newspapers are so small that the staff includes fewer than five people. Therefore, the editor often is not only the owner and the publisher, but also the layout person and the sales manager. In addition, the editor often serves as a reporter, covering news and writing most of the paper's content. Editors who have to fill that many positions at once are extremely busy, and are very grateful to find a writer who has some talent and is interested in learning the business or providing a few articles.

The main criteria an editor at a small newspaper uses to determine whether an article will fit her publication are local slant and reader relevance. A paper for seniors doesn't need material on choosing a preschool, but does need articles that explore Medicare issues and discuss local senior programs and events. With severe limitations on space and budget, the editor has to be positive that every article provides value to a large share of her readers. It's too easy for readers to stop subscribing, and thereby put a serious dent in the paper's budget.

The editor of a small newspaper makes all final decisions and provides all editorial direction for the publication. When a paper addresses a readership that's homogeneous—a readership in which everyone shares common beliefs and interests—the articles may all have a particular political slant, which, of course, must be reflected in the editor's decisions. Because these publications are so small, they often enjoy the freedom to support one specific agenda—as long as it's the one shared by their readers.

Small newspapers represent a great opportunity for new writers. Their editors are always in need of good content, and often have time to work with writers and show them the ropes.

How an Article Reaches an Editor's Desk

At a small newspaper, the editor is also often the mailroom clerk, so she may both collect the mail and make decisions regarding any submission. But even when there are other staff members, the office space is usually so small that any articles or proposals are immediately presented to the editor. If the submission piques the editor's interest, usually either she or the assistant will call the writer, discuss the article, and offer to buy it over the phone. Most small newspapers are produced on a weekly basis, so the article might not run for a while. However, the decisions are made quickly simply because the process doesn't involve the many levels of command found at larger publications.

Because small newspapers operate much more informally than their larger counterparts, not all articles reach the editor via the mail. Often, writers call the editor and pitch their ideas, and then stop by to present samples of their work. This casual way of doing business offers new writers a great opportunity to get a feel for both the editor of the paper and the newspaper business.

Things to Consider When Working With a Small Newspaper

The biggest drawback to working with a small newspaper is the pay rate. Don't expect to get much more than cab fare for an article. These publications simply don't have the budget or the advertisers to pay writers more than a few dollars per piece.

On the other hand, small newspapers offer some wonderful opportunities to the new writer. They are the hungriest for material to fill their pages, and the easiest place for an unpublished writer to successfully sell an article. Moreover, small papers often enable writers to try their hand at different kinds of articles. You can cover local town meetings, write about the new business in town, interview the pastor at the local church, and even pen a few obituaries if you want to. As long as your writing is good and your material is newsworthy, the small newspaper in your city or town is very likely to run the piece. This can give you the satisfaction of a byline and a lasting record of your publishing achievement.

My very first writing job was with a small weekly newspaper. Later, I moved up to a medium-sized city paper, and then to magazines and trade journals. It was a matter of amassing one clip at a time; gaining experience in a wide variety of writing projects; and then, once I figured out what kind of articles I liked to write, directing my efforts toward those types of publications. Many, many writers have cut their teeth on small newspapers before moving on to bigger markets.

The best way to contact an editor at a small newspaper is to call. If it's a weekly paper, call on the distribution day for the paper, because this usually falls in a small window of downtime. Be prepared to discuss a few ideas or to send in a couple of articles or writing samples.

Syndicates

A syndicate is an agency that sells the same article simultaneously to different outlets. *Dear Abby,* for example, is distributed by Universal Press Syndicate, and is the most widely syndicated column in the world. Many writers dream of mirroring Abby's success by having their work published in hundreds of newspapers across the country. While there are some opportunities at syndicates for freelance work, it is rare and difficult for a new writer to break into this market.

Some syndicates carry only certain types of articles, such as pieces on education, parenting, or financial topics. *Motor News Media,* for example, specializes in 650-word articles on automotive issues. The most popular article with syndicates is the short how-to, which is often used as filler material.

While it doesn't hurt to submit an article to a syndicate, keep in mind that most of the writers who provide material for them have been doing so for a very long time. The smaller syndicates, which hit less than a couple hundred newspapers at a time, are the most open to accepting single articles for publication. The most complete list of syndicates available can be found in the *Editor and Publisher Syndicate Directory,* which also includes information on different syndicates' content requirements. (See page 323 of the Resource Directory.) Keep in mind that highly specialized material which a syndicate may not be able to get from an average freelancer—material that requires expertise in fine art or wines, for instance, or that relies on the writer's obtaining an exclusive interview with a celebrity—stands a better chance than run-of-the-mill articles.

A step up from the newspaper is the city magazine. These regional publications profile people, services, and events in one community. They can be as small as chamber of commerce publications, and as large as full commercial magazines that focus on one state or city, such as *Boston Magazine.* These magazines are generally published for upscale audiences. They pay about the same as medium-sized magazines, and a little better than most newspapers.

Newsletters

Newsletters are the smallest of all the publications discussed in this chapter. Rarely does a newsletter extend past a dozen pages, and most are only four to eight pages in length. A newsletter's job is to provide a quick source of information about a subject, giving readers an easy way to stay current on trends or literature. This type of publication doesn't go into depth, but rather serves as an overview. Most have a central theme running through each issue, and often, the editor or the president of the company that's producing the newsletter writes a commentary that sums up the issue's purpose.

There are four main types of newsletters: consumer, professional, marketing, and association. Many newsletters have some kind of advertising or marketing built into their content, because this is the main source of revenue for the publisher. But not all newsletters are designed as revenue producers. Those publications that cover medical issues or address members of support groups, for instance, are created simply to provide subscribers with current information on their area of interest.

Depending on the aim of the newsletter, the content will differ. Companies or groups that are trying to reach a consumer audience create newsletters directed to their customer base. They are generally filled with helpful information, and may contain coupons or advertised specials. For instance, Toys"R"Us, the national toy chain, puts out a newsletter called *Parents University.* Inside are articles on parenting, along with bylines that do a "soft" sell for the manufacturer that sponsored the article.

A professional newsletter is distributed by a trade association or group, and contains industry information that is designed to keep readers current on new trends and technologies. The Screenprinting & Graphic Imaging Association International (SGIA) sends a monthly oversized newsletter to its members, with articles on awards, benefits of the SGIA, and changes in the printing industry. Much of the information can be used by member companies to run their businesses more efficiently.

Marketing newsletters are sent by companies to potential and current clients. The sole purpose of these newsletters is to serve as a soft marketing piece—to show that the company is doing a good job. For example, the newsletter might discuss employee awards, introduce new services offered by the company, and offer congratulations to clients who have reached milestones. Because the last thing that people want to receive is a giant pitch for one company, these newsletters often include articles that provide some value to the reader by covering industry trends or product usage.

Finally, association and organization newsletters are designed to inform readers about upcoming events, new resources and services, and advances in the field. The Muscular Dystrophy Association (MDA), for instance, sends a newsletter to parents of children who are affected by the disorder. This publication is part of the MDA's outreach efforts, and provides a resource for parents who have similar needs and problems, and want to keep up-to-date on advances in care and treatment. Other newsletters that fit in this category are those produced by churches and universities.

Most newsletters are run much like small newspapers. The staffs are extremely small, and often one person makes all the decisions regarding content. When an article is submitted, it is generally reviewed by the editor herself or, if there is a staff, by an assistant. The submission is evaluated for relevance to the newsletter, and if it's a good fit, the editor contacts the writer and asks to use or buy the piece.

Just as it's a good idea to call a small newspaper to gauge the editor's interest in your articles, it's smart to contact the editor of a newsletter before sending in your work. Ask for the submission guidelines, and discuss the types of articles for which the editor is looking. Then send in a piece that fits the editor's needs. Marketing and consumer newsletters are the least open to outside contributions, because these publications are usually generated by an advertising agency or an in-house staff. However, some of them do rely on freelance contributions to help fill their pages. Professional association newsletters, though, very often take content from members of that association. Association and organization newsletters, too, are often interested in work from outside contributors, and especially in first-person accounts from readers of the publication. The editors of these newsletters are generally willing to work with the contributors as they know that many of them are readers, not professional writers. Often, the editor will help you rework your article until it meets the newsletter's needs.

The best way to get your foot in the door of a newsletter is to write an article on your area of expertise or particular experience, and

There are four main types of newsletters: consumer, professional, marketing, and association. Of these, professional and association newsletters are the most open to freelance contributions.

Newsletter articles can often be used as clips when approaching other types of publications. Remember, however, that a letter to the editor is *not* considered a published clip. The best articles for your portfolio are those that have met some sort of editorial standard and that brought some educational value to the readers of the publication in which they appeared.

submit it to a newsletter that focuses on that area. Articles that provide industry-specific or consumer-specific tips for working or living better are the most likely to be successful. Just be sure to study the newsletter's back issues so that you get a feel for its content and approach. Several sources can fill you in on existing newsletters. The book *Hudson's Subscription Newsletter Directory* is one such source. Also check the Internet sites www.newletters.org and www.newsletteraccess.com/directory.html. (See the Resource Directory for more information on these sources.)

Remember that writers who submit work to newsletters are rarely paid for their material. However, depending on the type of credentials you hope to gain, the byline offered may be worth more than any check. If you are trying to build credibility in your field of expertise, or if you are an academic who needs a few writing credits, a newsletter can give you both the writing credits and the clips that you require to move on to other publications and establish a reputation in your field.

E-Outlets

This is not only the fastest-growing, but also the fastest-changing market in publishing. In some circles, it has yet to gain the prestige that print publishing merits, and not all magazine or newspaper editors view an online clip with the same respect they give a print clip. However, as the Internet publishing industry grows, this attitude is sure to change.

Every year, hundreds of *e-zines*—online magazines—start up, and just as many fold. Their needs and focus adjust with the market. Writers who want to break into electronic media need to understand the ever-shifting nature of this industry and be ready to adapt their articles and approach.

There are literally thousands of e-publications available, and like print media, there are both high- and low-level outlets. Sites like *Discovery Channel Online, Salon,* and *Women's Wire* tend to use well-known authors and experienced journalists for their main stories. A recent issue of *Salon,* for example, featured pieces by screenwriter Joe Eszterhaz and political expert David Horowitz. As with print magazines, the smaller, filler-type sections are the ones most open to freelance contributions.

Brush Up Your E-Vocabulary

Before you start writing for online sites, you should be familiar with different Internet terms. While new words pop up on a daily basis, the following basics should get you started.

attachment. A file attached to an e-mail message. With the number of viruses floating around, most editors don't want attachments. They would prefer you to save your article as a text file and paste it into the body of the e-mail message.

HTML. The language that most web pages are written in and coded with. You don't need a full course in HTML language to be able to submit web-ready material. A few basics, such as knowing to add <B> both before and after a line that should be set boldface, is enough to get you started. A great online resource for learning these basic web codes is www.sharpwriter.com, which contains several links to e-publishing style guides and formatting rules.

link/hyperlink. The address phrase that lets you click and immediately be taken to a particular Internet address. It is often highlighted in a different color so that people realize it's a "live" link, meaning that it works.

mailing list. An e-mail discussion group. There are many specialized groups that were started for the sole purpose of sharing knowledge within a field. These are great resources for writers who want to gain more information about their area of interest, whether that area is the craft of writing itself or an article topic such as technology, education, or travel.

URL. The address of a website. URL stands for Uniform Resource Locator.

E-zines offer immediate publication gratification, because online magazine sites update their content continuously and are always seeking quality submissions. Outside of newspapers, online publications are one of the best ways to break into publishing and establish clips immediately. However, one caution—read your contract very carefully and obtain opinions from other writers about the site before you start submitting online.

There are legitimate sites out there that use freelanced material—www.suite101.com, www.bluesuitmom.com, and www.thewriting parent.com, to name just a few. But new writers have to be cautious and determine what rights the site is buying. (See Chapter 11 for an explanation of contract rights.) A good number of sites buy all rights to a piece, meaning that the author can never reprint the article anywhere, not even on her own personal website. You need to fully understand and weigh this clause of the writing contract before you sign on the dotted line.

The online world changes faster than the print world. Sites listed today may be sold or closed tomorrow. The dot-com economic roller coaster affects the revenues of these sites, and closings are as frequent as openings.

Numerous sites offer even worse deals to writers. Pay-per-click and write-for-percentage sites, like Themestream and The Vines, put the burden on the writer to direct traffic toward her piece. While one or two articles on such sites can lead to bigger and better markets, don't fall into the trap of hoping that these sites will eventually build your career or your bank account.

And there are additional drawbacks to writing for online publications. First, few online magazines pay for articles, and what they do pay is often a fraction of the print payment rate. Copyright infringement is another hot issue with web publishing. At this time, there's no online protection device that prevents cyber thieves from lifting words off sites and then using them on their own sites. At any given time, I can find at least a dozen of my articles that have been stolen and put on other sites.

But publishing on the web offers a number of advantages, as well, the biggest benefit being permanence. Articles are stored in databases indefinitely and are accessible to readers as long as that page exists. You can link to your work in e-mails to editors, or you can build a personal web page and add the web addresses for articles you have had published online. When an editor wants to see additional copies of your work, it's as simple as clicking a mouse to reach the page. Just be sure to check the web addresses frequently to make sure the pages still exist.

In addition, the web can help you hone your writing skills, gain experience, and ultimately break into print publication. And if you're working for the top sites, which pay upwards of $500 per article, or utilizing e-zines to sell reprints over and over again, the Internet can also be a great way to add to your income level. "In the less than two years I've been on the Internet, my sales have more than doubled, my writing income in six months doubling from the whole of the previous year," says Kathryn Lay in her article "Writing the Net" for the e-zine *Writing for Dollars*. Kathryn has re-sold several articles to e-zines, and has used the Internet to find markets that she might not have known about otherwise.

Finally, response times are fast and content is updated frequently on the web, spurring a need for more articles. Even though the pay is usually low, the web offers a door for breaking into article publishing—as long as the writer is vigilant and cautious about the use of her content.

If you submit articles to a website, choose one that will show your work in its best light. Countless sites neglect to proofread articles before they are posted. If there are typos in your work, other editors will judge your writing abilities as substandard. Check and recheck anything you are thinking of submitting online, and then check it again once it's up on the site. If there is a mistake, notify the webmaster immediately so it can be fixed.

ACADEMIC PUBLICATIONS

Academic journals are designed to bring the latest in research, break-throughs, and case studies to readers in a certain field. Unlike trade journals, which are written to increase career and business knowledge in an industry, academic journals are created to advance the thinking in a particular area.

The world of academic article publishing differs from commercial publishing in terms of content and amount of available markets. The sheer volume of consumer magazines is staggering compared with the number of academic journals. However, as the Internet and other means of publishing integrate with academia, more and more opportunities are opening up on a daily basis.

In this arena, the most esteemed publishing credentials come from refereed journals. Like higher-echelon magazines, however, these offer the most challenges to the new writer who is trying to break into the market. Better choices for the new writer are the non-refereed journal and the online journal. But while it is more difficult to break into refereed journals, it is far from impossible. Impeccable research, fresh ideas, and good field credentials carry a great deal of weight with review boards.

According to the National Writers Union, 20 percent of writers work in the academic/scholarly writing arena. More than half of all writers have advanced degrees, with 37 percent carrying a master's and 14 percent holding PhDs.

Refereed Journals

In broad terms, a *refereed journal* is one in which all submitted articles and papers are reviewed by a board of experts that are usually drawn from the academic community. A detailed, anonymous critique of the piece is then written, with feedback provided to the author to request revisions or explain reasons for rejection. The *American Journal of Education* falls into this category. According to this journal's guidelines, it is most open to research reports, scholarly writing, and critical syntheses of educational scholarship, policy, and practice. These editors are looking for well-written, original, and concise pieces for inclusion in the journal.

When compiling a list of publications that might accept your work, it is sometimes difficult to tell the difference between a refereed and a *non-refereed journal*—an academic journal in which submissions are not formally reviewed by a board of experts. Check for the words "peer-reviewed" in the submission guidelines, and consider the journal's level of prestige. In general, refereed journals don't carry commercial

If the academic journal in which you're interested is listed in *Ulrich's International Periodicals Directory*, the *Ulrich's* entry will tell you if the publication is refereed. (See the sample entry on page 104.)

advertisements, don't take submissions from freelancers outside of the academic circle, and route all submission through a lengthy review process. Also look at the requirements for publishing within the journal. Some higher-level publications require writers to have particular degrees or certifications, or be members of the society that sponsors the journal. Overall, refereed journals expect more of their authors and are more precise in their requirements for publication.

Large Academic Journals

In academia, size classification for journals is not based entirely on circulation. The "large" journals—the journals to which it is the most difficult to successfully submit articles—are the ones with the best credentials and highest prestige in the field. These journals hit the biggest market concentration, meaning that a very high percentage of the academics in that field read these publications and turn to them for the latest information. The wider the distribution in the right circles, the higher on the scale the journal ranks.

For an outsider, this is not an easy determination to make. You need to examine the publications in your field and not only look at who is writing articles for each of them, but also consider who is reading these publications. If you have a mentor or a colleague who has been published, don't be afraid to ask her which journals are the most prestigious.

Keep in mind that the higher the level of the journal, the more difficult it is to get an article into publication. A large journal can afford to be very choosy about the material it publishes. The backlog of submissions at such journals can run as long as two years.

How They Work

Large academic journals often have large staffs. There are usually a few assistant editors for each of the editors, a managing editor, and an editor-in-chief. If the journal is very large and encompasses many areas, there may also be section editors. It is the job of the assistants, editors, and managing editor to sort through the multitude of submissions received by the journal, and pick the absolute best before approaching the editor-in-chief. The editor-in-chief makes the final decision on all materials. As already discussed, every refereed journal, regardless of size, also uses a review board to examine its submissions. Sometimes the board members are part of the staff, and sometimes the board is handpicked for each article based on expertise.

At a large academic journal, great attention is paid to details. Every submission is meticulously reviewed, discussed, analyzed, and checked for factual consistency. Depending on the circle of regular contributors, you may find that the doors will remain effectively shut to you until you can establish your expertise among your peers.

The editors are like gatekeepers, determining which material gets in and which is excluded. While this may limit the dissemination of knowledge in a given field, a set of checks and balances is important to maintain a level of consistency. The editors must judge if the articles meet one of academia's three basic goals—to continue or detail earlier research pieces in the journal, to challenge thinking and invite new discussion, and to contribute to the intent and scope of the journal.

These editors are not looking for think pieces or for general, sketchy articles that don't advance research in a field. They want detailed pieces from scholars who know their material and have created fully fleshed-out, comprehensive articles.

How an Article Reaches an Editor's Desk

As already discussed, at a large journal, there are several layers of editors and assistants who review all submissions, much as they do at large magazines. First, the submissions are screened by the assistant editors, who weed through the articles, sorting them into appropriate and inappropriate submission piles. Those articles that are clearly wrong for the journal—a study on genetics sent to the *Harvard Business Review,* for instance—are rejected right away, as are articles that don't meet the style and length requirements set forth in the publication's submission guidelines. To an editor, ignorance of the journal's rules shows a lack of research on the part of writer, and is a red flag that the article hasn't been thoroughly researched by the author.

Once that first, cursory review has been completed, those articles that are still in the running are passed up first to the editors and then to the managing editor. Each editor looks over every piece, determining if the article meets one of the three goals discussed earlier, and if the submitting scholar has the necessary credentials to merit publication.

If the article is still in the running, it is submitted to the review board. The members of the board then read over the piece and offer

Many large journals have a regular group of contributors who write most of the material in the journal. You may need to establish yourself in your field as an expert and build a strong reputation before your articles are accepted.

Take the time to study and follow the journal's guidelines for submission. Editors are annoyed by writers who don't send the required number of copies, or who make errors in length and subject matter.

their opinions as to whether the article should be accepted as is, should be accepted only if revised to the board's satisfaction, or should be rejected. The editor-in-chief makes the final decision, however, regarding the fate of each article, and sometimes, though it is rare, even asks for revisions on a piece that the board has rejected. The reviewers are there to advise and comment on the research, but only the editor-in-chief can accept or reject a submission.

THINGS TO CONSIDER WHEN WORKING WITH A LARGE JOURNAL

The higher the prestige level of a journal, the more submissions it receives. These journals are swamped with material, and can take months to get back to writers. You can increase your chances of a successful submission by studying the journal carefully and following its guidelines to the letter.

You might also consider sending a letter of inquiry before writing the article and submitting it. Many authors use conference papers as a springboard for scholarly articles. With the preliminary research already completed for the paper, it is easy to mail off a letter to see if the journal would be interested in a full-fledged article. This can net you a faster response and give you more direction for writing the later piece.

Most important, read several issues of the journal to make sure that your work accomplishes one of the three goals discussed earlier—that it adds to a current discussion, introduces new thinking, or contributes to the intent and scope of the journal. By being well acquainted with your potential market, investing the necessary time in researching and writing, and carefully reviewing for mistakes, you can avoid many of the pitfalls that so often prevent academic writers from achieving success. This is not to say that strong credentials, advisor recommendations, peer recognition, and awards don't carry a lot of weight with the peer-review boards, because they do. In the end, however, success in publishing depends on writing an excellent piece and submitting it to the right outlet.

While good research and writing can greatly increase your chances of getting published in a large refereed journal, be aware that few writers who have not yet built a reputation make it into the pages of these highly esteemed publications. The editorial staff is very choosy and has no scarcity of material from which to make its selection. You may need to gain stronger credentials or publishing experience before you can enjoy success there.

Don't expect to get rich from publishing in journals, regardless of the publication's level or size. Because most publications are supported by universities or associations and their distribution is limited to people in the field, revenue is low and payment is minimal, if any. In fact, at some journals, it is the writers who pay to have their work included. Most academics write articles for refereed journals as a means of increasing their exposure in the field and augmenting their curriculum vitae.

Most writers don't get rich, or make much money at all, through their academic publishing ventures. However, publication in a large journal can help you build a reputation in your field, and can provide a wide audience with valuable information.

Medium-Sized Academic Journals

Like large refereed academic journals, medium-sized journals cannot be easily defined, as these categories are not based on circulation. If you look at your particular field of study and rank the journals that address it in terms of prestige, circulation to experts, and author credentials, the middle of the list would encompass what is considered the medium-sized journals.

Many of these journals are quite popular with writers because the academic community recognizes that they are easier to publish within than the more prestigious publications. But that's not to say that it's a breeze to successfully submit to moderate-sized journals. Because these journals are refereed, the articles they receive are subjected to the same rigorous standards of review and analysis used by larger publications. A journal's reputation is based on the quality of the research it publishes, and at most journals, editors won't take a chance on an unknown writer unless the research is truly stellar and the author's credentials are very strong.

HOW THEY WORK

The structure of moderate-sized refereed journals is much like that of the larger refereed publications. There are fewer editors, however, and often only one assistant to the managing editor, who then reports to the editor-in-chief. There may also be an associate editor, who helps the managing editor with her workload. And, of course, the journal uses a review board, which may or may not be part of the staff, to critique each of the articles that pass the initial screening.

Moderate-sized journals use the same criteria as large journals to determine an article's suitability. An article must add to a current discussion, introduce new thinking, or contribute to the intent of the journal; and the work must be written by an academic who has the credentials to lend the piece some authority. A new professor, straight out of graduate school, is far less likely to be published in a mid-sized journal than someone with more experience and a long list of published articles in his curriculum vitae.

Again, great attention is paid to detail, and standards are high. Although it is slightly easier to publish in a medium-sized journal than in one that has greater prestige, you may have to make several attempts at publication. Don't expect success overnight.

How an Article Reaches an Editor's Desk

The process through which an article goes when it reaches a journal in this category is much like the process it goes through in a large refereed academic journal. First, the editors on the staff screen out the submissions that fail to fit the scope of the journal, to meet the submission guidelines, or to suit the journal's style. Then, if the manuscript has been properly prepared and covers a relevant subject, the article is forwarded to the appropriate review board. If all reviewers agree that the material is outstanding and needs little if any revision, the editor-in-chief usually accepts the article. If opinions differ, though, the editor may ask for another review or make the decision herself. No matter what the reviewers advise, the final decision always rests with the editor-in-chief, who has the option to accept the manuscript, reject the manuscript, or ask the writer for revisions.

At most publications, the first step of the editorial process is a quick review of your material to see if it fits the vision and needs of the journal. This is a simple "yes" or "no" answer for the editor. By doing your homework ahead of time, you can make it past this first review.

Things to Consider When Working With a Medium-Sized Journal

Medium-sized refereed academic journals have about the same advantages and drawbacks as larger journals. Pay is low, with the real payment being the prestige of having work appear in the journal's pages. And, if you have not yet built a reputation as a well-respected academic, the chances of having your article accepted are also small— unless your article is outstanding. Even at this level, journals receive the bulk of their submissions from known academics who are not new to the article-submitting process. These publications can pick and choose from among a wide range of submissions.

However, as in large journals, outstanding research and excellent writing will increase your chance of getting an article into print. And if your article is accepted, you will start amassing the publishing experience and credentials needed to get your work into larger journals.

Small Academic Journals

The smaller refereed journals may be highly focused on one niche, which limits their audience size, or may have the same topic focus as larger academic journals, but simply fail to attract as many readers. Generally, because the reach of these journals is limited, the prestige factor is lower.

How They Work

Small journals face many of the same problems in staffing and resources faced by small magazines and newspapers. They simply don't have the large staff enjoyed by major publications. Therefore, a small number of people usually juggle several different jobs at once.

These editors are interested only in material that addresses the scope of the journal and the interests of its readers. Here, the readership is even more defined than that of medium-sized journals, and thus, the articles have to be, too. The smallest journals may reach audiences of only a few hundred, and every article needs to serve the interests of those subscribers.

The editors of small journals want articles that provide their readers with useful information. A smaller journal offers more practical and applicable information than a larger journal, rather than presenting groundbreaking research. In short, the publication's job is to help readers disseminate information and apply it to their professions. For example, a writer for a large business journal might conduct a study on minorities in the workplace. Later, a writer for a small journal might take the data from the first study and apply it to yield information that its readers, business executives, can use—an article on how to encourage diversity in the workplace, or how to deal with affirmative action issues in an industry largely populated by one race. By combining the precision of the research with the analysis of experts in the field, the small academic journal can provide a treatment of greater depth than that offered in a trade journal, and of greater practical application than that provided in larger academic publications.

Submitting excellent written material, complete with any necessary graphs and data, is the key to gaining a journal publishing credit. Spend the extra time necessary to get it right before submitting.

How an Article Reaches an Editor's Desk

As mentioned earlier, at a small journal, each staff member wears many hats. Therefore, the editor to whom articles are submitted may also be the copyeditor, publisher, and layout person for the journal. As submissions come in, she reviews each one, noting first if it fits the journal's area of coverage. She also examines the article to see if it is in the proper format and set up according to the journal's guidelines. However, at a small journal, good writing or an interesting topic may override a rejection based on format. This does not mean that it's okay to ignore the journal's guidelines of submission, but it does mean that proper formatting is not as critical here as it is at larger publications. If the article makes it through this first screening, it is passed on to the review board for further discussion. As with other journals, the final decision is always the editor's.

Because fewer layers of editorial staff have to review each submission, decisions regarding acceptance, rejection, and revision tend to be made much faster at smaller journals.

This process happens faster at a small journal both because there are fewer submissions to deal with, and because the editor can make decisions without consulting several other editors in the office. For the most part, the process of submitting to a small journal is less formal than that at larger publications.

Things to Consider When Working With a Small Journal

As already mentioned, these publications receive fewer submissions than the bigger journals in the field. This is partly due to the journals' lower prestige, but may also be caused by the narrower focus of the publications. Sometimes, other academics don't even know that these journals exist. Thus, the subscribers are often people who are just starting out in the industry, and may feel that they do not yet have anything new and innovative to add to the field.

Because there are fewer submissions, these journals are always on the lookout for good writing and excellent research. This provides a wonderful opportunity for new writers. Keep in mind, though, that articles which propose new theories or challenge current thinking are often better suited to the larger audience of the bigger journal. Smaller journals, however, are great markets for articles that present applicable lessons from research, building on the information provided in other academic outlets and putting it in a "news you can use" form. Research on violence among children, for instance, can be combined with insights from educators or child psychologists and molded into an article about dealing with violent student tendencies in the classroom. Or perhaps a groundbreaking study on cancer treatments can be reslanted to focus on bone cancers for an orthopedic journal. These specialized journals, which have a smaller reach, can take research that encompasses larger topics and shape it into material that works for their particular readers.

Even when producing articles for small journals, take the time to research both your subject matter and the publication to which you're submitting your work. Then try calling the journal's editor to make sure that your idea fits the needs of the publication. If your first idea is rejected, follow up with another one. Always remember that editors at small publications are overworked and limited in resources. Everything you can do to make their job easier—from sending in appropriate material to being open to revisions—will make you a more valuable writer in the editor's eyes. If your research is complete, your writing is of good quality, and you make every effort to give the editor what she is looking for, you will eventually enjoy success.

The experience of working at a small journal can be a wonderful means of learning about the publishing process. You will see how an article is crafted and shaped into its final, published form and, most likely, will have the opportunity to work with the journal's editors throughout the process. For new writers, this can be invaluable. And, of course, the experience will add a publishing credit to your curriculum vitae.

Non-Refereed Journals

There are several differences between refereed and non-refereed journals. First and foremost, articles submitted to non-refereed publications are not formally reviewed by a board of experts. Therefore, they are not subjected to the same rigorous standards as those imposed on submissions to refereed journals. In addition, unlike their refereed counterparts, non-refereed journals may carry commercial advertising, include articles written by people who do not work in academia, and contain news and editorial commentaries.

Like publications in any category, different non-refereed journals are associated with different levels of quality and esteem. But it is often difficult to determine a non-refereed journal's level of prestige.

Many journals offer both refereed and non-refereed sections. *Fire Technology*, for instance, is a peer-reviewed quarterly sponsored by the National Fire Protection Association. The "Technical Notes" section, however, is non-refereed and offers a place to publish brief articles, literature reviews, tutorial papers, and other information about fire technology. This provides a way for beginners to break into print and establish a relationship with the journal, which eventually may lead to other opportunities.

Unlike consumer magazines, there are no set criteria by which you can evaluate a journal. In general, journals that hit a wide segment of the industry, are widely read by experts in the field, and take the time to carefully review all submissions, rank the highest with academics. Often, a mentor or colleague can fill you in on a journal's position in the academic hierarchy.

Because there is no review board, generally, an editor or associate editor reviews all submissions and determines their appropriateness for the publication. If revisions are needed, the editor sends a letter to the author asking for specific changes. If the editor doesn't think that the material fits within the scope of the journal, or if the subject has been covered by another article in the recent past, she sends out a rejection letter instead.

These publications offer a great way for unpublished academics to enter the journal market. "Non-refereed journals are easier to publish within, often need the copy and are rather like non-paying markets for writers who wish to get their work noticed and get experience in writing," explains Danusia Malina, Professor of Organizational Behavior and Development at University of Teesside, United Kingdom. In actuality, some non-refereed journals *do* pay for articles, although payment rates never approach the fees paid by consumer magazines. However, as with most academic journals, the lure is not the money but the prestige associated with being accepted for publication.

Another plus is that the publication process moves faster in non-refereed journals than in peer-reviewed publications simply because the editorial review process is shorter. If you have important research or a timely idea, your piece could be held up for more than a year at a peer-reviewed publication. Consider this point, and weigh the different journal options before submitting.

Always keep in mind that while many non-refereed journals are hungry for copy, this does not mean that the publications never ask for revisions. Most authors need to perform revisions of some type before their articles are accepted.

Online Academic Journals

This market is growing in leaps and bounds. Hundreds of academic journals are producing online versions that sometimes feature material different from what is offered in the print versions. One of the first to be a true virtual academic journal was the education-centered *Kairos*, which states in its guidelines that although it is refereed—the publication refers to it as "interactive non-blind peer reviewing"—its goal is to guide writers in developing their piece for publication on the site.

As an experimental medium, online journals have the ability to take more chances, both with their design and with their content. They can add video and audio clips, provide animation, and insert daily updates on any material. Links can be added, updated, or removed, depending on the needs of readers. Information can be augmented as necessary, or rewritten to fit new findings. The fluidity of electronic media makes it great for cutting-edge topics. In addition, distribution of your paper is instantaneous and broad because of the nature of web publishing.

Online journals open up many previously closed doors to publication. Authors who have a piece that may not fit anywhere else sometimes stand a good shot of publishing online. Online journals don't offer the same prestige as refereed print publications, and few, if any, pay. But these publications do provide a good outlet for beginning writers because they have unlimited room for content, a willingness to take a chance on untried formats, and a need for continual material. In addition, as *Kairos* states in its guidelines for submission, a credit in such journals offers the benefit of establishing the writer in a technological and innovative light.

Other Academic Outlets

Academic journals are not the sole market for scholarly writers. A number of commercial publications offer opportunities for unique think pieces and unusual approaches to different topics. Payment is also more likely in traditional publications than in academic.

The best places to start are the trade and technical journals discussed earlier in this chapter. "Alternative" publications make up another good market. These newspapers and magazines have smaller markets, but are constantly on the lookout for cultural, political, and literary material. *Mother Jones, Mother Earth News,* and the Chicago *Reader* are all examples of alternative publications.

In addition, literary or "little" magazines—publications like *Antioch Review, Frank,* and *Michigan Quarterly Review*—are open to unique

Many print journals are now offering online segments to broaden their reach. This is great for academics with a web presence or online curriculum vitae. When an article is published online, it's easy to add a link from your web page to the piece.

Don't forget to look into international publishing opportunities. *Ulrich's International Periodical's Directory* provides a wealth of information on non-American journals. (See additional data on this source in Chapter 4.) Many of these journals are eager for an American perspective on the issues they cover.

Little magazines are usually financed by individuals or groups who want to provide an outlet for intelligent and sophisticated writing, including the unique and avant-garde pieces usually rejected by large commercial magazines. If your article idea seems to fall into this category, your chances of selling to this market are great.

material from authoritative voices. Although payment usually takes the form of contributor's copies and the readership is small, these magazines are often 90 to 100 percent freelance written, providing a ready forum for people who wish to express ideas and opinions.

CONCLUSION

You now should have a firm grasp of the various markets available to you. While most writers dream of seeing their article printed in a publication like *Reader's Digest* their first time out, the reality is that unknown writers stand little chance of getting their work into major consumer markets of this type. If you are trying to find a home for a few articles, aim for smaller, lesser-known publications. If you are interested in building a career in writing, remember that whether your target publications are consumer magazines or refereed journals, the best means of reaching the top is to start at the bottom and work your way up. The upper levels can be reached, but it takes credentials, perseverance, and patience to get there.

GETTING AN ARTICLE PUBLISHED

A writer has to do more than dream of success if she wants to see her article in print. She has to get her work to the most appropriate publications and present it in the best way possible. Designed for the writer who has already written an article and wants to find a home for it, Part Two does just that: It details the steps you need to take to get your work into publication.

Chapter 3 begins the journey by helping you define your article's topic, approach, and audience. Then Chapter 4 helps you zone in on the best publications for your work. In Chapter 5, you'll learn to prepare an effective submission package, and in Chapter 6, you'll find a step-by-step system for sending your packages out to your target publications. Finally, Chapter 7 helps you deal with the responses to your work, whether they take the form of much-desired acceptance letters or less-desirable rejections.

In the following pages, you will:

■ Learn to identify and accurately describe your article's topic, approach, and audience.

■ Explore the many available market resource books, periodicals, and Internet sites, and use them to create a list of target publications.

■ Discover how to prepare a winning submission package and tailor it for each publication on your list.

■ Master a system for sending out submissions that will maximize your chance of getting your article into print.

■ Discover how to respond to acceptance letters like a pro.

■ Learn from rejection, master new skills, and get your article into publication.

It takes work to get an article published. Part Two will guide your efforts, helping you navigate the maze of the publishing world and successfully reach your goal.

CHAPTER 3

WHERE DOES YOUR ARTICLE FIT IN?

Imagine you've decided that your local newspaper would provide the perfect home for your article. As suggested in Chapter 2, you call the editor of the newspaper to see if he might be interested in the piece. He asks you to encapsulate your piece in a few sentences and explain why you think it would fit in his publication. What is your article's topic? What type of article is it? What specific audience are you trying to reach?

Consider if you would be able to answer these questions with confidence and clarity. If not, you will probably have a more difficult time getting your work published, and not only because you will show a lack of savvy during conversations with editors. As you learned in the previous chapter, some publications use freelancers to write only certain types of articles—op-ed pieces, for instance. If your article takes another type of approach—if it's a news story, for example—it would be a waste of time to submit the piece to that publication. Later on, when you write to or call your target publications, you will have to demonstrate an understanding of both your topic and your audience. If you fail to do so, you will show a lack of professionalism. In fact, there are many, many reasons you should know where your article fits in.

This chapter will help you pinpoint the topic of your article, the type of article you have written, and the audience that your article addresses. By identifying these three elements, you will be better able not only to find a publication that is interested in articles like yours, but also to convince the editor that your article would be of value to his readers.

WHAT IS YOUR ARTICLE'S TOPIC?

Whether you are compiling a list of potential markets for your work or preparing a submission package for one of your target publications, you need to have a very clear idea of the topic covered in your article. That may sound fairly obvious—and fairly easy, too. "What's so difficult about that?" you might ask. "My article is about weddings. My topic is weddings." But you need much more than a general notion of the subject of your piece.

First, it's important to recognize that the subject of an article *must* be limited simply because the length of an article is limited. Because a book can be several hundred pages in length, it can take a more general approach, devoting separate chapters to the history of weddings in America, the symbolic meaning of wedding rituals in Western society, the various types of ceremonies, and more. But because an article doesn't have the same luxury of space, it has to focus on one aspect of weddings.

Now you know why an article must focus on a limited subject. But why is it so important to be able to define that topic? To answer this question, let's look at two different articles on the same general subject of weddings. First, let's assume that you've written an article entitled "Creating Memorable Wedding Decorations." Such an article—broad in its reach, and suitable for all brides, young and old, wealthy and middle class—might work in a variety of publications, including, for instance, *Better Homes & Gardens* and *Brides.*

Now, let's consider an article entitled "Blending Custom Teas for One-of-a-Kind Wedding Favors." This article—more precise in its reach—speaks to a smaller, probably upscale audience. Thus, *Better Homes & Gardens,* which addresses the "average" person, would not be the best home for it. However, *Martha Stewart Weddings,* which is geared for an upscale crowd that wants something a bit out of the ordinary, might be just the market for this more specialized piece. As you see, your specific topic will have a marked effect on the audience and the publications that you target.

When you are defining the topic of your article, it's easiest to start with the general subject, and then keep tightening your focus until you pinpoint the precise subject of your piece. Let's turn to the general subject of cars, and assume that you have written a piece that falls within this general category, there are literally millions of different subjects on which you could write: antique cars, new cars, car manufacturers, car safety, how a car is made in a factory, engines, and on and on.

Now take a look at just one of these subjects: automobile safety. If you told an editor that you had written an article on automobile safety, you would certainly be providing more detailed information than you would if you defined your subject as just "cars." Nevertheless, even narrowing your subject to that of safety doesn't provide much useful information. On what aspect of safety are you writing? Are you writing about the history of car safety? Are you writing about the safety features that will be introduced in next year's cars? Are you covering only those automobiles that get three stars or less in Insurance Industry tests? Only those automobiles that failed safety tests? Only vehicles that failed in a certain year? Only cars that failed in the past, but now are passing with flying colors? All cars, foreign and domestic? Only luxury vehicles? Only sedans? Only sports utility vehicles? As you see, the more questions you ask, the more exact your focus will be—and the more useful your information will be to the editor to whom you are submitting your article or query.

If you're having trouble defining your topic, think of it another way: What is the reason people would want to read this article? What information will they glean from your words—information they might not have had before, or might not be able to find anywhere else? Fill in the blank: By reading this article, people will know more about _____. If you answer this question as specifically and accurately as possible, you should be able to clearly define the subject of your article.

> When trying to define the topic of your article, ask yourself what information the reader will glean from your piece. What questions will your article answer that another might not?

In the case of most articles, it is fairly easy to define the topic. An article on luxury sedans could not be mistaken for an article on any other subject. Be aware, though, that sometimes you have to look below the surface of the words on the page to find the true subject of the piece. You might remember a book called *Zen and the Art of Motorcycle Maintenance*. This book told the story of a cross-country motorcycle trip taken by a father and son. But was the book really about cross-country travel—or about motorcycle maintenance? Actually, the author of the book used the setting of a trip to explore the philosophical landscape, and the book was more or less a history of philosophy. So, as you can see, looks (and titles, too) can be deceiving. Similarly, your personal essay may seem to be about a night you spent out with the boys, but really be an exploration of men's relationships with women as discussed during a boys' night out. So be sure to pinpoint what your article is really about and to communicate this to editors in both letters and phone conversations.

Once you've defined your topic, be aware that your topic should define your article. A piece on the safety features of luxury sedans shouldn't stray from the subject and start discussing lower-priced cars or SUVs. And an article on tea bag wedding favors shouldn't turn into an exploration of wedding rituals. So if your article has already been written, by all means read it over to make sure it stays on track from beginning to end. And if you have yet to write your piece, keep your subject in mind as you complete your work. (For more guidelines on writing articles, see Chapter 10.)

WHAT TYPE OF ARTICLE HAVE YOU WRITTEN?

Editors and experienced writers alike use specific terms to refer to different types of articles. An editor may be looking for an "interview/profile" of a new actor. A writer might offer a "round-up" on the mayor's new policy regarding the city's treatment of homeless people. Whether you want to place only one article or launch a freelance writing career, it's important to understand these terms and to use them properly. If you have already completed an article, your understanding of article types will allow you to classify your piece so that you can select the best target publications—publications that accept that type of article from a freelance writer. If you have yet to write your article, by first choosing the form that your work will take, you will be better able to shape it to fit the parameters of that classification. And, of course, your familiarity with these terms and categories will enable you to communicate more confidently and knowledgeably with editors, both in letters and over the phone.

Although certain types of articles appear in both consumer publications and academic publications, for the most part, each of these areas uses its own unique approaches. Let's look first at the articles found in consumer and trade publications, and then at the article classifications used by academic journals.

Consumer and Trade Publications

Consumer and trade publications use a variety of articles to inform

Choosing the Right "Person"

When you read about the different types of articles in this chapter, you will learn that a how-to article is usually written in *second person,* while a humor piece is generally written in *first person.* But if you haven't been in English class for a while, you may have forgotten what these terms mean. The forms of first person, second person, and third person all have to do with the pronouns used within a written piece—you, me, he, she, etc. If your memory of these terms is still a little foggy, the following discussions should clear everything up and make sure that you choose the right "person" when crafting each of your articles.

First Person

When something is written in first person, it has the "I" viewpoint, meaning that it is seen from the writer's point of view. You can think of it in terms of closeness; first person is the person closest to you, i.e., you.

First-person writing is used often in personal essays, humor pieces, and other articles that describe experiences which you have directly undergone. This style builds a relationship with the reader, as if you were telling the story to a friend: "*I* learned a unique way to bake bread when *I* ran out of bread pans the other day. Spying an empty coffee can, *I* concocted the idea of coffee bread—cinnamon loaves baked in coffee containers, giving them a unique shape."

Second Person

Second-person writing has the "you" viewpoint. Again, you can remember this by imagining that you are talking to the second most immediate person to you—the person sitting next to you.

The second-person form is most common in how-to pieces—articles that give advice or information. It is designed to help the reader feel as if the writer is talking directly to him: "When *you* are baking bread in a coffee can, *you* need to turn the oven temperature down and reduce the cooking time by ten minutes. This helps *you* control the

cooking, providing a more even texture and a loaf that stays within the confines of the can."

Third Person

Third-person writing is the most distant of all the forms being discussed. In this type of writing, "he," "she," and "they" are the pronouns used. "I" and "you" are not used at all.

Third-person writing is generally employed in objective articles such as news stories and features, and is sometimes used in interview/profile pieces, as well. When you are trying to present important information or show an unbiased front, this is the style of choice: "Kim Hart said that newborn babies can't see anything that isn't in their immediate line of vision. *She* recommends that new parents interact face-to-face, with slower movements that give the baby time to interpret body language."

A certain sign of an amateur writer is the tendency to move from first-person writing to second-person writing to third-person writing—all in one article, without rhyme or reason. So choose your style carefully, and then use it as consistently as possible. This is not only technically correct, but also ensures that the tone of your article remains exactly what you want it to be from beginning to end.

and to entertain. Some of the following categories are most common in consumer publications, while some are more likely to appear in trade journals.

When trying to categorize an article, be aware that some articles combine features of two different categories. A profile of an expert like Bob Vila, for instance, would have a how-to component if it contained tips on do-it-yourself home repair. If this is true of your article, determine which approach is most dominant in your work and use that term to describe it.

The terms used below are the most common ones. However, you may find that your editor refers to one of these articles by a different name, as jargon can vary slightly from publication to publication. When in doubt, ask the editor for clarification.

Be aware that the following article types have been arranged in alphabetical order; the order in no way reflects your chance of selling such pieces to publications as a freelancer. Some publications have their staff writers provide the majority of the profiles, for example, and assign only reviews and filler pieces to freelancers. The key to success is investigating your market before you send in your article.

Cultural Commentary

A *cultural commentary* is a first-person piece that expresses the writer's opinion on a cultural issue or trend. These pieces can run fairly short—only a few hundred words—or can be several hundred words in length. An article that examines how America is driven by the quest to own luxury vehicles, even at the cost of personal safety, would make a good cultural commentary, as would a first-person article discussing our society's obsession with weight loss. Almost all consumer publications, from newspapers to magazines, run variations of this type of piece.

Cultural commentaries are written entirely by staff at some publications, yet mostly by freelancers at others—depending entirely on the editorial policy. Check the masthead against the bylines to see which is the case with your target publication.

Feature Article

A *feature article* is one that is presented as a special attraction in a magazine or newspaper. This piece is usually the cover article, meaning that there is a mention of it on the cover of the publication. Although a feature doesn't have to take a specific form, it generally gives a human-interest perspective. For instance, a feature might tell the story of a woman who has successfully battled cancer. Such a story is one that readers can relate to because it is about something that could happen in their own lives. Most feature articles are written in the third person, although some are styled in first person, with an "as told to" mention of the writer at the top. The word count varies from publication to publication and according to placement in the magazine. A cover feature can run 3,000 words, while a secondary feature runs around 1,000 words or so.

All publications use feature articles in one way or another. Most of these are provided by staff writers or by contributing writers who are freelancers, simply because editors need to know the article will be there on time and in good shape. When you are just starting out, filler pieces and other relatively short articles are a far better bet.

Filler Piece

A *filler* is a short article of 200 words or less that does exactly what its name implies—it fills a space. Depending on the publication, fillers can range from news stories that don't merit feature treatment—such as a story on the Make-a-Wish Foundation's need for extra funds—to humor pieces, anecdotes, puzzles, jokes, and poems. These articles are usually written in third person if they are news-related, and in first person if they are humor or slice-of-life pieces such as the ones printed in *Reader's Digest*.

Fillers represent a great opportunity for the writer who's trying to break into print. Almost every publication needs them to fill the spaces left by larger pieces.

Fillers represent one of the best ways for freelancers to break into a market because they are easy to sell and used by almost every publication. However, because they are usually needed in a hurry, publications rarely assign them to freelancers. If there are no freelanced fillers waiting in line, an in-house writer is asked to create a filler from a press release or other material.

How-To Article

A *how-to article* provides step-by-step information on completing a physical or creative project—fixing a car, planting watermelons, or decorating a cake, for instance. These articles, which can range widely in word count, combine information, advice, and, often, quotes from the people who provided the tips. A how-to is usually written in second person, because this creates a more immediate bond with the reader.

Because of the high demand for how-tos, many are created by freelancers. Most of the time, these articles are used by magazines and e-zines, but newspapers use some as well.

Humor Piece

Many publications are open to freelanced humor pieces. The key is to find the publication that is the best match for your brand of humor.

A *humor piece* is designed to do exactly what its name conveys—to entertain people and make them laugh. These articles can vary widely in style. Some are funny slice-of-life essays, while others are parodies. Some are tongue-in-cheek, while others are marked by sarcasm. Most are written in first person, and usually they run no more than 1,000 words in length.

A good number of humor pieces are created by freelancers. Just be aware that the type of humor used varies from publication to publication. *Salon.com,* for example, uses a witty, somewhat sarcastic tone in its essays, with writing that covers contemporary issues. *Country Woman* has more down-to-earth humor, with essays about funny life adventures. Find the publication that is the best fit for your writing, and you will increase your chances for success.

Interview/Profile

An *interview/profile* is an article based on a conversation with a celebrity or expert, and written either in a question-and-answer format or as a traditional third-person article, with quotes from the primary subject. These pieces can run anywhere from 200 to 2,000 words or more, depending on the publication.

Profiles are common in virtually all publications, from consumer magazines to trade journals to newspapers. Even e-zines and newsletters carry these popular articles. Just be sure that your interview subject is one of interest to the readers of the target publication. An interview with Kathie Lee Gifford, for instance, would work well for a women's magazine like *Woman's Day,* but probably wouldn't be a good fit for *GQ.*

Although freelancers can land profile assignments, keep in mind that big magazines and newspapers have little trouble securing these interviews, and usually just assign a staff writer or an editor to the story. However, if you are able to secure such an interview on your own and are writing for a smaller publication that might not have that kind of celebrity access, you stand a good chance of getting the assignment.

News Story

Written in third person, from an unbiased point of view, a *news story* provides serious coverage of a topical subject. These articles run 200 to 1,500 words in length, and rely on at least three sources to offer an impartial treatment of the topic. Stories like "Why Discount Retailers Are Making It Big," "Police Hunt Murder Suspect," and "Michael Jordan Considers Return to the Court" are all news stories because they offer a look at something that is affecting the reader's world today.

Trade journals and newspapers are the publications most likely to print news stories, with trade journals focusing on the news in their particular industry, and newspapers covering local, national, and global issues that affect large numbers of general readers. However, some magazines—*Time* and *Newsweek*, for instance—are dedicated to presenting these articles.

At newspapers, most news stories are covered by staff writers. At other publications, freelancers may provide some of the news stories, while contributing writers provide others. In general, however, because deadlines are so critical, editors assign news stories only to those writers whom they know to be reliable.

Op-Ed Piece

An *op-ed piece*, more formally referred to as an *opinion-editorial piece*, is a 400- to 600-word first-person work that expresses the writer's opinion on a particular topic. Some op-eds offer a supporting viewpoint on an issue that was covered in an earlier article; others are written to inform readers about issues facing society or the neighborhood. If you were a vocal supporter of the local PTA, and noticed that few parents were involved, you might want to write an op-ed about the benefits of being a member of that organization.

The most common outlets for op-ed pieces are local newspapers, although some magazines and newsletters run them, as well. Newspapers usually have one or two op-eds that are written by staff writers, but a good majority of op-eds in all publications are created by freelancers. There is generally very little or no pay for an op-ed, but the exposure can be beneficial.

Personal Essay

Virtually every type of publication uses personal essays—and many are open to freelance submissions. Just be sure that the tone and style of your essay matches that of your target publication.

Personal essays are 400- to 1,000-word pieces written in first person on either a personal problem that the writer has faced and overcome, or a meaningful event. These articles, which are also called *personal experience pieces*, differ from op-ed pieces in that the subject is always of a personal nature. Moreover, rather than expressing an opinion, the essay is usually written to show how the writer conquered a problem, survived a tragedy, or learned a lesson. A story on the devastating consequences of a car accident would make a good personal essay. Family and relationship issues are also popular topics.

Women's magazines are a very common forum for personal essays. E-zines, too, provide a good market, as the informal atmosphere of most Internet publications lends itself to the intimate tone of personal essays. Newspapers like *The Christian Science Monitor* also run these pieces. All types of publications are very open to freelance personal essay submissions.

Photo Feature

The *photo feature*—or *photo essay,* as it is sometimes called—is, as its name suggests, very light on writing and heavy on pictures. This type of article often has prominent status in the publication because the photos lend it great force. The writer usually provides a few sentences about each photo, letting the images tell the story. Sometimes, the photographer does both jobs—photography and writing. In other cases, a writer on the publication's staff provides the content. For the most part, photo features are not assigned to freelance writers because the photography dictates the amount of writing necessary, and it is often easier to assign an in-house writer or to let the photographer write the piece.

Review

A 200- to 2,000-word critique of a book, movie, play, product, service, website, or restaurant, a *review* is written in the first person and designed to provide the writer's perspective of the review subject.

Reviews are carried by most magazines, trade journals, newspapers, and e-zines. Some newsletters run them, too. For a site like Cars.com, you could provide a review of the new Cadillac on the market; for *Auto Weekly*, one that covers the autobiography of Lee Iacocca would be appropriate.

Although the pay for reviews is generally very low, reviews provide a great opportunity for freelancers—especially since they sometimes require relatively little research. In fact, a lot of writers who compile information for a news story or feature article later review the books they used to gather data, and sell the resulting pieces to other publications.

Round-Up

A *round-up* is a 500- to 1,000-word third-person piece that contains quotes from a variety of people on one subject, or in answer to a particular question. Sometimes, these articles are referred to as *surveys* and incorporate statistics, such as percentage of respondents who gave one answer over another. A number of women's magazines carry these entertaining articles, and often turn to readers or celebrities for the answers. For instance, a fun round-up might ask celebrities what one makeup item they'd take on a desert island. A more serious round-up might question senior citizens about their worst medical experience.

Although a few newspapers carry round-ups, they are generally found in consumer and trade magazines and e-zines. These articles are usually written by staff writers who call on sources from their reader database or from past interviews. In most cases, those round-ups that are written by freelancers are assigned to writers who contribute frequently to the publication.

Service Piece

Service pieces fall into the how-to category, but go further than just explaining how to do something. Usually running 500 or more words in length, a *service piece* is a third-person article designed to inform, educate, and advise the audience about an important issue or life skill like investing, working, or making a purchase. An article on finding a good mechanic would be considered a service piece. These pieces usually offer a sidebar of additional information and resources, including phone numbers and addresses.

Service pieces are used by virtually every type of publication, and are split evenly between freelancers and staff writers.

Technical Article

Written in technical language, a *technical article* covers issues that the typical layman's publication wouldn't examine in its articles. Technical articles vary in length, depending on the material being covered, and are always written in third person. As you might expect, these pieces are run by trade journals, specifically by those that cover technical fields such as engineering and computer programming. An article on "Streamlining the Internet-Fiber Connection" or "Programming in JAVA Script" would fit these outlets.

Because the language of a technical article is so complicated and specialized, in-depth knowledge of the subject is an absolute must. For this reason, the writer is usually a staff writer or an outside expert.

Tips Article

A *tips article* provides readers with hints and advice in a quick, easy-to-read format. Specifically, these pieces tell the reader how to do something better or more economically.

Depending on the format and tone of the publication, tips articles vary in approach. Some are written in first person; many, in second person; and a few, in third person. Tips articles are often short—less than 1,000 words—and are defined by a series of short paragraphs offering advice and resources. "Seven Ways to Save Money on Groceries," "Five Criteria for Choosing a Physician," and "Quick Tips for Cooking Success" are all samples of tips articles.

Virtually every kind of consumer and trade publication uses tips articles. And better yet, freelancers write the majority of the tips pieces published.

Like fillers, humor pieces, op-eds, and personal essays, tips articles represent an opportunity for the new writer. Virtually every kind of consumer and trade publication uses tips articles, and the majority of these pieces are contributed by freelancers.

Academic Journals

Often, when people think of academic journals, dissertations immediately come to mind. However, academic journals also carry many of the same types of articles that are printed in consumer publications. Depending on the focus of the journal, you might find a wide range of article types, or you might find just a few of the following categories represented.

Note that although I have sometimes indicated the general length of some types of articles, in many cases, article length can vary dramatically from journal to journal, based on space considerations. Be sure to check with each publication for word-count guidelines before submitting your work.

Case Study

A *case study* is usually a first-person fictionalized or real account of a dilemma, and the method used to resolve it. Many times, a case study focuses on personal and interpersonal crises. An article on dealing with difficult children in the classroom, on helping young executives bring their enthusiasm to work in a constructive manner, or on treating patients with a specific condition can provide guidance for peer readers who face similar challenges.

A case study is generally submitted by the person who was a firsthand observer of or participant in the experience being described. This writer has learned techniques that can benefit other readers.

Conference Paper

A number of writers use verbal presentations as "trial runs" for papers they'd like to write and submit to journals in the future. A *conference paper* is an article based on such a presentation. Sometimes, conference papers—as well as dissertations, discussed below—are published in collections that center on one topic, such as plant studies. These books are generally intended to appeal to audiences wider than that of the journal by incorporating material on related topics.

Because verbal presentations are less formal than written works, and omit the details usually included in journal articles, the text of such presentations is generally revised before it is published. However, some lectures are so well written that they are printed in journals as is. Carefully analyze your presentation and compare it with the written material printed in your target journal before deciding if it requires revision.

Verbal presentations made at conferences often serve as "trial runs" for submissions to academic journals. Most of these presentations must be revised before they are suitable for publication.

Dissertation

A *dissertation* is written to do one thing—to prove a thesis. In general, the first sentence of the dissertation is the thesis, and everything that follows is used to support that conclusion. The key to writing a good dissertation is making it original and substantive. You don't want to prove a thesis that has been proved before. Rather you want to examine information in a new light.

Dissertations are written in the third person and can run quite long—100 to 300 pages. Many scholars have their dissertations bound into books or submit them to publishers. Online markets are best for dissertations because they offer unlimited space, although some journals publish excerpts in their print editions, and some publishers collect several dissertations for publication in annual volumes.

A large number of schools are now promoting Electronic Theses and Dissertations (ETDs) to their students. These electronic forms allow for a greater concentration of tables, graphs, and references. The Networked Digital Library of Theses and Dissertations project is an online venture that links a number of schools' ETDs for research purposes.

Editorial

Like an op-ed piece run in a consumer publication, an *editorial* is written in first person and expresses one individual's view of a topic, usually in 900 words or less.

Editorials can cover a full gamut of subjects, but should always relate back to the journal's main area of coverage. For example, an academic journal that analyzes popular culture might include an editorial on the controversial advertising methods used by fashion designers like Calvin Klein. A journal for medical professionals might include an editorial on how HMO cutbacks are affecting research funding.

In some cases, all editorials are written in-house by the editor and/or his staff. Other journals accept outside contributions. Be sure to check with the journal before submitting, or to compare the masthead with the editorial bylines to determine if any of these articles are freelanced.

Feature Article

A *feature article* is similar to a news stories found in consumer publications. These pieces, which are written in third person, are designed to provide in-depth, comprehensive information on breakthrough thinking and its application in the reader's world. Pieces on the effects of information technology systems on the workplace, efforts to thwart mad cow disease, and studies on violence in high school children would all be considered feature articles.

Although you would find these same stories in a publication like *Newsweek*, the journal version would be far more detailed and be addressed solely to the readers of the publication, rather than the broad audience served by a newspaper or magazine. When written for an agricultural journal, for instance, the article on mad cow disease would detail new research and include tables and graphs that demonstrate research findings. It would also include information on how this research could be applied in practice.

How-To/Application

A *how-to/application* provides in-depth information on improving or remedying a particular situation. How-to/applications usually show these ideas in action, providing real-life examples of the application at work. Like consumer service pieces, these articles often offer tips and resources. But unlike a case study, which uses a specific real-life example to demonstrate lessons learned, or a personal experience article, which is written entirely in first person, the how-to/application incorporates information from a number of sources and experts, providing a well-rounded third-person article. For instance, an article on improving employee morale would incorporate tips from not just CEOs, but also human studies experts and perhaps employees themselves. By including information from numerous sources, this kind of article is designed to interest a wider swath of readers.

Outsider Opinion Piece

An *outsider opinion piece* is generally written in first person by someone outside the academic community, which is what makes it different from a personal experience article. The purpose of such an article is to provide a unique perspective, highlighting techniques or information that may have worked in the nonacademic world. The *Harvard Business Review,* for example, often uses this type of article to help executives solve workplace dilemmas. An expert in negotiations with employees could submit an article on this topic, providing information from his experiences. Or the CEO of Johnson & Johnson could

Outsider opinion pieces offer an excellent opportunity for writers who are outside the academic community. If you are an expert in your field and have a unique perspective on a problem covered by a specific academic journal, consider sharing your information with the publication's readers.

submit an article on trends he sees in health-care products, and offer advice to researchers on filling niches. These articles are always written by freelancers and, because most outsider opinion articles don't incorporate data like tables and graphs, are usually not as long as other academic articles.

Personal Experience Piece

Like a personal essay printed in a consumer publication, a *personal experience piece* is a first-person account in which the writer presents a problem that he faced, and then explains the solution he used to solve it. The goal of these articles is to teach applicable lessons to readers who might face similar challenges in their industry. Unlike a case study, which is accompanied by more in-depth research and findings, the personal experience article is shorter—generally under 1,000 words in length—and less detailed. For instance, a journal that covers international politics could carry a personal experience article from a writer who traveled to Russia and saw the impact of United States' policies on the rural poor. He would include his observations and thoughts on how politicians should rethink their strategies to benefit people at all economic levels. Or an oncology journal might print a doctor's account of treating patients with alternative remedies in conjunction with traditional therapies. The key to making a personal experience article work is to present information that's relevant to a number of readers while keeping the approach of the article personal.

Profile/Interview

Based on personal interviews, a *profile/interview* focuses on one individual, usually an expert with esteemed credentials. These articles can be written in either a question-and-answer format or a narrative, depending on the publication. Profiles of Disney's Michael Eisner and Ford's Jacques Nasser would both be appropriate articles in academic journals. Like most journal articles, the goal of a profile/interview is to advance the reader's knowledge of a relevant topic. Thus, a profile of a business executive might explain how that individual transformed the structure of his company, while the profile of a surgeon might detail how the doctor's education and earlier work contributed to his development of a life-saving procedure.

Research and Trend Report

Based on observation or experimentation, a *research and trend report* provides information on relevant trends, phenomena, companies, or individuals. These reports can often be used as the foundation for other academic articles. For example, a report on obesity in America can form the basis of an article on the consumption of milk products and their effect on obesity in laboratory animals or study groups. Or the report itself can be released in a journal such as the *New England Journal of Medicine,* and then utilized by other authors in articles on specific aspects of the topic.

Research and trend reports are generally compiled by organizations, although some come straight from the laboratory. They are welcomed by journals because they stimulate thinking, leading to the creation of further material.

Review

Like a consumer review, an academic *review* provides critiques—in this case, of software, texts, books, workshops, websites, and other resources of interest to the journal's audience. Reviews sometimes accompany a feature article on a particular topic, and sometimes run in the review section of a journal. Often, the review section is non-refereed and open to contributors. These articles are very short—usually only a few hundred words—and are often written in first person because they are subjective in nature.

Because the review section of an academic journal often is not refereed—meaning that submissions do not have to be approved by a board of experts—reviews can be a good means of breaking into higher-echelon publications.

Sample Syllabus or Curriculum

Journals dedicated to teachers or teaching issues often present a sample *syllabus,* an outline or summary of the main points of a lecture or course of study; or a sample *curriculum,* a course of study. Usually accompanied by notes and commentary from the teachers and students, these articles are intended to guide teachers in presenting material in new ways or in setting up classes for new subjects. First-year teachers find sample syllabi especially helpful because they provide a starting point. But experienced teachers who are facing a new challenge—who have to incorporate technology into a science class, or who are looking for innovative ways to teach Latin—also read these articles. Generally, these pieces are written by experienced teaching professionals and are accompanied by a number of resources, sample lessons, and tips.

Survey

Journals that analyze trends in different industries or fields of interest often include *surveys* that report the latest research in that field. To round out the survey, the article usually contains brief interviews, charts, opinion analyses, or short discussions of relevant research.

Unlike a research report, a survey asks a question of experts in the field and then compiles their responses. For example, a survey might examine the reactions of physicians to marketing by drug companies, and question how that marketing affects the doctors' prescription choices. Or it might ask graduate students how their publishing credits have affected their careers at the university. Results are reported in statistical form, with some analysis and commentary included. Any information provided by respondents to back up their answers is also presented. Many times, the survey is sponsored by the journal and performed by either a staff writer or an outside writer. Surveys are written objectively, in third person, so that the responses from the survey takers are not colored by the writer's opinions.

Theoretical Essay

A *theoretical essay* can be written in first or third person, and is designed to help advance the discussion of different theories, often by presenting evidence that supports or refutes a specific viewpoint. For instance, a journal that covers media topics could run a theoretical essay on the future of newspapers, focusing on the impact of the dot-com demise coupled with the rising cost of paper. Another journal might explore how birth order affects scientists and their research abilities. Designed to provoke thought, these essays explore subjects that may seem radical, yet have some grounding in fact. Like other academic articles, theoretical essays should incorporate research and statistics. Length on these essays varies, but because of their experimental nature, they are kept shorter than full scholarly articles.

WHAT IS YOUR ARTICLE'S AUDIENCE?

Every magazine, newspaper, newsletter, e-zine, and journal markets its publication toward a particular group of readers. And as you learned in Chapter 2, when editors review submitted work, they look for pieces that would interest that audience, and therefore sell issues. As a writer, you need to pinpoint your article's readership so you can direct your material toward the right publication; so you can demonstrate your understanding of your audience in communications with editors; and so you can, if necessary, make any changes in the tone, content, and language of your material to better fit your readers.

When determining the audience for your piece, don't make the common mistake of thinking that your article has universal appeal. Although we would all like to believe that everyone would profit from our work, the fact is that no article is really for everyone. Every article—whether on the cultivation of roses, the safety features of luxury automobiles, or breakthrough surgical techniques—is directed toward a particular kind of reader. The objective is to match your article with its intended audience and, then, ultimately, with the publications that serve those readers.

Consumer and Trade Audiences

The vast majority of articles are geared for the general consumer audience or the trade audience. So unless your article is a scholarly piece designed to advance the thinking in a specific field of academic endeavor, you can begin by focusing on the general consumer and on people in businesses or professions.

Once you've narrowed it down to the consumer and trade audience, it's fairly easy to determine which of these two general markets you're addressing. If your article is geared to improve job performance in a trade, business, or profession, you'll want to target the trade audience. If, however, your article has broader appeal, your reader will be the general consumer.

Let's assume that your readers are among the millions that buy consumer publications. You have now narrowed down the field a bit, but you have to go much further, because no publication addresses every member of the consumer audience. The best way to further define your reader is to ask yourself who would be interested in reading your article. The answer to this question will be largely based on your topic, and in most cases, it will be obvious. A piece that highlights the latest glittery nail polishes would appeal to teenagers and women

Many new writers make the mistake of thinking that their articles will appeal to everyone. The key to success is first determining your article's audience, and then matching your article with publications that address those specific readers.

in their twenties. A how-to article on picking a great cruise would appeal to an older audience comprised of people with enough money to afford relatively expensive vacations.

Be aware, though, that, depending on your approach and the specific information you provide, an article on a single topic may appeal to more than one audience. To clarify this, let's consider an article on children's car safety seats. On the surface, such an article seems to be geared for new parents. And certainly, if the article is a general how-to piece on choosing or installing a car seat, the audience would largely be new parents. However, an article on the same topic might also address other audiences. A brief how-to on using a car seat, coupled with some information on how today's restraints differ from those used a generation ago, would be good for grandparents. A legal slant on car seats and their importance would be best suited for day-care providers. When pinpointing your audience, therefore, be sure to carefully examine your particular slant—how you've presented the material, and what specific material you've chosen to include. Your spin can have a big effect on audience composition.

Now let's look at an article designed for a trade journal. Again, remember that although the topic is an important clue, your particular slant on the topic must also be kept in mind. Consider, for instance, an article on the latest commercial heating and cooling systems. At first glance, this might seem to only appeal to commercial contractors, and it would—if it focused on installation or on the specifications of the system. However, an article on how a new system can save a business money would work for managers. And a short how-to on do-it-yourself maintenance of the system would appeal to small business owners and maintenance workers.

Be aware that your article may appeal to more than one audience, depending on your chosen approach.

An Academic Audience

If your article is designed to bring the latest in research, breakthroughs, or case studies to readers in a specific field, you have targeted an academic audience. As you know, though, this general audience is comprised of people from many different fields with many different specialties. Your job is to pinpoint the readers who would be interested in your article.

Just as when you defined the audience for a consumer article, you must first look at the topic of your piece, being as specific as possible.

An article on cancer research could appeal to a broad group of physicians. If, however, that article concentrates on clinical applications of that research, with a definite focus on trials and outcomes, you are speaking to hematologists and oncologists. If it focuses only on bone cancer, your article is suitable for doctors who specialize in that area.

When analyzing your audience, you must also take into account the depth of your research and the language used in the piece. The more detailed and technical the information, the higher the education level of the audience must be. Also consider your goal in writing the article. Did you write it to instruct or to encourage discussion? In other words, are you speaking to those who are practicing in the field and are interested in new and better treatments, or are you addressing researchers? Once you've analyzed not only your topic but also these other elements of your article, you will be better able to determine the person for whom you're writing.

If you are unsure of your target readers, ask a peer to review your article and help you make this determination. If you're still not sure, ask yourself who would benefit the most from the information in your article? If you are writing on medical research breakthroughs, are you speaking to surgeons, clinicians, or nurses? To pharmacy executives or teaching hospitals? Again, not only your topic, but also the specific information you present and the intent of your piece, will decide the audience of your article.

Be as accurate as possible when naming the audience for your academic article. Oncologists and hematologists, as opposed to physicians in general, would probably be most interested in a piece on groundbreaking cancer research.

What Is the Profile of Your Audience?

You have narrowed your audience down. Perhaps you've determined that the audience for your article is comprised of new parents or grandparents. Or perhaps your article addresses researchers involved in the study of a specific type of cancer. While this is certainly helpful information, in most cases, it is beneficial to go a little further and create a *profile* of your audience. Rather than stating a general audience category, such as parents, a profile provides the readers' *demographics*—that is, specific characteristics such as age, gender, income level, level of education, and region of the country. It may also include other features, such as a specific area of interest.

To examine the process of profiling, let's turn to a subject of interest to the consumer audience—the subject of luxury sedans, for instance. What type of person would be interested in an article on this topic? The most obvious feature of this reader would be income level. In order to afford a high-priced car, the reader would have to be in the upper-middle class at least. What age would this person be? If the reader has the disposable income needed to afford a luxury sedan, he would most likely be middle-aged. Another clue to his age is the fact that the piece focuses on luxury sedans, rather than sports cars. Although this certainly varies from person to person, older people, rather than wealthy young men, are most interested in big luxury cars like Cadillacs and Lincoln Continentals. Gender? Again, there are exceptions, but while both men and women drive cars, it is mostly men who are interested in *reading* about cars. And, finally, there's the question of educational background. This, again, can vary, but if the reader has reached middle-age and enjoys a better-than-average income, there is a very good chance that he has earned a college degree. You could even focus on a certain area of the country, such as the coasts, where the use of luxury vehicles is more prevalent. The profile of your article's average reader, then, is an upper-middle class, middle-aged man, probably with a college degree, and possibly with a home on the east or west coast.

If your topic is flower gardens, and you have written a how-to article, you want to look at the average gardener. While many people of all ages enjoy gardening, the people with the most time to spend outdoors are older, with children who are grown or independent. Men tend to work on landscaping, while women are the predominant flower gardeners and planters. It does take some disposable income to invest in a flower garden, but not much, so your reader is probably in the middle class. In addition, your reader probably lives in the suburbs, where there is more land available for plantings. Education is less of a factor here, because working with earth and plants does not require a great deal of specialized knowledge. In addition, a how-to article is written so that everyone can understand the directions, making it a universal piece. Thus, your how-to article on planting a successful flower garden would be addressed to an older woman, living in the suburbs, with an average income and education.

Don't underestimate your reader's intelligence. When in doubt, leave industry terms and jargon in the piece. Then, if you think it's necessary, include definitions in a sidebar.

As you consider various articles, the readers that might be interested in them, and, eventually, the publications in which they might appear, you will find that in the case of some topics, certain features of the audience profile may be more important than others. While a consumer-oriented article on makeup, for instance, is probably gen-

Profiling Your Audience

On pages 85 to 86, we looked at two article topics and developed two audience profiles. This practice of audience profiling may seem tricky at first, but the more you do it, the easier and faster it will become. Below, to help you out, I've listed three sample article titles and types (service piece, tips article, etc.), each of which is followed by a brief audience analysis and, finally, a reader profile.

When reading the following analyses, keep in mind that these profiles are not based on intuition. Rather, they are based on market information compiled by relevant publications, as well as a number of reports found on the Internet. But the resulting profiles are well worth the work, as they truly reflect the audience that would ultimately read such articles.

Topic One: Taking Care of a New Baby (How-To Article)

Couples of all ages, from late teens to early fifties, can have questions about the care of a newborn. If your article specifically addresses very young or mature parents, your reader profile will be different. However, the *average* new parents are in their mid-twenties, with some college education. They tend to be very familiar with the Internet and use it often; *American Baby's* advertising survey found that 80 percent of their readers research baby products on the Internet. At that age, parents are often still in the lower-middle class income bracket, and are working hard to make ends meet. They may live in any region of the country. These parents want information that is quick, easy to read, and filled with both print and Internet resources. Finally, most of the parents who read articles about children and child care are female. *Average audience member:* A lower-middle class woman, in her middle to late twenties, who uses the Internet and print media for her research.

Topic Two: How to Find a Great Retirement Home (Service Piece)

People who are interested in buying retirement homes are either a few years from retirement or have just retired, meaning they are in their mid- to late sixties. They are generally worried about their disposable income, and sometimes drop one level in income after they give up their jobs. Their education level varies, although those who can afford a retirement place in a resort area tend to have college degrees, which is what enabled them to hold higher-paying positions. These readers are more familiar with print media than online resources, although this trend is gradually being reversed. Men tend to research these decisions at the outset, and then bring their wives into the decision-making process. Geographic region varies. *Average audience member:* An older male, middle to upper-middle class, who uses primarily print and some Internet sources for information.

Topic Three: Ten Tips for Choosing a College Major (Tips Article)

The people most concerned with choosing a college major are high school juniors and seniors. They have little or no real world experience and require a great deal of guidance in finding their niche. They also want to be entertained, and look for a quick read that will allow them to easily find the information they need. Students who go on to secondary school are more prevalent on the coasts, but students in all areas of the country are interested in this topic. They often come from families in higher income brackets, but are by no means restricted to that group. Gender is pretty evenly split, and most readers in this group have web savvy and value information on Internet resources. *Average audi-* *ence member:* A high school student who uses the Internet and is looking for fast information.

As you can see, depending on your topic and approach, your audience can vary. By understanding your reader profile, you can better tailor your article to fit your reader, and can more successfully target the best publications for your work.

der-related; other articles, such as those on cat care, appeal to people of both genders, as well as to a wide range of ages, income levels, and levels of education. Nevertheless, always keep in mind that although cat lovers may come in all ages and genders, the publications that cover the subject of cats may actually serve specific demographics. For instance, the audience of a certain cat magazine may be largely comprised of women who belong to the upper income levels. Therefore, if at a later time you find that you're having trouble finding an editor who's interested in your article, you may want to check the demographics of your target publications to see if your work is geared for the appropriate audience. Perhaps you emphasized the wrong side of the demographic equation, focusing on information that would serve a relatively small portion of the audience. Whenever possible, try to address the majority of your readers.

How do you determine the demographics of a publication? It's really fairly easy to do so, as magazines, newspapers, and journals have already analyzed their readerships for you. First, check the advertising information that can be found either in the ad section of the publication's website or in your resource books. If these strategies don't provide the data you need, call the publication and request a copy of its media kit, which will include a market breakdown.

As mentioned earlier in the chapter, once you've created a reader profile, you can better judge if the tone, content, and language of your article is appropriate for your audience. If you're writing for a trade journal whose readers are likely to use certain professional jargon, your article should use the shared language that the readers expect to find in industry-related pieces. And if your audience is composed of upper-middle class women with college degrees, the reading level of the piece should be higher than it would be if it addressed teenage girls. One thing to keep in mind: Many new writers underestimate their readers, writing "down" to them. Unless your editor specifically asks for an article that covers the basics, assume that your readers are intelligent, and that they see the news, read other publications, and are generally familiar with your material. Then use a combination of the appropriate jargon and layman's language. The editor is looking for quality in your research and writing. Any word changes can be made during the revision stage, as the editor helps you craft your article to fit his specific audience.

How Big Is Your Potential Audience?

As discussed in Chapter 2, unless their publication intentionally targets a very limited group, most editors want articles that will appeal to a fairly good-sized audience. By estimating the number of people potentially interested in the subject of your article, you can often gain the ammunition you need to convince an editor that your article will help sell copies of his publication. Perhaps just as important, this data can allow you to judge if the topic you have chosen actually has a sizeable market.

There are a variety of means by which you can estimate audience size. If, for instance, you have decided that your article addresses middle-aged women who live in the southern part of the United States, you will probably find that government websites have the statistics you need. Another good option is to connect to an Internet search engine such as Google.com or Ask.com, and type in "women statistics." Numerous websites that contain information on this demographic can be found there. Be sure to be specific, though. If you want statistics only on women over the age of sixty-five, don't type in the more general word "women." Try "retired women" or "retirement-age women" instead.

If you don't have access to the Internet or can't find the exact information you need on the web, other avenues of research are available. For a more defined audience—say, cat owners—try calling the organizations that address that audience, such as the American Humane Association and The Humane Society. In fact, during your research for your article, you may have asked for press materials from organizations such as these. If so, the press kits may provide just the information you need. If not, refer to the *Encyclopedia of Associations*, published by The Gale Group. (See page 324 of the Resource Directory.) Found in the reference section of most libraries, this multi-volume source can guide you to organizations that focus on your article's topic.

Finally, other books and articles on your subject may provide you with useful statistics on your audience. If you decide to use these statistics in your own article, though, be sure to verify the information with your quoted source.

Once you've estimated your audience size, keep this information handy. Then, if possible, work these statistics into your cover or query letter to demonstrate to the editor that you have researched the potential readership. This will go a long way not only toward showing that your article has a market, but also toward proving that you have the capabilities to handle the entire piece.

CONCLUSION

The writer who truly understands his article's topic, approach, and audience has greatly increased his odds of seeing his work in print. Not only will he be able to choose the most appropriate magazines, newspapers, or journals for his piece, but he'll also be better able to communicate with the editors of those publications and provide them with the information they need.

Now that you have more clearly defined your article, you are ready to find it a good home. The next chapter will introduce you to valuable resource materials and guide you in using them to find publishers who can help you realize your dream.

CHAPTER 4

ℱINDING THE RIGHT PUBLICATIONS

Chapter 2 provided you with an overview of the different markets available for your article. You now know that certain types of publications—newspapers, online magazines, small consumer magazines, and non-refereed journals, for instance—are the best bets for a writer with no or few previous publishing credits. And after reading Chapter 3, you should have zeroed in on your article's topic, audience, and approach. Now it's time to zone in on those publications that are the best match for your article. In this chapter, you will learn about the different market research resources available to you, and you will learn how to use them to create a list of target publications.

RESOURCE BOOKS

With the technological advances available today, market information is as plentiful as publications. The newsstands and bookstores display trade magazines designed to help budding writers find markets, and the Internet offers hundreds of sites that provide tips and up-to-the-minute information about current demand. But for the vast majority of writers, the most important sources of market information are the resource books.

The resource books discussed below have long been considered the standard references in the field. Although other books are available, these are the most comprehensive and the most valuable for new and veteran writers alike. But while every one of these publications is excellent, it is unwise to limit yourself to a single resource book. Each reference contains slightly different information and can provide a different slant on the market. Luckily, most writers' resource books are available in the library, giving you free access to the data you need.

Writer's Market

Industry professionals often refer to this book, published annually since 1921, as "The Writer's Bible" because it covers so many publications—a total of over 1,750 consumer magazines and trade journals—and because it provides so much helpful information on each one. *Writer's Market* is available in every bookstore and library. Used copies can be found, but your best bet is to use the most up-to-date copy found in your library, or, if you expect to get a lot of use out of the text, to buy a new copy, as it's relatively affordable.

This book is chock full of information on all areas of interest to a writer: book publishers in both the United States and Canada; small presses; book producers; consumer magazines; trade, technical, and professional journals; scriptwriting; newspaper syndicates; greeting card and gift idea companies; contests; awards; and organizations. It is updated annually and has changed format over the years to reflect the needs of the writing community.

Every market listed in Writer's Market is a paying market. Dollar symbols printed at the beginning of each entry indicate whether that publication's pay rate is relatively good or relatively poor.

The beginning of *Writer's Market* offers tips on selling your writing, including annual dissections of query letters—both letters that work and ones that don't. In addition, profiles of and interviews with editors are sprinkled throughout. The real value of *Writer's Market*, however, is in the publication information. Listed alphabetically and divided by general category and then again by subject matter, this resource covers a wide range of publications, all of which are open to freelance submissions and are paying markets. The publications of greatest interest to article writers can be found in two sections of the book—*Consumer Magazines* and *Trade Magazines*.

One of the best additions to *Writer's Market* in recent years has been the large symbols that immediately tell you several things, including what the publication pays and whether it represents a good opportunity for freelancers. At a glance, you can determine if the market is even open to you. In addition, tips from editors let you know the best way to get your foot in the door.

Resource Rundown

A good market resource accomplishes several things. It presents all the basic information about the publication, gives you tips on submission, and lets you know about "opportunity" publications—markets that accept a high percentage of freelance material. Look for resource books that offer the following facts about each publication.

☐ **Title of the Magazine or Journal.** These titles are usually a good clue to the publication's area of coverage: *Parents, Car and Driver, Business North Carolina.*

☐ **Focus and Audience.** This tells you the publication's area of interest and the readers to whom it directs its material.

☐ **List of Editors.** This list usually includes only the editors who acquire material—not every person employed by the publication.

☐ **Contact Information.** This lets you know where and to whom you should send your submission or query.

☐ **Circulation.** This tells you the number of people who receive the publication.

☐ **Payment Information.** This data tells you what the publication pays for an article.

☐ **Percent of Freelanced Material.** Here, you'll find out how much *outsourced material*—material from sources outside the publication's staff—is bought by the publication.

☐ **Basic Guidelines.** These guidelines are the "rules" for submission—essentially, what sections are open to freelance material, what specific format your submissions should be made in, etc.

Although most writers view resource books as their primary source of market information, you should not rely solely on books for the data you need. Because of publishing schedules, much of this information is months old by the time it appears in print. Editors leave, magazines shut down, and guidelines change. Once you have decided to query a specific publication, *always* obtain a current copy of the magazine or newspaper, at either the newsstand or your library, and check the information again. As a further safeguard, call the editorial office and verify the editor's name and position, as well as the address of the publication.

A few years ago, Writer's Digest Books, which publishes *Writer's Market,* started offering the book with a CD-ROM filled with all the information in the text, as well as a searchable encyclopedia of terms and answers to beginner's questions. In 2000, Writer's Digest changed that offering to make the CD-ROM into a means of connecting to the web database with instant updates and searchable markets. (You can preview this at www.writersmarket.com.) While the Internet version of *Writer's Market* costs a bit more than the print version alone (bar-

Although *Writer's Market* offers an online version for a few dollars a month, writers who are publishing only an article or two will do just fine with the print version, which is available in both bookstores and libraries. In addition, the paperback version offers some real advantages over the online edition. A tangible copy doesn't crash. And if you later choose to pursue a writing career, the paperback will be available to peruse whenever you're waiting for an appointment or just trying to develop ideas.

gains can be found, particularly in September when the new editions are released), it offers tremendous advantages over the paper version. If you are hoping to sell multiple articles, the online *Writer's Market* will allow you to update your market listings on a daily basis; find back issues of the tips library; bookmark and categorize your listings; link immediately to a publication's web page, if it has one; and search for complementary markets. "If a magazine closes, moves or spins off another title after the book comes back from the printer, we can hop onto the Internet and make that change," said editor Kristen Holm in an interview with *Inscriptions* magazine.

Although entries do vary, within both the print and online versions of *Writer's Market*, you will generally find the publication's name, address, phone, fax, and website; the editor's name; and the contact person's name and title. You'll also find a brief description of what the magazine covers, as well as the audience it targets. In addition, *Writer's Market* includes data on the year the magazine was launched, its circulation, the editor's response time to queries, and the publication's payment schedule. Different columns and departments are highlighted, with approximate word counts and other relevant information provided.

In the back of *Writer's Market* is a section devoted to contests and awards as well as unique writing opportunities, such as providing greeting card copy. Book, website, publication, and organization resource lists are also presented in the back, giving you a full range of information on writing.

Using the Writer's Market to Create Your List

Now that you know the different listings contained within *Writer's Market*, you need to understand how to use this resource. The best way to explain the process is by using an example. So here's the scenario—you have written an article, and, using the information presented in Chapter 3, have determined your work's topic, audience, and approach. The topic is creating a roomy home office space, the audience is comprised of established and aspiring home office workers, and the piece is a how-to article.

When you have a few free hours, you sit down with a borrowed or purchased copy of *Writer's Market*. Because your article can fit into both consumer and trade magazines, you flip through both the *Con-*

sumer Magazines and *Trade Magazines* sections, scanning the various categories in each. In the *Consumer Magazines* section, you find that the most appropriate listings are in the Consumer Service & Business Opportunity category, and that there are also some good listings in the Business & Finance category. In the *Trade Magazines* section, you see a couple of possible markets in the Business Management category. If you want to tailor your article to address people in specific trades, you also check out categories such as Real Estate, Journalism & Writing, and Insurance. So you start a list of all the publications that would potentially be interested in your article.

When you are through with your first review of *Writer's Market*, you have a tentative list of target publications. At this point, though, you have only names, and no other information. To learn about the publications, you examine the entries themselves. After reading through the information provided, you remove the names of those publications that are not appropriate, and obtain contact information and other important data for those that are. In your list, include as much of the following information as possible:

- Publication name

- Address

- Phone number, fax number, e-mail address, and website

- Contact for submission package

- Area of publication and circulation

- Percentage of freelanced material

- Any other pertinent information you come across during your search

If you don't have all the information you need at this point, don't worry. Before you send out your submission package, you will be contacting the publication to verify all the information and double-check the editor's name.

The sample entries presented on the following pages show a fictional version of the types of listings you can expect to find in *Writer's Market*. Let's briefly review these samples to see how you should go about assessing publications and paring down your list to include only those companies that best suit you and your article.

Judging from its title, the publication *Home Office Magazine* seems like a good candidate for your list. According to the entry, shown below, it "covers all aspects of starting and running a home business." However, a careful reading of the entry shows that relatively few of the magazine's articles—only 20 percent—are freelance written. Moreover, the entry states that, like most large consumer magazines, the publication "only works with established, experienced writers." Since you are a new, unpublished writer, you decide to pass this magazine by, so you cross *Home Office Magazine* off your list.

Next, you look at the entry for *Business News of Charleston*, found on page 97. One of the few newspapers listed in *Writer's Market*, this publication seems more promising, as 40 percent of its articles are freelance written and it does not limit submissions to known writers. Plus, you notice that the newspaper publishes how-to articles and

SAMPLE ENTRY
WRITER'S MARKET
LARGE CONSUMER
MAGAZINE

$ $ HOME OFFICE MAGAZINE, 2256 Furnish Rd., Congers, NY, 10920. (914) 555-0567. Fax: (914) 555-0568. E-mail: dmcdonnel@homeoffice.com. Website: www.homeoffice.com. **Contact:** Dan McDonnel, editor-in-chief. **20% freelance written.** Only works with established, experienced writers who have a strong background in home office issues. National magazine directed toward home office workers. "*Home Office Magazine* covers all aspects of starting and running a home business. We are designed to be a single resource for the home office worker." Estab. 1998. Circ. 650,000. Pays on publication. Publishes ms. an average of 8 months after acceptance. Byline given. Buys first, one-time and second serial rights. Editorial lead time 3 months. Submit seasonal material 4 months in advance. Accepts queries by mail only. Accepts simultaneous submissions. Sample copy for 9x12 SAE and $2.00. Writers' guidelines for # 10 SASE.
Nonfiction: Book excerpt, general interest, how-to, new product. No non-home office related topics. **Buys 100 mss/year.** Send complete ms by e-mail or mail. **Pays 50 cents/word for assigned articles; $100–200 for unsolicited articles.**
Reprints: Accepts previously published submissions.
Photos: Send photos with submission. Offers one-time payment for photos accepted with ms.
Columns/Departments: Marketing; Money; Time Management; Technology; Working with kids. All columns are 400–600 words in length. Send complete ms. **Pays $50–150.**
   The online version of the magazine carries additional content and features a special web work section. Contact: Sheila Green, online editor.
Tips: "Read several issues to determine our writing style. Have a good knowledge of the home office market. Add sidebars and resource lists for added information."

BUSINESS NEWS OF CHARLESTON, P.O. Box 331, Charleston, SC. (843) 555-8901. Fax: (843) 555-8900. E-mail: chris@cbusnews.com. Website: www.cbusnews.com. **Contact:** Chris Masters, features editor. **40% freelance written.** Weekly newspaper covering local news and national trends in small business. *"Business News of Charleston* is always looking for articles that have a local slant or cover issues of general interest that can apply to our readers. Every story must have some tie to Charleston." Estab. 1998. Circ. 110,000. Pays on acceptance. Publishes ms. an average of 3 weeks after acceptance. Byline given. Buys first, one-time and second serial rights. Editorial lead time 1 month. Submit seasonal material 4 months in advance. Accepts queries by e-mail and mail. Does not accept simultaneous submissions. Sample copy for 9x12 SAE and $1.50. Writers' guidelines for # 10 SASE.
Nonfiction: How to, interview/profile, new product. New section on tele-commuters opened in Spring 2001. **Buys 25 mss/year.** Send complete ms by e-mail or mail. **Pays 20 cents/word for assigned articles; $50–175 for unsolicited articles.**
Reprints: Does not accept previously published submissions.
Photos: State availability of photos with submission. Reviews contact sheets. Negotiates payment individually. Requires captions, model releases and subject identifications. **Columns/Departments:** Around Town, Business Sense, What I Learned, Work from Home. Columns are 200–400 words in length. Send complete ms. **Pays $50–100.**
Fillers: Facts, quick tips, short humor and reviews. Length: 200 words. **Pay varies.**
Tips: "Our audience is comprised of business people with a high technology focus. Keep that in mind when writing. Be sure to have a tie to Charleston in your story, or add local resources to a general piece."

SAMPLE ENTRY
WRITER'S MARKET
MEDIUM-SIZED BUSINESS NEWSPAPER

that it has a special section on telecommuters. So you keep *Business News of Charleston* on your list, adding all of the contact information, and noting the fact that your article will have to be reworked a bit so that it includes some sort of tie-in to the Charleston area—possibly a list of local resources.

Now, you turn to the entry for *Telecommuter Business Journal,* which you find in the *Trade Magazines* section of the book. (See page 98.) Since this publication is devoted to the person who works at home, it seems like a natural for your list. And because the publication is small and obtains most of its material from freelance sources, you should have a good shot at getting your article into print. Moreover, the journal has an online newsletter, which offers an additional market. *Telecommuter Business Journal* is a "keeper" and belongs on your list.

TELECOMMUTER BUSINESS JOURNAL, 1100 College Blvd., Randolph, NJ, 08809. (973) 555-9876. Fax: (973) 555-0231. E-mail: info@telecom.com. Website: www.telecom.com. **Contact:** Mark Connor, managing editor. **90% freelance written.** Bimonthly trade journal for telecommuters. Estab. 2000. Circ. 6,000. Pays on publication. Publishes ms. an average of 6 months after acceptance. Byline given. Buys first and one-time rights. Editorial lead time 3 months. Submit seasonal material 4 months in advance. Accepts queries by e-mail, mail and fax. Accepts simultaneous submissions. Sample copy for 9x12 SAE and $5.00. Writers' guidelines for # 10 SASE.

Nonfiction: New product, how-to, technical. Only interested in material for telecommuters. **Buys 10 mss/year.** Query before sending ms. **Pays 10 cents/word for assigned articles; $10–50 for unsolicited articles.**

Reprints: Accepts previously published submissions.

Photos: Send photos with submission. Offers no additional payment for photos.

Columns/Departments: Profile; Telecommuter Dilemmas; Time Management; Technology. All columns are 400 words in length. Send complete ms. **Pays $10–15.**

There is also an online newsletter that accepts articles. No payment, but author receives a byline and link to his or her website. Contact: Janet Jenkins, online content editor.

Tips: "Writers should know and understand the telecommuter market. Those who work from portable and home offices face different challenges than traditional workers. Read several issues of the journal before submitting."

After checking the publications on your original list, you have eliminated some and kept others. Your list now contains ten to twenty publications, depending on how specialized your topic is. You could end your investigation now, but you know that there are other excellent resources that could yield further markets for your article. So you continue your search, this time turning to *Online Market for Writers.*

Online Markets for Writers

Although set up much like *Writer's Market,* this resource book focuses solely on online markets. The beginning of *Online Markets for Writers* contains helpful tips about publishing online and discusses a variety of issues that tend to be faced by e-writers rather than print writers. The next portion of the book is dedicated to market information. In addition, writers can obtain current updates and an e-mail newsletter with market information by visiting the authors' website: www.marketsforwriters.com.

Online Markets has a separate chapter devoted to the top ten markets for e-writers, along with advice for breaking into these markets from writers who currently publish on those sites. Like *Writer's Market*, this book provides a wealth of information on all the listings, including the publisher's name and address, the editor's name and contact data, the type of material published, particular editorial needs, and the payment schedule. In the back is an extensive listing of information resources.

All the publications included in this book are online. However, many also publish a print version of their magazine, making this book a particularly great choice for writers who want to publish their articles in both print and online markets.

The online market changes faster than New England weather. Every day, new e-zines pop up and others fold. This is a market where you have to be extra vigilant about checking current information before submitting.

Using the Online Markets for Writers to Create Your List

When you sit down to use *Online Markets for Writers*, turn to the *Subject Index* located at the back of the book. For the article on creating a roomy home office space, search for publications that cover the home worker market. In this book, there isn't a category for business e-zines, but if you look at the Technology and Lifestyle listings, you'll see listings for markets that address technology workers and home workers.

Next, flip to the A-to-Z listing of publications and read about the markets you selected from the *Subject Index*. You may end up adding another ten or fifteen markets to your list, because the e-zine world is virtually limitless. Be sure to go to the website, verify all the contact information, and look for updated writer's guidelines. See the sample entry below for a fictional preview of what the book contains.

Home Worker Online: The E-Zine for Work at Homers.
http://www.homeworker.com.
38 Commercial St., Boston, MA 02110
"Please, no phone calls or faxes. Contact by e-mail is preferred." Ken Little, editor.
"The premiere resource for people working at home or thinking about it. We feature stories on managing your business, working around life and existing in a home environment. Lots of support and ideas for lonely workers." 50 percent freelance written. Established July 1998. Buys one-time rights.
 E-mail for queries: info@homeworker.com
 Editorial needs: new product, how-to, personal essay
 Advice from Market: Almost all of the content is written by people in the trenches, i.e., people working at home. Know your audience.

SAMPLE ENTRY
ONLINE MARKETS FOR WRITERS

Ulrich's International Periodicals Directory

Ulrich's International Periodicals Directory is one of the longest-standing and most comprehensive guides to the periodicals market. It lists nearly 250,000 consumer and trade magazines, academic and scholarly publications, monographic series, newsletters, newspapers, electronic publications, e-zines, and many other types of serial publications and services, both domestic and international. You can usually find the most recent edition of *Ulrich's* in the reference section of your library. This is a lifesaver, as the guide costs several hundred dollars. In fact, the book is so expensive that if you live in a small town, you will probably have to go to the main library to gain access to *Ulrich's* because a copy may not be purchased for every branch. The library's copy should be more than adequate for your needs.

In 2000, *Ulrich's* developed a web update format. In addition, the publisher, R. R. Bowker, launched www.ulrichsweb.com, an Internet version of the book, complete with advanced search, browsing, and indexing options; as well as Ulrich's on Disc, a CD-ROM version with the same search options. Although the Internet service is fee-based, keep in mind that many libraries offer free access to the electronic option, which you can use on the library's computer or, in some cases, on your home computer by accessing the library's website. Be sure to ask your library if these services are available.

The main advantage that the Internet version of *Ulrich's* has over the print version is the ease with which it enables you to find appropriate publications. If you want to know which agriculture journals accept book reviews, for instance, it's as simple as typing a word or two into the search criteria and letting the computer do the work. In order to find that same information in the print version, you would have to carefully read every entry in the agriculture section. The Internet version also provides a link to the online version of Journal Citation Reports, a service that ranks journals based on the frequency with which their content is cited in other outlets. This gives you an easy way to evaluate the credentials of peer-reviewed journals in the science and social science fields.

Both the print and online editions of *Ulrich's* contain pertinent information. The data is organized under detailed subject headings, split into broader media categories. Each entry contains the title, address, contact information, and publisher data for the periodical. In

Many libraries offer free access to *Ulrich's* and other fee-based resource guides. Sometimes you can access the database on your home computer through the library's website. In other cases, you have to go to the library and use its computers.

addition, any Internet information, such as a web address, web edition, or e-mail contact, is provided. Rights, permissions, circulation, and types of documents published are also included.

While a review of *Ulrich's* is not essential for every writer or every article, this resource should be consulted whenever you want to locate academic publications, newsletters, and newspapers—markets that aren't fully covered by resource books such as *Writer's Market*.

Using Ulrich's to Create Your List

With hundreds of thousands of listings provided in several separate volumes, *Ulrich's* can be confusing to navigate, making it difficult to find the subject under which suitable publications are listed.

The searchable CD-ROM and the web version of *Ulrich's* are the easiest to use, so if your library offers them, by all means, take advantage of the free access. Ulrich's on Disc, the CD-ROM version, allows you to search by twenty-four different criteria, providing more precise results. The disc and online versions also contain previews of reviewed journals and expanded descriptions for up to 80,000 others. You can generate lists of journals by publisher, discipline, country, format, and more for evaluation and comparison, plus you can download or print the records for future reference.

If you are using the print version of *Ulrich's*, plan to spend some time flipping through its pages. First, you'll want to turn to the *Subject Index*, which is always in one of the last volumes of the series. (As *Ulrich's* has grown over the years, adding further volumes, the index has moved to higher-numbered volumes.) Here, you will find literally hundreds of listings of different subjects. Since the topics of academic articles are usually different from the subjects of consumer publications, let's use a different article example this time—say, an article on chronic ozone exposure and its effect on seaweed.

When trying to find publications for your piece about seaweed, your initial thought may be to look under the subject Biology and Botany, so turn to that one first. When you scan the publications in that section, you'll find several listings that contain information on marine plants. To find additional listings, you might have to dig a little further. Try listings that spin off your original subject—environmental biology, environmental studies, and botany, for instance. Alternative categories are often listed under main categories, providing you with additional ways of finding appropriate publications.

Make a list of all the publications that seem appropriate. Then, to find the information you need on each of the target publications, turn to the *Title Index,* which is also found in one of the higher-numbered volumes. This will provide the page number of the full entry for each of the publications in which you're interested.

When you turn to the actual entries, write down all of the pertinent information—basically the same information you would record for a consumer publication, with an added note stating whether the publication is refereed or non-refereed. Be sure to include the following data:

■ Publication name

■ Address

■ Phone number, fax number, e-mail address, and website

■ Contact for submission package

■ Area of publication and circulation

■ Refereed or non-refereed status

■ Any other pertinent information you come across during your search

Although it's important to record all of the pertinent data for each publication on your list, never forget that the information in your resource books may not be entirely up-to-date. Before you submit your article, you'll want to contact each publication, verifying the contact data and filling in any blanks.

Don't worry about having every bit of information. Before you submit your article, you will call and verify address and contact data. This will be the best time to make sure that the data on your list is current. Be aware that this step is especially important when using *Ulrich's* because, although this unique resource is impressively comprehensive, the contact information is often out of date. Since this is true to an extent even for the Internet and CD-ROM versions, this step should not be skipped.

Ideally, the list you create will include twenty publications or so. However, if your topic has a very narrow focus, you may find that only a few journals that cover that area. If you locate only a handful of candidates, you have two options: You can widen the scope of your article, or you can consider some of the international publications that produce a version in English. The listings for foreign editions state if they publish an English version or not, so be sure to read closely.

Ulrich's is a great resource because it lists so many periodicals published throughout the world. It does have limitations, however.

In order to carry such a broad spectrum of information, the entries provide just the most basic information—no tips on gaining entry to the journal, no word-count guidelines, no submission criteria. *Ulrich's* is not designed to be a full submission resource, but a shared book for libraries, universities, and writers who have different data needs. The following fictional entry will give you an idea of what you may find. Below, you'll see the entry exactly as it would appear in *Ulrich's*. On page 104, you'll see a feature-by-feature breakdown of the exact same entry, with excerpts from the entry provided on the right-hand side, and explanatory notes presented on the left-hand side to help you pull out the information that you need.

As you'll see by examining the sample *Ulrich's* entry, various facts—the journal's circulation, the year in which the journal was established, and the fact that it is either refereed or non-refereed, for instance—can help you determine a journal's level of prestige, and therefore the likelihood that it will accept your manuscript. If you are interested in science and social science journals, you can gain further information about the prestige of a journal by checking the Journal Citation Reports website, mentioned earlier. Also refer back to Chapter 2, which provides tips for gauging the status of any journal with which you are not familiar.

Is the sample journal right for your article? By looking at the subject matter covered in the description of the sample journal, you can see that the journal publishes original results in seaweed biology. Therefore, if your article is bringing something new to the forefront,

---

581   USA   ISSN 1093-2189

JOURNAL OF SEAWEED SCIENCES. Text in English, Spanish, French. 1927. Bi-m. USD $56 to individuals; USD $62 to Canada; USD $70 to institutions. bk. rev. (book reviews), charts, illus., index. *Refereed.* **Document Type:** *Academic/Scholarly.*
  Description: Presents the results of original seaweed biology, including development, evolution, genetics, ecology, and systematics.
Formerly: (until vol. 42 1996): Seaweed Yearbook (0021-8071)
Indexed: Biol.Abstr., Gen,Sci., Plant.Path
  -BLDSC (4583.696189)
Published by: University of Detroit Press, Journals Division, PO Box 300, Detroit, MI, 00234. TEL 000-555-7898, FAX 000-555-7899, subscriptions@udetroit.edu. http://www.journals.udetroit.edu. Ed. Carole Maxwell. Page 385; trim 11 x 8.5. Circ: 2,500.

SAMPLE ENTRY
ULRICH'S
ACADEMIC JOURNAL

ULRICH'S **SAMPLE ANNOTATED PRINT ENTRY**
ACADEMIC JOURNAL

DEWEY DECIMAL CLASSIFICATION/COUNTRY CODE/INTERNATIONAL STANDARD SERIAL NUMBER (PERIODICAL IDENTIFICATION NUMBER)	581 USA ISSN 1093-2189
PUBLICATION NAME.	**JOURNAL OF SEAWEED SCIENCES**
LANGUAGES IN WHICH JOURNAL IS PUBLISHED.	Text in English, Spanish, French.
YEAR JOURNAL WAS ESTABLISHED. HAVING BEEN ESTABLISHED SO MANY YEARS AGO, IT IS LIKELY TO BE WELL RESPECTED IN THE ACADEMIC COMMUNITY.	1927.
FREQUENCY OF PUBLICATION. HERE, THE BI-M MEANS BIMONTHLY, OR ONCE EVERY TWO MONTHS.	Bi-m.
SUBSCRIPTION COST. THE ENTRY USUALLY INCLUDES THE COST TO INDIVIDUALS AS WELL AS FOREIGN COUNTRIES AND INSTITUTIONS. INSTITUTIONS PAY A HIGHER RATE THAN INDIVIDUALS BECAUSE SEVERAL HUNDRED READERS POTENTIALLY HAVE ACCESS TO EACH ISSUE.	USD $56 to individuals; USD $62 to Canada; USD $70 to institutions.
CLASSIFICATIONS OF THE MATERIAL PUBLISHED IN THE JOURNAL.	bk. rev. (book reviews), charts, illus., index.
INDICATES THAT JOURNAL IS REFEREED, AND THEREFORE PREFERS WORK FROM KNOWN WRITERS WHO ARE RESPECTED IN THEIR FIELD.	*Refereed.*
CLASSIFICATION OF THE PERIODICAL—IN THIS CASE, ACADEMIC/SCHOLARLY.	**Document Type:** *Academic/Scholarly.*
DESCRIPTION OF THE PUBLICATION AND THE SUBJECTS IN WHICH IT IS INTERESTED. YOUR SUBMISSION SHOULD FALL INTO ONE OF THESE CATEGORIES.	**Description:** Presents the results of original seaweed biology, including development, evolution, genetics, ecology, and systematics.
PUBLICATION'S PREVIOUS TITLES.	Formerly (until vol. 42 1996): Seaweed Yearbook.
THE JOURNAL IS INDEXED, AND THE INDEX IS ALSO CARRIED BY OTHER PUBLICATIONS, WHOSE NAMES ARE ABBREVIATED FOR SPACE CONSIDERATIONS.	**Indexed:** Biol.Abstr., Gen,Sci., Plant.Path
THE VARIOUS SERVICES THAT PROVIDE REPRINTS OF MATERIAL FROM THE JOURNAL.	BLDSC (British Library Document Supply Centre)
ADDRESS AND ADDITIONAL CONTACT INFORMATION FOR THE PERIODICAL'S PUBLISHER. THIS IS IMPORTANT TO INCLUDE IN YOUR LIST. JUST BE SURE TO DOUBLE-CHECK ALL DATA BEFORE SENDING IN YOUR SUBMISSION.	**Published by:** University of Detroit Press, Journals Division, PO Box 300, Detroit, MI, 00234. TEL 000-555-7898, FAX 000-555-7899, subscriptions@udetroit.edu. http://www.journals.udetroit.edu
THE EDITOR'S NAME. AGAIN, DOUBLE-CHECK THIS INFORMATION, AS EDITORS TEND TO CHANGE OFTEN IN THE PUBLISHING INDUSTRY.	Carole Maxwell
SIZE OF PUBLICATION, BOTH IN PAGE COUNT AND DIMENSIONS.	Page 385, trim 11X8.5
CIRCULATION GIVES A CLUE REGARDING THE SIZE OF THE JOURNAL. IN THIS CASE, THE JOURNAL APPEARS TO BE LARGE-SIZED AND WELL RESPECTED, GIVEN THAT THE NUMBER OF PEOPLE INTERESTED IN THIS SUBJECT IS LIMITED.	Circ: 2,500

this would be a good place to submit your article—*if* you are a known writer or have produced a truly outstanding piece of work. However, if you are writing an article on seaweed utilization, and not providing groundbreaking information, you'll want to look for a journal that specifically requests articles on applications and usage.

Always take the extra step to research the journal through the library or its website. A thoughtful analysis will reveal what a journal publishes, and, just as important, what it has printed in the recent past. This should enable you to eliminate a few inappropriate publications from your list. If your article could appeal to a wider trade audience, you might want to continue your research by looking through *Writer's Market*, discussed earlier, and *The International Directory of Little Magazines & Small Presses*, discussed below.

The International Directory of Little Magazines & Small Presses

As you learned in Chapter 2, if you're a new writer, it's a good idea to start out with smaller publications. An excellent resource for this type of search is *The International Directory of Little Magazines & Small Presses*. This directory includes listings of more than 5,000 small presses, magazines, and journals. Most entries—which can be found through both subject and regional indexes—contain information on payment rates, frequency of publication, editorial staff, contact information, and types of material published. This resource is reasonably priced, so if you plan on sending a great deal of material to these kinds of publications, it might be worth the investment. If not, you should be able to find a recent copy of *Little Magazines & Small Presses* in your library.

Small magazines and journals are always looking for well-written material. Just be sure to tailor your submission to meet the needs of each publication's audience.

Using Little Magazines & Small Presses to Create Your List

The first place to turn in *The International Directory of Little Magazines & Small Presses* is the *Subject Index*. In your search for publications that might be a good match for your article on creating a roomy home office, you look under the general category of Business. There, you find about a dozen publications that cover offices and home workers.

Next, you flip to the A-to-Z publishers listing and read about those twelve or so magazines you have selected, adding any appro-

Part-Timer Magazine, Ruth Ahearn, Editor; Jane Smiley, Managing Editor, PO Box 1324, Sarasota, FL 34277, 941-555-9876, Fax 941-555-6743. 1975. "Part-Timer Magazine is a national magazine that focuses on people with part-time businesses. We're looking for compelling, well-written pieces that focus on starting a part-time business, especially in terms of resources, starting out tips and business ideas. Maximum length is 2,000 words." Circ. 25,000. 4/yr. Pub'd 4 issues 2000; expects 4 issues 2001, 4 issues 2002. sub price: $12; per copy: $5; sample: $5. Back issues: $6. 4pp; 8½ by 11. Reporting time: 2 months. Simultaneous submissions accepted: yes. Publishes 20% of manuscripts submitted. Payment: $15–$25 articles and stories. Not copyrighted. Pub's reviews: 2 in 2000. Ads: $250/$150/$95 ¼ p.

priate publications to your growing list. In the fictional entry shown above, the publication prints relatively few freelance submissions, and pays very little per article. However, because of the magazine's focus, you might want to add it to your list as a secondary target in case the more promising publications don't work out.

Gale Directory of Publications and Broadcast Media

If you are interested in submitting your article to newspapers, the *Gale Directory of Publications and Broadcast Media* is a great place to start. *The Gale Directory* contains listings of different newspapers, radio stations, and television stations throughout the country, as well as a few—though not many—trade journals and magazines. While it doesn't provide the complete information offered by *Writer's Market* and the other resource books discussed earlier in the chapter, it does offer the data you need to begin your search.

The *Gale Directory of Publications and Broadcast Media* is available in libraries and is a hefty volume. Listings are organized by publisher, subject, and region. If, for example, you wanted to find a weekly newspaper that might publish an article on cultivating plants in the Southeast, you could look under particular cities, or you could search for newspapers under the appropriate topic in the *Subject Index*. Within each listing, you'll find a brief description of content, as well as information on publishing frequency, online information, and contact data.

Once you've created a list of publications from this resource, your next step should be to research the newspapers through the library or through the Internet. Some libraries carry microfiche editions of city papers for different states, and more newspapers are adding a web presence to their print edition. If neither of these sources yields a copy of the edition, you might want to consider ordering one from the newspaper's office. You can then call the editorial department to learn the publication's policy regarding freelanced material.

The Standard Periodical Directory

Billed as the "largest authoritative guide to US and Canadian Periodicals," *The Standard Periodical Directory* contains listings for 75,000 magazines, newsletters, newspapers, journals, and directories, restricted just to the North American market. The information it presents is straightforward, and includes contact and publishing information, broken down by categories. *Standard* also notes whether a publication runs advertisements and where the magazine is available. *Standard* is prohibitively expensive for individual purchase, but may be found in the reference section of most libraries.

Like *Ulrich's International Periodicals Directory, Standard* has built a complementary website: www.mediafinder.com. You can search the site free of charge, or you can pay a subscriber fee and search by circulation, publication type, advertising or list rental rates, print/production specifications, publisher, printer, or list management company. You can also download information from any search result list.

RESOURCE MAGAZINES

The books discussed earlier in the chapter are great primary resources, but because publishing is such a fast-changing industry, resource books are often outdated as soon as they hit the shelves of your library and bookstore. Fortunately, writers' magazines—available in bookstores and libraries—are a great means of bridging the information gap. Whether you want to find a home for just a few articles or you're hoping to build your article-writing into a career, flip through the following publications for monthly market updates, tips on improving your writing skills, suggestions for better marketing your articles, and information on what is happening in the field today.

A subscription to a good writers' magazine can help keep you updated on the ever-changing writing industry and enable you to learn from other writers.

ByLine

Founded in 1981, *ByLine* is devoted to the beginner. Each monthly

In addition to *ByLine* and *Writer's Digest*, two other magazines may be of value to you. *The Writer* and *Writer's Journal* do not provide in-depth, up-to-the-minute market information, but do offer some industry information and a number of articles on the craft of writing. Page through these resources at your local bookstore or library.

issue contains articles on both the craft and business of writing, offering a full perspective on the world of articles.

ByLine is committed to helping new writers obtain that first credential, and actually offers a number of opportunities for publishing within the magazine itself by accepting articles by novice and student writers, as well as fiction, poetry, and personal essays. If you have a success story you'd like to share, if you have written a profile of another writer, or if you have tips for breaking into a new market, by all means, consider submitting your article to *ByLine*.

Every issue of *ByLine* features an in-depth piece on one area of publishing. It is therefore a good idea to flip through back issues until you spot one that pertains to your targeted market. In that issue, you'll probably find information on changes in the industry, along with tips for selling your article to editors.

Writer's Digest

Writer's Digest is dedicated to writers at all levels, in every genre. Calling itself "a guide to getting published," this monthly publication includes columns on everything from setting up a home office to selling articles in a nontraditional market, as well as information on recent market additions and changes, online market listings, notices of contests, and interviews with editors. Its companion website, www.writersdigest.com, presents much of the same information, and also offers a weekly newsletter with quick tips.

Annually, *Writer's Digest* releases its "Top 100 Places to Get Published," a list of the best markets for new writers. On a semiannual basis, the magazine updates that list. Features like this make *Writer's Digest* the most complete and popular of all the writing magazines on the market, and of immense value to the new writer who wants an insider's view of the world of article publishing.

INTERNET RESOURCES

The Internet has literally thousands of helpful sites targeted to writers, providing a veritable feast of information for anyone who's looking for the best publication for her work. All kinds of market-related data—including updates on new markets—are just a mouse click away, as are links to publication guidelines and opportunities to commiserate with other writers.

The biggest benefit of online resources is that they are updated constantly. Magazine information is at least a month old when it reaches subscribers; book information can be even older. But many sites make it their mission to stay abreast of the latest changes in article markets.

Be creative when you look for marketplaces on the web. Angela Giles Klocke, editor of *The Writing Parent*, recommends that you use search words like "Writers Wanted," "Who's Looking for Writers?," or "I Want a Writing Job." The following sites are sure to help you in your hunt for appropriate markets.

PubList.com
www.publist.com

PubList.com, The Internet Directory of Publications, offers a comprehensive database of 150,000 domestic and international publications, including magazines, journals, newsletters, and other periodicals. Also included is free but limited access to information in *Ulrich's International Periodicals Directory*.

The focus of this site—which you can search without charge—is largely on academic journals, making it a great aid for the writer who wishes to publish in the academic arena. However, consumer publications are also included. Every time you log onto the site, a different journal is profiled in the "Feature Title" section.

On PubList.com, you can browse through periodicals listings in ten different main categories, which are further subdivided and categorized. Within each subcategory, magazines and journals are listed alphabetically and by country of distribution. Clicking on a title gives you four different information selections: main, publisher, advertising, and full record. The main page provides basic information about the publication, including classification (trade, consumer, etc.), office address, website, frequency of release, and editor's name. The publisher page brings up contact and address data for the magazine's publisher. The advertising page offers circulation information, advertising calendars, and the types of advertisements run by the publication. The full record page consolidates all of the above, and adds any other subject areas covered by that magazine.

The search function on PubList.com is quite extensive, allowing you to find any periodical that fits your specific requirements. In addi-

Good online resource guides update their information regularly, provide links to publications, and offer avenues for finding additional information.

Keep an eye out for new magazine listings. For a beginning writer, these offer some of the best opportunities to sell articles because the staff is usually minimal and there are few queries being submitted. While the first two or three issues of a new magazine are filled with planned material, the editors are often dependent on outsiders for future content.

tion, PubList.com offers a "Pre-Launch" section, which previews publications that are about to be released. The site also provides links to publishers, article-ordering services, and a number of reference services. This is a great resource if you aren't able to get to the library, or if you want to run a fast search of potential periodicals.

Writer and Market
http://writerandmarket.searchking.com

Writer and Market is one of the most complete sites for writers on the web. Well maintained, frequently updated, and exhaustive in its scope, this site is a great writer-defined search engine and portal to other Internet sites. What differentiates this site from other writer resources is that it provides online links to consumer magazines, newspapers, and e-zines that accept outside content. In fact, Writer and Market includes only publications with online links, so publications that don't have a web presence aren't featured on this site.

The market listings in Writer and Market consist of a brief overview of the magazine's focus and a link to the publication's site. Via this site, you can find out if a publication has an online version, and then get a sampling of what the print magazine covers.

In addition to providing links with various publications, Writer and Market serves as a portal to a vast array of other popular writers' sites, such as Wooden Horse, Writer's Digest, and Writers Write. These sites present further market information, and also offer free weekly newsletters that list writing opportunities.

Klocke Publishing Presents
www.klockepresents.com

Home to a number of writer-based e-zines, Klocke Publishing Presents provides a wealth of resources and market information. The markets are divided into three categories: writing opportunities within the site; paying markets either online or in the world of print publishing; and nonpaying markets. Clicking on a market link brings up extensive writer's guidelines—a plus for this site. Another plus is that this site is continually updated. You can either visit the site frequently to check for updates, or subscribe to one of Klocke Publishing's newsletters, which will advise you of any new information.

Klocke Publishing has several sites and companion publications, addressing different types of writers. The Writing Parent site features a print publication with a condensed online version that carries articles, tips, and advice on writing with children at home. The Writing Child site offers a similar publication, featuring the works of young authors (the assistant editor is ten) and information on markets for that age group. Bright Ink News features writing selections from adults, as well as information about new markets and writing opportunities. And Kazoodles is a simple newsletter containing listings of e-zines, books, and sites on writing.

A number of online resource sites offer articles on the craft of writing. Many also provide free e-newsletters highlighting new markets and listing writing tips.

NARROWING YOUR LIST

While the writers' resources discussed within this chapter provide important information on each market, nothing can replace studying the publication itself, whether it is a magazine, academic journal, newspaper, newsletter, or e-zine. To be safe, examine the last six months' worth of issues, if possible, to see what material the publication has used in the past, and to avoid duplicating a recently run article. Obviously, this is an easier task with magazines than it is with newspapers. However, back issues of local papers will be available in your library, and the publications' websites may allow you to get a sampling of out-of-town papers.

To fully understand each of your target publications, first study them individually, and then compare them with one another. How are they alike? How do they differ? If you look carefully, you will find differences even among publications that fall within the same general category. "A *Woman's Day* story is very different in topic and tone from a *Redbook* article; a *Ladies' Home Journal* story is different from a *Woman's World* piece; and *O* magazine has a distinct voice of its own," says Shana Aborn, senior editor for *Ladies' Home Journal.*

Use the same approach with newspapers, journals, and e-zines. All have minor variations or differences that set them apart. For instance, while *The Boston Globe* and *The Boston Herald* may appear to cover the same area and address the same audience, they differ considerably in terms of style, content, and approach. The *Globe* is more conservative and more hard news-driven, while the *Herald* is known to be a little more quirky and experimental, containing fun articles that don't hit heavy subjects, as well as a heavy concentration on local and national celebrities and characters.

This is a time-consuming practice, but is important if you are serious about getting your article into print. By examining a publication, you will be able to more accurately define its audience, to determine the topics it's most interested in covering, to understand the manner in which it usually approaches its topics, to judge the type of contributor it's seeking—and much, much more. You will then be able to decide if your article is a good match for that publication, and, if necessary, to tailor your submission package to the needs of that market.

Depending on whether you're reviewing consumer publications or academic journals, you will want to use slightly different strategies to achieve the best results. The following discussions should get you headed in the right direction.

Consumer Publications

If you are unable to find the volume and issue numbers on the cover of your target publication, check the top of the table of contents. Or, in the case of a magazine, look at the Statement of Ownership and Copyright, usually found in the back of the publication.

Analyzing a consumer publication means *really* reading the publication. And the best place to start is the beginning.

First, take a look at the cover. Does it list a volume and issue number? The volume number tells you how many years it has been published, and the issue number tells you how many editions have been published this year. Keep in mind that newer publications have a greater need for freelanced material.

Sometimes, the cover also helps define the publication's focus, audience, and more. For instance, in small print, the cover of *Parents* magazine tells you that it's "America's #1 Family Magazine." The cover of *American Baby,* on the other hand, says it's "For Expectant and New Parents." Also pay attention to the headlines on the cover. These indicate the kind of articles that the editors most like to run and what they hope to see in submissions.

Now open to the beginning pages and, if there is one, read the letter from the editor. This is a great place to determine the overall tone of the publication, the personality of the editor herself, and the types of contributors that the publication is seeking.

Move on to the profiles of the contributors for that issue. Are they experts in their respective fields? Are they new freelancers? Many times, a short interview is included in this section, providing readers with an inside look at how this particular issue came to be. Some e-zines don't carry this information in the issues themselves, but place it somewhere on their websites.

Now compare the *masthead*—the list of staff members—with the *bylines* on the articles—the names of the writers. Which sections were produced by staff members? How many pieces were written by *contributing editors* or *contributing writers*—freelancers who are hired on a long-term basis, usually under contract? Which articles were written by other freelancers? In newspapers, a clue to this are the words "Special to XYZ Newspaper" or "For the XYZ Newspaper" under the byline of the author. This means that the pieces were written by outside contributors.

Before you move on to the articles in the publication, take a close look at the advertising. Do you see more ads for household products or more for investment firms? A careful analysis of the advertisements will help you determine if the publication is geared for middle-class readers or for a more upscale audience. (To learn about the importance of understanding your audience, see Chapter 3.)

Finally, study the articles themselves. Note first if the articles use only advertisers as resources for article interviews and profiles. Although this type of article seems biased, it's an economic reality for some publications that rely on their advertisers, more than newsstand sales, for income. When you are submitting, be aware that you may be asked to include advertisers in your rewrite or to compromise your writing to reflect the advertisers in a positive light. Decide if you feel comfortable with this before sending in your work.

Then study the articles' tone and style. What words would you use to characterize the material in this publication? Hip and irreverent? Serious and intellectual? Warm and personal? If your article does not seem a good match—and if you feel that it can't be changed or that you prefer not to alter it to fit—this publication may not belong on your list.

> A careful analysis of the advertisements in a publication can tell you a great deal about its average reader, helping you determine if that market is a good match for your article.

Academic Journals

Before you actually pick up copies of your target academic journals, you will, of course, want to carefully review the information found in your resource books. And you will want to consider the papers published by your colleagues to determine where the most important articles in your field of study are being printed. Ultimately, though, you will want to examine the actual journals or to scan the archives of electronic journals to determine their suitability for your manuscript and your goals.

To begin your review, look at the title page of the journal. In academic journals, this page usually contains a brief statement of purpose that sums up the publication's area of focus. Also check the front and back covers for an "Instructions to Authors" page. This will indicate what material is and isn't published in the journal. For example, the purpose of the *Harvard Business Review* "is to advance the theory and practice of management." The journal does this by printing articles that offer important new ideas and original thinking; providing best-practice models and hands-on techniques; reporting on cutting-edge research; and giving firsthand examples of companies facing these challenges.

Finally, look at the articles themselves to see how they are developed; to note if they include supplementary materials such as photographs, sidebars, and resource listings; and to determine their approach. Study the writing and the depth of information so that you can tailor your work as necessary—or so you can find a better match for your article.

SEND FOR WRITER'S GUIDELINES

After researching possible markets through resource books, resource magazines, and Internet sites—and, of course, after examining the target publications themselves—you will have the final list of publications to which you will submit your article. At this point, you will want to send for the writer's guidelines that most publications make available to potential contributors. It's vital that you have these before you start submitting any material. The last thing you want to do is make an error that will immediately earmark a great article for rejection. Having the guidelines in hand can also help you further refine your list, because you may find that your article doesn't fit one or more criteria of some of your target publications.

It is vital to secure a copy of the writer's guidelines for each of the publications on your list. These guidelines—which spell out the publication's rules regarding submissions—will help you shape each package to meet the editor's basic requirements.

Writer's guidelines cover a number of important points. They specify desired word count, detail the publication's freelance options, spell out the means by which finished articles should be submitted, and provide other information of which all freelance writers must be aware. The entries in *Writer's Market* often tell you exactly how you can go about obtaining these guidelines. In some cases, though, these guidelines can be found on the publication's website or on the *Writer's Market* website. If in doubt, place a call to the publication's editorial office. An editorial assistant should be able to tell you if you must send for the guidelines or if they can be obtained elsewhere.

CONCLUSION

You have now created a list of potential publications for your work. These publications should be the ones best suited to handle your work considering its topic, audience, and approach. Ideally, they should also be open to the work of new writers. If you have taken the time to develop this list carefully, it will greatly increase your odds of seeing your article in print.

Now, though, you want to put this list aside and turn your attention to preparing the all-important submission package. Chapter 5 will guide you in preparing a package that will put you and your work in the best possible light, inviting the interest of editors.

CHAPTER 5

$\mathcal{P}$REPARING YOUR SUBMISSION PACKAGE

I f you have read through and followed the directions in Chapter 4, you now have a carefully prepared list of target publications, each handpicked to match your article. Your next step is to create a winning submission package—one that will invite an editor's attention.

Although publication guidelines vary, the majority of submission packages should include the following: a cover letter; a copy of your article; clips of previously published articles, if you have any; and a self-addressed, stamped envelope for the editor's response. When submitting material to an academic journal, it is often a standard practice to also include a curriculum vitae. This chapter will guide you step by step through the creation of each of these components, and will help you tailor these components for different publications so that every package is appropriate for the editor who is receiving it.

THE COVER LETTER

The cover letter is your submission's salesperson, journeying far and wide, working hard to help make that sale for you. Before you send him out into the world, you need to make sure that his suit is pressed, his speech is ready, and his experience is evident. If not, the door could be slammed in his face before he gets out one word.

The following guidelines will help ensure that every cover letter you send will be well written, interesting, and professional in both content and appearance. As you read these guidelines—and, of

Whatever you are writing, including your cover letter, keep in mind the Reporter ABCs—Accuracy, Brevity, and Clarity. Everything you write to or for publications should adhere to these three principles.

course, as your write your letter—keep in mind that the cover letter should best be kept to a page in length. A long letter is an irritation to a busy editor who has a looming deadline and a hundred other envelopes waiting to be opened. Get to the point and demonstrate why your article is perfect for his publication.

In general, cover letters for all traditional media—magazines, newspapers, trade publications, and academic journals—follow the same format. Those for e-mailed submissions should be shorter, but should do the same job of "selling" the article to the editor. Note, though, that the vast majority of articles submitted to print publications should be sent by regular mail. (See the inset "To E-Mail or Not to E-Mail?" on page 223 for further details.)

Composing the Cover Letter

A submission package cover letter is composed of very specific parts, each of which serves a specific function. By making sure that your letter includes all of these components and that each does exactly what it is supposed to do, you will greatly increase your chances of getting your article into print.

As you write your letter, try to match its tone to that of both the publication and the article you are submitting. A personal essay geared for publication in *Woman's Day*, for example, has a different sound to it than an article on management styles written for the *Harvard Business Review*. Use humor if it's appropriate, or keep things businesslike and professional, if that is the customary voice for that publication. Note how the sample letters in this chapter vary, depending on the type of article being submitted and the editorial flavor of the publication. (See "Sample Cover Letters" on page 123.)

The Salutation

Don't try to guess at a female editor's marital status in your salutation. "Ms. ———" is the least offensive and most professional option. You risk angering the editor if you try to be too creative or make faulty assumptions.

Every letter should, of course, begin with a salutation such as "Dear Mr. Jones." I can't stress enough the importance of making sure you have the correct name of the editor to whom you are submitting your package. By putting in his predecessor's name or getting the spelling of his name wrong, you will immediately show the editor that you didn't thoroughly research the publication. On the other hand, by using the correct editor's name on both the cover letter and the outside of the package, you will appear professional and help ensure that your submission gets to the right person. (More about getting the appropriate editor's name in Chapter 6.)

Keep your salutation simple. "Dear Mr. Doe" is perfect. Unless your goal is to sell something completely off the wall and unique, don't get cutesy or unusual in your cover letter. If the publication requests that you make your submission to a panel of editors, but you are unable to obtain a specific name by calling the publication, use a more general "Dear Editors" salutation.

The Introductory Paragraph

This paragraph is your first chance to demonstrate your voice to the editor and to sell your article. It should, as stated earlier, match the tone of your article and be a good reflection of your skills as a writer. Editors at top publications are swamped by submissions. The better your cover letter, the better your chances of convincing them to move past the top sheet and on to the work you have enclosed.

Depending on what you are submitting, the first paragraph of your letter will vary slightly. Serious-minded publications merit a matching approach—to the point, with very little room for flair. But a cover letter for a publication that's looking for humorous pieces should reflect some of that humor in its approach, and doesn't need to follow as strict a format.

In a cover letter for a submission to a consumer or trade publication, the first sentence of the first paragraph should state the subject of the article. When a manuscript is unsolicited—meaning that it was not requested by the editor—it is essential to make this sentence as strong and intriguing as possible so that it motivates the editor to read the attached article. Too many writers start out with weak sentences, and hurt their chances of acceptance by making a bad first impression. If you think of the cover letter as an ambassador for your work, you can see the importance of making sure it does a good job of convincing the editor that your article is worthy of review.

After the strong introductory sentence, expand on your topic slightly, giving a bit more information and a strong hook to make the editor want to see more. Following this, write a sentence that demonstrates your familiarity with the publication: "I have seen articles on similar topics in *Your Journal,* but not one that establishes a direct link between learning and musical instruction." This shows that you have done your research and studied the last few issues of the publication.

Compare these two opening sentences: "Enclosed is my article on the use of music in the classroom as a teaching aid," and "Music can be a powerful motivational and teaching tool in the educator's arsenal, a theory I explore in detail in my enclosed article." Which sentence grabs your attention? Which better captures the essence of the work?

Don't forget to include the word count of your article in your letter. Run your word processor's word count feature on the text of your article only, not on any headlines or contact information. Editors use this to judge whether a piece will fit in the space they have available.

If you can compare and contrast your work with a specific article, you may wish to do that as well. Remember to keep your sentences brief and to the point.

Use the last sentences of this paragraph to suggest where the article might fit in the publication's pages and editorial schedule. This, again, will demonstrate that you have done your research. "In your guidelines, it says that your June 'Hands-On Lessons' column will cover instrument use in the classroom. I think my article would be a perfect fit for that section."

Also be sure to state the word count of the article. This is a vital piece of information. Many editors reject submissions that are too long or too short—again, because they show that the writer didn't study or follow the set guidelines.

If you are an academic submitting an article for consideration to a journal, your first paragraph should be somewhat different from what was just described. The opening paragraph of a cover letter to an academic journal should always state the basic premise of the article. As the *Harvard Business Review's* guidelines put it, "What's the 'so what?' What is new, unusual, useful, counterintuitive, or important about your message?" Moreover, in Chapter 2, you learned that a journal editor is looking for articles that introduce new research, add to current journal discussions, or advance the premise of the journal. So your introduction should also clearly show which of these three roles your article is filling.

Like consumer magazine editors, academic journal editors want to see that submitting authors did their homework. Be sure to mention the section of the journal in which your article would best fit, and to include a word count or page count if one is specified in the journal's guidelines.

The Second Paragraph

If you can't find a copy of a publication's editorial calendar online, go to the section for advertisers. The advertising schedule usually contains a listing of the proposed editorial content for each issue.

This is where you show the editor that you understand his audience and can demonstrate the relevance of your article to his publication. For an article providing information or news, try to obtain statistics that demonstrate people's interest in the topic. For example, your letter might state: "A study done by XYZ Association found that 90 percent of high school teachers would incorporate music in their lessons if they had techniques and sample curriculum to utilize." This concrete data shows that you have done your research, and that the journal's readership would be interested in the topic of your article. If your article is a personal essay, use this second paragraph to show that the publication's readers would benefit from your experience.

What's important here is convincing the editor that your work fits his readers and will provide value to them. It's not enough to simply deliver information; it has to be presented in a manner that helps the reader in some way. People read magazines, newspapers, and other publications for information that will help them in their field of work or in their lives. You have to show how your article will provide them with the facts, advice, or guidance for which they're looking. By proving to the editor in the early paragraphs of your letter that your article will benefit and be of interest to his audience, you will convince him to read further.

The Third Paragraph

In the first paragraph, you covered what your article was and where it would fit in the publication. In the second paragraph, you told the editor why reading the article would be beneficial to his audience. In this paragraph, you must show why *you* are the best person to write this article.

Use this paragraph to showcase any background—your education, your work, or your life experience—that is relevant to your article. Note that the key word here is "relevant." If you are an obstetrician writing about advances in birth techniques, for instance, your background is clearly relevant to the article you have written, and establishes your credibility as the author of your article. But if you are an elevator mechanic writing about the best way to grow marigolds, your professional experience should *not* be highlighted in your letter, as it is in no way relevant to the topic of your article. In such a case, it would be far more helpful to mention life experience, such as the fact that you have been gardening for twenty years and have won several prizes for your flowers. Never forget that no matter how meaningful a personal accomplishment is to you, it won't score points with an editor unless it is related to the submitted piece.

If you have publishing credits—meaning that you have been previously published in magazines, newspapers, or other publications—this is the place to mention them. Editors value writers who have experience with the publishing industry and knowledge about how it works, because the chances are good that such writers will turn in

Cover letters to newspaper editors follow the same format as letters to magazines. For e-zines, however, you should condense your cover letter into two or, at most, three paragraphs, because this publishing format dictates shorter, tighter writing. Again, you always want to reflect the type of writing presented in the target publication.

If you have no writing experience at all, don't mention that in your cover letter, as it will only draw attention to the fact that you haven't been published. See the sample letter for an unpublished writer on page 124 for an example of how you can handle this third paragraph.

quality work before the deadline. But be selective when presenting your credentials, and include only those that are most prestigious and relevant—not everything that comes to mind. Your job is to impress the editor, not to overwhelm him with minutiae about your writing background.

If you don't have any published work experience, don't panic. Editors understand that all writers have to start somewhere. Just be sure to relate your background to your topic, and to make the first two paragraphs of your letter the longest and strongest. Unpublished writers need to do more work on the selling end of their letter.

Unless you are submitting your article to an academic journal, do not add a resumé or curriculum vitae, and avoid the temptation to make this third paragraph too lengthy. Be choosy about what you include and make sure it is relevant to both the publication and your piece. (For information on creating a curriculum vitae, see page 136.)

The Fourth Paragraph

The fourth paragraph of your cover letter is your conclusion. Consisting of two or three sentences, this should be the shortest paragraph of your letter. These sentences should include a thank-you for the editor's time and consideration; a mention of whether the article is a multiple submission or an exclusive one; and a note about enclosing an SASE and clips, if you have them. (To learn about multiple submissions, see page 143 in Chapter 6.) Finally, provide a few closing words about how you are looking forward to the editor's response.

The Closing

Keep this brief and professional. A simple "Sincerely" or "Respectfully" is enough. Skip a line for your signature, and then type out your name beneath that. Before sending out your letters, don't forget to sign each letter above the typed name. Finally, if desired, place an enclosures note—Encl: clips—two spaces below your typed name to emphasize the fact that you have been published and that your clips have been attached.

Formatting the Cover Letter

The appearance of your cover letter is important. First, choose clean, white, good-quality 8½-x-11-inch paper (20-pound is okay, but 24-

pound is a heavier and better stock). Cream paper is also acceptable, but never use brightly colored paper, and resist the temptation to use decorative stationery. To an editor, that type of paper spells amateur. Also avoid erasable bond as it smears easily.

Print on only one side of the paper, using a font that is clear and easy to read. Although Times New Roman is often referred to as the industry standard, you can try fonts like Book Antiqua or Courier as well, as long as they are clean and readable. Be sure to use a 12-point type size. Editors spend their entire days reading and appreciate the large-size letters.

If you have letterhead that contains your contact information, you can use that stationery as long as it is plain and professional in appearance. You can also create your own letterhead with your word processing software. It's okay to put your contact information—address, phone number, e-mail address, etc.—in the top right-hand corner of the letter, in standard business position. But if you have multiple phone numbers and addresses, it is better to consolidate this data below your name rather than grouping it unattractively at the top of the letter.

The margins of your letter should be one inch all around. Set up the letter itself in a business format, meaning that the paragraphs are left-justified and single-spaced, with an extra space between paragraphs instead of an indent.

Put the date in the left-hand corner of your letter. Two spaces below the date, place the editor's name and title, followed by the name of the publication and the address. Skip a line, write the salutation, and then skip another line. The four paragraphs of the body of the letter follow from here. Finally, add your closing and signature, and the enclosure line, if you choose to use one. All the elements of your cover letter should work together to present one cohesive, polished image.

Sample Cover Letters

Following are several sample cover letters for you to review and use as guides in writing your own. Each addresses a specific type of submission situation, showing through example how you can tailor your letter to suit your background and experience, as well as your article and the publication to which you're making your pitch. Remember, though, that these letters were written by me and thus reflect my voice and style. Your cover letters should be a reflection of your talent and be infused with some of your personality.

When formatting e-mailed cover letters, it is standard to place the contact information at the *bottom* of the letter, beneath your signature. This allows the editor to get straight to the heart of your letter when he opens your e-mail.

(Current Date)

Kathryn Carter, Editor
Natural Resources Journal
40 West Water Street
New York, NY 10011

Dear Ms. Carter:

> ### For the Unpublished Writer With Real-World Experience #1
>
> This letter aptly demonstrates that a lack of publishing credentials doesn't have to be a hindrance. Instead of mentioning his lack of experience, this writer emphasizes the relevance of his article to the journal he's contacting, and explains his background and involvement in the journal's field of interest.

In Indiana, a battle is brewing to reclaim the state's lakes from the zebra mussel. These tiny creatures are taking over 20 percent of the area's waters, threatening the fish and wildlife population with their parasitic presence, a danger covered in my article, "Zebra Mussels: Deadly Invaders." How the mussels got to Indiana is a hotly debated topic, pitting fishermen against environmentalists. My enclosed 800-word article details the history of these animals and the impact they have had on freshwater lakes. I think it would fit well in your "News and Comments" section.

A study conducted by Southern Illinois University addressed this growing threat to natural resources and developing techniques to battle zebra mussels. The study found the zebra mussel problem is growing at a rate of 15 percent per year, threatening at least five different local fish species. My article provides information to help combat the problem and prevent it from spreading. Readers concerned with environmental issues will find these techniques informative and useful in the protection of their own lakes and ponds.

I am an active member of several environmental organizations and an environmental biologist with the Athens Nature Institute. I have studied this area extensively and have subscribed to journals such as yours to broaden my knowledge base.

Thank you for taking the time to review my article, which has been submitted to other publications as well. I have enclosed a SASE for your reply. I look forward to hearing from you.

Sincerely,

John Fisher
33 Breakwater Road
Athens, GA 22347
Phone: 123-555-1212; Fax: 123-555-1213
E-mail: johnf@internet.com

(Current Date)

Nellie Niceties, Editor
The Parent Newspaper
127 Adult Lane
Centerville, GA 11735

Dear Ms. Niceties:

For the Unpublished Humorous Writer #2

This letter is a good guide for an unpublished writer who is submitting a personal essay to a major magazine. Because the tone of a personal essay is more relaxed and intimate than that of a news story, the letter is, too. This cover letter reflects the writer's personal style, which is both informal and humorous, and invites the editor to read the enclosed essay.

What do you get when you have two kids, one chocolate brownie and a battle brewing over an imagined discrepancy in Dad's dividing skills? You get "Brownie Wars," my personal essay on trying to keep peace while teaching my children about equality. My enclosed 600-word essay is a humorous slice of life about trying to balance parenting with life lessons. I think it's a good fit for *The Parent Newspaper's* "Solutions" section, which often features essays on sibling skirmishes.

My article provides a comical look at one of the common battles in my house—the She Got More Syndrome. A poll conducted at my local play group, using ice cream sundae samples, revealed that 110 percent of the children thought another kid got more than they did (four-year-old Julia James insisted on voting twice). My essay gives parents a new approach to this problem, which hopefully results in more equitable portions and happier kids.

As a work-at-home father, I have muddled through the murky waters of parenting with a good sense of humor and a lot of patience. Whenever I get a chance, I clear the jelly off my monitor screen and vacuum out the chocolate chips from the keyboard so I can write about my adventures of fatherhood.

Thank you for taking the time to review my submission, which has been sent solely to your publication. I managed to wrestle the stamps out of my two-year-old's hands and have enclosed a self-addressed, stamped envelope. I'll be sure to get to the mailbox before the kids so I can be the first to see your reply.

Sincerely,

Harry D. Parent
2425 Busy Lane
Rushmore City, IN 46802
Phone: 156-555-0911; Fax: 156-555-0912
E-mail: harry@kidzone.com

(Current Date)

Business Reviewer
60 Company Way
Boston, MA 02190

Dear Editors:

For the Unpublished Academic Writer #3

The final sample letter is for the unpublished writer who has an advanced degree in a field that is relevant to the article being submitted. Editors respect an authoritative voice—a writer who is knowledgeable about his area of concentration. Information about your background and education can enhance your chances of acceptance.

When management styles clash, the entire organization suffers, as my enclosed article, "Management Style Wars," discusses. This can lead to an internal meltdown, undermining the success of the entire company. My article pinpoints the triggers that cause these problems and teaches managers to avoid them before these issues undercut the morale of the company. In the past, the *Business Reviewer* has run articles on issues similar to this ("Managing Away Bad Habits," January 2000) but not on the level I am proposing. My 1,500-word article would fit well in your "Best Practice" section.

A study in the July 1999 issue of the *Journal of Business Research* found that 95 percent of all CEOs have some problem with upper-management personality clashes. However, that article did not present a workable solution. My article identifies five main types of managers and their confrontational tendencies. With simple evaluation techniques, any upper-level manager can apply the same classifications to his team, and effectively lead and manage each of these individual personalities. My article goes into great detail about management types, offering proven techniques for optimizing work performance and communication skills.

As a professor at the Eastern Nazarene School of Business, I have taught this subject and researched it in depth for my classes. In my work as a consultant with IBM, I have helped their management team apply these tactics, with incredible results. Four weeks after my presentation on "Management Style Wars," morale levels increased 40 percent, according to independent researchers who were brought in to study IBM's corporate culture.

This submission has been sent only to your publication, per your "no simultaneous submissions" request. In addition, I have enclosed an abbreviated copy of my curriculum vitae and a self-addressed, stamped envelope. Thank you for your time and consideration. I look forward to your response.

Sincerely,

Dave Bigsuit
87 Corporate Lane
Boston, MA 02240
Phone: 138-555-3040; Fax: 138-555-3048
E-mail: dave@whitecollar.com

(Current Date)

Hugh Flier, Managing Editor
The Busy Pilot
Airport Publications
3000 Jet Road
LaGuardia, VA 22300

> ## For the Previously Published Writer #4
> Publication credits are a help to any writer who is trying to place an article—as long as the credits are from publications that are well respected within the profession. The following sample letter refers to the writer's publication credentials, showing that the writer is familiar with the publishing process and has the ability to meet deadlines with professional materials.

Dear Mr. Flier:

ABC Airlines struggled for ten years to make a profit before finally launching a route targeted to a specific niche—family members making last-minute travel plans. My enclosed 800-word article, "ABC Airlines Zeroes in on a Booming Market," details the company's rocky beginning and eventual success, providing a learning model for other regional airlines. I think it would fit well in your August special edition on Regional Aircraft Product Support.

Statistics from the regional air carriers say travel in this market is experiencing a downturn. It's a struggle for many smaller airlines to compete against mergers between air giants. My article provides an informative look at one airline that is bucking the national trend.

A professional pilot for Xerox Corporation for twenty years, I have written a number of articles for *Aviation World News* as well as for *Low Flying Pilot*. My articles have covered such topics as corporate flying, pilot safety, and small plane operational techniques.

Thank you for taking the time to review my submission, which has also been sent to two other journals. I have enclosed copies of two of my published articles and a self-addressed, stamped envelope for your reply. I look forward to hearing from you.

Sincerely,

Dawn Cessna
22 Airport Road
Baer Field, IN 49801
Phone: 198-555-3212; Fax: 198-555-1213
E-mail: cessna@pilotonline.com

(Current Date)

Kevin Tripp,
    Editorial Director
Coast to Coast News
Traveler Publications
220 Vista Drive
White Cliffs, NC 05678

> ### For the Writer Unpublished in Print, But Published Online #5
>
> If you have online clips from sites that either are well known or have won awards for their content, it is certainly worth mentioning them. Keep in mind, however, that not all print editors are aware of current online publications. In case the editor you are contacting is either unfamiliar with or unimpressed by your e-credits, be sure to do a strong selling job in the first two paragraphs of your cover letter.

Dear Mr. Tripp:

At any time of year, Italy is a romantic destination. Pairing a trip to that magical country with a bicycle tour, however, gives you a recipe for a memorable vacation. My enclosed personal essay, "Pedaling Around Italy," recounts my family's adventures traveling via bicycle through the wondrous countryside of Italy. My 800-word article would fit well in your monthly section, "Unforgettable Pitstops."

Readers who are thinking about a tour of Italy would enjoy reading about our unique, open-air adventure. The bike company that hosted our tour said that almost every participant is anxious to return to Italy for another bike trip because it's the best way to see the country up close. We will never forget our encounter with the old baker who pressed bread into our arms as we were about to pedal away, or the farmers who waved flowers at us as we passed. This article gives readers a view of Italy they would miss on a bus tour.

I have written numerous articles for online travel sites such as www.expedia.com and www.travelwriters.com. My piece on mountain biking was showcased on Expedia as the top getaway idea for the month of June. A writer by trade, I am also a member of the Sierra Club and an avid hiker.

Thank you for taking the time to review my essay, which is a multiple submission. Enclosed, you will find samples of my work and a self-addressed, stamped envelope for your reply. I hope you enjoy the tale of my Italian journey as much as I enjoyed taking the trip. I look forward to hearing from you.

Sincerely,

Hillary Traveler
16 Journey Street
Anywhere, HI 90087
Phone: 124-555-7896; Fax: 124-555-6853
E-mail: hiltrav@global.com

(Current Date)

Dave Research,
  Editorial Director
Finding Your Family Tree
  Magazine
230 Elm Street
Cincinnati, OH 45009

For the Writer Submitting an On-Spec Article #6

If you eventually decide to establish a freelance writing career, you will mostly likely submit article *ideas* instead of full articles. Sometimes, an editor may be intrigued by your article idea, but not want to make a commitment to buy the piece until he sees it. In such a case, he will ask you to send in the article *on-spec,* meaning on speculation. The following letter reminds the editor that he requested the work so that he will pay special attention to the submission rather than passing it on to someone else.

Dear Mr. Research:

Thank you for your letter of July 18 requesting to see a finished copy of my proposed article, "Tracing Your Roots in Europe." As I detailed in my query letter, this article is a how-to for people interested in exploring their genealogy on the other side of the world.

Last year, I took a bike tour through Italy. While there, I spent a great deal of time researching my ancestors. The roadblocks I hit in accessing information and my creative ways of circumventing them became the basis of this article.

I have always had a strong interest in genealogy as well as travel. I have written numerous articles for online travel sites, such as www.expedia.com and www.travelwriters.com. My piece on mountain biking was showcased on Expedia as the top getaway idea for the month of June, and my story about my family's bike expedition through Italy will be in the September issue of *Coast to Coast News.*

Thank you for taking the time to review my submission, sent exclusively to you. I have enclosed a self-addressed, stamped envelope large enough to return my article, if necessary. I look forward to hearing from you.

Sincerely,

Hillary Traveler
16 Journey Street
Anywhere, HI 90087
Phone: 124-555-7896; Fax: 124-555-6853
E-mail: hiltrav@global.com

THE ARTICLE

In Chapter 4, you composed a list of those publications that are best suited to your article and your experience. Does that mean that you can now send off your completed article as is to each targeted publication? Unfortunately, no. As discussed in Chapter 4, every publication has its own writer's guidelines—specific requests regarding spacing, article length, and more. If you want each of the publications on your list to consider your article, you'll have to tailor your article to match each one's needs and requests. Then you'll want to format it in a way that spells "professional writer." The result will be an article that makes editors sit up and take notice.

Checking the Writer's Guidelines

Although most writer's guidelines provide roughly the same specifications, there are variations. Be sure to read the guidelines of each publication carefully, noting any unusual requests.

After compiling your list of target publications in Chapter 4, you sent for the writer's guidelines for each magazine, newspaper, and journal on your list. Hopefully, you have these guidelines on file, because now they're going to come in handy.

Writer's guidelines provide specific information about how each submitted article should be set up in terms of line spacing, word count, margins, etc. Newspapers and journals generally have the most specific guidelines, because their structure is more formal than that of many magazines. The guidelines of magazines tend to be a bit looser.

The writer's guidelines of most publications are rather clear-cut and relatively similar to one another. Nevertheless, there are variations, so be sure to read them closely and to note any unusual requests, such as special spacing requirements. Most editors view writers who fail to follow these guidelines as being highly unprofessional and unlikely to produce a decent article. Moreover, all editors have an internal checklist of "no-nos"—mistakes that result in immediate rejection. To avoid putting up unnecessary roadblocks to success, be sure to follow all guidelines to the letter.

While it is important to read and follow each and every one of a publication's requests, pay particular attention to word-count requirements. Whether you're writing to a consumer publication or an academic journal, submitting an article that's too short or too long usually results in rejection. Remember that the effort you expend now, double-checking guidelines and tailoring your submission, will be amply rewarded later when you see your first article in print.

Reviewing the Publications

When you wrote your cover letter, you took the time to match the tone of the target publication. Now reread your article to make sure that it, too, has the right voice for the magazine, newspaper, or journal. Is the style of the target publication warm and personal? Funny and irreverent? Straightforward and to-the-point? The more closely you match the publication in this regard, the greater your chance of being accepted.

Although your entire article should be tailored to match the style of the target publication, pay particular attention to your headline and to the first and last paragraphs of your piece. Try to keep your headline in the same tone and at about the same length as those that appear on the cover of the newspaper or periodical. This will allow the editor to more easily envision your article in his table of contents. Then make sure that the first and last paragraphs—the most critical elements of your article, after the headline—are not only clear, focused, and interesting, but also similar to those found in the publication. Each of these steps will bring you a little closer to publication. (For detailed information about writing headlines and other components of an article, see Chapter 10.)

If the articles in the publication always carry a sidebar, either include this material with your submission or note in your cover letter that you can provide it if the editor so desires. Offering this "extra" after the editor has bought the main article can get you a bit more pay, so it may benefit you to mention it but to defer writing the actual material until asked to do so in a contract.

Formatting the Article

Now it's time to make your article look as good as your letter. There's always a temptation to print the article on fancy paper, but that won't do anything except mark you as an amateur. The key here is to let your *writing* stand out, as that is what the editor is looking for and all he cares about. And the best way to do that is to present a clean, quality image.

As you did with your cover letter, print the article on good quality 8½-x-11-inch paper, using a 20-pound or 24-pound weight. Choose white paper with clear, dark ink, because that provides the best contrast for the tired eyes of a busy editor. The heavier the

In the old days, writers underlined anything that would be italicized in the finished piece. With the advances in word processing software, this is no longer necessary. Use italics where they are needed.

weight of the paper, the more durable it will be during the editorial review process.

Type on only one side of the paper, and be sure you have 1-inch margins all around. Editors often mark up your manuscript, either with revisions for you or with notes for the copyeditor. By leaving adequate margins, you will provide enough space to enable the editor to do his job.

Double-space your paragraphs and use regular half-inch indents. As when formatting the cover letter, use 12-point type and select an easy-to-read font like Times New Roman or Courier. And unless the writer's guidelines clearly state otherwise, insert one space after each period instead of the old double space.

Be sure to include all of the pertinent information—information that identifies you and your article—at the top of the first page of your article. The basic facts that should be presented here include your name, address, and other contact information, as well as the word count of your article. Also, if desired, list the rights that you intend to sell, even if they haven't been negotiated. This will put you in a position of *offering* certain rights to the publisher, rather than waiting to see what he offers you. While the editor may, of course, insist on buying more rights than you originally offered, it never hurts to show that you understand the rights process and are savvy enough to negotiate the best deal for your work. (See Chapter 11 for information on rights and other contract issues.) Finally, include a copyright notice, listing yourself as the copyright holder. Referred to as *common copyright*, this is a visual reminder that you have the rights to that work—even if you have not registered your article with the United States Copyright Office. (For more information on protecting your work, see page 152 in Chapter 6.)

I generally provide the pertinent information just discussed in a table format, and hide the grid lines so it looks more attractive. The sample article on pages 134 and 135 shows how this information should appear, and clarifies other aspects of article formatting, as well.

Make sure that each subsequent page of your article contains a keyword for the article title, and a header with your name and with the page number (Example: PROCRASTINATE/Kawa-Jump 2). There is no need to put your contact information on every page.

Center your headline below your contact information, and immediately below this, type in your byline—"By: Shirley Kawa-Jump,"

How to Handle Academic Articles for Submission

The requirements regarding the format of articles submitted to academic journals are more stringent than those for consumer and trade publications. Each area of study has its own specifications. Before submitting, it's always best to check the appropriate reference book in your field—the *Publication Manual of the American Psychological Association,* for instance.

It is also important to determine whether the target journal utilizes APA (American Psychological Association) or MLA (Modern Language Association) style. APA style information can be found in the *Publication Manual of the American Psychological Association;* MLA information is in the *MLA Style Manual and Guide to Scholarly Publishing,* published by the Modern Language Association of America. The writer's guidelines created by your target journal should inform you of this. Once you know, make sure that your submission fits the stated parameters.

Every academic journal expects the different sections of the article to be presented in a specific order. Some university guidelines require figures, tables, and footnotes to be inserted within the text. In general, though, the page order for an in-depth academic article with data and text—dissertations, feature articles, and research and trend reports, for instance—is as follows:

- [ ] Title Page
- [ ] Abstract
- [ ] Text
- [ ] References
- [ ] Appendices
- [ ] Author Note
- [ ] Footnotes
- [ ] Tables (if any were used)
- [ ] Figure Captions
- [ ] Figures

When the format and style of your article match those requested by the target publication, you immediately present an image of a careful researcher and writer. While this may not get your article into print, it will help ensure that it gets past the initial review—and therefore one step closer to publication.

for example. If you are planning on using a pseudonym, it should appear below the byline. Place the words "Writing As:" before the pseudonym so that the editor knows that you are using a pen name.

Start your article directly beneath your name. Left justify all of the text and indent a half inch for all new paragraphs. At the end, don't type "The End." Instead, simply let the article end. If your article has been written well, it will be clear that this is the conclusion.

Sample Article

To appear as professional as possible, you want to set up your article in a clean, clear format. Some publications have unique requirements—some, for

In this sample article, the information at the top of the first page includes all of the contact data, as well as the rights I want to sell to the publication and a copyright notice. Directly below that is the headline: Beat the Urge to Procrastinate. The byline has my real name; the "writing as" line, a possible pseudonym, Stella Author.

Shirley Kawa-Jump
100 Anyplace Street
Anytown, MA 02287
Ph: 781-555-4532
Fax: 781-555-4030

767 words
Rights: One Time
Copyright 2001 by Shirley Kawa-Jump
e-mail: shirley@shirleykawa-jump.com

Beat the Urge to Procrastinate

By: Shirley Kawa-Jump
Writing As: Stella Author

I have a confession to make: I procrastinate as much as the next person. I'll avoid a pending deadline by cleaning out the bathroom cabinet, taking a trip to the mall or simply overdosing on junk TV. The problem is that I'm a working writer, and I'm responsible for a sizable chunk of the household income, so procrastination is not a good idea.

Still, I do it. And I'm not alone. "I procrastinate about almost everything, even though when I do something right away it always feels so good! If something is going to be unpleasant, though, I will procrastinate," says writer Holly Gumpher Fawcett.

How do you overcome procrastination and learn to move forward with your work? After a writing career that has spanned more than twenty years, I've developed a few tips that have worked well for me.

☐ Accept that you are a procrastinator: If you know you have faults, you can work around them. Understand that your tendency is to put things off and work hard to encourage yourself to do the opposite. Just be careful to build in enough extra time to accommodate your habits. "I've learned through experience how long certain projects take, and I procrastinate accordingly," says humor writer Jennifer Doloski. "I have, however, been burned by procrastinating under the assumption that my sources will be available when I'm ready to work, and it doesn't always happen."

☐ Take Baby Steps: If you need to get three queries out this week and feel overwhelmed by the task, do one tiny thing at a time. Just outline the first one on Monday, then write the opening paragraph on Tuesday. Wednesday, finish it and outline the second one, and so forth. "You know that analogy about the eagle with the branches in its talon?" asks Melanie Gold, a freelancer and Associate Editor with the National Association of Colleges and Employers.

instance, ask for 1½-inch margins instead of 1-inch margins—but by and large, you can't go wrong by using standard formatting. The following article has been set up according to the guidelines discussed on pages 131 to 133.

PROCRASTINATE/Kawa-Jump 2

"Singularly the branches are weak, but together they're unbreakable. I reverse that. A seemingly impossible project can be done if you break it down into parts."

☐ Take the work with you: Often, the problem is in your environment. Some people feel all their self doubts and fears come back the minute they sit in front of their computer. If that's the case, then pick up your pad of paper, your pen and some Post-Its and journey to wherever you feel most comfortable. I've worked on the couch, in the library and even in a coffee shop as a reward and a break from my office. A change of pace can also restart those creative juices.

☐ Get the beginning done: When I have a huge article to write and only have a minute to work on it, I'll often write just the lead. For some reason, once that opening is done, the rest of the article easily falls into place when I come back to it later. Even though I've only composed a paragraph, it feels like the bulk of the work is done and the project isn't so overwhelming anymore.

☐ Put a mental boss on your shoulder: Working at home or on your own schedule is too much temptation for most procrastinators. It's far too simple to opt for baking cookies over writing essays or sending invoices. Writer Cheryl Duksta pretends she has a To-Do list from a boss. "What helps me is to create a list and pretend that it's my boss. I don't think; I just follow my list."

☐ Do the icky stuff first: If you have a long list of projects and have a couple that you are dreading doing, do those first. Author Melissa Hill says she uses a prioritized list and deals with the unpleasant jobs early. "If say, number 1 is no fun, [say to yourself] I'll just do it for ten minutes. After ten minutes, you're kind of in the flow of the thing and you end up just finishing it up."

☐ Make bargains with yourself: I've set all kinds of rewards for myself to get dreaded projects done—from a Hershey bar to a walk around the block. The key is to find something that motivates you enough to get your work done so that the reward is worth the effort.

You can learn to overcome bad procrastination habits and make yourself a much more productive writer. The key is knowing who you are and finding the right approach for your style of work. Before you know it, you'll be getting ten times more work done than ever before—and seeing ten times the results of your efforts.

On the second page of the article, I have added a header that contains a keyword, "PROCRASTINATE"; my last name; and the page number. If the pages of the article become separated, this header will allow the editor to easily put them back in order. The article itself is set in a clear, legible font with double-spacing and one-inch margins.

YOUR PUBLISHED CLIPS

If you want your clips returned, be sure your SASE has enough postage. If you don't need them back, you can put a note on the cover letter to that effect, if you like. However, most editors assume that you won't want your clips back after they have been folded, mailed, and handled.

If you have already enjoyed seeing one or more of your articles published either in print or online, by all means include copies of one, or at most three, of your published articles in your submission package. (If your articles appeared online, print out hard copies to accompany your submission.) Although your submitted article may be adequate to convince the editor to buy your piece, sometimes editors need additional proof of a writer's skill. Your *clips*, as they are called, will show him your talent as a writer and your range of ability. Your published articles may prove to be especially decisive if the editor likes your idea but wants the article rewritten to reflect a different slant, or if he already has an article in the queue on that topic and is looking for a writer to cover another topic.

Never send original copies of your published articles out as clips. The chances of their being returned are slim. Clean, clear photocopies are fine. If it's at all possible, try to keep these photocopies to one page—but don't sacrifice readability by reducing the print. Instead, make the copy double-sided. This will make it as easy as possible for the editor to review your published work and make a decision.

YOUR CURRICULUM VITAE

When sending articles to academic journals, it is often standard practice to include a copy of your *curriculum vitae*—a summary of your educational and professional background. When submitting very short articles, such as reviews, it usually isn't necessary to include a curriculum vitae. However, when submitting longer articles that encompass research and conclusions, your background and expertise will definitely make a difference to the editor. Some academic authors have multiple speaking and publishing credits, with vitae that stretch into dozens of pages. This is more than most editors want to see. Instead of sending a sheaf of papers, limit yourself to a couple of pages at most by including only your most prestigious achievements. (See the sample curriculum vitae on page 137.) This is the best way to showcase your background and demonstrate to the editor that you have the necessary knowledge to write the article.

Remember, though, that not every writer should enclose a vitae with his submission. Vitae are demanded by academic journals only, and should not be included with consumer and trade articles.

THOMAS SHEPHERD, D.V. M.

EDUCATION

1981, University of Missouri, Degree: Doctor of Veterinary Medicine

POSTDOCTORAL TRAINING

1986–1987, Internship, University Veterinary Hospital (Berkley, CA)
1987–1991, Residency, Surgery, University of Missouri Animal
Hospital and Clinic, Department of Veterinary Surgery

PRIVATE PRACTICE

1994–Present, PetCare Clinic, Madison, Wisconsin

PROFESSIONAL ASSOCIATION MEMBERSHIPS

Madison Humane Society, Board of Directors
American Animal Hospital Association

PUBLICATIONS

"Early Results and Complications of Chemotherapy in Canines,"
Shepherd, T., Rock, M. G., Simpson, P.L. Canine Care Journal, 1993

"Feline Tooth Care: Current Perspectives," Shepherd, T., Simpson,
P.L. Journal of the Southern Veterinarian Association, Vol. 3, No. 2,
pp 95–107, 1994

"Running a Successful Practice," Vet News, Vol. 9, No. 1, pp 12–13,
1996.

"Hip Dysplasia in the Adult Golden Retriever," Animal Care Clinic
Bulletin 21, Winter, 1997.

SAMPLE CURRICULUM VITAE

THE SELF-ADDRESSED, STAMPED ENVELOPE

It is considered standard procedure to include a self-addressed, stamped envelope—known as an SASE—in your submission package. The editor will use this business-sized envelope to mail his response to you. Be aware that if you don't include an SASE in your package, you should not expect to receive a response from the editor. In addition, this kind of oversight is a sure way to irritate the person receiving your letter.

Unless you specifically request the return of your entire submission package, and include sufficient postage, the editor will send back only a response letter. Because few editors take the time to mark up the manuscripts they are rejecting, it's generally a waste of money to pay the extra postage.

POLISHING THE PACKAGE

Editors don't want to reject your work. They are always on the lookout for good writers of professional caliber. If two submission packages on the same exact topic come in on the same day, the editor will choose the one that is more professionally researched, written, and executed—not the one that is studded with typing errors and that neglects to pinpoint the article's intended audience.

Once you have put together the different components of your submission package, you may want to start sending packages out right away. But wait. Remember, you get only *one* chance—and a brief one at that—to favorably impress an editor. Take the time to make sure that everything is perfect.

First and foremost, check your materials to be sure that there are no spelling or grammar problems. This proofreading step is essential and shouldn't be hurried. Ideally, you should proofread everything at least twice, once on your computer screen and once in printed form. Your mind can sometimes fill in the missing words in a sentence. By reading your material over several times and checking the details, you will catch these errors. Remember that everything you send to an editor is part of your overall presentation. Your letter, your article, and even your envelope should be clean and neat, and as error-free as possible.

I once made the mistake of sealing the envelopes on a series of query letters without proofreading them first. I had even mailed a few out before catching this mistake: "I a freelance writer." When I'd read the letter on my computer, I had mentally added the missing word, not seeing that it wasn't actually there. Needless to say, not a single assignment resulted from this mailing. I learned my lesson about proofreading that day.

When all of the components of your package are letter perfect, you may be tempted to put them in a fancy binder or folder. *Don't*—and don't fasten the pages together with a rubber band or staple, either. Editors don't like anything that limits their ability to read and write on a submission or that makes the whole package heavy and awkward to handle. Simply use a paper clip to keep the various sheets together. The editor will find it easy to remove the clip, look at the pages individually, and mark the copy up with sugestions and comments, if necessary.

Remember that your writing should be what most shines through in your submission package. Don't let your letterhead, your typeface, or impressive "packaging" take center stage. No amount of elaborate formatting or stationery can compensate for poor writing. In fact, it may only serve as a distraction when you are trying to capture the editor's attention.

CONCLUSION

If you've followed all the guidelines in this chapter and created a clean, professional, and well-written package, you have done everything right. Now it's time to send your package out into the world. Chapter 6 presents a proven step-by-step system for submitting your carefully created package to your selected publishers—a system that will maximize your chance of having your article published.

CHAPTER 6

USING THE SQUARE ONE SYSTEM

Chapter 5 guided you through the writing of an effective submission package. You've written a strong cover letter; you've tailored your article according to the submission guidelines of the publications you've targeted; and if you're lucky enough to have them, you've compiled your clippings. If you're like most writers, you're now more than eager to send your package out into the world. But what's the best way to get this accomplished? Enter the Square One System.

The Square One System for submission is a carefully planned program that guides you in sending out your proposal in groups, with the first group going to those publishers that you feel are most likely to help you meet your goal of publication. By breaking the submission process into steps, this system makes the process easier, and enables you to benefit from any editorial feedback you receive along the way. Just as important, the Square One System ensures that everything is done right, maximizing your chance of getting your article into print.

STEP ONE: PRIORITIZE THE PUBLICATIONS ON YOUR LIST

In Chapter 4, you put together a list of those publications that would be the most appropriate markets for your article. Depending on how specialized the topic of your article is and on whether you are target-

When prioritizing the publications on your list, base your decisions not only on your research, but also on your instincts and your personal preferences. If you like a particular publication and read it regularly, chances are that you have a good sense of what the editor is looking for in terms of content and tone.

ing commercial publications or academic journals, you should have from fifteen to twenty publications on your list. The next step is to prioritize your entries. Give each publication a number, with the first one being the most promising—the one where you think you stand your best chance of garnering an acceptance. The last publication on the list should be the one that you think is the least promising.

Base your decisions both on your research in resource books and your gut instincts. You know the caliber of your writing and you know what kinds of articles are printed in these publications. Perhaps just as important, you know your own tastes. If you like a publication and are already familiar with it, you may have a better chance of placing your article within its pages because you have an intuitive sense of what the editor wants and likes to publish. In addition, the magazines you like the most will naturally be the ones you put the most effort into during the submission process. It's human nature to strive harder to please the editor of a publication you admire. But—and this is an important but—always try to be realistic and to keep in mind that the smaller, lesser known publications are the ones most likely to buy work from an unknown writer.

When you have completed Step One of the Square One System, your prioritized list should contain all of the publications that appeared on your original list, but should name them in order of preference. In Step Two, you'll work with the first five publications on your list—your A List—verifying the information needed to send out your first submission packages. In subsequent steps, you'll work with the second group of five, your B List; and, finally, all of the remaining companies, your C List.

STEP TWO: DETERMINE THE CORRECT ADDRESSES AND EDITORS

In Chapter 2, you learned that it's vitally important to send your package to a specific editor, rather than just any name on the publication's masthead. Don't assume that if you send something to the wrong editor, she will take the time and effort to forward your material to the right one. Instead, you'll want to find the name and title of the appropriate person and mail your submission directly to her. And, of course, to make sure that package reaches that editor, you'll have to find the correct address—the address of the building that houses the

The Multiple Submission Debate

Whether it's called a *multiple submission* or a *simultaneous submission*, the premise is the same: a writer submits one article or idea to many publications at once. Ask writers and editors about this practice and you'll get as many opinions as there are pages in this book. Some writers and editors feel strongly that sending tailored submissions to one place at a time is a better practice. But in truth, it all depends on how big the market is for your particular article and what the policy is at each of your target publications.

The fact is that multiple submission is an economic necessity for most career writers, and is a helpful practice for the noncareer writer who wants to maximize her chance of getting an article considered and purchased. Whether you're publishing for money, for prestige, or for fun, the practice of sending out multiple submissions means that several pairs of eyes will see the piece—and, hopefully, someone will like what she sees. As a bonus, if an editor is interested in your article, she may try to review it more quickly if she knows that it is being considered by other publications.

While it's rare, multiple acceptances do happen. When I first started submitting to magazines, I sent the same query to eleven different publications, all of which accepted multiple submissions. Two editors from two different magazines called me—on the same day—wanting to

buy the piece. I had to do some fast negotiating and offer a different slant to one publication to make that double sale. In the end, both editors bought and ran the story. Neither was angry that I had submitted elsewhere because my letter had informed them that they were receiving a multiple submission. (For more detailed information on handling this situation, see page 163 in Chapter 7.)

Your decision regarding multiple submissions should be based on your target list of publications. If the number-one publication on your list specifies "no simultaneous submissions," send your piece there first and wait for the editor's response. If, however, your top few publications accept multiple submissions—or don't specify a preference—go ahead and send your package to all of them. However, as explained in Chapter 5, your cover letter should inform the editor that your article has also been submitted to other publications.

It is risky to blatantly ignore an editorial policy that says "no multiple submissions." If you don't tell an editor that your work has been submitted elsewhere, and then end up withdrawing it or giving another publication the "scoop," you could anger the editor. Above all, you want to be straightforward and professional with editors so that you can establish a good reputation to match your quality writing.

editorial offices, and not the advertising office or the publishing company's corporate headquarters.

When you compiled your list of publications, you jotted down the accompanying contact information that you found in your

The Electronic Submission Package

While electronic correspondence has not become a big hit with print publications, it's a necessity with most Internet-based markets. Thus, the majority of electronic publications ask that all of their correspondence—including all submissions—be sent to them via e-mail. (For information on sending queries and submissions to *print* publications via e-mail, see the inset "To E-Mail or Not to E-Mail?" on page 223.)

Don't assume, however, that all electronic publications are the same. Before you send an e-submission, check with a resource guide like *Writer's Market* or verify through the site's guidelines that it accepts submissions by e-mail. Most will state their preference.

The e-submission process is virtually the same as the regular submission process, with a few minor differences. Obviously, you don't include an SASE because the response, too, will be sent electronically. And if your software allows, you can add the "request receipt" option so you will know that your proposal has reached its destination.

Remember that with the high prevalence of computer viruses, most editors will delete your e-mail unread if it has an attachment. Your best bet is to send your cover letter and your article in the body of the e-mail, single spaced and formatted in Text Only, so that you don't end up with any odd characters from translation errors. In the subject line, be sure to put the word "SUBMISSION" in capital letters, followed by a colon and a brief title for your piece. If you don't, the editor might think that your query is *spam* (junk e-mail) and delete it unread. Paste your article directly below your letter. At the end of the submission, type [END] so the editor knows that nothing has been lost in cyberspace.

Keep your e-mail letters as professional as your print letters. Don't use emoticons like smiley faces. Refrain from e-mail shorthand and abbreviations. This is still a submission package, and is your best chance to convince an editor that your material is worth publishing. Make sure that every aspect of your material, right down to your signature line, conveys this message.

resource books and magazines—the address, phone number, and name of the editor that might be interested in your article. Even if you did a careful job of copying this data, keep in mind that in the publishing world, change is as frequent as summer thunderstorms. The editor of the parenting section today could be the book reviewer tomorrow. The magazine could be bought by another publisher and moved to new offices. In fact, any one of a million changes can take place between the publication date of the resource guide and the day you send your submissions out into the world. For this reason, you need to double-check everything, right down to the zip code, with a quick phone call.

When you make your call, don't ask for the editor. Editors are busy people who don't want to be bothered with verbal queries from writers they don't know. They would much prefer to see your material in writing so they can examine it and pass it along the chain of editors discussed in Chapter 2. Ask the person who answers the phone—generally, an editorial assistant—about the name of the current editor for the section you are targeting. Be sure to get the spelling of the editor's name correct and to verify the publication's address. If the assistant won't give you a name, don't fret. You can work around this bit of information if you have to. Just address the article to the Lifestyles Editor, the Book Review Editor, or whatever. Or, if the publication has requested that you make your submission to a panel of editors, simply use a more general "Dear Editors" salutation. Now repeat this process with the rest of the publications on your A List, carefully double-checking and revising your initial contact data as needed.

STEP THREE: FILL OUT YOUR TRACKING CHART

You now have all the information you need to start sending your packages out to the magazines, newspapers, and other publications you have targeted. But don't put those packages into the mail without first taking the time to set up and fill in your Tracking Chart, a sample of which is shown on pages 146 to 147. At this point, of course, all you can fill in is the first three columns. Start by putting in the editor's name and the publication's name, address, phone number, and other contact information. Then fill in the circulation of the publication, which will allow you to measure your success with publications of different sizes; and the expected response time, which you'll find in the writer's guidelines that you earlier obtained from the publication. Later, as you send packages out and receive responses, you'll be able to fill in the Date Sent, Follow-Up, and Response/Date columns.

As your responses come back, make sure you compare the information in the editor's letters with what you have on your Tracking Chart. This is just one more way to make sure you have current submission information.

If you choose to create the Tracking Chart on paper and write the information in by hand, be sure to leave enough room between the entries for notes. You can also create the Tracking Chart on your computer using spreadsheet software or even tables within a word processing document. Then print out a copy to keep on your desk for easy reference.

You may wonder why it's desirable to keep track of your mailings and responses. Although you may be one of the lucky writers who

TRACKING CHART

Publication/Editor/ Contact Information	Circulation	Expected Response Time
Julian Childs Quick Cook Magazine 11 Menu Lane New York, NY 10001 Phone: 212-555-1122 Fax: 212-555-2211 E-mail: Quickcook@food.com	17,000	1 month
Nora Chef One Pot Cooking 4756 Crockpot Street Boston, MA 02170 Phone: 212-555-1133 Fax: 212-555-3344 E-mail: Potchef@food.com	6,000	1 month on queries; 2 months on ms.

Be realistic about the expected response time noted in a publication's guidelines, as this is actually the *desired* response time. Busy seasons and deadline rushes can set editors back for weeks. If your response is delayed for a couple of weeks, be patient and give it some more time.

immediately receives a positive response from the publication at the top of your list, chances are that it will take some time to actually get your article into print. In the meantime, you'll probably be sending out a lot of letters and receiving a good many letters in return. A conscientiously filled-out Tracking Chart will allow you to keep tabs on each of your submissions so that, at a glance, you can easily determine when you sent a package out, and what, if any, response you have received. You will then know when to send out follow-up mailings or to submit elsewhere if your first mailings don't produce the desired results. And if an editor calls with questions about your submission, you'll have a ready reference at hand. The Tracking Chart will prove even more helpful if you decide to develop your article writing into a career. At that point, your chart will enable you to evaluate your success rates at various types of publications, and to target the best markets for future submissions.

Date Sent	Follow-Up	Response/Date
2/23/--		Accepted, 3/30/--
2/23/--	SASP sent 4/20/--	Not interested, 5/7/--

STEP FOUR: MAIL OUT
YOUR FIRST FIVE SUBMISSION PACKAGES

It is now time to send out submission packages to the five publications at the top of your list. First, finalize the five letters by adding the date, the name and address of the publication, and the editor's name and title. (See the sample cover letters on pages 124 to 129.) Proofread the letters one more time. Make sure you didn't accidentally transpose any numbers in the zip code or make a mistake in the editor's name. Also check all the sheets going into the envelope to be positive they don't have any stains or tears. When you are 100-percent sure that everything is perfect, make a copy of each cover letter, and place it in a file. Then place your submission packets in the envelopes and seal them. Don't use staples or tape; just use the gummed area at the edge of the flap, and seal the package well.

While most print publications prefer to receive submissions by postal mail, many electronic publications prefer e-mail. To learn more about this, see the inset "The Electronic Submission Package" on page 144.

The best option for mailing an article is a catalog envelope. These are a little bit bigger than a sheet of paper, measuring 10 inches by 13 inches, and provide plenty of room for a thick enclosure. If your article is only a couple of pages long, a 9-x-12-inch envelope works well, too. Bigger than the standard business-sized envelope, both of these sizes will keep the article flat and neat.

If your handwriting is legible, it's fine to write out your return address and the mailing information. If not, invest in printer labels that you can format on your computer and affix to the envelope, or simply type out the envelopes on a typewriter. If the editor requested your article, put the words "Requested Article" in the bottom left-hand corner. This ensures that your work won't be lost in the editorial department or buried at the bottom of the Inbox. Don't be tempted to rush at this point. A submission package enclosed in an envelope that bears the wrong zip code is not going to do its job no matter how effective the cover letter may be.

To make sure that your mail gets to its destination in a timely manner, send domestic mail first class and international mail by airmail. The last thing you want is your manuscript being lost or held up because it went a slower route.

Finally, fill in the Date Sent column of your Tracking Chart, and sit back and relax. You deserve it.

STEP FIVE: BE PATIENT!

Now that you have those first five submission packages in the mail, put them out of your mind and try not to worry about them or anticipate the editors' responses. Don't forget that response times vary dramatically and are affected by vacations, deadlines, and turnover at the publication. The responses will arrive; they just may not arrive as quickly as you would want them to. So try to cultivate patience during this time.

In the upper left-hand corner of your SASE, put the title of your article. Below this, write the return address of the magazine. Then, when the envelope comes back in the mail, you will know at a glance the article to which the publication is responding.

As you receive responses—letters of either rejection or acceptance—be sure to record the date in the Response/Date column of your Tracking Chart. When filling in the last column of your chart, don't forget to note any requests from the editor, such as: "Make revisions" or "Send a copy via e-mail."

Occasionally, you will get a personal letter from an editor suggesting revisions of the piece. This feedback is valuable and should

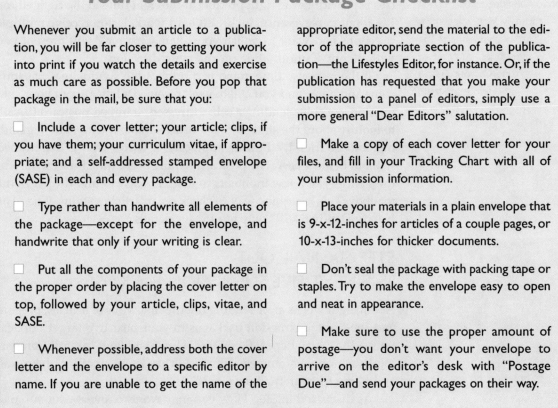

Your Submission Package Checklist

Whenever you submit an article to a publication, you will be far closer to getting your work into print if you watch the details and exercise as much care as possible. Before you pop that package in the mail, be sure that you:

☐ Include a cover letter; your article; clips, if you have them; your curriculum vitae, if appropriate; and a self-addressed stamped envelope (SASE) in each and every package.

☐ Type rather than handwrite all elements of the package—except for the envelope, and handwrite that only if your writing is clear.

☐ Put all the components of your package in the proper order by placing the cover letter on top, followed by your article, clips, vitae, and SASE.

☐ Whenever possible, address both the cover letter and the envelope to a specific editor by name. If you are unable to get the name of the appropriate editor, send the material to the editor of the appropriate section of the publication—the Lifestyles Editor, for instance. Or, if the publication has requested that you make your submission to a panel of editors, simply use a more general "Dear Editors" salutation.

☐ Make a copy of each cover letter for your files, and fill in your Tracking Chart with all of your submission information.

☐ Place your materials in a plain envelope that is 9-x-12-inches for articles of a couple pages, or 10-x-13-inches for thicker documents.

☐ Don't seal the package with packing tape or staples. Try to make the envelope easy to open and neat in appearance.

☐ Make sure to use the proper amount of postage—you don't want your envelope to arrive on the editor's desk with "Postage Due"—and send your packages on their way.

be put to use immediately. If the editor says that she liked your idea but found the material unfocused, or if she thought that you needed to add more statistics, consider her suggestions seriously. Then, if they make sense to you, revise your article accordingly. You will probably find that the resulting piece is stronger and more marketable. When you start on your next round of mailings—Step Six of the Square One System—use the updated article. And if the editor indicated that she would be open to seeing a new draft, resend the reworked piece to her. Your changes may be the ticket to the sale.

If you get one or more positive responses, congratulations! You should now turn to Chapter 7, which will help you take the next steps on the road to publication.

If you're lucky enough to receive feedback from an editor, be sure to consider it carefully. Her suggestions may give you just the direction you need to tune up your article and find it a home.

If you receive only rejections, don't let it get you down or stop you from moving forward. Remember that 90 percent of publishing articles is providing the right product at the right time to the right editor. It's about perseverance, luck, and hard work. If you receive multiple rejections and want to polish your plan, Chapter 7 will present you with plenty of information on changing direction.

If the response time noted in a publication's guidelines has long come and gone, and you still haven't received a letter about your submission, consider sending a self-addressed, stamped postcard (SASP) to inquire about the status of your article. Make it witty, not demanding, and be friendly. Editors appreciate a writer who is determined without being a pest. The postcard requires very little time on the editor's part—just a few moments to mark an answer and drop it in the mailbox. This is a quick way to check on an article's status. (See "The Handy Dandy SASP" on page 151 for details.)

STEP SIX: MAIL OUT
THE NEXT FIVE SUBMISSION PACKAGES

About eight weeks after sending out the first wave of articles, prepare and send out submission packages to your next five target publications—the B List. Repeat Steps Two, Three, and Four carefully, preparing five more customized submission packages, mailing them out, and filling in your Tracking Chart.

As discussed in Step Five, you may want to revise your submission package based on any feedback you received from editors. Take the same care the second time around as you did with the original package. Read through the new letter and article, checking again for errors in spelling, grammar, and punctuation. Change the headline if the focus of the article is different, and, if necessary, amend your headers and footers to reflect the new headline. Everything should be as consistent and professional this time as it was in your first mailing.

Keep yourself motivated, and don't let any rejections you may have received get you down. Publishing articles is a tough business, but not an impossible one. It may take a few repetitions of the Square One System before you make that first sale. Once you do, however, you will find it that much easier to publish subsequent articles if you have an interest in doing so.

The Handy Dandy SASP

After painstakingly preparing your list of publications and crafting your submission packages, it can be very frustrating when responses fail to arrive in the expected period of time. At that point, many writers pick up the phone and try to contact the editor to check on the submission. But this is the fastest way to annoy her and receive a rejection letter. Editors are so pressed for time that a call from a writer they don't know can upset the daily schedule. Most likely, by pressuring the editor to read your piece, you will simply push her in the direction of crossing you off the list as a potential contributor.

The easiest, most effective way to check on an article's status is to send an SASP (self-addressed, stamped postcard). On the card, simply type a message telling the editor that you mailed a submission to her publication, and noting the date of your mailing so that she can check her files. Be sure to mention your article by name. Then, to make it as easy as possible for the editor to get back to you, provide her with a series of responses, placing a check box next to each one. All she needs to do is make a mark or two and drop the card in the mail.

Make sure that your SASP is friendly and professional, and don't be afraid to add a touch of humor. This is an easy way to lend personality to your message, and may inspire the editor to find your article and give it a second (or first) look. Editors like the response postcards because they are quick and easy, and one that gives them a chuckle is even better.

To account for busy schedules and deadlines, wait three to four weeks past the stated response time before sending out the postcards. And once the postcards have been mailed out, try to wait patiently for your answers. If the editor is currently evaluating your submission, she may take a few days to get to the SASP.

Here's a sample of a card that provides the necessary information and has a humorous edge:

Dear Mr. Smith,

My article, "How to Fix a Faucet," mailed to you on June 14, is waiting on your desk, eager to provide advice to your readers. I realize that you are busy and have thousands of submissions, but I wanted to check on the status of my submission in case any of your readers is having a plumbing problem. Before there's a minor flood, could you confirm the receipt of my work by checking off one of the boxes below? Thank you.

☐ I have received your submission and have no use for plumbing repairs.

☐ I enjoyed your submission, even fixed my own faucet with your information (thank you), but don't have room for it in the magazine.

☐ I enjoyed your submission and am considering it for publication.

☐ I didn't receive your submission. Send it quick! I have a growing puddle beneath my sink.

☐ I didn't receive it. I don't want it. Don't send it. If I have a leaky faucet, I'll get out the Yellow Pages.

STEP SEVEN: MAIL OUT
THE REMAINING SUBMISSION PACKAGES

Wait for another eight weeks to pass, recording any feedback and sending out follow-up postcards as needed. At the end of that time, if you still haven't received an acceptance, go back to your original list and repeat all of the steps necessary to send out the remaining submission packages. If you have less than ten publications left on your list, return to your resource books and find another batch of five or ten publications—from magazines to online sites—that could be potential homes for your article. You may need to rewrite your original piece to fit these new markets. "How to Fix a Leaky Faucet" may become "Saving Money on Plumbing Bills." In this case, you'll be starting again at Step One.

PROTECTING YOUR WORK

As you send copies of your articles out to so many people, you may feel just a bit panicky. Are you losing control over you work? Might someone steal it? If you feel a little protective of your article, you're certainly not alone. The fear that someone might steal a written work is one that is shared by authors around the world, and has been since the printing press was invented in the fifteenth century, making printed materials more readily available and the printing process more affordable. However, do keep in mind that the chances of your work being stolen are relatively slim. It is a well-known fact that anything written down is, by law, the property of the author. Magazines, newspapers, and journals tend to abide by this law, and will offer a contract for use of submitted work. They won't just take your work and use it as their own.

Nevertheless, it pays to be familiar with the law. And if the possibility of theft remains a concern for you, consider means by which you can further protect your work.

Copyright Basics

A copyright is a federal law that protects original "works of authorship," which can include anything from a poem, to a drawing, to a computer program—to an article. Your ideas and concepts are not protected, but your finished work is. Under copyright, no one can reproduce, adapt, distribute, perform, or display your work unless you formally grant him or her the right to do so. Moreover, a copyright is yours as soon as you put your work down on a piece of paper or in a recording. It is yours whether or not you have registered your work with the United States Copyright Office.

Establishing a Common Copyright Through Standard Notation

You can help protect your work by simply placing a copyright notation on the work itself. This is referred to as a *common copyright*. It's important to understand that this notation isn't necessary to establish copyright. As explained earlier, copyright was established as soon as you wrote your article. However, this notation does serve as a visual reminder that you have the rights to that piece of work.

If you examined the sample article in Chapter 5, you saw that at the top of the page, the article contained a notation of common copyright: Copyright 2000 by Shirley Kawa-Jump. You can also use the copyright symbol in this notation, printing the notation one of the following ways: © 2000 Shirley Kawa-Jump, *or* Copyright © 2000 Shirley Kawa-Jump. Any of these notations will serve the intended purpose of reminding the reader that you are the author of the work, and therefore own all rights to it.

Registering Copyright With the Federal Government

If the option of common copyright does not provide you with an adequate feeling of security, or if you have a special reason to fear infringement of your work, you have another alternative: You can register your work with the United States Copyright Office. Formal registration gives you certain legal benefits. If anyone does violate your copyright by publishing part or all of your work, the formal copyright registration will speed up any legal battle and avoid complications. And if the work is registered with the copyright office within three months of its appearance in print or before any violation of your rights occurred, you will be awarded the money to pay for any attorney expenses, as well as compensation for the wrongs committed against you. A willful copyright infringement, where it's clear that the user stole your work on purpose, carries with it damage awards up to $100,000 per infringement.

The copyright on your work is automatic, but remember that there aren't any copyright police patrolling the magazines and websites of the world, looking for violators. For that reason, you should post a copyright notice on everything you create, particularly material you place on a website or bulletin board. This reminds readers that the work is yours and can't be reproduced without your permission.

It is simple to register your article with the Copyright Office in Washington, DC. And you can register the work at any time—even years after your article is written. Even better, you can apply for a copyright on an entire collection of works at one time, such as a year's worth of your articles.

First, you will have to fill out an application form, which can be downloaded from the Internet or obtained through the mail. (See the Resource Directory for further information.) You will then send the completed application form, a copy of the manuscript, and a check covering the copyright fee. The office will mail you a certificate of registration once your application has been reviewed and accepted. Be aware that neither the fee nor the manuscript will be returned to you.

It should be noted that, despite the extra protection afforded by copyright registration, most article writers do not choose this option simply the because the registration fee and the time spent applying for a copyright can negate any income that might be generated by the article—unless you send in a large group of articles at one time. Also keep in mind that only your *words* are copyrighted, not your idea or your article's title. Therefore, if you submit an article presenting "Twenty Ways to Amuse Your Children on a Rainy Day," and a magazine rejects your article and then proceeds to print one with the exact same title, this would not be an infringement of your copyright *unless* the printed article used your exact words.

A Word of Caution

Some writers recommend other means of protecting your work. Some obtain a notary public's stamp for each page of the article. Since every notary has an excusive ink stamp that contains his or her identification number, the notary seal shows that the work was in your possession on the recorded date.

Other writers mail themselves a copy of their work, and then keep the still-sealed envelope in their files. Like the notary stamp discussed above, the sealed, postmarked document serves as visual evidence that the piece of writing was complete and in your possession prior to the postal stamp date.

Although some writers have enjoyed success using these techniques to prove original authorship in court, it should be noted the National Writer's Union and various groups of freelance writers claim that neither of these practices is supported in the courtroom, and that both are subject to potential fraud. If the writer has a postage machine, for instance, she can change the date on a mailed package. However, although they are certainly not foolproof, if theft is a concern to you, you may want to consider these as additional means of protecting your work. Do, however, avoid submitting an article that bears the stamp of the notary public, as this would most certainly mark you as an amateur. Instead, keep the notarized document in your files.

If you establish a freelance writing career—or even if you find yourself writing and submitting articles once or twice a year, as a hobby—over time, you will probably become more comfortable with the process, and less concerned with possible abuses. Nevertheless, by being aware of the law and of the various ways in which you can protect your work, you will have a greater understanding of the writing business and be better prepared to handle any problems that come your way.

CONCLUSION

The Square One System was devised as a guide to getting your article into publication. It will help you stay focused, organized, and dedicated to reaching your goal. If you follow the system with care, and add a little perseverance, your odds of seeing your article in print will be dramatically increased.

Once you implement the Square One System, you will start receiving responses, both positive and negative. Chapter 7 was designed to help you handle those responses and to chart a new course of action if the results prove to be disappointing.

You, as the creator of your work, own the copyright to it until you assign that copyright to another party. Simply by creating the material, you have copyrighted it.

CHAPTER 7

EVALUATING THE RESULTS

There's a thin envelope in your mailbox, labeled with the return address of one of the publications to which you sent a submission packet. Inside could be anything from a form letter rejecting your article to a congratulatory offer to publish it—or even better, a contract. Take a deep breath and open up the envelope. This chapter will prepare you to handle any response you may receive.

There are three possibilities to consider. First, the editor loved what you submitted and has sent a letter of acceptance, coupled with either a contract or an offer of terms for you to consider. Second, two or more editors want to publish your piece, putting you in a multiple acceptance quandary. Third, your article has been rejected. While the last option is the least desirable, it is an unfortunate reality for every writer. This chapter will help you deal with all three scenarios and revamp your approach if the pile of rejection letters is starting to get uncomfortably high.

IF YOU RECEIVE AN ACCEPTANCE

Congratulations! You did it! An editor or editorial review board has read your material, recognized your talent and your message, and decided to publish it for all the world to see. There is no greater validation of your skill as a writer than a letter accepting your work.

Go ahead and celebrate this achievement. Frame your acceptance letter. Call all your friends and your grandma in Oklahoma. Then sit

As you continue to receive responses, don't forget to update your Tracking Chart with your results so you know exactly where your work stands at all times. Filling in "accepted" always provides a wonderful ego boost.

down and get to work filling out your Tracking Chart and studying the editor's letter for any special requests.

Checking the Publication Details

In addition to notifying you that your article has been accepted, a letter of acceptance usually covers a number of important points. It is imperative to read and understand these points, and to take whatever steps are necessary to ensure that your article gets into print.

Generally, acceptance letters tell you when your article is slated to run and what your payment terms are. Add two columns to your Tracking Chart, noting when you can expect to see your article in print and when you can expect your check to arrive. But realize that the dates regarding payment aren't written in stone, and give the check a little extra time to arrive. Check runs don't always match what the guidelines say.

Another issue that is usually covered in an acceptance letter is rights bought. And, of course, a contract may be included. If you are not familiar with these issues, turn to Chapter 11, which explains the specifics of publishing agreements. That chapter will help you understand the terms of your contract, and will give you the ammunition you need for the negotiation process if you are in a position to argue for a change in terms.

Finally, the letter may request a rewrite, whether large or small. Below, you'll learn more about handling requests for changes in the article itself.

Dealing With a Rewrite Request

If the editor has asked for a rewrite, look at your work with an editor's eye and compare it with what is already in the publication. Analyze how the recommended changes will help your article fit the publication's tone, style, and premise.

Sometimes, an editor will ask for a rewrite or the addition of other materials such as a sidebar or list of resources. If you are unclear about any of the editor's requests, dash off a quick e-mail or call and ask for clarification. If you must call, be sure the phone contact is brief, to the point, and not filled with small talk. As I've said before, editors are busy and will respond best to writers who show that they understand the time constraints under which the editors are working.

When you review a request for revisions, always remember that editors are the greatest experts on what should be included in the pages of their publication. If they ask for a rewrite, they have a good reason. Don't immediately refuse to do what is asked of you. Consider the editor's comments for a few days, reread the publication, and determine if those changes will make your article better fit its style. Nine times out of ten, the editor has made the right judgment. Your article will be the better for it, and by making the requested alterations, you will demonstrate your professionalism.

The majority of rewrite requests are minor and involve little more than doing supplementary research or adding a sidebar. Occasionally, an editor will return a well marked-up copy of your manuscript, asking you to make many changes. The editor may want you to structure the article differently or to present a new slant on the information. Don't panic at the sight of all that red ink. An editor who has taken the time to mark up your copy and provide both feedback and direction is trying to help you succeed, not crush your ego. (See "Learning From Rejection" on page 169 for more information on editor feedback.)

If you submitted your article to a refereed academic journal, the peer review board will either accept the submission as is or send you a letter of recommendations for revision. While the requested changes may be extensive, keep in mind that they are not intended as a personal attack on your particular writing style. "You have to be prepared to accept constructive criticism, particularly if it is negative, and revise your manuscript accordingly," says Karen Mohr, profiled on page 10. "This takes time; revising a manuscript may take as much or more time than writing it in the first place. Decide how much time it will take you to write the paper, multiply by 2½, and that's the minimum time it will take to go from submission to acceptance."

In refereed journals, the intent of the revision process is to fine-tune your article until every paragraph not only supports and proves your theme, but also maintains the interest of your audience. Remember that the reputation of any journal—or any other type of publication, for that matter—can spiral downward quickly if several bad issues make it into readers' hands. It's the job of the editor and the review board to make sure that every article is held to the same standards of excellence. The revision requests of the board are designed to help your article become the best it can be.

Whether you have submitted your work to an academic journal or another type of publication, if you feel that you absolutely can't make the rewrite the editor is asking for because it will either dramatically alter the message of your article or negatively affect your

Always be professional and courteous in your dealings with an editor, even if you disagree with his opinion. It's in your best interests to establish a good reputation for yourself.

Pay special attention to the deadline the editor specifies in his response letter. Do not miss this deadline or you will have difficulty convincing the editor that you are a reliable writer. Get it in on time, or better yet, turn the article in early.

writing, you will have to withdraw the article from consideration. Don't burn any bridges when you write your withdrawal letter. Remember that editors move from publication to publication, and they don't forget which writers were difficult to work with. If possible, offer another slant on the editor's rewrite or a different article in its stead. See page 161 for a sample letter that withdraws the piece originally submitted, but offers two new articles in its place.

After all the requested changes have been made, read through your piece to make sure it flows smoothly from section to section. Editorial rewrite requests usually take the form of guidelines for improvement. Rarely will an editor critique your piece word by word. He assumes that if he directs you to "expand on your point in paragraph three," you will know how to do exactly that. (If you do need help in reconstructing the article, turn to Chapter 10, which will lead you step by step through the structuring and writing of a good article.)

Finally, give the article another reading to check for typographical errors—get a friend to give it a glance, too—and follow the tips below to send the final draft to the publication.

Mailing in the Completed Article

In this electronic age, most editors request that you forward a copy of your article on disk or by e-mail. Don't rush this step. Instead, take care to meet the editor's requests and the publication's needs.

E-Mail Etiquette

Most publishers have a ban on opening attached e-mails because of the potential for launching a computer virus. Always paste a Text Only version of your article into your e-mail. As an extra precaution against cyberglitches, fax or mail a copy of the article to the editorial office.

If you have been asked to e-mail your article to the publication, first save your document in ASCII or Text Only, which strips the file of formatting—boldface, italics, etc.—and converts it to a single-spaced, plain document. Don't worry about the removal of the formatting. This simply makes the document easy to read by any computer, and is the preferred method of submitting an accepted piece. After the editor makes any changes, the copyeditor will format the article according to the magazine's style.

As a precaution against computer viruses, most publications will not open files attached to e-mails. So your next step is to copy and paste your article into the body of your e-mail message. In the subject line, type "REQUESTED ARTICLE" followed by your article's title so that the editor knows it is not an unsolicited e-mail. Then add a short

22 Lake Street
Boston, MA 02266
Phone: 145-555-1344
Fax: 145-555-1980
E-mail: simmonsd@internet.com

(Current Date)

Jane Doe, Managing Editor
Woman's Life Magazine
1500 Broadway
New York, NY 10019

Dear Ms. Doe,

Thank you for your letter accepting my article, "How to Fix a Faucet." I read your request for a rewrite and regret to inform you that I will not be able to make those changes. I felt that adding a lengthy section on "Suing the Pants off your Plumber" would change the tone of the article to one that had a heavy litigation slant. That wasn't my original intent for this piece, and is a direction that I would rather not take with this article.

However, I have another article on "Selecting a Preschool" that would also work in your publication. I have enclosed it for your review. In addition, I am offering to rewrite "How to Fix a Faucet" into an article that covers more plumbing basics, making the piece more valuable to your readers.

I struggled with the decision to turn down your request for a rewrite. In the end, however, I felt that I had to protect the true meaning and tone of my article. Please let me know if we can reach a resolution on this situation.

Sincerely,

David Simmons

If you have the option of requesting a receipt with your e-mail program, add this feature to any e-mail you send to an editor. By enabling the editor to respond with the click of a mouse, you will eliminate the need for a follow-up call.

note at the top, thanking the editor for his response and mentioning that the article is inserted below. Proofread one more time, because converting to text sometimes adds or changes a character. Finally, double-check the editor's e-mail address—and then send your article through cyberspace.

Postal Mail Etiquette

If you are asked to send the article via disk, the editor will specify the format in which he wants the document saved. If he doesn't, give the publication a quick call and ask the editorial assistant what the preference is. Usually, editors want a Text Only version as a precaution, along with one saved in your word processing program.

If you are worried that your disk might get lost in the mail, the cheapest and easiest way to keep track of it is to send it Priority Mail through the U.S. Postal Service and pay the nominal fee for a tracking receipt. This option allows you to go online or call the post office, and find out if your package has been delivered.

Add a short cover letter, like the one mentioned above, thanking the editor for his response and mentioning the enclosed disk. Be sure to clearly label the disk with your name, the article's title, and the requesting editor's name. Then enclose the disk in a hard cardboard or well-padded envelope to protect against breakage, print the words "REQUESTED MATERIALS" on the outside so that the package doesn't end up on an assistant's desk, and send the disk off.

After the Acceptance

Once the excitement wears off, be sure to update your Tracking Chart. Then, unless you wanted to get only that one article into publication, get back to work applying the Square One System to another article or query idea. And be sure to change the third paragraph of your cover letter to mention your accomplishment.

Sometimes, a first sale brings with it a phenomenon not so fondly referred to as "Second Sale Syndrome." Because writing is such a personal endeavor, success can bring about fears that your first sale was just a lucky break, a fluke. Don't let this hold you back from pursuing another sale. Editors pick writers based on their skill level and their talent for presenting an idea or article. If you sell a piece, it means that you had something wonderful to offer. Keep believing in yourself and you will have another sale to add to that list before you know it.

A letter of acceptance brings with it a nice boost in your confidence level. This can keep you writing and submitting even when you get a rejection letter. Your work will now be published and, if you like, you can use this accomplishment as a step toward future success.

IF YOU RECEIVE MULTIPLE ACCEPTANCES

As discussed in Chapter 6, while the practice of simultaneously submitting the same material to different publications is discouraged by some writer's guidelines, most editors realize that it's a common practice for career and noncareer writers alike. If you have applied the Square One System correctly and thoroughly researched your market, however, your submissions will be tailored to each specific magazine's needs, both in tone and subject matter covered, making multiple acceptances an easier issue to deal with because each editor will receive a slightly different product. In addition, if you have followed the guidelines presented in Chapter 5, your cover letter informed every editor that yours was a multiple submission, so that no editor can claim to be surprised if you later inform him that the article was accepted by more than one editor.

When sending out multiple submissions, always try to have a backup plan in place, just in case you receive several acceptance letters.

If you receive two acceptance letters for the same article, look at the rights that each of the editors is asking to buy. (See Chapter 11 for specifics.) If one editor wants *first serial rights*—in other words, he wants to publish the article first, after which the rights will revert to you—you can settle the issue easily as long as the other editor does not express a preference. Simply send the first editor the article with a letter or signed contract awarding his publication first rights, and explain that another publication also bought the piece and will be running it after the first magazine does.

Unfortunately, though, some publications want first dibs on anything they decide to buy and do *not* want a competitor running the same item at any time. In other words, they want *all rights*. If this is the case, you have two choices: Select one magazine to publish your article and withdraw your article from consideration at the second, or offer a different slant on the same subject to your second-choice magazine.

If you have to choose between two publications (or more), both of whom have requested your article, it's time to return to the questions you asked yourself in Chapter 1. Don't look at monetary reward as the sole criterion in making this choice, but consider all your publication goals. Perhaps it has been your dream to see your article in print in a certain magazine. Or perhaps publication in a certain journal would help you build a reputation in your field. Such considerations should figure heavily in your decision-making process.

What is your main goal in sending out articles for publication? Whatever the answer, keep it in mind as you choose the publication that will run your article.

Once you've thought about your personal goals, turn to your Tracking Chart and your resource books. Which magazine or journal has the highest circulation? Which hits your targeted audience better? Which offers the best chance to move further up the publishing ladder, if this is your goal? Also consider which publication plans to run your piece first and which seems easier to work with.

Whatever you do, don't consider allowing two publications to print the same piece if one or both are buying all rights. They will undoubtedly find out and may sue you for withholding information. In any case, you will never be able to publish another article with these editors. Instead, make the best decision you can, and then sit down and draft a letter of withdrawal to the "losing" publication. Don't let this matter linger. The editor is planning on your article for a future issue and needs adequate notice to find another one to fill the space.

A letter of withdrawal should be sincere and professional, offering a true apology. It's also a good idea to use the letter to submit another article, on an exclusive but time-limited basis, to the editor. See page 165 for a sample letter that meets these criteria.

IF YOU RECEIVE A REJECTION

Rejection is never pleasant, and if you've been entertaining dreams of receiving a series of glowing acceptance letters, a stack of rejections can come as quite a blow. It should help to realize that every writer faces rejection at least once, maybe even thousands of times, over the course of a career. Rejection is an integral part of publishing, and is more common than acceptance simply because there are far more submissions than slots. If you understand that not everything you write will be perfect for every publication you send it to, you will see rejection as a business decision on the editor's part, and not as a personal criticism. Then you will be able to learn what you can from any rejections you receive, and to change course as necessary to reach your goal of publication.

Put Things in Perspective

All editors have to evaluate all submissions in terms of their publications' interests. Even if an article is outstandingly well written and filled with fascinating information, the editor may reject it because it doesn't meet the publication's needs at that particular time.

22 Lake Street
Boston, MA 02266
Phone: 145-555-1344; Fax: 145-555-1980
E-mail: simmonsd@internet.com

(Current Date)

Sharon Wise, Managing Editor
All Women Magazine
163 Garden Ave.
Yonkers, NY 10009

Dear Ms. Wise,

Thank you for your letter accepting my article, "How to Fix a Faucet." I regret to inform you that I must withdraw my article. It was bought by a similar publication three days before I received your letter. However, I have another article on "Selecting a Preschool" that would also work in your publication. I have enclosed it for your three-week exclusive review.

I enjoy your publication and sincerely apologize for this inconvenience. I hope you like "Selecting a Preschool" and look forward to working with you in the future.

Sincerely,

David Simmons

Your great article could be rejected simply because it arrived on the wrong day. Maybe a similar story was assigned the day before to a staff writer, or perhaps that section of the magazine was cut at the last editorial board meeting. Whatever the reason for the rejection, you shouldn't take it personally. "I think many writers mistake a rejection of their ideas as a rejection of themselves. It's not. When you get

If you think of a rejection letter in terms of a business decision on the part of a magazine or newspaper, it is easier to understand that the editor has nothing against you personally. The door to that publication is not closed to you forever, just for this article.

a rejection, there could be a hundred reasons why the editor didn't buy your idea," says Karen Asp, M.A., a health and fitness writer for magazines such as *Shape* and *McCall's*. (See the profile on page 11.)

Of course, editors are human, so personal preferences do sometimes figure into this equation. I once received a "Dear Writer" letter from an editor who said that she didn't like my style of writing. When that editor moved on to another magazine and a new editor took her place, I was able to make a sale. The new editor liked my style, plus my persistence, and was more than happy to work with me.

And, of course, you may get the occasional unprofessional response. One time, I got my original query back in the mail for an idea I'd proposed to a women's magazine. Two editors had written a conversation across the top of the page: "Seems like a good idea. What do you think?" wrote the first. "Too simplistic. Reject it," wrote the second. That was the sum of my rejection letter, all scribbled on my own carefully thought-out and agonized-over query letter. Another time, I got my manuscript—a *requested* manuscript, no less—back in the mail, sans cover letter or even a form letter, with the word "Rejected" written across the first page in bold red marker. I knew then how it feels to be a chicken failing the USDA test for quality. It happens to all of us. The point is not to let it stop you from submitting again.

By and large, though, most of my rejections have been standard form letters or gracious personal letters. The latter are the ones to pay attention to and take advantage of because it is rare for a busy editor to take time to write a personal note to a writer. (See "Learning From Rejection" on page 169.)

Shana Aborn, senior editor at *Ladies' Home Journal,* advises writers to take rejection gracefully. Don't get indignant or threatening, don't send a sarcastic follow-up, and don't beg for a re-read. "And editors don't like being put on the spot, so please don't call to ask for a detailed critique 'just so I can better tailor my future ideas to your needs.' If an editor includes an explanation or a suggestion in the rejection letter, take it as a very encouraging sign. Otherwise, keep following the magazine world to see for yourself what ideas are selling now."

Whether the rejections you receive are form letters, personal messages, or quickly scribbled phrases, it is essential that you pick yourself up and try again. Yes, rejection stings. You wouldn't be human if you weren't at least a little bothered that someone didn't buy your material. But keep in mind that one rejection letter, or even a thousand, doesn't spell failure as a writer. Ask anyone who has been in this business for more than a few weeks to show you his collection of rejection letters. If that writer has been actively working to get his articles published, then without exception, that file is thick enough to wallpaper a three-bedroom house. Karen Asp says the worst thing a writer can do is give up. "If you believe with all your heart that you can write and can do it well, if you have the passion, and if you're willing to persist, be patient, and learn, then there's no reason why you won't succeed."

The secret to success is simple: *Your desire to publish has to be stronger than your fear of rejection.* By understanding the market and conquering your own doubts, you can learn from and work through rejection, rather than putting away your pen for good.

Reexamine Your List of Publications

If you are receiving multiple rejection letters and feel stymied by your lack of progress, it's time to take a closer look at what you are doing. And the first thing you'll want to look at is the list of publications you compiled.

Take out your list, and try to examine it with a realistic eye. Perhaps you have aimed too high, and should target smaller publications. Remember that for every writer, it takes perseverance and many small steps to reach the top. Beginning writers will get their best responses from smaller publications. Or maybe the publications are not too big, but you have not aimed for the sections of these publications that are open to outside contributors. Again, a more realistic approach may be in order.

Maybe your article's topic was a bit too far out of the publication's reach. A newspaper, for instance, covers a particular geographic region. If your article dealt with something that happened outside of that area, the editor probably wouldn't be interested in it. A magazine dedicated to cats might not be interested in a story about a dog who befriended a cat, depending on the editor's preferences.

You also need to look at the audience. Maybe your article was written too simplistically or at too high a level for the average reader of that publication. Perhaps it didn't address *enough* members of that audience to merit publication. An article on growing heirloom vegetables may be too defined for a general interest publication like

Keep all of your rejection letters, and not just for mementos. If you ever have to undergo an IRS audit or get questioned about the postage category on your tax return, you will have tangible proof that yes, you did use that many stamps in one year.

Remember that big publications don't offer the best opportunities for new writers. Try submitting to smaller markets, like local newspapers, to get those first few sales.

Parade because only a small segment of the readership is likely to care about the topic.

If you feel that the submission strategy, and not the package itself, is the problem, return to the earlier chapters of the book. Chapter 2 explains how the article market works and pinpoints the best markets for new writers, and Chapter 4 helps you find the right publications for your work. By reexamining the guidelines presented in those chapters, you should be able to create a strategy that works for you.

Reexamine Your Submission Package

If the publications you selected seem appropriate for your article and your level of experience, it's time to take a critical look at your submission package itself, and especially at your article. Is your article structured properly? Is your writing as vivid as it can be? Did you prove the different points of your premise? Are you lacking in substantiation or hard facts? Does your conclusion fail to leave the reader with a strong impression?

It can be difficult to even admit that such a problem may exist, and even more difficult to diagnose and fix it. Sometimes, one of the editors who rejected your article will give you some clues in his letter. (See "Learning From Rejection" on page 169.) But if the editors failed to provide any helpful feedback, there are many things you can do to pinpoint your problem and to improve your writing in general, and your mastery of article writing in particular. Let's look at some of them.

Get a Second Opinion

If all you are receiving is negative responses to your submissions, you might want to consider having a friend or another writer review your submission package, including your article. What you are looking for, of course, is honest input that you can learn from and apply to this and future submissions. Since a close friend or a relative will be more likely to praise your work, but not offer any constructive criticism, the best person to critique your work is a professional writer. If you don't know any professional writers, try someone who is in a related field— that is, a field related either to writing or to the subject area addressed by your article. An English teacher, for instance, can provide valuable pointers on grammar and structure, while someone who reads the

Learning From Rejection

If an editor takes the time to include a personal note in his rejection letter, *pay attention*. This is very rare, and occurs only when the editor sees some potential in your work. It's designed to help you learn, and hopefully, submit something even better the next time around. Plus, it can open the door to future sales at that publication.

Start by putting your emotional reaction aside, and objectively looking at the editor's suggestions and comments. The editor might, for instance, say that your article was lacking in hard facts. Then take action, searching the library or the Internet to find the necessary data, and rewriting the article as needed.

If you choose to send the article in again to the same editor, tell him that you appreciated his rejection letter and applied his advice to your piece. If you decide not to rewrite and resend the rejected article—either because you can't find the additional information needed or because the editor explicitly said that he didn't want to see the article again—be sure to use the editor's input on your next submission. Again, thank him for his time and feedback in your cover letter. Editors appreciate it when writers acknowledge a personal letter. If you don't have anything new to submit, you may choose to send a short thank-you note to an editor who clearly spent a great deal of time on your submission. This is a professional way to express your gratitude, and may be remembered by the editor if, in the future, you decide to send another submission to that publication.

At academic journals, the editorial review committee usually composes a review of the submission, pointing out any weaknesses and strengths. Again, use the review as a guideline for a rewrite and for any additional articles you send to that journal.

Above all, don't take the rejection personally. Look at your article objectively, trying to see it through the eyes of the experts in the industry, and then revamp the piece as needed. You may find that your stack of rejections leads to an ever-growing stack of acceptance letters.

publications you're targeting can offer a reader's perspective, rounding out your feedback.

It can be very beneficial to establish an ongoing relationship with someone who reviews your work, because he will get to know your writing style and your goals. Repay the favor by critiquing his work—or simply by taking him to dinner. You can have your work reviewed either online or in person, depending on where your critique partner is located. If you are exchanging work online, however, be cautious and know the person you are e-mailing. It's far too easy for your work to be stolen, particularly if you are sending it directly to a stranger's computer.

Family and friends are wonderful at offering positive feedback, but often don't provide much in the way of helpful criticism. If at all possible, go to another writer to learn about craft, and let those close to you provide the compliments.

Criteria for a Critiquer

When looking for a critique partner, it's important to choose one who will be honest but not hurtful. It can be difficult to strike a balance between feedback and negativity. A professional understands this and treats the work of other writers with care. A friend can do the same, but might not be aware of the "rules" of critiquing that are employed by writers. Before you and your partner start exchanging work, you might want to discuss a few guidelines, using the following criteria as a starting point. Tell your critique partner that you are looking for someone who can:

☐ **Understand the market.** If you are writing humor pieces and your critique partner is unfamiliar with that market, he may give you feedback that isn't helpful.

☐ **Not try to impose his own writing on your work.** The goal is for you to learn how to improve your writing, not to have a critique partner completely rewrite your article in his voice. If your partner fails to understand this, you may need to find someone else. You want to learn how to write great articles yourself, not to watch someone else do it for you.

☐ **Point out your weaknesses.** This should be done honestly, and without malice. You don't need a critique partner who says, "This is terrible." You need someone who can say, "Your lead sentence is a little weak. Why not try opening with this second sentence instead?"

☐ **Talk about your strengths.** You also need feedback on what you are doing right. This will help you understand what you are good at so you can capitalize on your greatest skills.

A good critique partner is there to help, not harm. While criticism is never easy to take, as long as it is constructive and paired with honest compliments, your writing will benefit.

Read, Listen, and Learn

Even if you aren't planning on being a writer by trade, it makes sense to study the craft. Anyone who is trying to use words as a means to educate others, make money, or express their opinions, should invest time in learning the fundamentals of good writing.

Those resource books you've been using are valuable for more than just the market listings. Most of them also have sections on how to craft an article for a specific market and how to match your writing to that of the publication. The monthly writers' magazines provide the same kind of information. And don't overlook the information provided in other sections of this book! Chapter 10 explains the basic format of a good article and discusses its various components, from the headline to the conclusion. You'll even find a sample article that models article structure for you.

To further enhance your skills, you will want to read a variety of articles and to analyze them as you read. Everything from the morning paper to the evening news, from the content on the Internet stock site to the mini-magazine that comes packaged with your day planner, is something to study. What you are looking for is the magic of construction. Whether they are personal essays, humor pieces, or news stories, what do these articles have in common? How did they grab you as a reader, and keep you engrossed until the very end? Finally, what can you learn from these articles and apply to your own work?

One great technique that I strongly recommend is reading an article out loud. Take the lead story in the morning newspaper, or even the tiny filler in the review column of your favorite magazine, and read it aloud, listening for how the article shifts and changes, drawing the reader in and keeping him there until the end. What words did the writer use to give the sentence impact? How did the construction lead to a firmer ending?

Then take your own work and read *it* aloud. Quite often, this will enable you to pinpoint that one thing you were missing or to hear the sections that fall flat.

While you are reading and studying, make sure you keep writing. Practice with different styles of articles until you feel you have hit the perfect stride for your skills and goals. Every writer has to work to find his voice and strength. When you discover the style that is exactly right for you, you'll know it because it will feel as comfortable as an old pair of slippers.

As you read, listen, learn, and continue to write, your skills will naturally improve. It comes down to the same mantra you hear repeated to athletes, musicians, and all other professionals: practice, study, and practice some more.

Join a Writers' Group

Writers always benefit from involvement with people who have similar interests. That's why it can be so helpful to take part in a writers' group. Although, of course, your particular focus is on article writing, groups like the National Writers Union and the American Society of Journalists and Authors don't always have local chapters. If this is the

While Strunk and White might seem ancient, their advice in *The Elements of Style* is timeless and should be heeded by every writer. This book teaches the reader to use powerful words to deliver effective messages.

case in your area, by all means consider other types of groups. Yes, articles have their own special construction and format, but good writing is good writing. You'll find that you can learn much from writers in other genres.

A study of good fiction can teach you a great deal about the power of one word over another in bringing an article to life.

How can knowledge of other types of writing help you in crafting an article? As one example, techniques used in fiction can teach you how to make your nonfiction more powerful. The goal in a good novel is to show, not tell, the reader what is going on, and then let the reader draw his own conclusions from the material before him. And excellent nonfiction works the same way. Say you are doing a profile on a movie star. You don't *tell* the reader she was nervous, you *show* the reader: "Jane Smith fidgeted in her chair, shifting from side to side. A moment later, she leapt to her feet, dashed to the wet bar and poured a double Scotch before the first question was even asked." These techniques can make your nonfiction ten times stronger. You can paint a picture with your words, not just lay out a series of facts.

Poetry is another good medium to study when you are teaching yourself how to write. The beauty of poetry is in its brevity and clarity. In very few words, the poet expresses his meaning and captivates his audience. All writers have the same goal—to reach the audience with a memorable, informative piece. Substituting one word for another, or for ten, can make a big difference in your work.

Writers' groups also provide wonderful opportunities for you to learn about the *business* of writing. Networking is often a big part of each meeting, with writers giving one another information about new markets or tips on selling to specific publications.

Not all writers' groups are conducive to learning and sharing, though. You need to search for the one that gives back as much as you put into it. Look for a group that offers workshops and combines a wide variety of genres. This will give you the most options for exploring different techniques. Then sit in on a meeting or two to see if the group offers the atmosphere that you're looking for.

To find a writers' group in your area, begin by scanning your local newspaper for advertisements and looking for press releases announcing upcoming meetings. Be aware, though, that some groups are so small that they do little, if any, publicity and may not be listed in the newspaper. So you'll also want to ask about groups at your library and bookstore. Some libraries carry lists of local groups to pass out to interested patrons. Bookstore owners and employees frequently know local writers, and are one of the best sources of information on groups in the area.

While interacting with other people in a real-life setting is wonderful, it may not be possible for you, depending on your schedule. In that case, consider participating in an online group. Again, look around and don't leap into a group without testing it out first. Be a "lurker" in the beginning, observing and not commenting until you are sure the group is right for you.

Online groups are often very chatty, and depending on the number of members, can generate hundreds of posts a day. Look for a group that stays on track, rather than digressing to discuss the neat trick their dog learned last week or the merits of shopping at one store over another. To learn about professional writing, you should try to surround yourself with people who are doing exactly that.

One of the great things about online groups is their immediacy. If you need a question answered or you have to find a source by the end of the day, you can post to the list and have ten different answers in an instant. If you've received your eighth rejection letter of the week—or your first acceptance!—an online group will be there to shore up your confidence or cheer your achievements in seconds. Another plus of online groups is that they're quite easy to leave. So if one isn't working out for you, don't hesitate to sign off and try another.

To find a writers' group online, go to sites like www.topica.com or www.yahoogroups.com and browse the listings under Arts and Entertainment. You can also use a search engine like www.ask.com and type in "Where do I find writers' groups?" The answer will include hundreds of links to in-person and online groups.

Look Into Classes, Conferences, and Workshops

One of the biggest complaints editors have is that the writers who are submitting material to them don't understand the construction of an article and haven't mastered basic writing skills. Writing classes, conferences, and workshops are a terrific means of learning all of these basics.

If you want to improve your general writing skills, inquire if your local college offers courses in grammar and writing. Depending on their focus, these classes may take you step by step through a grammar book, or may help you develop your ability to organize material and express yourself clearly in writing. Night courses are usually available, and some colleges have continuing education programs designed expressly for adults.

You may also want to look into courses that are specifically concerned with article writing and the basics of journalism. These classes will teach you the rudiments of researching and writing articles, and will also give you a chance to interact with people who have similar interests. The simple fact that you have paid to attend a class may motivate you to work harder on developing your writing skills.

While in-person classes have many benefits, traditional classes can be expensive and time-consuming. If your budget and schedule are keeping you out of the classroom, you might want to consider an online class. There are dozens of these, available through sites such as www.paintedrock.com and www.freelancesuccess.com. Some are free, while some require a small fee. Most offer course work in addition to instruction and online lectures. The benefit of online classes is that they give you the freedom to complete work at your own pace and e-mail it in when it's convenient. Internet classes generally last for four to six weeks, and include online participation once or twice a week.

Also check out the various writing classes available on television. BookTV offers informational question-and-answer sessions with published authors in a variety of genres. Cable and satellite TV presents PBS You (also called PBS U), which provides classes in News Writing and other topics. For more information and a schedule of airdates, go to the website www.pbsyou.org.

Also consider attending writers' conferences and workshops. Depending on their focus and format, these gatherings can provide you with tips on writing through workshops and discussions; insights into the world of print and electronic publication; and encouragement from peers and professionals. Workshops and conferences can also keep you up-to-date on industry happenings, new techniques, and who's who in the business.

To find a conference near you, or in your area of choice, begin by calling your local state arts council and area colleges to see what they have to offer. Many groups sponsor writers' retreats, conferences, and get-togethers.

The Internet can also provide information on writers' conferences and workshops. You can use the search engine of your choice, or you can visit ShawGuides at writing.shawguides.com. This resource will allow you to browse through a list of writers' conferences and workshops by month or by state. Or sign up to receive ShawGuides' periodic listings of workshops and conferences in your area.

Writers' magazines are another source of information about conferences and workshops. *Writer's Digest* hosts an annual writing con-

> Which type of class is right for you? Look honestly at the amount of time you have available and your level of commitment. Weigh that against interacting in-person or through cyberspace.

ference in Maui and offers local and online classes that vary in length from one day to several weeks. Also check your resource books. In the back of *The Writer's Handbook,* for instance, you'll find listings that provide a brief synopsis of what happens at each of these retreats, explain what's expected of participants, and give information on costs. The focus and content of these conferences vary widely. Some conferences are geared to professional writers interested in honing their skills and networking with peers, while some address beginners by providing basic instruction in all types of writing. Still others offer a blend of classes, inviting both new and experienced writers to mingle and interact.

Consider Self-Publication

If you feel strongly about the worth of your written work, and have been unsuccessful in getting it published through the more traditional channels, you might consider self-publication. Various options are possible. You can, for instance, place your article on an Internet site that provides a venue for self-published writers, or you can produce a homemade magazine or newsletter.

Be forewarned, however, that self-publishing has some drawbacks. First, self-publishing often lacks credibility with editors because there is no critical editorial review. Therefore, no matter how well written or researched your self-published article is, it should not be used as a clipping in any future submissions. Second, in self-publishing ventures, you must do all the work yourself, editing, typesetting, and distributing the publication to your audience. This will clearly make demands on your time, your money, and your technical expertise.

Despite these drawbacks, many writers choose self-publication as a means of making their work available to their audience. Fortunately, anyone who chooses this option can find guidance and support from a number of resources. (See the Resource Directory for further information on each of the following organizations and publications.)

Several Internet sites have been designed to provide venues for writers who want to publish their own articles and possibly make a little money off their work. Many of these sites advertise in writers' magazines or post on writers' information sites. Also search for them under "self-publishing." For every "view" you get—a reading by an online visitor—you receive a few cents. Of course, it takes hundreds of views to make any kind of profit, and the sites aren't guaranteed to be around forever. However, the experience and the exposure can be good for new writers. Just be sure to proceed with a great deal of caution and to read your contract carefully before agreeing to post your work on the site.

If you are interested in starting your own literary magazine or small newspaper, you'll find a vast listing of resources in the *Laughing Bear Newsletter*. Designed to provide news, information, and inspiration to the small press community, *Laughing Bear* offers both a print newsletter and a helpful website. One of *Laughing Bear's* many services is a Directory of Organizations for Small Presses and Self-Publishers, which can lead you to educational programs for independent publishers, make you aware of marketing opportunities, and more.

If you are an expert in your area, you might consider starting your own newsletter. The best resource for information is the Newsletter & Electronic Publishers Association (NEPA), an international group established to serve publishers of subscription for-profit newsletters and specialized information services. Founding member Howard Penn Hudson, owner of the Newsletter Clearinghouse, publishes the annual *Subscription Newsletter Directory*, which lists all the subscription newsletters in the country, and is the author of the book *Publishing Newsletters*. Visit the NEPA website to learn how the organization can provide you with guidance and support through education, training, and networking.

Several books have been created to inform and guide people who are interested in learning more about the self-publication of newsletters and magazines. One, written by Cheryl Woodard, is *Starting and Running a Successful Newsletter or Magazine*. This excellent book covers everything from finding start-up money, to increasing advertising and sales, to creating an online publication. Woodard is a knowledgeable source, having been the co-founder of *PC Magazine*, *PC World*, *Macworld*, *Publish* magazine, and *Macworld Expos*.

Another helpful resource is *The Newsletter Sourcebook* by Mark Beach and Elaine Floyd. In addition to providing examples of successful newsletters, the *Sourcebook* contains a great deal of useful information on layout and design. And many of the principles offered for print newsletters can also be applied to online publications.

If you do decide to self-publish your work, consider securing a written endorsement from a reputable organization or peer. This can lend credibility to your work, and give it the attention it merits. Some

Self-publishing is a real option for the writer who is having difficulty finding an interested publication. Online self-publishing, of course, offers the simplest option, and is far easier than printing and distributing a homemade newsletter or magazine.

self-published writers have even attracted the attention of editors and gone on to secure publishing contracts. Nevertheless, if you hope to be published in a recognized publication, it's important to continue pursuing traditional publishing routes, because the chances of an editor's coming across your self-published material aren't high. Editors are consumed with day-to-day tasks and deadlines, and rarely have the time or inclination to go looking for writers.

As when considering any medium, investigate all your self-publishing options and weigh them carefully before making a decision. Look at the long-term ramifications, keeping your personal goals in mind. Will your self-published material reach your target audience? If so, how will your audience interpret the venue? If you're interested in establishing a career in writing, what benefit or drawback will this have on your future plans? Only a decision based on a complete understanding of your choices will help you achieve success.

If you choose to self-publish in either a print or online format, make sure to put a copyright notice on your work. This will tell readers that the work is yours and can't be copied without your permission. (See "Protecting Your Work" on page 152 for further information.)

Get Involved in a Publication

Writers who have a full knowledge of the world of article publishing—who understand a publication's day-to day workings and know how decisions are made regarding article acquisitions—have a real advantage over writers who are strangers to the publishing world. An excellent way to get that kind of knowledge is to take a full-time, part-time, or volunteer job at a small newspaper, magazine, journal, or newsletter office.

If you are an academic who works at a college or university, find out if your department produces a publication. If so, involvement in its production—even at the copyediting level—not only will help you understand the publishing process, but may also enable you to cultivate relationships with editors who can assist you in getting your work into print.

In the world of nonacademic publications, local newspapers are a wonderful option, as they are so often in need of extra staff members. Pay may be minimal or even nonexistent, but if your objective is to learn about the newspaper industry, this is the place to start. You may even find an editor who is willing to take you under his wing and teach you the ins and outs of article writing.

Yet another option for the nonacademic writer is the newsletter of any association in which you may be involved, either at the local or national level. Again, even a relatively low-level position will give you an opportunity to learn about the publication, to become more knowledgeable about the newsletter's area of interest, and to network with people who can provide information and support.

Finally, consider the world of online publications. E-zines often need people who are willing to either edit submissions or handle the flurry of e-mail sent to the editor. Like all of the other options mentioned, such a job will enable you to get a foot in the door and learn the business from the ground up.

CONCLUSION

By now, you should have some helpful perspectives on rejection and acceptance, and know how to deal with each. If your submission package has thus far had less-than-satisfying results, always remember that one rejection—or one hundred—doesn't mean that you are a bad writer. It doesn't even necessarily mean that you are doing anything wrong. It could be a matter of timing, approach, or material. Whatever the reason, don't let rejection stop you from pursuing your writing. Keep using the Square One System, altering your approach as needed, and you will see your name in print.

If your submission package has met with success, be proud and, if desired, continue to hone your skills and explore the world of publications. Once you have a few publishing credits under your belt, you may want to consider the possibility of becoming a freelance writer. If so, Part Three will provide you with the information and guidance you need to build a part- or full-time writing career.

BUILDING A FREELANCE CAREER

While some writers are content to see only an occasional article in print, others dream of establishing a freelance career in article writing. If you want to turn your passion into a business, Part Three is the place for you.

Chapter 8 begins at the beginning by explaining how you can develop great article ideas and tailor them for specific markets. Once you have your idea, you'll want to turn to Chapter 9, which will guide you in turning your concept into a winning query. Soon it will be time to research and write the article, which is what Chapter 10 is all about. You'll also want to visit Chapter 11, which explains standard contract terms and even provides the ABCs of contract negotiations. Finally, Chapter 12 offers the guidance you need to make career-building decisions.

In the following pages, you will:

- Learn to develop article ideas that sell.

- Discover how to spin one idea into many to multiply your sales.

- Learn how to write an effective query package that presents both your idea and you in the best possible light.

- Master the arts of researching and interviewing.

- Discover how to write consumer and trade articles like a pro.

■ Develop contract savvy.

■ Decide whether you should specialize in one area of writing or enjoy working on a variety of topics.

■ Explore ways in which you can put your writing ability to use to maintain a steady flow of income and develop your writing skills.

A freelance writing career can be both personally and professionally rewarding. If this is your dream, the following chapters can help make it a reality.

CHAPTER 8

DEVELOPING IDEAS FOR ARTICLES

E very article begins as an idea, and in the world of freelance writing, this idea usually springs from the mind of the freelancer herself. The writer then composes a query letter proposing the article, and sends it off to an editor. And a sale is made—*if* the idea sparks the interest of the editor. If not, it's back to the drawing board.

The fact is that not every idea will work as an article. If your ideas are to result in sales, each must fit the specific market—in other words, the publication—for which it's intended. And it either must propose something that no one has covered before or treat an old topic in a new way. That, in fact, is the key element that separates an idea which makes a sale from one which lands in a rejection pile. If you are giving the reader new information or taking a unique approach to old information, you're providing the reader with something of value. And this is exactly what editors look for when they wade through the piles of submissions on their desks.

This chapter will help you develop article ideas designed to make sales. It will also guide you in tailoring your ideas to fit specific markets, and in spinning one idea off into another so that you can generate a constant stream of winning proposals.

WHERE DO IDEAS COME FROM?

Many new freelance writers sweat and strain, searching for a great idea for their article. But the truth is that you don't need divine inspiration to come up with a salable concept. You can find a host of terrific ideas just by taking a look at the things that are part of your daily life. Your job, your home, your kids, your friends and acquaintances, your favorite magazines and newspapers, your pets—all of these provide fodder for articles. The challenge lies in seeing what's around you in a light that reveals its potential as article material. Where do article ideas come from? Let's look at a few possibilities.

Your Interests

Start with what you know. What are your interests and hobbies? These make great subjects for articles.

You are your own best source. Start with the things in which you are interested and of which you have a good understanding, and use them as a basis for your articles. For example, if you are an avid collector of presidential biographies, then over the years, you have amassed information about presidents, biography writing, and collecting. You've probably been in a few antique stores or hunted for bargains at garage sales. To protect your finds, you might even have taken a mini-course in preserving old volumes.

Boom. You have at least a dozen ideas to work with and turn into article pitches. Now let's take just one—book collecting—and look at the different ways you could turn that into a salable piece:

- For seniors' magazines: "Are There Valuable Books in Your Attic?"

- For children's magazines: "How to Start a Basic Book Collection"

- For women's magazines: "Get Your Children Interested in Book Collecting"

- For general interest magazines: "Spotting Valuable Books in the Ten-Cent Yard Sale Pile"

Each of these ideas could be tweaked slightly to fit individual markets. As a point of interest, the above stories are also article ideas that have worked for me in the past. I don't collect books, but I do know someone who specializes in rare and old books. His expertise has resulted in at least a dozen articles over the years.

Now let's look at this same pastime from a different perspective. Can you list ten things you wish you'd known when you started your hobby? If you can, this, too, could be the basis for one article—or ten, depending on the complexity of your interest. Either way, the activities you enjoy participating in are a natural source of article ideas.

The People in Your Life

Don't overlook the people that you know through work and other activities. While having the editor of *Time* as your next-door neighbor could be quite beneficial to your writing career, a number of friends and acquaintances could give you a hand in other ways. Often, their interests, expertise, and experiences can be the basis for an article.

Maybe you know an accountant who specializes in debt reduction or a lawyer who just won a landmark case against small town government. Perhaps the second grade teacher at your local school has been able to increase reading scores with a new program. Or maybe the neighbor across the street has developed a unique way of growing roses. People all around you are doing interesting things that others would like to know about.

Before you pitch an article to a publication, however, be sure to ask permission of the person about whom you're writing. If you land the assignment first and *then* ask your friend for permission, you will have to disappoint the editor if your friend says no. Realize that you don't have to go into detail when you ask a neighbor if it's okay to use her story. Just say that you are thinking of writing a query to *XYZ* magazine and wonder if it would be okay to write about her technique for cultivating roses or for increasing reading scores. A heads-up before sending out a query is only fair.

Many of the business people in your area would also make great subjects for articles. As a plus, they are usually receptive to being featured in the media because it means a nice plug for their business. Again, be sure to ask if they are interested before pitching the article.

If you meet someone interesting, be sure to get her business card and make a note to yourself about what she does. Then slip the card into your idea file. You never know when it might come in handy.

Always ask permission before sending out a query about anything that involves someone you know.

Your Area of Professional Expertise

Most of us are experts in some area because of our chosen careers. This area of expertise could be a great subject for an article—especially if it is something in which tens of thousands of people would be interested. And the fact that you have professional training and experience will make a big difference to the editor who reads your query. For instance, if an editor has a choice between a piece on medical breakthroughs written by a doctor and a similar piece submitted by a layperson, chances are she will choose the doctor to write the piece because of greater reassurance that the information provided is correct, as well as greater credibility in the eyes of the reader.

What is your profession? If you're a carpenter by trade, your knowledge can be applied to a great how-to article for do-it-yourselfers.

In addition, as a professional in your field, you probably already own or have access to numerous books and articles on that subject. It's also likely that you have friends in the field or are familiar with other experts. Therefore, a good portion of your research is as good as done. While a nonexpert might have to scramble for the information needed to complete the piece, much of the necessary material is already at your fingertips.

In your letter to the publication you've targeted, always mention anything in your education and professional background that is relevant to the story you are proposing. This will show the editor that you have both the knowledge and the interest necessary to write a good article on that subject. If you've won awards or accolades for your achievements in your field, include a quick summary of these, as well.

Reading Materials

You are surrounded by reading materials, from advertising leaflets to newspapers to magazines. And a quick glance at even the headlines of these publications could help you spin off a number of ideas.

For example, let's say that today's newspaper is covering an upcoming national election. Literally hundreds of ideas—some fun, some serious—could come from that topical subject.

You could, for instance, take it to a local level and pitch a story to the editor of your neighborhood newspaper about the impact of the election on your town. You might cover a local group campaigning for candidates, or you might do a round-up of opinions among the patrons of the downtown coffee shop. (To learn about round-ups and other article forms, see Chapter 3.)

Newspapers are great fodder for magazine ideas. You can take what you read in your daily paper and then expand upon it or look at it from a different angle. Just keep timeliness in mind when developing the idea, since the magazine article will come out a few months down the road.

Then take that idea a little further. How does an election year affect donations to charities? Consider contacting the United Way and the Red Cross to see if they have noticed any difference. That would make great material for a magazine or business journal.

Online, each of these approaches could be shortened and readapted. A round-up could be conducted in a chat room instead of a coffee shop. You could write reviews of the best election sites or provide information on voting. These are just a few article ideas you could glean from one feature in one day's newspaper. There are virtually thousands of ideas in your daily paper that are just waiting to be developed into interesting, salable pieces.

New Trends, New Research

All writers should remain abreast of trends and new research. Certainly, this is true of writers for academic journals, who must maintain a continual interest in what is happening in their field to keep ahead of the competition. So if you notice a trend or have a unique perspective on current research, consider making it the focus of your next article. This is exactly the type of piece editors are looking for when they search the submissions pile.

In addition to keeping a finger on the pulse of the academic field, it helps to keep up with what the commercial media is writing about, not just to provide fodder for your research, but also to understand what is important to the community at any given time. When there were several incidents of teenagers shooting one another in classrooms, a number of experts rushed to complete research and publish findings on the workings of these young people's minds. These articles were used as a basis for discussion in both the academic and nonacademic worlds.

It's also vital for writers of commercial articles to stay on top of trends and new events because these represent an ideal opportunity to break into a publication—particularly newspapers and e-zines, because they have faster response times. If you are the first to hear about a new program or an innovative product, pull together some material and contact editors of appropriate publications. With breaking news, you might run into a couple roadblocks as a new writer. It's a Catch-22: The fastest way to capitalize on a breaking story is to call, fax, or e-mail the editor to be sure she hasn't already assigned someone to the story before you write it. News is new for only a short time, and you have to move fast. However, if you don't have established relationships with editors or strong writer credentials, this kind of spontaneity can be seen as an intrusion and irritation. Your best bet? Take a breaking story and turn it into something that could run further down the road. A critical new finding in medical research for cancer could become a broader story on treatments and options, or even a profile of the research team that made the finding. Think beyond the immediate, but still make your pitch by traditional postal route right away so the editor sees that you are on top of what's hot.

Even though you want to immediately act on breaking news, it's wise to maintain files on areas as they change and develop. Many

When you study the publications around you for inspiration, be sure to use only the ideas. *Plagiarism*—the act of copying another's work and then publishing it as your own—is not only illegal, but also wrong. Except when using quotations, make your work original and use your own words.

times, I have found that research reports which came out a year or so ago are still important because the findings are being put into real-life practice. I then successfully revisited old "new" stories by using a different slant and exploring how the issue had changed with the passing of time.

The Targeted Publication

Always look at the last few months' worth of issues to analyze a publication for trends and repeated themes. These should be used as a basis for your approach.

One of the best places to find ideas is the publication you are targeting. You don't want to copy what is already there. Rather, you want to use what you see to develop complementary articles. The newspaper in your town might run a series of new business profiles, or the e-zine you subscribe to may decide to add a section on accounting. If you have material for these sections, you can formulate an approach that matches what the publication has offered in the past.

Although you'll want to examine at least one single issue carefully, you should always flip through the last few months' worth before you begin your brainstorming. Take *Writer's Digest*, for example. By reviewing the last several issues, you would find that this publication regularly provides articles on magazine and Internet writing. Each issue contains a profile of a successful writer and tips on improving your fiction skills. Plus the publication offers articles on topics such as the fair use of trademarks and how-tos for corporate writing. With this in mind, you might come up with the following article ideas:

- A profile of a successful writer, agent, or editor. If you're in a writers' group—in-person or online—one of the members might make a good profile subject.

- A review of the latest software for writers.

- Tips on creating good newsletter copy. This, of course, is a good subject only if you are familiar with it.

- A primer on tax codes or legal issues for writers. Again, this subject demands suitable expertise.

No matter which publication you are targeting, take a look at the last few issues and try to formulate a long list of ideas. Not all of them will work as articles right away, but many of your thoughts could have great potential down the road.

PERPETUAL MARKET NEEDS

Articles on certain ideas are in demand all the time. If you've had a subscription to the same magazine for a couple of years in a row, you've probably noticed a repetition of topics from season to season. These perpetual articles provide a great way for an innovative and creative writer to break into the publication.

Evergreens

Virtually every magazine and newspaper runs stories that are called "evergreens." These are stories and articles that are recycled year after year, and are usually run to coincide with certain seasons. Women's magazines, for instance, carry annual mid-summer features on choosing the best school, and annual pre-Christmas tips for planning holiday festivities. January issues of most magazines contain advice on sticking to New Year's resolutions and information on tax law changes. February newspapers have information on gardening and some sort of Valentine's Day piece.

> Strive for unique spins on old topics. Try to find something that hasn't done before.

Evergreen articles offer a great opportunity for the beginning writer. Editors are always on the hunt for a new twist on an old tale. Each year, they wonder how many different ways they can write about Christmas cookie baking without being redundant or boring. Sit down and brainstorm to come up with several ideas that are unique and interesting. Use your resources to look at several years' worth of issues, both from the targeted publication and from its competitors, to see if anything similar has been printed in the past. Make a list of the different slants each has used. Then develop your own slant. If you're trying to sell to a newspaper, look at national magazines to see how they have handled a similar issue. Then see if you can come up with a local angle. For example, if you come across a magazine piece on gingerbread cookies, rethink it as a piece that would interest your neighbors. Maybe there's a cookie baker in town who makes gingerbread cookies that are decorated to look like real people. If you do come up with a novel approach to an evergreen, submit it several months in advance so the editor will have time to slot in your article.

The Hot Categories

Evergreens are not the only article ideas that are continually popular. Pick up any issue of any consumer-oriented publication in any given

Virtually every magazine on the market wants articles that give readers ways to save money, save time, or make money. Keep these themes in mind when pitching to editors.

month and you are guaranteed to find at least one story that fits one of the following categories: saving money, saving time, or making money. Remember the article on growing roses mentioned earlier in the chapter? How about turning it into "Pruning Roses in Half the Time"? Or use your knowledge of pet care to write "Finding a Vet Who Costs Less" or "Starting a Pet-Sitting Business."

If you've found a unique way to save money during travel or if you've discovered an innovative way to shave five minutes off your dinnertime preparations, write about it. These are the kinds of stories editors like to run because they present common information in a new and useful way. Targeting a specific magazine? Come up with a dozen ideas that fit these categories, pick your top three, and write those queries first.

Beyond the three major categories mentioned above are several other categories that always have an audience. Look at the newsstand and you'll notice a number of recurring themes driven by the demands of an aging populace. Articles dealing with health, money, retirement, family, entertainment, and travel are always popular, across the board. Whenever you think of an idea along those lines, jot it down and then try to refine it further to fit your target publication. Start idea files, and keep copies of everything you come across that has to do with each topic. When you have enough information to write the basic outline of the article, it's time to turn to Chapter 9 and learn how to compose a good query letter.

Whatever the category or specific subject of your article, always keep in mind that the key to selling your idea is to take a unique approach. That's where analyzing past issues can be a big help. The worst thing you can do is pitch an idea that the publication ran only two months ago. Take the time to do it right, and find out which topics *haven't* been covered.

The Not-So-Hot Categories

While it's great to choose a topic that's hot, it's important to avoid a topic that has been overdone. What topics are we talking about? That's hard to say, as trends come and go so quickly that subjects are constantly moving from the "hot" category to the "overdone" category. But if you've read about something hundreds of times, chances are good that the editor and the publication's readers have, too. Over

the years, subjects that have gone from hot to not-so-hot have included Princess Diana (and later, Princess Diana's death), fondue cooking,
feng shui, e-shopping, and more. In the heydey of each of these topic's
popularity, editors were virtually swamped with articles and queries
on the subject.

Does this mean that when several publications are running pieces
on a particular topic, the subject should not be touched? No, but it
does mean that if you want to make a sale, you'll have to come up
with an angle that's a little different. For instance, just when feng shui
was waning in popularity, I came across a woman who was employing the practice in her work as an image consultant. I called the editor at the newspaper where I worked, and pitched an article on
applying feng shui principles to choosing a wardrobe. She immediately bought the article and ran it on the front page of the Living Section. Not only did this have a local angle, since the feng shui image
expert was in the readership area, but it also took a unique approach
to a tired subject. So if you really want to tackle a somewhat overdone
subject, try it. But by all means, take an unusual tack.

> Fresh ideas or new twists on old themes are your best bet when trying to break into a market. If it's been done before using the same exact approach, editors won't be interested.

RECYCLING OLD IDEAS

In the writing world, there is a well-known axiom: "If you sold it once,
you can probably sell it again." An article on photography techniques
that you originally sold to a parenting magazine might now be resold
to other outlets in different markets. This is the most lucrative way to
work and a great method for carving out a niche, if you decide to take
that route. (See Chapter 12 for information on building a writing
career.) Yet another great way to recycle old ideas is to take one idea
and spin it off into several. By planning ahead, and by overinterviewing and overresearching, you can easily take one article and turn
it into a number of sales. Let's look at both of these options.

Reprints

Both in traditional and online magazines, there is a vast market for
reprints—articles that previously appeared in different publications.
Not all markets can afford to pay for original articles, and reprints represent a quick, easy, and cheap way for an editor to fill her pages.

Generally, writers are paid half the original fee for a reprint. If
you were paid $100 for the article the first time it was published, the

reprint rate would be $50. Some publications set a specific rate for all reprints, regardless of their original source and first payment terms. Some pay a set amount per printed page. Check the guidelines in your resource book to find out what the going rate is.

Before you try to sell an article as a reprint, refer to your original contract. (For more information on contracts, see Chapter 11.) If you sold "all rights" to the first publication, you can't resell the article. The term "all rights" means exactly what it says. All rights belong to the original publication in perpetuity (forever). The publication can run the article as many times as it wants in print, online, in a flyer, on a billboard—virtually anywhere it wants to—for that one initial fee. This is the worst deal for a writer and should be avoided at all costs.

However, if you have retained some rights—particularly, second serial rights—you can go ahead and sell the article as a reprint. When you send in your query, be sure to include a photocopy of the printed article, state when and where it first appeared, and offer to e-mail or mail a fresh copy to the publication upon acceptance.

You invested a lot of time and energy in the researching and writing of that first article, so it makes sense to try to resell it. All savvy writers understand that the true money for an article comes in the reprints and spin-off articles they develop. They have to do the research only once, and then can sell the same piece again and again for very little additional effort. It does take some time and effort to scout out reprint markets, but the payoff can be big.

Reader's Digest is the top-paying market for reprints, offering several hundred dollars per article. Because of this, it is also one of the hardest markets to sell reprints to. Easier ones include *Capper's*, a biweekly paper, and the *Big Apple Parent* newspaper.

Spin-Offs

Another great way to increase your return on an article is to take one idea and spin it into several different ideas. I have done this a number of times, always with great success. It takes a little more market research, but if you plan ahead, you can overinterview and overresearch with the intent of developing future articles.

The key is to know where you are going before you start. The best multiple sale spin-off I ever made was based on a profile of romance writer Mildred Riley. Mildred didn't start writing until after retiring from a nursing career. In addition, she specialized in African-American historical romances, which were just beginning to grow in popularity at that time. The initial article, which appeared in my local newspaper, focused on Mildred's career as a writer. Then, with a little ingenuity, I managed to spin that one piece into several, including:

- Two pieces for retirement magazines on her "second career."

- A piece for a magazine devoted to African-Americans on the hot new trend in romance novels.

- A piece for a parenting journal on making time for romance, with advice from romance writers.

- An updated article for another local publication when Mildred's new book appeared.

- Two additional articles, printed in writers' magazines, that provided advice for the writer.

I've kept all the notes from my interviews with Mildred, and every once in a while I pull out a quote I haven't yet used and put it in an article dealing with one of the above subjects. Each and every time I use material from one of these interviews, I make sure to call the author and ask her permission, as well as get an update on her writing career so I can include current biographical information.

If you think you have an article idea that can fit many markets, sit down and make up your potential market list *before* you start your research, slotting different angles for each publication. Then write a brief synopsis of each angle and outline the piece so that you know early on what additional material you will need to write the article. When you get the first assignment, overinterview and overresearch so the work is already done for those subsequent pieces. (See Chapter 10 for tips on conducting effective research and interviewing.)

REFINING YOUR IDEA

Once you come up with an idea for an article—whether it's a totally new idea, an "evergreen," or a spin-off from an old article—you'll want to work on refining it to make it more appealing to the editor to whom you plan to send your proposal. During this part of the idea-development process, it is important to keep two considerations in mind. First, be aware that you must adapt every idea to fit the particular market you are targeting. So many potential sales are lost because the writer didn't take the time to fit her idea to the publication's needs! Second, be aware of the importance of narrowing the focus of your topic rather than proposing an article that covers a broad subject. In this case, too, never lose sight of the fact that each publication is different, with a different audience that requires a different "spin."

Fitting Your Idea to Your Market

Think back for a moment to Chapter 4, where you sat down and examined every aspect of a magazine to analyze the publication for tone, style, focus, and audience. Every detail you found in that analysis will be utilized in the development of your idea, and in the writing of your query in Chapter 9.

To begin this discussion of markets, let's take a look at a magazine called *Smart Business*. This is a wonderful publication to examine because it started out as one type of magazine and then evolved into something quite different to fit the changing marketplace and the changing needs of its readership.

Prior to 2000, *Smart Business* magazine was *PC Computing*. The focus of the magazine, published by Ziff Davis, was to provide comprehensive information and analysis of computer hardware, software, and peripherals.

Then in 2000, in a letter to its readers, the editorial board explained that adequate information on computer hardware and software was available in competitor magazines and the Internet. While product reviews and news are still a good portion of the magazine, the publication has shifted its focus to provide business owners with the information they need to run their businesses more efficiently in a technological age.

How does all this affect your ideas and your submissions? Well, if you are writing articles about the computer industry, you will have to adapt your approach and your idea to fit this magazine's new focus. In 1999, you could have pitched a story entitled "How to Select a Laser Printer" and possibly landed an assignment with *PC Computing*. But now that the magazine has experienced a rebirth as *Smart Business*, a better bet would be "Laser Printers That Boost Your Productivity" or "Ten Tips for Deciding Whether Your Business Needs Laser or Ink-Jet."

It pays to study your target publication—and, just as important, to study a *recent issue* of the publication. Never assume that the issue you read last year is reflective of today's needs. *Smart Business* is a perfect example of a publication that shifted with the times to keep up

Baby boomers are fast becoming the biggest audience for everything. Always keep that segment of the population in mind when developing ideas for adult magazines.

with its audience. A writer who doesn't do her research can end up wasting hours first writing an article, and then waiting for a response that will probably be a no. Carve out time from your daily writing schedule to study your market. It will pay off in the end.

Let's look at another way in which a market analysis can help you fit your idea to a publication. In Chapter 4, I advised you to take a close look at the advertisements in a publication, as they will tell you a great deal about the publication's readers. Now let's assume that you're writing an article on remodeling bathrooms—an article that will cover the purchase and installation of new bathroom fixtures. When studying possible markets, you first look at a magazine whose ads for mid-priced cars and similar products show the readers to be solidly middle class. You know that if you decide to submit to this publication, you will have to include information on finding fixtures that are reasonably priced, and possibly even sold at discount rates. When you open the next publication, however, ads for Rolex watches and Rolls Royce automobiles clearly demonstrate that the magazine appeals to higher-income readers. While this publication, too, might be interested in such an idea, the article would have to take a different tack. In this case, you might focus on finding one-of-a-kind plumbing fixtures for an upscale bath remodeling.

As you did in Chapter 3, develop a mental portrait of the magazine's audience and make a list of the types of articles that would interest it. Then take your basic idea and adapt it to fit that publication.

Narrowing Your Topic

In Chapter 3, you learned that the subject of an article must be limited because the length of an article is limited. It should therefore come as no surprise to learn that some article ideas are rejected because they are too broad. An article on Antarctica is a hard sell, for instance, because the topic isn't defined well enough. Not only is there simply too much information on Antarctica to cover in an article, but a piece that takes a general approach such as this has no "hook" to grab the reader and draw her in. Remember that editors want new and unique information, or an interesting angle on an old story. It is therefore much easier to convince an editor to buy an article that profiles the survival techniques of an endangered species living on that continent, or the story of one family's lonely winter in a cabin in Antarctica, than it is to sell a story that looks at the whole of Antarctica.

If you actually read the magazines to which you are sending proposals, it's a pretty safe bet that what interests you will also interest the editor.

The same is true of any piece. To an editor of a publication covering the oil industry, a general overview of the history of oil drilling is much less likely to sell than one that explores how the process of drilling oil affects the finished product, or one that explains how the refining process affects the ultimate price of the oil. An even tighter version of that article would be a profile of a new company that is carving out a niche in the oil industry. This is exactly the kind of success story that *Entrepreneur* and similar business magazines are always seeking because it provides a role model for readers who are starting their own companies and looking for advice or inspiration. When developing your articles, try to think in terms of information the reader can use to improve her life, business, or financial picture, and then narrow your broad idea into a kernel idea that helps the reader relate to the subject of the story.

Does this mean that broad ideas *never* make sales? No. Broad ideas can work; they are just more difficult to sell. Consider, for instance, a general concept like "How to Finance Your Business Venture." Many magazines could use this kind of piece, particularly ones geared to small business owners and entrepreneurs. However, a better approach would be to develop smaller versions of the same idea, and then sell them to different outlets. For instance, you could write an article on "Finding Seed Money," or one on "The Top Five Financing Mistakes," or one on "What a Business Incubator Does." Literally hundreds of different terms and tips could be pulled out of your one large idea.

Think of an upside-down pyramid when developing story ideas. Start broad, and then gradually narrow it down to fit the market.

So once you've come up with an article idea and you've looked at the markets, you'll want to find an angle—an approach that will interest the readership of the publication. The approach needs to be timely, and needs to fit a particular place in a specific market. You can't just say, "I want to write about cars." You have to choose a certain aspect of automobiles to write about, be sure that the information you are dispensing is valuable to a reader, and find the right section of the right publication for this particular article. Then you must decide on the type of article you want to write—an op-ed piece, cultural commentary, or round-up, for instance. (See Chapter 3 to learn about the various forms that articles can take.) Once you have consolidated all of these elements, you have more than just an idea—you have a *salable* idea.

CONCLUSION

Ideas for articles are all around you. The best way to find them is to pay attention to the things you read, the people you meet, and the markets you are approaching. Carry a notebook and jot down thoughts that come to you as you go through your daily life. Keep files of interesting tidbits that could become stories. Flip through the newspaper and other publications with an eye toward article development. In short, make yourself open to ideas and they will come.

I Would Like to Thank the Academy . . .

Nearly everyone has heard of the Pulitzer Prize in Journalism, the most coveted award in the world of articles. Just how do writers come to win this symbol of excellence—as well as the many other awards conferred for achievement in this field? Although the judging for top journalism awards is very strict, most are run much like contests, with the field open to anyone who writes for the type of publication being recognized.

Below, you'll learn about three groups that present the top honors in journalistic writing. For the most part, these elite awards are given to newspaper reporters, but a few are open to writers in other media. Whether or not you hope to someday join the ranks of winners, it's fascinating to learn about the awards that helped set the standards in the business, providing inspiration for writers at all levels of skill and experience.

The Pulitzer Prize

Established by newspaper publisher Joseph Pulitzer as one of the provisions of his 1904 will, the Pulitzer Prizes in Journalism are by far the most prestigious awards in the field. Entries for a Pulitzer must have appeared in a daily, Sunday, or weekly United States newspaper. Nominations can be made by the newspaper staff, or even by a reader.

There are fourteen different Pulitzer Prize categories, ranging from a distinguished example of reporting local news to outstanding investigative reporting by a team of writers. Entries are judged by a panel of journalists in accordance with a number of criteria, including accuracy and depth of coverage. The initial jury chooses three nominees in each category, and final selections are made by the Pulitzer Prize Board. Winners receive a certificate and $7,500. More information can be found on the Pulitzer's website: www.pulitzer.org.

National Journalism Awards

Created in 1953 by the Scripps Howard Foundation, the National Journalism Awards comprise eighteen different categories, including human interest writing, editorial writing, environmental reporting, and public service reporting. The Ernie Pyle Award for human interest writing, for instance, is used to honor the newspaper story that most clearly exemplifies the style and craftsmanship of the late Ernie Pyle, who wrote during World War II. The judges in this category look for both warmth and a faculty for telling a story.

Virtually all of the National Journalism Awards are for newspaper writing, although one category does cover electronic media like radio and television. Entries are judged by a committee selected by the foundation. Prizes for all eighteen winners total $50,000. For more information, visit www.scripps.com.

AAAS Science Journalism Awards

The top achievement in the field of science reporting is the American Association for the Advancement of Science (AAAS) Journalism Awards. Created in 1945, the AAAS awards are given to individuals—not institutions or publishers—for their coverage of the sciences, engineering, and mathematics.

Six AAAS awards are presented annually, one each for large newspapers, small newspapers, magazines, radio, television, and online outlets. Entries can include stories on life, physical, and social sciences; engineering and mathematics; and policy issues that are grounded in science or technology. Articles are then judged by committees comprised of reporters, editors, and scientists. The winner of each category receives a cash prize of $2,500. For more information on the AAAS awards, visit the website at www.aaas.org.

The above awards, of course, represent the pinnacle of achievement in the field of journalism. But these are not the only honors conferred upon journalists. If you're curious about other prizes available for excellent writing, contact the writer's groups listed in the "Groups and Organizations" section of the Resource Directory, or flip through resource books such as *Writer's Market* for more information.

CHAPTER 9

$\mathcal{W}$RITING A QUERY THAT MAKES A SALE

In Chapter 8, you learned how to develop ideas for your articles and how to carefully tailor them to fit specific markets. Unfortunately, though, coming up with a great idea—or even writing a great piece—is not enough. To get your article into print, you need to sell your concept to an editor. That's the job of the query package; it is designed to convince the editor not only that the story you're proposing is a good one, but also that you're the right person to write it. It's a tough job for a few pieces of paper, but it can certainly be accomplished.

This chapter will guide you through the creation of an effective query package. It will take you step-by-step through the process of writing the most important and essential component of the package— the query letter—and it will help you craft various other package elements that some editors require before they make a decision about your proposal. It can take as much time to compose this package as it takes to write the article itself. But when done properly, the result will be a sale and—if your article is as good as your query—a possible string of future sales to the same publication.

THE QUERY LETTER

The most essential element of a query package—the element that cannot be omitted—is the query letter. The purpose of this letter is to sell the idea of your article to the editor and, just as important, to sell you

As you write your query letter, always keep in mind what it should *not* be. A query should not be a letter that showcases your entire background and family life; a chatty missive that addresses the editor as if he were a member of your family; or a blatant sales piece that screams your idea. A good query letter is written in a businesslike but intriguing style, demonstrating your skill as a writer and your ability to handle the idea you are pitching.

as a writer who has the knowledge and skills necessary to produce a great article.

Jessica Hartshorn, features editor at *American Baby* magazine, gives this description of the perfect query: "It should be a short explanation of what you want to write. Ideally, you've already thought of the lead and it's catchy. Ideally, you've already interviewed one expert and can tell us what he or she has to say on the subject. And in the rest of the query, you give us enough of an outline of the story that we're confident you can write it and research it well."

Shana Aborn, senior editor at *Ladies' Home Journal,* warns writers to avoid vague queries and to provide a more comprehensive package when approaching a major consumer magazine. "As an editor, I don't want to have to beg a writer for more information, an outline or a source list. I want to see it there in front of me. I want to be confident from the query letter that the writer really knows his or her stuff. Remember, as a freelancer, you're competing against hundreds of other writers trying to impress the same magazine, plus a few dozen who are lucky enough to be regular contributors. Don't handicap yourself by not giving the editors what they need."

The following guidelines will help ensure that the query letter you send will be concise, will be both persuasive and professional in tone, and will provide the editor with all the information that he needs and wants.

Composing the Query Letter

Like the cover letter detailed in Chapter 5, the query letter is composed of specific parts, each of which accomplishes a specific task. By making sure that your letter includes these components and handles them effectively, you will maximize your chance of making a sale.

Before you begin your query letter—in fact, before you begin creating any component of your query package—be sure to read the target publications' writer's guidelines, which can be found in your resource books or obtained on the publications' websites or through other means. (See page 114 of Chapter 4 for more information.) These guidelines will specify if any of the publications wants a detailed, and therefore longer query, and whether your letter should be accompanied by an outline of the proposed piece. (For more about outlines, see page 217.)

Quick Query Letter Tactics

Keep the following suggestions in mind as you follow the steps for creating your query letter. When you've finished writing your proposal, come back to this list and make sure that you didn't skip anything.

☐ **Get to the point quickly.** Don't ramble on for two paragraphs about your idea. Make sure that the first paragraph clearly presents the concept that is at the heart of your article.

☐ **Grab the editor's attention right away.** Be sure that your opening paragraph not only is informative, but also is compelling. If it's not, chances are that the editor won't choose to read any further.

☐ **Don't throw in the kitchen sink.** Include only what is relevant and intriguing—not every fact you know about the subject.

☐ **Research, research, research.** Read at least six months' worth of issues of the publication to get a flair for what has been run and how the writers approach their topics. Use the same writing style—chatty, informative, unbiased, or whatever—in the query letter that you've seen in the publication's pages. You also want to discover if the newspaper, magazine, or e-zine has run articles on similar topics and to understand how your article will be different so that you can convey this information to the editor.

☐ **Know what you are talking about.** You don't have to be a world-renowned expert on your proposed topic, but you should have a good working knowledge of it.

☐ **Don't show off your vocabulary.** Keep the big words, the flowery adjectives, and the overused adverbs to a minimum.

☐ **Don't skimp on the meat.** By leaving important information out of your query, you will end up with a proposal that lacks substance. Be sure to provide evidence of your basic research (in the form of statistics or quotes), a short list of the experts whom you propose to interview, and a thorough overview of the approach you intend to take. Also clarify how your article will offer value to readers by presenting either new information or a new perspective on old information.

☐ **Don't make the letter all about you.** Keep biographical information to a paragraph at most, but be sure to include a brief recap of any relevant background or publishing experience.

☐ **Don't tell the editor how to do his job.** Phrases like "You really need to run this" or "I know your readers will love this information" will only serve to irritate the editor. Tell the editor what he needs to know about your proposed article, and then let him reach his own conclusion.

As you write, keep in mind that your query letter should be one page in length unless the publication's guidelines specify a longer format. Some magazines want what is called "detailed queries," meaning they'd like a thorough discussion of what you plan to write about and how you will treat each section of the article. In that case, the letter can run to two or three pages long. Other publications request that you write an outline, which would be separate from the one-page query. Generally, major newspapers and magazines are the only ones who ask for in-depth information, and they usually specify whether they prefer a detailed query or an outline. Most other publications want query letters that do not exceed a page in length.

The Salutation

Like any letter, your query letter should begin with a salutation such as "Dear Mr. Jones." It is essential that the letter bear the correct name of the editor you are querying. If you misspell his name or address the letter to "editor" or to a predecessor, you will immediately show the editor that you didn't bother to research his publication. Look for the editor's name in your writers' resources and the back issues of the magazine. Then call the editorial office and double-check the name, as well as the publication's address, with the receptionist or an editorial assistant. (See page 142 of Chapter 6 for more information.)

Although typing out the salutation seems like a simple task, you might be surprised to learn how many writers alienate editors in this portion of the letter by trying to be creative, cute, or overly familiar. Never write "Dear Bob" and never try to guess a female editor's marital status. "Dear Mr. Smith" or "Dear Ms. Smith" are the appropriate forms of address. If the editor's gender is not clear, use the full name: "Dear Leslie Smith." Editors would rather see their correct name at the head of the letter than a misguided attempt at a salutation.

The Introductory Paragraph

This is commonly referred to as the "hook." In your first paragraph—actually in your very first sentence—you should show the editor that you are a skilled writer who has the ability to get the reader's attention and keep it throughout an article.

It might scare you to hear this, but the fact is that many editors don't take the time to read past the first few lines of a query. They are too busy to spend much more than a few seconds on each of the thousands of letters that cross their desks.

To make sure that you captivate an editor for those few seconds, it's important to spend the majority of your time crafting that hook paragraph, because it's the one that will count the most in the query letter. You have a couple of options. You can start with a paragraph that duplicates the *lead*—the opening paragraph of the article. (See Chapter 10 for information about the lead.) Or you can take a more creative approach and use a shocking statistic or a quote from an interview source as a way to get the editor's attention.

By far, the safest way to proceed, particularly when you are new or approaching a more traditional venue like a newspaper, is with a sample lead opening. This will allow you to show the editor that you read his publication, are able to mirror the voice and approach of its articles, and can write a compelling introduction that will capture the reader's attention. It's your best chance to demonstrate that you can do the job.

This paragraph should be about four or five sentences in length, and should reflect the style used in the target publication. Some e-zines have very short, snappy openings, and your paragraph should be the same. If the publication opens its articles in the first person, or always starts with an anecdote, be sure you do exactly that in the first paragraph of your query. When writing a newspaper pitch, you want to capture all the basics of your story—the classic Who, What, When, Where, and Why—in that first paragraph.

When proposing a lengthy article, such as a dissertation, to an academic journal, this first paragraph should provide an abstract of your research—in other words, a summary of important points. If you are writing a shorter academic article, such as a review or editorial, the first paragraph should provide the same type of sample lead you would use when querying a commercial publication.

Sometimes you can't duplicate the article's lead, either because the lead is too long or because you haven't completed enough hard research. In that case, be creative and begin with a startling statistic or quotation. While this is a good place to show what you know about your topic, be careful not to dump too much information into the beginning and overwhelm or bore the editor. Keep the first paragraph intriguing, interesting, and compelling—and leave the editor wanting more.

If you take the creative route, be sure that the remaining sentences of your opening paragraph expand on your hook. It's fine to keep this section brief if your intention is to give the editor just a taste of the article and grab his interest. However, take care to develop the idea

Be sure to do any necessary preliminary research for your query and include relevant statistics, if possible. The better you demonstrate you can do the job, the more likely the editor is to give it to you.

Don't leave the editor hanging after you write a great hook. Expand and develop that idea in your query.

more fully in the ensuing paragraphs so he will see that you have the resources and knowledge needed to tackle the assignment.

The Second Paragraph

Don't lose the momentum of your query as it develops. Keep your tone professional and confident, and leave the editor wanting to read the entire article.

If you wrote a good lead, you have won half the battle by capturing the editor's attention. Now you need to show him why this article will fit his magazine. Whatever you do, don't say, "I know you don't normally run pieces like this," because that will be an immediate sign to the editor that you didn't take the time to do your homework and find the right outlet for your idea. Editors exclude certain pieces for a reason—because they aren't what the publication's readers want and expect. Everything you pitch to a publication should fit its parameters.

Without overdoing the praise, demonstrate briefly that you have researched the publication and have pinpointed this as an area of interest for its readers. For instance, you might say: "Your article in the July issue on miracles generated a great deal of reader mail, demonstrating a reader interest in stories exploring spirituality." If you have done your research, you already have a copy of each target publication's editorial calendar and can point out which issue might be a good fit for your article.

Your job will be ten times easier if you are pitching a timely article that coincides with an upcoming anniversary or holiday. If this is the case, be sure to mention the event and, if possible, prior years' issues and their treatment of the subject. Remember that editors love to see a new spin on an old favorite. If that's what you're proposing, be sure to show how your article will be unique.

Any statistics or demographic information you have on your topic can be included here. The Invisible Web at www.invisibleweb.com offers links to hundreds of databases and search engines that can help you find information to strengthen your query.

The second paragraph should also present your article's headline so that the editor has a title for later reference. I often boldface the headline to make it stand out among the rest of the text. Make sure that your headline, like your sample lead, is written in the same style as the headlines used by the publication. (For more information about headlines, see Chapter 10.)

Your goal in the second paragraph is to prove that your article will provide value for the reader in the form of either information or entertainment. People don't buy magazines, journals, or newspapers to let them sit around and collect dust—they read them. Every article you pitch should give the reader some return on his investment.

The Third Paragraph

It's not enough to suggest an idea for an article; you must also tell the editor exactly how you propose to research and write it. Who are you going to interview? What organizations will provide data for your article? How long will the finished article be? What format will it take? This is the information that should be conveyed in the third paragraph of your query letter.

When listing your sources, avoid making promises that you may be unable to keep. Never, for instance, guarantee a quotation from Joe Smith if you don't know how to contact him, and haven't the vaguest idea if he's even open to an interview. Although your promise may land you the assignment, if you fail to deliver, you will probably never win another one from that publication.

Be aware that while most magazines and e-zines want writers to take a national approach to stories, newspapers need material that is directly related to their readers' home area. Therefore, when querying a paper, always make sure to give your piece a local angle and, if possible, to cite an interview source from the region served by the paper.

In paragraph three, you also want to discuss the article's proposed length and any accompanying material you will be submitting, such as a sidebar or photographs. Again, be sure to read the publication's guidelines thoroughly so that you don't query a 3,000-word piece when the magazine wants articles of only 500 words or less. The editor will make the final determination on length and format, but you should make sure that you have matched the information in your query to the stated needs of the publication.

The Fourth Paragraph

This paragraph should be the "Why Me" section of your query. It may come fourth or fifth, depending on the article you are proposing. If your article will be longer than 1,000 words, and if the guidelines for the publication specify a detailed query, the fourth paragraph should continue in the same vein as the third and offer more information on

Draw attention to your article by boldfacing its title in your query letter. Unlike a cover letter, detailed in Chapter 5, a query isn't accompanied by a completed article, and thus has to speak for itself. If you have a catchy title and a great idea, the bold headline will make this immediately apparent.

what the article will contain. In that case, provide your background information in the fifth paragraph. For shorter articles, three paragraphs on the idea are plenty.

The paragraph that discusses your credentials should be short, but should demonstrate your capabilities and background. Mention any writing credits and any work experience that is relevant to your article. If you have no or few writing credentials, be sure to focus on significant work and life experience, which is greatly valued by some publications. *American Baby* magazine, for instance, will often buy an article from an untried writer as long as he is a new parent, and therefore knows what the publication's audience is going through as they care for their own kids. Similarly, a newspaper like the *The Wall Street Journal* is eager to find writers who have a strong background in business issues. If your letter is well written and professional, the editor may be willing to take a chance on you even if you don't have many publishing credits.

If you have any other publishing credits—if you've written a book, for instance—mention these too, but briefly. Editors value previous experience within the publishing industry because it means that the writer understands the importance of deadlines and quality work.

Be sure to keep this paragraph brief and to the point. Don't mention everything you've ever written—include a select list that puts you in the best light and is relevant to the publication you are approaching.

> If you have no writing experience at all, make no mention of this in your query letter. Instead, show why your real-life or work experience makes you the best writer for the assignment. See Sample Letter #1 for the Unpublished Writer on page 208 for an example.

The Concluding Paragraph

The concluding paragraph should consist of no more than two or three sentences. First, tell the editor when you can complete the proposed article. This should not be viewed as an ironclad guarantee, but simply as an estimate. "I could have the finished piece to you within four to six weeks" is fine.

Don't threaten the editor or impose any kind of deadline. Saying things like "If I don't hear from you by July 10, I am pulling the idea and sending it to *Newsweek*" accomplishes nothing.

Add a sentence thanking the editor for his time and consideration in reading your query. Then mention your enclosed self-addressed, stamped envelope (SASE), and clips. Finally, say that you are looking forward to his response.

The Closing

Use a standard one-word professional closing: "Sincerely" or "Respectfully." Like the salutation, this is not a time to get cute or unique. The body of your query is the place to showcase your skill as a writer.

After the closing, skip a line for your signature and type in your name beneath that. You can consolidate multiple phone numbers and addresses below your name, if you have so many that they look crowded at the top. Don't forget to sign each letter above the typed name before sending out your queries. Finally, if desired, place an enclosures note—Encl: clips—two spaces below your typed name to emphasize the fact that you have been published and that your clips have been attached.

For the First-Time Submitter

If you are an unpublished writer, you need to put extra time into your query. Why? You will have to sell yourself even harder to the editor so that he will take a chance on you even though you don't have a slew of clips to send in as proof of your ability. The research needs to be clear and evident in your letter.

Go the extra mile. Call up a few potential sources, explain that you are writing a query letter, and ask them for some statistics and a quote that you can use to pitch the article to the editor. Don't reprint what other publications have written or take quotes from your expert's best-selling book. This won't show the editor that you have the stuff it takes to research and write the whole article. Most sources are agreeable to providing preliminary information for a query, and will be glad to help you out. Then, when writing your query, include whatever statistics or facts you have gathered and list the people who have agreed to talk to you.

It can be tough to launch a writing career—to convince editors that although you are a new writer, you have the ability to produce a good article. But if you submit a strong, compelling query, there is an excellent shot that the editor will have a positive response.

Formatting the Letter

Like a cover letter, which was detailed in Chapter 5, your query letter should be neat and professional in appearance. Choose a clean, white, good-quality 8½-x-11-inch paper—20-pound stock or, even better, 24-pound stock. Don't use an erasable bond, because it tends to smear. And never use colored paper or decorative stationery.

Print on only one side of the paper, and choose a clear and easy-to-read font such as Times New Roman. To further maximize readability, be sure to use a 12-point typeface.

The margins of your query should be one inch all around. Set up the letter itself in a standard business format, with single-spaced lines and left-justified paragraphs. Skip an extra space between paragraphs rather than using paragraph indents.

I created my own letterhead with my word-processing software, putting my name, address, and contact information at the top. If you choose to do the same, refrain from adding "Freelance Writer," "Writer Extraordinaire," or any other such title to your letterhead. It's okay for business cards, but when used on your query letter, it will just mark you as an amateur.

If you don't have letterhead, you can put your contact information in the top right-hand corner, in standard business position, or beneath your signature if you have multiple contact options, such as work, school, and home. Don't list every phone number at which you can be reached, from your mom's home phone to your own cell phone. List just the ones that offer the most direct link to you or your answering machine.

Position the date in the upper left-hand corner of your letter. Two spaces below the date, type the editor's name and title, followed by the name of the publication and the address. Don't leave this valuable bit of information out because some publishers, like Gruner & Jahr, publish several different magazines. Your query could easily get lost in the mailroom shuffle if you don't include complete information. Also avoid sending multiple copies of the same query to editors throughout one publication, as if you were throwing a handful of darts at a dartboard. One query is enough.

Skip a line, and type the salutation. After the salutation, skip another line. The three to four paragraphs of the body of the query come next. Finally, add your closing and signature. Be sure to print or type your name clearly below your signature.

Take the time to proofread your query letter at least twice, once on your computer screen and once in printed form. On the first go-through, your eye will often insert words that aren't there. A "the" or an "of" is easy to skip, and may be missed by your software's grammar checking option. And if you transpose letters and type "form" instead of "from," your spell check won't pick up that error, either. Remember that your query letter is your calling card, and that you won't get a second chance with that letter if it is sloppy or filled with grammatical errors. Everything you send to an editor should be crafted with care.

Editors are faced with daily choices between dozens of articles. Give the editor a reason to award the assignment to you by submitting a professional letter that clearly demonstrates your research and writing skills.

If you aren't good at catching your own errors, ask a friend to give your work the once-over. If you have a writing critique partner, ask him to proofread your submission. Constructive criticism can make a big difference in the quality of your finished piece.

Sample Query Letters

Following is a selection of letters that illustrate how the above guidelines can be followed to create strong, effective queries. Each covers a specific type of situation, showing how you can tailor your letter to suit your background and experience, your article, and your target publication. You'll also want to take a look at the inset on page 212, which compares an actual query that didn't work with the rewrite that eventually made the sale.

As you read through the following sample letters, remember that they should serve only as guidelines. It's important to let your voice and style show in your letter so that the editor can get a preview of your particular writing abilities.

Tips for Letter Perfect Queries

Throughout this book, I emphasize the need to submit written copy that's error-free. The following tips will help ensure that your query letter—and everything else you send to your target publications—is the best it can be.

☐ Read your copy once; then read it again. It's easy for your eye to skip over mistakes. To catch as many errors as possible, read everything several times.

☐ Put the letter away for a day or two. When you return to the letter, you'll see it with a fresh eye, making it easier to catch mistakes.

☐ Run a spell check. While this can't catch every possible problem, it will find many of them.

☐ Give the letter to a friend. Sometimes it's difficult to see your own mistakes. Another person may find it easy to detect what you've missed.

(Current Date)

Karen Stone, Editor
Stay At Home Mom
210 Crockpot Avenue
Mountain View, IA 52556

Dear Ms. Stone,

When Carol Parsons worked in an office, she carried pepper spray when she had to enter the parking garage at night, kept her house on an alarm system, and made sure she shredded confidential documents when she was through with them. But when she started working at home, she stopped worrying so much about security. "I had the perception that I was safer," she said. She was wrong. Carol's identity was stolen by a cyber hacker, and she is just now able to repair some of the damage to her credit, and her peace of mind.

I'd like to propose a short article for the "Managing at Home" section of *Stay At Home Mom* on **Home Office Security: Are You Vulnerable?** Nearly 80 percent of the nation's home office workers are left vulnerable by security loopholes and unawareness of hacker abilities. Your March 2000 article on setting up a home office covered the importance of firewalls for computers, but didn't cover other cyber vulnerabilities.

In my article, I plan to detail the various methods that hackers use for infiltrating a system, and to include a sidebar of safety measures, for both parents and children, as well as sites that offer tips and free testing systems. My proposed 800-word feature would incorporate interviews with Jim Steady, CEO of Safe Internet; Joe Daring, an ex-hacker; and Carol Parsons.

As a systems analyst for IBM, I have seen many people make the mistake of thinking they are safe when they aren't. In my industry, this frightening attitude of complacency is growing, not shrinking.

I could have this article to you within three to four weeks of your acceptance. Thank you for your consideration. I have enclosed an SASE for your response, and I look forward to hearing from you.

Sincerely,

Lisa Frost
100 Snow Street
Wintertown, MA 00000
Phone: 617-555-0000
E-mail: jane@frost.com

(Current Date)

Dan Parsons, Editor
Self Employment
   Opportunities Magazine
10 W. Jefferson Street
New York, NY 10007

For the Published Writer Submitting an Outline #2

If one or more of your articles have been published, by all means capitalize on your experience by mentioning your credits in your query letter. This letter informs the editor of the writer's considerable experience, and also mentions the enclosed outline, which some publications request in their writer's guidelines. The outline itself can be found on page 218.

Dear Mr. Parsons:

Looking for a way to have fun, make money, and edge into the expanding craft field? If so, the time is right. As the world becomes more high-tech and hands-free, millions of people are turning to the comfort and quality associated with handmade goods. For the crafting industry, this is great news. "We've seen a dramatic shift in the last couple of years in the number of people buying crafted products," said Jean Simpson, program and public relations manager for the Association of Crafters in Toledo, OH. "People are getting back in touch with themselves and the environment." And they're doing that in a big way. According to Sally Delagrange, director of communications for the Hobby Group in Castleton, MI, the crafts supply market alone grew from $6.56 billion in 1990 to an estimated $10 billion in 1996.

My article, **Stitching Up Profits in the Craft Industry,** would cover this trend and profile several successful crafters. The June issue of *Self Employment Opportunities* covered embroiderers who make money with their hobby, and I think this would be a good complement to that article.

Stitching Up Profits in the Craft Industry would profile four successful crafters in 2,000 words, and include a resources sidebar for readers. I have attached an outline of the proposed article for your perusal.

As a multi-published, full-time freelance writer, I have written articles on a variety of business issues. My work has appeared in the *Boston Business Journal, Design Times, Indiana Business Magazine,* and other publications.

I could send the completed article to you within four weeks of your letter of acceptance or contract. Enclosed you will find an SASE for your response. Thank you for your consideration, and I look forward to hearing from you.

Sincerely,

Shirley Kawa-Jump
100 Tree Street
Anytown, MA 12345
Phone: 617-555-1111; Fax: 617-555-2222

(Current Date)

Jim Healey, Technology Editor
Business Smarts
245 Lori Lane
Harveytown, MI 09876

Dear Mr. Healey,

Right this minute, a cyber thief could be accessing your home office computer, stealing those pictures of your seven-year-old's birthday party and selling them on the Internet to pedophiles. Think it isn't possible? Think again. Many people leave themselves open to attacks on their home computer because of the fuzzy feeling of security that comes with working near the family room.

"Is Your Home Office Safe?" was the headline in your July/August Home Office Technology section. But there's another angle of Home Office safety many readers might not have thought about. I'd like to take this subject a step further with my article **Home Office Security: Are You Vulnerable?**

Home office workers are especially vulnerable to attacks because they often lack firewalls and other network security measures that exist in a corporate environment. With home Internet connections, many people feel safe and don't think anyone will want to access their files or data. But cyber thieves will use almost any means, including chat rooms, hacking, and web-page raiding, to find things like:

- Pictures of children

- College term papers

- Financial records

- Credit card information

- Software

My 1,500-word article will detail various methods hackers use to infiltrate a system, and will also provide a sidebar of sites that offer tips and free testing systems. Interviews with experts and with home office workers who have faced security issues will be included, as will information on the following safety techniques:

1. Be aware of your weak spots. If you're networking or running a server on your desktop, you need to take additional precautions. Both open up loopholes, according to Dean Smart, owner of Cyber Security, Inc. in Boston.

2. Keep yourself up to date by reading about breaks in security. Try the Carnegie Mellon CERT site, www.cert.org, for information on Internet security. Internet expert Jake Lincoln says, "Too few people remember to update or intensify their security when they access the web at home. It's like leaving your back door wide open."

3. Don't forget to frequently update your virus protection and other software, too. Norton offers a home office firewall program that alerts you to potential hackers, puts a stop to their infiltration, and offers advice for future prevention. Other computer software manufacturers offer similar products that provide varying degrees of security. "Knowing what software is perfect for your needs is as simple as asking yourself three questions," says Smart.

4. Unplug your computer. "This seems like simple advice but many people leave their machine connected to the Internet 24/7," says Lincoln. If you're not there to monitor the computer, turn it off. No hacker can break into a computer that isn't on.

I am a professional freelance writer with an extensive background in business articles. During my twenty-five-year career, I have authored more than 300 articles in this area, publishing in national and local magazines and newspapers.

I could have **Home Office Security: Are You Vulnerable?** to you within three weeks of your letter of acceptance or contract. Thank you for your consideration. I have included copies of my published articles and an SASE for your convenience. I look forward to hearing from you.

Sincerely,

Adam Atkinson
57 Keen Street
Mystic Port, ME 03345
Phone: 780-555-6780
E-mail: adam@mysticonline.com

Hits and Misses

When responses to your queries start coming in, take a moment to evaluate which letters were most effective and which didn't do their job. Be ruthless in your evaluation of each query. Did you adequately explain your idea? Did you describe enough of your relevant background to give the editor the confidence she needs in your abilities? Did you show your familiarity with the publication?

Often, when a query is receiving negative responses, you can analyze the problem, rework the letter, and make a sale. Such was the case with the query below. My first query lacked a hook and supporting

The Query That Didn't Work

Herb Masters, Editor
Successful Writers
234 Adams Street
Springfield, MA 09870

Dear Mr. Masters:

For beginning writers, there is no task more daunting than earning that first byline. A good number of freelancers who enter the field expect to land stories in national magazines immediately. Many overlook the possibilities and experience available in the world of newspapers.

I would like to propose an article on **Seven Reasons to Freelance for Newspapers,** based on my own experience as a newspaper reporter. The steady paycheck provided by stringing for several papers in the Boston area has allowed me to switch to full-time freelancing this year.

The article would run approximately 800 words and could be sent to you within 14 days of your letter of acceptance or contract.

I have worked extensively for area newspapers and regularly have articles appearing in *The Middlesex News, The Boston Business Journal* and other papers. I have also been published in a variety of magazines, from *Design Times* to *Self Employment Opportunities*. I enclose copies of my published clips for your perusal.

Thank you for your consideration. I have enclosed an SASE for your response. I look forward to hearing from you.

Sincerely,

Shirley Kawa-Jump
100 Tree Street
Anytown, MA 12345
Phone: (617) 555-1111; Fax: (617) 555-2222
E-mail: shirley@shirleykawa-jump.com

evidence. It also failed to show why the publication's reader would care about the topic. So I rewrote the letter, adding a stronger hook as well as statistical information that included industry research. The result was an almost-immediate sale to a new magazine—not one of the publications that had received the first letter. (Please note that the editors' names and addresses below are all fictitious.)

When reading the following letters, note all the differences you can between the letter that missed and the letter that hit. Then apply the same analysis to your own work so that you can make every query letter as strong and effective as possible.

The Query That Made the Sale

Tina Brandt, Managing Editor
Writers Like You
200 Fieldstone Lane
Waynedale, OH 53013

Dear Ms. Brandt:

The words *writer* and *starving* often seem to go together. However, there is a way to keep food on the table and money in the bank: branching out into newspaper work. As a full-time (and not starving) writer myself, I write an average of seven newspaper articles a week, keeping regular paychecks appearing in my mailbox.

According to a recent study by the National Writers Union, the average freelance writer makes a paltry $7,500 a year. Boosting that income is an achievable goal for the more than 200,000 people who call writing their career. As a reader of *Writers Like You,* I know that many of the publication's letters to the editor are from writers who want to find the key to a steady income. My proposed article, **Seven Reasons to Freelance for Newspapers,** would help them find that key.

With 1,800 daily and 7,500 weekly newspapers available across the country, the opportunities are vast in this area. What many writers might not realize is that newspapers are a gold mine for published clips and regular pay—two points that I will make in my 800-word article. It will be written in first person and contain tips from my own personal experience as well as resources for more information.

As a professional writer for fifteen years, I have worked extensively for area newspapers and regularly have articles appearing in *The Middlesex News, The Boston Business Journal* and other papers. I have also been published in a variety of magazines, from *Design Times* to *Self Employment Opportunities.* Copies of my published clips have been enclosed for your perusal.

Seven Reasons to Freelance for Newspapers could be sent to you within 14 days of your acceptance. Thank you for your consideration. I have enclosed an SASE for your response. I look forward to hearing from you.

Sincerely,

Shirley Kawa-Jump
100 Tree Street
Anytown, MA 12345
Phone: (617) 555-1111; Fax: (617) 555-2222

(Current Date)

Dan Johnson, Editor
National Business Newspaper
18 E. 41st Street
New York, NY 10007

> ## For the Published Writer Submitting a Follow-Up Letter and Query #4
>
> If you've sold an article to an editor once, don't let an opportunity go by to offer another article. Because the writer has already worked with the editor, and the editor is familiar with the writer's work, the following query is a little friendlier than the previous sample letters, and also slightly departs from the usual query format. The mention of the previous article—which is placed in quotes instead of being boldfaced to avoid detracting from the new idea—reminds the editor of their existing working relationship.

Dear Mr. Johnson:

It was a pleasure working on "Carving a Slice out of the Mail Order Pie" for the June issue, and I appreciate the opportunity to work with *National Business Newspaper.*

I would like to propose another idea for a future issue: **Setting Up a Serious Office Without Spending Serious Cash.** One of the biggest expenses for a new business owner is that first office. The price of furniture, computers, even the space itself, can run into the tens of thousands. Many fledgling owners simply don't have the upfront capital to spend on desks and chairs. For businesses needing a complete professional look, renting an executive suite may be the key. The advantage of doing so is in the on-staff secretarial, graphic design, and reception staff—all of which are included in the lease. According to president John Loan, that is exactly what Offices Away, an executive suite leasing company, strives for. "We're basically helping business owners share a resource," he said, "whether it be a high-tech piece of equipment or a conference room."

Entrepreneurs need to know that there are inexpensive ways to look like a million bucks, an issue that is frequently covered in your "Home Offices on the Cheap" section. **Setting Up a Serious Office Without Spending Serious Cash** would profile Janet Harlan, an entrepreneur using virtual space; James Meridian, a small business owner who found leasing to be the best cash flow option; and Offices Away, a national network of temporary space. I envision the article running approximately 1,500 words and including a sidebar of resources and quick tips for business owners.

As you know, I have an extensive background in business articles and have covered home office issues for your magazine and for *Business News.* I have been a professional writer for 20 years and formerly worked in my own small business as a printer.

I could send this article to you within 14 days of your letter of acceptance or contract. Again, thank you for the attractive copy of my article. It was a pleasure working with you on that piece. I have enclosed an SASE for your response and look forward to hearing from you.

Sincerely,

Pam Singer
12 Mockingbird Lane
Indianapolis, IN 46208
Phone: 317-555-1244
Fax: 317-555-2242

> ### For the Published Writer Submitting to an E-Zine #5
>
> E-zines generally accept queries by e-mail, which requires a slightly different format, as well as a shorter letter. The subject line of your e-mail should clearly mark it as a query so that the editor doesn't see it as spam (junk e-mail) and delete it. Type QUERY: Your Article Title in the subject line, with the word "query" capitalized so that the purpose of the communication is clear. Place your contact information at the end of the query, rather than the top, so that the subject of your article is the first thing to pop up in the editor's e-mail window.

(Current Date)

Karl Tinman, editor
WizardofOz.com

Dear Mr. Tinman,

If Dorothy were to be lost in Oz today, she'd need a lot more than a pair of ruby slippers to navigate her way to the Emerald City. At the very least, she'd need a Palm Pilot and a GPS system to help her past the apple-throwing trees and flying monkeys. Even better would be a stun gun, to ward off all the evil predators lurking along the Yellow Brick Road.

My essay, **Dorothy in a Techno Oz**, would take a light-hearted look at the classic Baum story, providing a version of the tale for the new millennium. With the anniversary of the release of the novel coming up at the end of the year, I think it would be an apt topic for your e-zine.

Give me 700 words of space and a couple weeks to write it, and the essay can be running on WizardofOz.com. I can send along a Text or Word file, depending on your word-processing weapon of choice.

I have written for a number of satirical sites, including Salon.com. Links to my work can be found at: www.funnyguy.com/harold.

Thanks for reading this and if you're interested, drop me a line. Toto and I are waiting anxiously for your response.

Sincerely,

Harold Baumfan
21 Emerald Street
Saint Paul, MN 00987
Phone: 300-555-1237

(Current Date)

Yvette Reynolds, Editor
Journal of Adolescent Angst
34 Boylston Street
Boston, MA 02110

For the Published Writer Submitting to an Academic Journal #6

As mentioned earlier in the chapter, academic publications want queries for longer, research-intensive articles to begin with an abstract—a summary of important points. This helps the editor immediately determine if the writer put in the necessary legwork to write the proposed piece. In addition to starting with an abstract, the following query demonstrates that the writer researched the publication, and knows which experts she plans to interview and how she intends to craft her article.

Dear Ms. Reynolds,

Today's teens face twice the risk their parents did of developing high blood pressure, a major risk factor for atherosclerosis. This hypertension, which is developing at a shocking rate in baby boomers and is expected to grow tenfold with the next generation, points to a stroke rate that is 75-percent higher than the rest of the nation. Half the people who suffer from heart disease die, but teens are too consumed with their lives to stop and ponder the consequences of their behavior. However, a new study released by the *The New England Journal of Medicine* indicates that consuming enough milk and cheese early in life can cut this risk in half. My clinical research into this data, complete with medical chart audits and thorough patient analysis, confirms this information with the adolescent population.

My article, **Long-Term Benefits of Calcium in Teens**, examines the report from *NEJM* and pairs that with the findings of the research team I head at the University of Medicine in Boston. This article would be a good fit for your "Improving Health" section, and fit well with the Adult Diseases theme of the August issue.

For this article, I will interview Dr. Eli Dairy and Dr. Mary Bovine, two prominent physicians in this area of research. In addition, I will include a series of graphs and tables that demonstrate our findings in the laboratory, and in the cafeteria at Lincoln High, where we discussed this issue with teens. I expect the piece to run 15 pages, including annotations.

I have been a part of the Calcium Research Team for ten years and have published in a multitude of venues, including the *Journal of Bone Health* and *Calcium Journal*. Please see my attached curriculum vitae for specifics on my background. I have studied this topic in the field and in the lab for more than two years, and have solid data to share with your readers.

The completed article could be sent to you at the end of May. I have enclosed an SASE for your response. Thank you for your time and I look forward to hearing from you.

Sincerely,

Dean Atkins
222 Sycamore Lane
Pembroke, MA 02360
Phone: 781-555-0987

THE OUTLINE

Sometimes, the publication's guidelines require that every query include an outline of the proposed article. In other cases, an interested editor asks that the writer follow up his initial pitch letter with a detailed outline. This request is most common at the largest publications or when the query has been made by a new writer, because the editor wants solid, comprehensive evidence of how the writer plans to approach the article before it is assigned.

When you write an outline for an article, provide an overview of all of the research material you have already accumulated, and try to be as precise as possible regarding the information you will include in the article. The Sample Outlines on pages 218 and 219 demonstrate two different but equally effective ways in which your material can be presented.

Formatting the Outline

When creating the outline for your query package, keep in mind that all elements of the package should be consistent in appearance. Therefore, whatever paper and typeface you used for the query letter should also be used for the outline.

At the top of the page, place the word "Outline," followed by the title of the article and your name. If the outline runs more than one page, on all subsequent pages, be sure to add a header that includes a shortened version of the title and a page number.

Although you can certainly use a standard outline format, complete with Roman numerals, it isn't necessary to do so. The editor is more interested in learning how your article will be developed and whom you will be interviewing than he is in your mastery of the outline form. If you cover the meat of the article by providing a paragraph or two about each point you plan to make, you will be fine.

If you haven't yet outlined your article, doing so will be a helpful exercise, as it will force you to consider how you will develop your theme. Just don't make the outline too detailed; leave room for revisions. The purpose of the outline is to give the editor a clear enough idea of the article to make an informed decision about your proposal, not to provide every single fact that will be included in the final piece.

Editors at large magazines and newspapers often want writers to submit either a detailed query letter or an outline. These are designed to give the editor a clear picture of the proposed article so that he can determine if the piece would be a good fit for his publication.

Sample Outline #1

The first time you send a proposal to a major magazine, your outline should be detailed and complete. In fact, the rule of thumb is that the higher the status of the publication, the more detail the editor will want from a new author. This outline would be perfect for a first-time submission to a high-profile publication as it lists all of the sources that will be used for the article, explaining why each is relevant and how that subject's story will serve to illustrate the point of the piece.

Outline of Stitching Up Profits in the Craft Industry
By Shirley Kawa-Jump

I. Introduction
    a. Statistics on Crafting Industry
    b. Quotes from Associations on Opportunities

II. Profile #1: Kim Krafter, host of "The Kim Krafter Show" on HGTV.
Home and Garden Television (HGTV) in Knoxville, TN, is one of several channels offering craft-related programming. Host Kim Krafter, spokesperson for National Crafts Month for the past twelve years, does 70 shows a year, with two guests per episode. The featured projects are constructed from readily available materials with easy-to-follow instructions.

III. Profile #2: Leanne Weaver
When Leanne Weaver's husband, a basket salesman, lost his job in 1965, she started a home party business called Basketmakers. With 100 baskets in hand, she held her first party, netting only $20 in sales. She encouraged her guests to host their own parties, a la Tupperware style. Within her first five months in business, Weaver trained 25 salespeople and grossed over $300,000. A later appearance on "The Craft Success Stories Show" helped spur her business.

IV. Profile #3: Donna Snow
The hottest trend in the craft industry today is home decor, according to major craft organizations. Donna Snow, owner of Amazing Decorative Painting Company in Phoenix, said the growing interest in personalized home decorations is helping her net $40,000 a year. She started out decorating pieces she found at flea markets and yard sales, building up her portfolio. She now does custom work for clients.

V. Profile #4: Janet Colt
Janet Colt entered the arena of crafting by accident. She wanted to find a wooden train for one of her children. When she couldn't, she created her own. Friends and family began asking for their own. She and her husband, Bob, now have a successful business.

VI. Conclusion

VII. Sidebar of Resources

Sample Outline #2

Outline of Are You Driving a Luxury Deathtrap?
By Ned Tines

1. Introduction: 30% of all luxury cars are unsafe, resulting in thousands of injuries and deaths every year. The top names for luxury sedans have been linked to fatal accidents that are rarely publicized, out of an industry desire to maintain its image. Lincoln Parker and his family never suspected their luxury car would also become their coffin.

2. One Family: An interview with Lincoln, the only surviving member of his family. His two children and his wife lost their lives when the air bags failed to deploy in what should have been a minor accident.

3. The Industry Take: Executives at Luxury Autos refute claims that their cars are rated unsafe by the Insurance Safety Institute. President John Gaines says his cars are safe enough for a two-year-old to drive.

4. The Data: Reports from the ISI differ from Luxury Autos internal records. Simulated head-on crashes resulted in fatal injuries for test dummies. Jim Perkins from the ISI calls Luxury Autos and two other brands "worse than driving a tuna can."

5. The Aftermath: What consumers can do today if they suspect their car is unsafe. This will be followed by a sidebar of resources and a link to the ISI's report.

Not all outlines need to be lengthy. If you have worked with the editor in the past, or if you are sending a proposal to a medium-sized publication, you can use a briefer outline, encapsulating the main points of each section of the article in a sentence or two. Just be sure to state whom you plan to interview and to explain their relevance to the story.

YOUR PUBLISHED CLIPS

Whenever you send in a query, whether to a commercial publication or an academic journal, it should be accompanied by examples of your published work—assuming, of course, that some of your articles have already appeared in print or online. Ideally, the clips you submit should be on the same sort of subject matter as the article you are proposing, thereby demonstrating your expertise in that area. For example, if you are pitching to a parenting magazine, you would include copies of any articles you have written for online parenting sites or print magazines addressing women's or childcare issues. But don't panic if you don't have clips in the area of the proposed article. Just include the best examples of your work, and use your letter to stress your interest or your expertise in the subject of the query article.

The best number of clips to include is two. One isn't a big enough representation of your skill as a writer, and four or more clips will make the package too bulky and probably end up in the trash.

Arrange your clips on a single sheet of paper, using both sides if necessary, and keep your articles neat and easy to read. Bylines and publication names should be clearly visible.

It may be necessary to cut and paste your articles onto new sheets so that the clips are kept to a single-sided or double-sided page, if at all possible. If you do have to cut and paste, keep your articles neat and easy to read, and make sure that the bylines and publication names are visible.

Never send originals, because it's doubtful that you will get them back. Editorial offices are swamped by submissions, and loose papers often get misplaced or tossed away. Always send photocopies. However, don't bind your clips or send them in any kind of portfolio or folder. Editors don't want anything extra cluttering up their desk or weighing down their briefcase when they bring queries home to review.

What if your clips are all online? If you are sending your query by regular mail, include a printout of the Internet article. You can include URLs to your other work in your query letter, but this should be in addition to, not in place of, a printout of your work. Again, try to keep the length to one page and make sure that the copy is neat, clean, and readable.

If you are sending an e-mail query and have only *print* clips, this presents a different kind of problem. In this case, offer to fax or postal mail a copy of your clips to the editor. Many editors prefer hard copies of clips so that they can be kept on file for future reference.

THE AUTHOR BIOGRAPHY

Within the space of a brief query letter, it's impossible to mention more than a few of your published articles. An *author biography*—or *author bio*, as it is usually called—enables you to present a longer list of credits, and to provide other information as well.

Begin your author bio with "About the Author" copy that provides a two- to three-sentence summary of your writing experience. (See the Sample Author Bio on page 222.) This should be followed by a section called "Select Publishing Credentials"—a carefully chosen list of your most prestigious published articles. In the case of each entry, include the name of the article, the name of the publication in which it appeared, and the date it was published. If you have an article that is due to come out, it's fine to list that, too, along with the expected publishing date. If you have a website on which your work is available, add that to the bottom.

Carefully consider the option of including an author bio. It can clutter the envelope and become separated from the query in the review process. Use a bio only when you have extensive credits, and then list only those credits that are most relevant and impressive.

If you are an academic writer, it is standard practice to include a curriculum vitae instead of an author bio. This will provide the editor a good overview of both your credentials and your publishing history. For more information on the curriculum vitae, and for a sample vitae, see pages 136 and 137 in Chapter 5.

Formatting the Author Bio

Like the article outline, the author bio should be printed on the same paper and in the same typeface as the query letter. Place your name, address, and other contact information at the top of the page, either centered or flush with the left-hand margin. Below that, add the "About the Author" headline and copy. Follow this with the list of published articles and your website, if you have one.

Remember that the author bio should be relatively short—less than a page in length. If you find that your typed bio is longer than a page, read it over critically and eliminate the less prestigious articles as necessary, or shorten the summary of your writing experience. The purpose of this piece is to provide further details about your experience—not to overwhelm the editor.

An author bio is not a must; in fact, it can add unnecessary clutter to your query package. A bio is useful, though, if you have a number of published works to your credit or if you want to draw special attention to one area of expertise.

Susan Haskell
2234 Sugartree Place
Boston, MA 02170
Phone: 617-555-1200; Fax: 617-555-1345
E-mail: susan@boston.com

**SAMPLE
AUTHOR BIO**

About the Author

Susan Haskell specializes in writing about parenting and child-care issues. As a mother of six and a full-time freelance writer, she has a great deal of experience in both writing and parenting. She has written more than 200 articles for national parenting publications and is the co-author of *All You Ever Wanted to Know About Kids* (Random House).

Select Publishing Credits

"Avoiding Toddler Meltdowns," *Parents* magazine, June 2000.

"Making Dinner Enjoyable and Fast," *Child* magazine, April 1999.

"My Life as a Car Pool Mom," *Work at Home Mom*, due to appear in September 2002.

"The New Car Seats: Innovation or Irritation?" *Parents Paper*, July 2000. Reprinted in *Mom Times*, January 2001.

For more information on Susan or to see samples of her writing, visit: www.susanhaskell.net

---

In the return address section of your SASE, write the title of the article. If you have made several submissions to the same publication and receive form letter rejections, this will immediately tell you the piece to which the editor is responding.

THE SELF-ADDRESSED, STAMPED ENVELOPE

It is standard procedure to include a self-addressed, stamped envelope (SASE) with your query. The editor will use this business-sized envelope to mail his response to you. Editors simply do not have time to address envelopes and lick stamps so that they can contact every author who sends in a query—including those they are rejecting. That's why this component of your package should never be omitted. If you don't include an SASE, you will not receive a response from the publication.

To E-Mail or Not to E-Mail?

The Internet allows us to send information off to nearly anyone with the click of a mouse. This fact inspires many writers to speed things up (they think) by e-mailing off queries and submissions to their target publications. Still other writers eagerly fax in their proposals, confident that they are not only saving on postage but also sending their ideas off in the fastest way possible.

Unfortunately, print publications still work in a traditional manner. For this reason, queries and article submissions should always be made by postal mail, not by e-mail or fax, unless the writer's guidelines or the editor himself has specifically stated that the publication welcomes e-mail and fax submissions.

There are many disadvantages to submitting a query through the Internet. Glitches can easily occur, causing your piece to be mistranslated by an e-mail program and end up garbled or lost in cyberspace. Also, most e-mail submissions need to be made in text format (also known as ASCII), which doesn't show your work in its best light because it removes all formatting, including bold, italics, and underlines.

If you send material by fax, you're also taking a risk, because it is impossible to know the quality of the machine at the other end. Noise in the phone line, ink cartridge problems, and machine reading errors can alter your proposal and spoil that all-important first impression.

However, if the editor requests it, you can do follow-up submissions by fax or e-mail. Some editors may ask to see additional copies of your work or request a more detailed outline of your proposed article. These kinds of things can be e-mailed or faxed *if* the editor makes it clear that it's okay with him. But if you're worried about the possibility of technological errors, put a hard copy in the mail. It may not be fast, but it will get your work to the editor without gibberish or blurred type—and usually without fail.

WHAT'S THE NEXT STEP?

After you have carefully created a query package for each of the publications on your list, your next step is to send your packages out to the editors. Chapter 6, "Using the Square One System," will guide you in sending your queries off in a way that saves time and money, allows you to keep track of both your mailings and the editors' responses, and enables you to profit from any feedback you receive along the way. Just as important, this step-by-step program will help ensure that everything is done correctly, maximizing your chance of making a sale.

Once you've sent out your queries, try to forget about them. Move on to the next project. If the weeks pass and your mailbox remains empty, consider sending a postcard specifically designed to check on the status of your query. (See "The Handy Dandy SASP" on page 151 for details.)

CONCLUSION

Learning to write a strong query is essential if you are to successfully build a freelance career. A good query does the combined job of selling not only your idea but also you as the writer. Take your time when you create this package, and especially when you write your query letter, because it is often your only chance to get the editor's attention and convince him that you are the best writer for the job. Once you have mastered the query, the article-selling process will be much easier.

Although it may take longer than you wish for the first responses to trickle in, ultimately, they will arrive. And, hopefully, you'll find that you've made a sale. If so, you'll want to turn to Chapter 10 for advice on researching and writing your article. If a contract is included with the acceptance, Chapter 11 will help turn legalese into English and, when possible, guide you in negotiating for better terms. And if multiple queries have resulted in multiple sales, turn to Chapter 7, which will show you how to make a sale (or two!) while keeping all the editors happy and willing to work with you on future projects.

CHAPTER 10

RESEARCHING AND WRITING THE ARTICLE

The editor has contacted you by mail or phone, responding to your query with an acceptance. This is the break you've been looking for, and you can barely contain your excitement. Go ahead and celebrate. A sale is a huge achievement!

Next, take a deep breath and concentrate on the business at hand. First, you'll want to make sure you understand exactly what the editor wants. Then you'll have to complete the interviews and other research from which you'll glean the information for your piece. Once you've finished your research, it will be time to write your article. And finally, you'll want to take steps to generate future work.

Sound like a tall order? It is, but don't panic. This chapter was designed to help you achieve all of these goals, from nailing down the editor's requirements to creating a great article to pitching ideas for future ones. So turn on your computer, and get ready to complete your assignment.

BEFORE YOU BEGIN

While you might want to sit down and begin researching and writing right away, it's important to take a few minutes and cover some preliminary ground. Specifically, it's vital that you clear up any questions you have about the requirements of the editor, learn how to calculate word count, and determine the publication's style. As a result of doing this "homework," your article will be stronger and better written, and will do a more effective job of projecting the image of a professional writer.

Clearing Up the Details

When talking with the editor, try to remain calm and focused. Make a list of questions and keep it nearby to help you stay on track.

If the letter of acceptance sent by the editor is straightforward and the task before you seems clear, you won't need to contact the editor. However, you may find that you have questions regarding the completion of the assignment and need to call the editor for clarification. And, of course, the editor may call you to discuss the piece, or may ask you to call her. If so, be prepared for this conversation because it is easy to get flustered and forget something important.

Before your phone call, compile a list of any questions you have so that you can get all the information you need at one time. A sure way to annoy an editor is to call her over and over again with questions about the article. In an ideal world, everything is hammered out in one phone call or e-mail.

It's also a good idea to carefully examine your letter and contract before contacting the editor. Many of the questions you are likely to have are probably addressed in one of these documents. What rights is the publication buying? What are the payment terms? How many words should your article be? What format should it be written in? First person? Third person? As a personal essay or as a service piece? Should it have any particular slant or present the information in an unbiased manner? Don't forget to consider these important issues. And if any of your questions hasn't been cleared up by the contract or letter, add them to your list.

When you speak to the editor or to her assistant, start by going over the parameters of your article to be sure that you didn't misinterpret the contract or acceptance letter. And if you didn't receive a contract or letter—not all publications send them—remember that it's *your* job, and not the editor's, to make sure that you get these details correct early on. This will prevent the need for a lengthy revision, and will also avoid any misunderstandings about payment. If you did receive a contract but are unsure about some of the terms, now is the time to ask for clarification. (Also see Chapter 11, which explains the different contract terms and offers tips for negotiating a better deal.)

Next, ask the editor about "art." This is the industry term for any graphics, photographs, or other images that might accompany the

Cover all the details of the article assignment, the payment terms, and the contract in one conversation with the editor so you can avoid repeated calls later on.

article. Some publications assign a photographer to the story and handle all the arrangements in-house. If the publication's budget is small, however, you may be asked to have the interview subjects forward photos of themselves, or you may be asked to take the pictures yourself for additional money. If you aren't comfortable taking the photos, tell the editor, and if possible, offer to find someone who can do the job.

Another extra to ask about is a sidebar. If you've studied the magazine, then you know if they use *sidebars*—boxes of information that are set apart from the main article. Sometimes a staff writer compiles this information, and sometimes the writer does. Again, you want to clarify the editor's expectations. (See page 257 for details about sidebars.)

Most editors like sidebars for several reasons. The boxed information draws attention to the main article and also provides a quick resource for people who either don't have time to read the whole piece or want to save some of the information. Sidebars should provide value to the reader, either by offering further information or by presenting a quick summary of the article's main points. They don't take very long to write and often boost your income. By offering one, you will show the editor that you have studied the magazine and understand the value of this additional mini-article.

The final extra you should ask the editor about is a *source list*—a list of the sources you used to research the article. Major publications employ fact checkers who verify everything written in the article, both to fend off the possibility of a lawsuit and to protect the reputation of the publication. Small publications don't have the budget for this service. However, regardless of the publication's budget, offering the source list to the editor to facilitate the fact-checking process will show that you are a professional who takes the time to verify everything before you write it. In fact, even if the editor doesn't ask for a source list, it's a good idea to prepare one. (See page 259 to learn more about source lists.)

When all your questions have been answered, be sure to thank the editor for the opportunity. Don't end on a sour note by saying something like, "I hope I'm up to the challenge!" This will scare the editor and make her think she's made a mistake. Throughout the conversation, be confident and upbeat to demonstrate that you are the right one for the job.

A sidebar is a short piece that accompanies an article and provides helpful hints, resources, or a summary of the article's main points.

Always keep a list of all your sources for quotes and research. Some magazines check these facts before publishing them.

Understanding Word Count

Depending on the type of publication for which you're writing, word count may be calculated in a variety of different ways. Newspapers and some magazines go by the column inch rather than using a word-by-word count. This tells them how much space the finished piece will take up—a critical fact that editors use to determine advertising space.

To figure word count by the column inch, simply multiply the number of inches the editor has allotted you by 40. So if you are given 20 inches of column space, that equals roughly 800 words. A typical column inch measures $2\frac{1}{4}$ inches in width (across) by 1 inch deep (down). If the publication you are working for is laid out in wider or narrower columns than most of the other papers on the stand, go

---

Ask the Editor

The first time you talk to an editor on the phone, you are likely to be nervous and forget much of what you wanted to say. The checklist below will help ensure that you get all the information you need to complete the assignment, and that you sound focused and professional throughout your conversation.

During your call, you will probably want to ask:

1. What is the deadline for completion?

2. What is the estimated word count for the finished piece?

3. Which issue are you planning to run my article in?

4. Will you need a sidebar of either resources or quick tips?

5. Who will handle the photos and graphics? Do you need me to provide anything or to find someone who can?

6. Are there any sources you want included?

7. Did you want me to follow the slant I proposed in my query letter, or do you have a different approach in mind?

8. How do you want the finished piece submitted? Should it be sent via e-mail? As a text file? As an attachment, or pasted into the body of the message? Mailed on a disk? Saved in what format?

9. Do you want me to fax or mail a hard copy of the article as a backup?

10. Will you need my list of contacts and sources for fact checking?

11. Will the article be available on the publication's website?

12. What rights are you buying?

13. What are your payment terms?

14. To whom should I submit my invoice?

ahead and measure one inch down in a column and count the number of words in that space.

You can do your word count by hand, or you can use your computer's word-processing software. Before running the word count feature, be sure you have highlighted only the article text, not any of your contact information or the headline of the piece. This will give you a more accurate number. Some word-processing programs require you to run the grammar check before the software provides you with a word count. Be sure to go through the options for this feature first and have it set to count everything but the punctuation.

If you don't have a word count option, or if you are working on a typewriter, simply calculate the average number of words per line and multiply that by the number of lines. Count all the lines in the article, even the short ones, because there will inevitably be several lines that have more words than the average. The resulting word count will be pretty close to the real number.

In any publication, and particularly in one that relies on advertising as its main source of revenue, space is at a premium. The pages are laid out in a certain style with a certain typeface, and these specifications can't be changed just because a writer decides she needs to add another 200 words to her article. That's why it is imperative that you come within a few words of the count specified by the editor. If there is a compelling reason why your article won't meet the word count, discuss this change with the editor *before* writing your article. But always keep in mind that professional writers do their best to abide by the stated count.

Understanding the Publication's Style

All publications adhere to certain style and format guidelines. These guidelines cover everything from punctuation (should you use a serial comma or omit it?) to numerical style (should you spell the number out or use the numeral?).

When you are first assigned a piece or when your proposed article is accepted for publication, the editor will probably send you a style sheet with instructions for submissions. But be aware that these sheets rarely spell out every style detail. It is up to you, the writer, to read the publication and get a general sense of its approach, and then scrutinize the style sheet and understand all of the terminology used

> When performing a word count of your article, count only the words in the article itself—not your contact information or the title of the piece.

Most publications now require that you put only one space after a period, rather than two. This saves on "white space," which can be used for other articles or for ads. Be sure your article is formatted accordingly.

there. To help fill in the gaps left by the style sheet, you'll want to refer to the appropriate style guide. Most publications use either the *Associated Press Stylebook and Libel Manual* or *The Chicago Manual of Style*. Find out which one is used at the publication for which you're working, and refer to the manual as needed during the writing process.

DOING THE RESEARCH

While some articles are more research-based than others, all articles require research. Even an op-ed piece on the day-care debate should be researched so you can understand both sides of the controversy before explaining your opinion. Naturally, the better and more complete your research techniques, the more information you are likely to gather on your subject, and the more valuable your finished piece is likely to be.

Depending on the topic of your article, different types of research will be appropriate. In most cases, in fact, you will have to use several forms of research to gather the data for even a single article. For instance, if you were to write an article on the growing popularity of goat farming, you might first look in a book and/or search the Internet to learn about goats in general, and goat farming in particular. Articles available on the Internet would be a great source of important statistics. Then, once you had acquired the necessary background information, you could line up interviews with some local farmers to get information directly from the source. To get a big-picture perspective, you might also want to talk to various people who oversee the industry—people in dairy and farming organizations, for instance.

It's important, both for your credibility and for the publication's, that all your facts are correct, and that any data you quote is verifiable. Therefore, whether you are getting your information from publications, from the Internet, or from interview subjects, it's vital to take careful notes and to check and double-check your data. Painstaking research habits will not only lead to more informative and interesting articles, but will also build your reputation as a reliable and resourceful writer.

Research is a large subject, and a complex one. To make it easier to approach, the following discussions first cover non-interview sources—books, periodicals, the Internet, and more—and then examine the important art of interviewing.

Using Publications, Organizations, and the Internet

Some new writers anticipate finding all the information they require in standard library materials—in books and back issues of newspaper and magazine articles. Others assume that they'll find all they need via the Internet. The fact is, though, that each of the many existing resources will be helpful to you at certain times and are used as a complement, not a replacement for, interviews with people or real-world research. That's why it's so important to learn what is available and to know when you should turn to each type of research vehicle.

The Internet

The range of material available on the Internet has become so broad and easy to access that the web is fast becoming the starting point for all research, with periodicals and books coming second. In fact, most subjects, to one degree or another, lend themselves to Internet research, sparing you a good deal of legwork.

The Internet is a great first stop for research. It can give you a good overview of your subject, lead you to possible interview subjects, provide valuable statistics, and more.

One basic and easy way to find information via the Internet is to start with a good search engine and type in a key word. Looking for information on goat farming? Simply type in "goat farming," and the search engine will provide you with a varied selection of online articles and sites. Of course, key words as general as these might bring up everything from a farm in New Zealand to a report on commercial goat industries. Depending on what you're looking for, you might want to use more specific words such as "goat farming statistics" or "goat farm locations."

One of the best sites for narrowing a search is the general question-and-answer site Ask Jeeves, found at www.ask.com. This site allows you to pose a question such as, "What agency compiles goat farming statistics?" You are then directed to dozens of online sources that may offer the specific information for which you're searching.

The Internet can also be a great means of getting your vocabulary up to snuff when you write articles on technical or business topics. A number of good online sites—including www.dictionary.com and www.contentious.com—explain technical terminology in layman's words. A careful review of these sites can help you more fully understand other materials on your subject and also enable you to better conduct your interviews.

Business articles are among the easiest pieces to research on the Internet. Visit the Society of American Business Editors and Writers homepage at www.sabew.org, and click on web links. There, you will find hundreds of links to sites that provide statistics, research, and general business data. If you want to find a site that explains the basics of stocks or you want to research a public company, this page will link you to that information.

Several Internet sites list experts in many fields, guiding you to appropriate interview subjects. To start your search, try either ProfNet Global at www.profnet.com (a service provided by PR Newswire), or Pitsco's Ask an Expert at www.askanexpert.com. To find additional experts, try PRWeb at www.prweb.com, WebWire at www.webwire.com, NewsBytes at www.newsbytes.com, and the Internet News Bureau at www.newsbureau.com. Most of these sites also offer e-mail newsletters and updates on the topics of your choice, usually free of charge.

Caution: Not every Internet site is reputable. Use only the most dependable sites— sites created by major periodicals, universities, associations, and the government, for instance— and try to verify any data found online.

While the Internet is a wonderful research vehicle, it's important to keep in mind that not every site offers credible information. Since virtually anyone can post material online, it's advisable to view each site critically. As you might expect, government sites, university sites, association sites, and sites created by major periodicals offer the most reliable information. Sites created by individuals, however, should be regarded with suspicion. But regardless of the site, it's always a good idea to verify any information with your interview subjects or a recognized association. This will help ensure accuracy and, just as important, help protect your reputation as a writer.

Books

Books can be a great source of basic information. Remember my earlier example of the article on goat farming? A good book could give you a fundamental understanding of goats and goat farming, and could also acquaint you with the appropriate vocabulary for the industry so that you could more easily converse with your interview subjects. Most libraries carry industry-specific dictionaries, as well as books that explain highly technical information in easy-to-understand terms. Just keep in mind that in most cases, the most up-to-date book available is your wisest choice.

In addition to providing valuable information, books can also lead you to experts on your topic—either the author of the book or the experts referred to in the text. Book authors, especially, are often glad to be interviewed because the article will provide both them and their work with publicity. Your best bet is to contact the author through the book's publisher, who is listed within the first few pages of the volume.

Periodicals

Periodicals—newspapers, magazines, and journals—can be a wonderful source of both information and inspiration. Note that you don't want to quote another article on your subject. Instead, you want to find some good starting points for research—perhaps the name of a leading expert in the appropriate field or the title of a recent study or report. In addition, it's always a good idea to examine the approach taken by the competition so that you will know how to make your article different.

One good place to begin your study of publications is your local library, where you'll find the *Reader's Guide to Periodical Literature*, a standard reference that can steer you toward articles on various topics. *Reader's Guide* is available in book form, as well as in CD-ROM and Internet versions. Most libraries also subscribe to various online services—Info Trac, FirstSearch, and EBSCO, for instance—that will not only inform you of relevant articles, but also supply the full text of the articles themselves.

Also try newspaper archives. All newspapers maintain a "morgue" where they keep files on different stories. If you are on assignment with that newspaper, you can search the morgue for anything pertinent to your subject. For a small fee, you can also search online archives at major metropolitan papers like *The Boston Globe*. If you are writing for one particular area, sign up for the daily news briefs from the newspapers or magazines that focus on your field. For general news, sites like the *The New York Times* offer a daily digest of the top stories. These quick tidbits of news can also provide inspiration for future articles.

Many fee-based article-location services can be used free of charge at your local library. In addition, by accessing the library's website on your own computer, you may be able to use these services at home. Ask your librarian what's available in your area.

Associations and Organizations

Associations and organizations make it their business to provide reliable information, including valuable statistics and industry data. Many of them conduct their own research, or work in conjunction with universities that do. This type of source can give your article great credibility.

If you are writing an article about an industry or an issue, turn to the group that represents that field, like the Dairy Farmers of America or the American Booksellers Association. Often, an appropriate group can be found simply by typing keywords like "dairy farmers association" into a computer search engine. If you aren't online, visit your local library and look for the organization phone directories, starting with The Gale Group's *Encyclopedia of Associations.* Guides such as this can help you find an association or organization in virtually any subject area.

If the organization in which you're interested has a website, you'll probably be able to find a good deal of helpful information online. If not, call the group directly. Among other things, an association can usually provide you with a press kit, which compiles frequently requested information on the group. And, of course, organizations can often put you in contact with reliable interview subjects. (For more on this, see "Finding Your Interview Subjects" on page 236.)

Studies and Reports

One of the most important components of any good article is statistics and fact-based research. This data helps you prove the premise of your piece, lending credibility to both you and your work. And the primary source for this data is studies and reports.

Universities and organizations, mentioned above, often can provide the most current studies and reports. A number of universities publish press releases, research findings, and statistics through the Newswise website at www.newswise.com. In addition, many professional organizations, such as the American Academy of Orthopaedic Surgeons, send out their information to science, medical, and business reporters through this site.

The federal government also issues reports and statistics, although their figures aren't updated as frequently as you might desire because a great deal of United States information relies on the census and tax returns. To find this data, visit the FedStats website at www.fedstats.gov. More than seventy federal agencies have teamed up to place data on this site as a sort of one-stop shop for reporters and others. Another option is to contact the appropriate federal organization. If you were writing an article on nationwide nursing staff shortages, for instance, you might wish to contact the Bureau of Labor and Statistics to learn which areas of the country have been hardest hit by the problem.

When searching for statistics for your article, always remember that it's essential to get the most up-to-date information available—especially when covering the fast-changing world of technology. A 1988 report on Internet use among teens should not be included in an article written in 2002. In fact, when writing about technology, the best statistics are those from this year. Even better would be figures from this month.

When You're Stumped

Editors expect the writers they hire to know where to find information. However, editors do understand that sometimes writers hit brick walls when researching a topic. So if you have tried every standard resource—from books to periodicals to the Internet—and still can't find the information you need, give your editor a quick call or send her an e-mail. Explain the situation, giving her a quick rundown of your search efforts. Then ask if she has some ideas for additional sources. But never dump the entire burden of research in the editor's lap. The actual legwork is your job.

Interviewing

Not all articles rely on information gleaned through interviews. For instance, first-person articles such as personal essays and op-ed pieces often don't require outside input—although even this varies from publication to publication. In the case of most articles, though, there is no question that you will need to conduct interviews to round out your piece.

The key to a good interview is to be prepared before you ask your first question. In order to write your query, you had to conduct some basic research. Later, when you got the assignment, you completed additional research to gather more statistics and current data. At this point, create a thorough outline of your article and see how many sources you need to fill in all the information you will require. To write an unbiased story, you should have at least three sources, ideally offering slightly different viewpoints on the subject you are covering. Once you decide what your article will encompass, your next

When writing about technology issues, it is vital to get the most up-to-date statistics available. The best sources for this are those in the know: universities, think tanks, associations, agencies, and professional organizations.

step will be to find the people who have the information you are seeking and to interview them.

Be aware that it is not always easy to arrange and conduct interviews that will enhance your article. Especially if you are writing about a controversial topic or one that requires a high degree of expertise from the interview subjects, you will need a certain amount of skill to get the information you're after. But like all other abilities, interview skills can be learned and cultivated. The following discussions will help you get started.

Finding Your Interview Subjects

If you've been keeping a file of information on your article ideas, you already have a list of potential sources. Any organization, association, university, or business mentioned in the data you gathered could help you find experts and other individuals who might make good interview subjects. The people who work at these companies and associations are usually very receptive to helping writers because the publicity is beneficial to their organization.

Let's assume that you are writing an article on cancer survivors. A good place to start your search for interview subjects would be your local hospital or American Cancer Society office. Make a call and ask for the marketing or public relations department. Sometimes, these offices are internal; in other cases, an outside marketing and advertising agency handles all media requests. Most health organizations have a list of people who have survived and are willing to talk about their battle with a disease. These spokespeople are interested in furthering education about their illness, and often make terrific interview subjects because they understand the power of the media. In addition, the organization itself can provide you with supporting information and research data.

When contacting an organization, always ask for a copy of its press kit. Most include basic information about the topic you are researching and can provide inspiration for future articles as well.

Don't be leery of talking to an organization's marketing department. While part of its job is to promote the organization through direct mail and advertising, marketing professionals understand that writers and reporters need unbiased information. A good marketing person knows that if she tries to make a hard sell to a reporter, the publication will go elsewhere for a source. Her job is to facilitate media contact by offering information, resources, and interview subjects. In most cases, she will gladly provide you with a copy of the organization's press kit, and will also schedule interviews for you and follow up with any additional materials.

Be sure to use the Internet to assist your search for interview subjects. "When I recently did an article on assignment from a major woman's magazine, I was required to interview experts," recounts Kathryn Lay, profiled on page 9, in her article "Writing the Net" for the e-zine *Writing for Dollars*. "Through the organization's website, I found phone numbers, as well as . . . e-mails to find the contacts I needed. Their website was loaded with information that I had immediate access to, rather than waiting for days or weeks for brochures to be mailed. My workload was cut and my experts more accessible." (For information on specific websites that can lead you to experts, see page 232.)

If you are interested in personal anecdotes, contact your friends, family, and any Internet list friends. But if you opt for subjects met on the Internet, keep in mind that many people online claim to be something other than what they actually are. For this reason, you should always talk to the person on the phone or in person, verify her credentials through research or phone calls, and only then conduct the interview by e-mail. And whenever possible, talk to verifiable, respected sources so that your articles maintain their credibility.

Remember that the sources you find may be able to provide valuable information not only for your current article, but for future pieces, too. If a subject might fit in a couple of different categories—for example, if you find a doctor who specializes in treatments for cancer *and* is an award-winning writer—make copies of her contact information and place it in each of your relevant idea files. Always ask for business cards, and always keep the cards where you can find them. You never know when they'll come in handy.

Preparing for the Interview

A good interview starts before you ask the first question. If you are to get the information you need, you'll have to be prepared. That means outlining the article early in the process, deciding which area of expertise each particular source will address, and composing a list of questions that focus on the topic that this particular subject will address. (See "What's Up Doc?" on page 238 for basic questions that all interviews should include.) Have more questions ready than you

While marketing people are a great source of basic information, always try to contact an executive in the organization for the actual interview.

Keep accurate records of everyone you talk to when researching your article. The publication's fact checker will appreciate a comprehensive list, complete with contact information.

What's Up, Doc?

There are certain questions that every good interviewer should ask. If you write up a list ahead of time and bring it with you to the interview, you won't forget anything important. Following are sample lists of questions for two basic types of articles—factual articles and human interest pieces. You'll note that while the first list seeks to obtain cold facts, the second is intended to help the subject open up about a traumatic event in her life. One list or the other should cover most interviews.

Note that both lists of questions are designed only to provide a framework for your conversation. Be sure to adapt the questions as needed to fit each situation, and to ask any questions that arise from the subject's responses.

Sample Questions for a Factual Article

1. What is the correct spelling of your name?

2. What is your job title?

3. What is the name of the company you work for? Is that Inc. or LLC (limited liability corporation)?

4. Do you have any special degrees, qualifications, or credits that I should be sure to list in the article?

5. Can you give me an overview of (insert subject of article here)?

6. What are the benefits of (insert subject of article here)?

7. What are the drawbacks of (insert subject of article here)?

8. What do you see for the future of (insert subject of article here)?

Sample Questions for a Human Interest Article

1. What is the correct spelling of your name?

2. What city or town do you live in?

3. What do you do for a living?

4. Has that career come out of your experience or been affected by what you went through?

5. Tell me a little bit about (insert subject of article here).

6. What was the biggest challenge of that experience?

7. What lessons did you learn from that experience?

8. How has it shaped you as a person?

9. What is your advice to others undergoing the same experience?

think you'll need. Not everyone you talk to will provide good quotes or be able to clearly explain what she means. It's always wise to have a backup set of questions, as well as a plan for finding other sources.

Try to avoid asking questions that result in a "yes" or "no" answer. Instead, keep your questions open-ended. Use one of the reporter basics—Who, What, When, Where, Why, or How—to open each one. By starting your questions with one of these words ("Why did you . . . ?" "How do you feel about . . . ?"), you will give the subject room to talk and explain herself. Most people love to talk about themselves or their area of expertise. Your job is to open the door wide enough to invite them to do so.

Once you've prepared your list of questions and thought about how you're going to pose them, you're ready for the interview.

Conducting the Interview

The manner in which you conduct your interviews is every bit as important as adequate preparation. By approaching your subject in an appropriate way, taking good notes, and double-checking facts *during* the interview itself, you'll make both the interviewing and the writing process much more easy, pleasant, and effective.

STANDARD INTERVIEW GUIDELINES

When you first approach someone for an interview, be sure to tell her the subject of the article, the publication for which the piece is being written, and the date on which it's scheduled to be printed. Remind the interviewee that she will be quoted in the piece and, just as a precaution, ask again if the subject wants to participate in the interview. This process may seem unnecessary or tedious, but it can help avoid later discussions about whether the remarks were made on or off the record. Some major magazines have all interviewees sign a release statement, showing that they granted permission for their words to be used, but most publications don't bother with this step. Should a dispute arise, the writer's notes and tapes are considered adequate evidence of the statements made during the interview. Once this business is out of the way, it's time to move on to the questions.

Open the interview with "soft" questions that ease the subject into the process. For many of the people you interview, this will be their first time talking to a reporter or writer. It's disconcerting to start out with the "Where were you on the night of the murder?" kind of questions. All that will do is alienate the interviewee and put her on guard.

For example, ask about the person's occupation or hometown, or request general information about her company or organization. Always verify the spelling of her name, even if it seems like a basic

Always try to ask questions that encourage the interviewee to give a longer response. It is far better to have too much information than too little.

Start with the easy, friendly questions. Easing into the interview will make both you and your subject more comfortable.

name. Smith can be Smyth, Smythe, or another variation. Don't rely on spelling from other people, or even from your editor. The best source for this kind of information is the person you are interviewing. If possible, get a copy of her business card, as well, so you have reference material for future use.

After the subject answers a question, don't be too anxious to jump in and move on to the next item on your list. Sometimes the wisest thing to do during an interview is to be silent. People are uncomfortable with silence and will rush to fill that empty air with words. Some of your best quotes will come during these quiet moments when the subject feels compelled to talk.

Once the basics are covered, you can move on to the other questions on your list. Feel free to deviate from your planned questions if you find that your source's information differs from what you expected, or that she isn't giving a helpful response. For example, in an interview with your state senator about the rising costs of prescription drugs, you might ask the question, "What kind of legislation are you sponsoring to help combat this problem?" If the senator avoids the question or uses terms you don't understand in her answer, ask for clarification. "What do you mean by that? Is this issue part of your campaign platform?" If she starts going off on a tangent that has nothing to do with your article, gently steer her back to the subject at hand by saying something like, "Thank you for that information, but what I really need is specific information on legislative action."

If your subject says something especially interesting or quotable, mark it with an asterisk as you are taking notes. That will make it easier to find the quote later. Also, be sure to number the pages of your notes and jot a headline at the top like "Senator 3," so you can keep your notes in order.

Verify all statistics quoted by your expert source during the interview. It's easy to make a mistake, both in speaking and in writing numbers, so check with the source to be sure.

When your subject states a fact or provides a statistic, be sure to verify it. Just repeat what she said and make sure you have the numbers right. This extra step will give you accuracy insurance.

One good interview strategy is to ask the same question of all of your sources so you can choose from different answers. With technical issues, for instance, it's usually a good idea to get explanations of complicated terminology from more than one person to be sure you have a thorough definition.

No matter what kind of article you are writing, approach all interviews as if you were a reporter for a newspaper. This means checking and double-checking all facts and data, making sure you have a good representation of all viewpoints, and covering all the important arguments.

THE ART OF OVERINTERVIEWING

In Chapter 8, you learned that you can turn one article into many by spinning a single idea into several different ideas. (See "Spin-Offs" on page 190.) One of the keys to using this article-generating strategy is to initially overinterview your subjects, thereby gathering enough information for several pieces.

Successful overinterviewing starts during interview preparation. If you know ahead of time that you will be pitching an article to different markets, write up your questions list to cover all the various bits of information that are relevant to those publications. You may, for example, remember that in Chapter 8, I explained how I turned a single interview with a romance writer into several articles, each with a different spin. During my interview, I asked the writer about the challenges of starting a second career, her techniques as a writer, her view of the African-American romance novel trend, and her belief in romance as a genre and as a way of life. Her responses then served as the basis of two articles for retirement magazines, two articles for writers' magazines, an article for a publication with an African-American focus, and more.

When you approach the interview itself, it's a good idea to tell your subject that you are pitching the idea to other publications at the same time. First, it will help her understand why you are asking so many questions. Second, it will help her frame responses appropriately for each audience.

Keep in mind that every article should have fresh quotes and be written with its own particular slant. If you don't make each piece original, the editor may be angered by the fact that you have essentially sold her a reprint. If you need a similar quote for all the different publications you are targeting—for example, a quote on what the interviewee plans for the future—an effective strategy is to ask the question a couple of times during the interview, separating it with other questions so that your subject gives a slightly different answer each time. You may be surprised to find just how many responses you receive.

> Every article should have its own quotes. Don't plagiarize yourself.

Finally, consider spreading the interview out over a few sessions or sending the questions in separate e-mails, if you are doing an online interview. Although this will take more time on your part, it will be easier on your subject, and will give her time to formulate additional answers. Plus, it may help avoid overwhelming her with one lengthy in-depth interview.

Using Different Interview Formats

Although the basic interview guidelines discussed earlier apply to all interviews, certain specific guidelines apply to interviews that are conducted in specific ways—in person, by phone, or online, for instance. Let's look at each of these possibilities.

INTERVIEWING IN PERSON

When interviewing a subject in person, try not to put your tape recorder right in front of her. Tell the interviewee that you are taping the interview, and then put the recorder out of her direct line of vision so that she is not constantly reminded that her words are being recorded.

If at all possible, try to conduct your interviews in person—especially when you are first launching your writing career. This type of interview has a number of benefits. First, when you are talking to someone face to face, it is easier to clarify points, understand the subject's perspective, and gather all the necessary information. One-on-one interviews also allow you to see a person in her environment and observe her body language. This can help you determine the validity of her information and, later, inject the subject's personality into the article.

In-person interviews can be easier on the subject, too. Many people find it far more comfortable to talk to a "real person" rather than a disembodied voice on a phone or an e-mail address.

Another plus is that when you conduct your interview in person, you will probably end up with more material. An in-person interview usually lasts longer and has more depth and spontaneity.

A final advantage to interviewing your subject in-person is that these interviews tend to end with the small talk that normally concludes any social situation. This will give you yet another opportunity to gather material for your articles. Some of the best quotes I ever received were delivered at the end of an in-person interview, just as I was walking out the door. However, since this time is usually considered "off the record," be sure to ask your expert if it's okay to quote what she just said.

I highly recommend tape-recording all in-person interviews, with the subject's permission, of course. This will guard against any inaccuracies and provide you with a second record of the meeting. I take notes while the tape recorder is humming—which saves me the time of transcribing the tape recording—and then verify quotes by listening to the tape when I later write the article. One way to make this easier is to keep the tape recorder nearby you so you can jot down the counter number for the location of the quote. This will allow you to find specific lines much more quickly and without a lot of rewinding and fast forwarding.

Some major publications, like *The New York Times* and *Ladies' Home Journal,* actually require that their writers tape copies of interviews to guard against lawsuits and misquotes. So before you conduct your first interview for a publication, give your editor a call and inquire about the desired procedure.

Before leaving an interview, hand your business card to your source and ask her to call or contact you with any further information, if she wants to. Many times, an expert will send you more material on the subject as an afterthought, or will call with any additional facts she comes across. This can be a nice bonus for your article. Always let the interviewee know when and where the article will appear, and thank her for her time and information. And if she was especially helpful, consider sending a thank-you note either directly after the interview or later, with a copy of the article.

Always hand out your business card at the end of the interview so that the interviewee has a way to follow up if she wants to provide additional material.

Interviewing by Phone

Although in-person interviews are ideal, there will be times when you have to conduct your interviews over the phone. To make these interviews as effective as your in-person meetings, you'll want to keep several points in mind.

When setting up the time for this conversation, try to accommodate the interviewee's schedule. Be sure to give her an estimate of how much time it will take and what material will be covered so she can be prepared. On your end, be sure that your calling area will be quiet and free of distractions.

During the interview, keep your list of questions close by and either tape the interview, take notes, or type your notes into your computer as you talk on the phone. This last method can be particularly helpful during the writing process as it provides both a hard copy and a computer copy of your conversation. (For information about tape-recording an interview, see page 242.) Your goal, of course, is to accu-

A number of recorders are designed to tape telephone conversations. However, always get your source's permission before taping an interview.

rately record all information and quotations. Slow down the interview if need be, or pick it up again at another time. Don't try to rush the conversation to fit in the available time, and don't count on your memory to fill in any blanks in your notes. By the time the interview is over, your mind will be swimming with facts and you'll be unlikely to recall the subject's exact words.

When the interview is over, read back any quotes of which you aren't sure. This is the best time to clarify terminology or wording—when the conversation is still fresh in everyone's mind. Then mail your business card to the interviewee so that she can contact you if she has further information, and let her know where and when the article will run. Finally, thank her for her time and, if she was especially helpful, follow up with a thank-you card. This small courtesy will pay off the next time you call her for a quote.

INTERVIEWING ONLINE

As people become busier, e-interviews are growing in popularity with writers and subjects alike. The benefits are many. For the writer, e-mail interviews are simple to accomplish, save much note taking, and offer the advantage of easy follow-up. For the person being interviewed, the e-mail format permits her to tackle the questions at any time, which is not only convenient, but also allows for the careful consideration of each answer.

The biggest advantage of e-mail interviews, however, is that they offer protection against misquoting. If someone essentially writes their own quotes and then e-mails them to you, both parties have a copy of what was said. This greatly reduces the chance that the writer will be sued for libel down the road.

However, e-mail interviews are very different from face-to-face and phone interviews. The medium is impersonal and doesn't allow for the same interaction permitted by in-person and phone conversations. You don't get any true idea of the personality of your subject, so you can't add that personal touch to the story. This is particularly a problem when the topic of the story is an emotional one, as the coldness of the e-mailed answers will prevent you from bringing that person to life in your article.

Some people hate doing e-interviews, while others prefer them to any other kind. Your best bet is to call first, find out what the subject's preference is, and go on from there. If the interviewee agrees to the online interview, be sure to tell her when you will be sending the questions, what the main premise of the article is, and what the deadline is for the responses. That way, she will know what to expect.

The best way to conduct an online interview is to e-mail the list of questions to the subject, and ask for the responses to be returned by e-mail as well. You can, of course, conduct interviews with instant messaging software, but be sure you can record the chat so you don't have to take notes and type at the same time. Then send a copy of the file to the interviewee so she can verify what she "said."

Even if you mentioned the deadline for the responses during a previous contact, note the deadline again when you send the questions off to your subject. Keep the note professional and direct, and once the responses have been received, always follow up with a thank-you for the person's time.

OTHER INTERVIEW METHODS

Although in-person, phone, and e-mail interviews are the most popular, there are other methods of interviewing people. When the subject is busy or on the road, and therefore difficult to reach by phone, the fax interview offers an immediate, easy option. This type of interview is an especially good choice when dealing with celebrities and experts, because the hard copy can be distributed to all the appropriate people, including publicists and office managers.

If you aren't in a rush to get your information, and your subject prefers to write out her responses rather than speaking them, send your interview questions through the mail. The benefit to conducting an interview in this manner is the level of detail you can send and receive. It's easy to include copies of relevant information in your packet to the interviewee, and vice versa. And like e-mail and fax interviews, this format allows the person you are interviewing to compose thoughtful answers, which could result in a richer response.

The final interview option is the Internet message board. If you are working on a story that requires numerous responses, posting your question on a message board may provide the material you need. One caution: Not everyone who posts on the Internet is honest, so be sure to follow up with a phone call to the interviewee, if possible. A message board is best used to find people who meet your article's criteria *before* you conduct the interview in a more traditional manner.

Never conduct an e-mail interview without first talking to the subject on the phone or in person. This is your best guarantee against fraud because many people on the Internet claim to be someone quite different from who they really are.

If They Won't Talk to You

It happens to every writer: The person you wanted to interview won't talk to you. Perhaps she doesn't trust the press, possibly because she had a bad experience in the past, or perhaps she feels that she has nothing to contribute to your piece. Either way, a reluctant interview subject can wreak havoc with your deadline and your article.

One option, of course, is to simply find another person to interview. In that case, you will need to go back to the beginning and start with the source that gave you the first person's name. If that fails, go online and search for another expert.

There are times, though, when the person who won't talk to you is the *only* one who can provide the answers you need. When this is the case, try to determine the reason for the subject's reluctance. If she has been burned in past interviews with the press, her feelings are understandable. Not all writers and reporters are ethical, and not all of them take the time to get the facts straight. Your job is to assure the interviewee that you will be honest and accurate. By employing some of the practices discussed earlier—letting her see a copy of her quotes before they are printed, verifying any facts, etc.—you can allay those fears. Try to accommodate a skittish source; it will pay off in the end with a better article.

If the person you want to interview feels that her input won't help the article, reassure her that it will. Tell her exactly what information you hope she can contribute, and reiterate how her area of expertise will be an asset to the finished piece. If she continues to resist, ask if she has a colleague or friend who would be better suited for the article.

Some business people are reluctant to talk to writers because they have very little experience with the media and are overwhelmed by the interview process. Many times, you can help these subjects overcome their reservations by pointing out that a mention in the magazine or newspaper will essentially provide free publicity for their business.

Every once in a while, you may find someone who refuses to talk to you no matter what you say or do to make the process easier. When that occurs, it's wise to move on and find someone else. Never badger a source. Just take this obstacle in stride and look for another interview subject.

If your interview subject is reluctant, consider if ethically, you feel right about pursuing her for the story. If the article you are writing deals with a tragedy in that person's life, and she would rather not discuss it, maybe it's time to call your editor, say the story can't be done, and move on to something else.

WRITING THE ARTICLE

Now that you have completed all your research, it's time to write the article. In the beginning, you may struggle for hours over every word, trying to get the piece perfect. This is normal and part of the learning process. Your best bet is to go back to your outline, fit your research in, and write from that framework. If you didn't create an outline, compose one right now, and follow it faithfully in your work.

Before you write, be sure you are thoroughly prepared. First, type up your notes from interviews and other research so that you won't have to waste time puzzling over your handwriting during the writing process. Then, position your style guide close by as a ready reference. Finally, sit down and briefly analyze the articles in your target publication. Gauge the tone of the articles, and see how much empha-

Defamation Definitions

When using interview material in your article, be aware that it is your responsibility to make sure that all quotations are accurate and that you've written nothing libelous. The Constitution's First Amendment protects your right to freedom of speech. It does not, however, allow you to write whatever you want about someone else without paying the price for defamation.

Exactly what is defamation? To defame someone is to damage her reputation, character, or good name. The laws against defamation stem from the belief that a person has the right to be free of the malicious publication of false statements that injure her reputation.

There are two types of defamation: libel and slander. *Libel* is a defamatory statement that is written or printed in a publication. It can appear in a letter, an article, or even a posting on an e-mail list. Basically, if you write it down and post it for anyone else to see, you better be sure you have evidence to back up what you are saying.

Slander is the oral form of defamation—speaking aloud things that defame another. Even the act of repeating something defamatory about another person can fall into this category.

How do you guard yourself against charges of defamation? Research everything, have verifiable evidence for whatever you say in an article, and don't ever accept another person's word when the issue is someone's reputation. You can't just call someone a drug dealer, for example, unless you can prove your accusation, and prove it well.

Besides researching and double-checking your work before printing it, always keep copies of your notes long after the story appears. Just in case someone calls you on a quote or a statement years later, you must be prepared to defend yourself. The best defense is to watch the words you use, never use anything you are unsure of, and be mindful of the impact of what you write.

The structure of academic articles varies, depending on the type of article being written, the academic discipline being addressed, and even the specific journal to which the piece is being submitted. Information on the required style can be obtained from the journal itself, the journal's website, or the appropriate reference book—either the *Publication Manual of the American Psychological Association* or the *MLA Style Manual and Guide to Scholarly Publishing.* (See the Resource Directory.) This section, therefore, focuses on the structure of articles written for consumer and trade publications only.

sis they put on research, how heavily they use quotes and statistics, and what length the sidebars are, if any. Keep these points in mind as you write, referring to the publication as necessary to refresh your memory and to look at particulars—the headlines, leads, etc.—as you work on those portions of your own piece.

The Parts of an Article

Articles are generally composed of four parts: the headline, lead, body, and conclusion. The headline and lead introduce the article and define its focus, while the body backs up the premise. The conclusion ties all the information together into one neat package.

It's important to make sure that all parts of your article work together to form one cohesive unit. A good article is circular, meaning that the ending reflects the beginning. This echo of the beginning makes the article more memorable for the reader and brings all the points made in the piece back to the original slant.

After you finish reading the following discussion of article structure, turn to the inset on page 260 to see a sample completed article. Alongside the article, a numbered key highlights the different sections of the piece and also explains how the information was presented to make the article as strong and effective as possible.

The Headline

While your *headline*—the title of your story—may not end up on the finished piece, it's important that you write one anyway. Besides giving you and the editor a working name for the piece, the headline will also serve a larger purpose. By encapsulating your entire piece in a few words, the headline pinpoints the theme of the article. If you feel your writing wandering, you can use the headline as a reference to judge the relevance of each paragraph.

The best articles are circular, meaning that the conclusion reflects the message of the headline and the opening paragraph, literally bringing the reader full circle.

A good headline is kept to seven words or less and uses strong, active phrasing. "Criminal Was Put in Jail Last Week for Ten Murders," for instance, is far less effective than "Serial Murderer Sentenced to Life Times Ten." When I say that the second headline is more effective, I really mean that this headline acts as a hook, pulling the reader in. A good headline also reflects the tone of the story, which in this case is solemn, but may instead be humorous, irreverent, or upbeat. Some headlines—like the one in the sample article on page

Using Copyrighted Material in Your Article

Sometimes, during your research for an article, you may come across a passage in a magazine or book that has the exact information you need for your piece. While you may be tempted to reproduce that material in your article, think twice before doing so.

Under current copyright law, no material can be quoted without permission of the publisher unless the material falls under the *fair use* provisions, which allow for limited copying of published works without permission. While at one time these provisions were fairly liberal, at this point, fair use generally allows people to quote from copyrighted material only for news reports, reviews, classroom instruction, and discussions. Nevertheless, in practice, many publishers often follow the older, more generous fair use laws, and permit the reprint of copyrighted material that's less than a paragraph in length. Note, though, that the situation is different when the quoted material takes the form of song lyrics or poetry. In these cases, reprint permission from the copyright holder is generally required even when the excerpt is very small.

Where does that leave you, the writer? Keep in mind it is always a wise practice to get reprint permission from the publisher of the quoted work. Also be aware that because people interpret fair use laws in different ways, and because of the time involved in getting reprint permission, most editors of consumer publications do not want you to quote from other people's work. Editors expect you to do your homework and obtain your own information, your own original quotes. If, considering these facts, you *still* feel that the quoted material would add to the value of your article, by all means contact your editor. She will be able to tell you her publication's policy so that you can make the best decision for your work. And if you do end up obtaining reprint permission for a quotation, be sure to give the editor a copy of the permissions letter so she knows that the excerpted material will not be a problem.

If you would like further information about the use of copyrighted material, you'll find help in your local library. *The Copyright Permission and Libel Handbook* by Lloyd J. Jassin and Steven C. Schecter is just one of the books that can help you determine if the quoted material requires reprint permission and, when necessary, guide you in securing the publisher's consent.

260—are followed by a colon and a subhead that more clearly defines the subject of the piece. Like the headline, the subhead should serve to entice the reader to continue.

The Lead

There is nothing more crucial to the success of your article than the first few lines. If you don't give the reader a compelling reason to get past the headline, you haven't accomplished your goal as a writer. While the headline may briefly hook the reader, the opening paragraph, known as the *lead*, has to pull the reader in and inspire her to read further.

The lead also has to provide enough information to outline the story that follows. It's a sad fact that few people read the entire text of newspaper and magazine articles. Most read the opening paragraphs and skim the rest, or read just the points highlighted in the sidebars and bullets. Therefore, your opening paragraph should present the basic premise of your article, but in a concise, engaging manner.

The lead should also set the tone for the article and demonstrate your voice and skill to the reader. In short, a good lead packages everything—the article premise, your talent, and an overview—into one interesting paragraph.

Don't feel you have to be Shakespeare to write a good lead. In fact, as a general rule, stay away from esoteric language. Remember that readers want information they can absorb quickly and understand easily. Try to write in an appealing style that seems natural and unforced, and doesn't cause the reader to grab a dictionary just to get past the first line.

> If you're having trouble with the lead, write the parts of the article with which you feel comfortable, and then go back to the beginning.

A good lead isn't bulky. It doesn't try to compact every fact in the article into two or three sentences. Provide enough information to get the story moving, but leave the reader wanting to know more.

To determine what your lead should be, go back to your original notes and query. What is your reason for writing this article? What point did you want to prove or make to your readers? That is what you need to convey in this opening paragraph.

Now, look at the material you have accumulated. Do you have a great anecdote, statistic, or quote? These kinds of openings can be powerful if they capture the essence of the article.

Also analyze the style of the particular publication and see if the opening sentences of its articles share a common thread. "One tactic used in many e-zine articles is to make the first sentence a question. A question demands an answer, and it demands the reader's attention," writes Michael Southon in "How to Write Ezine Articles That Get Published," an article in *Bright Ink News.* This kind of opening paragraph is somewhat unusual and, used sparingly, can be an effective means of drawing the reader's attention, no matter what kind of article you are writing.

Sometimes, a play on words can create an effective lead. In a column in *Smart Business* Magazine, Wendy Taylor and Marty Jerome wrote about the benefits and drawbacks of lockup agreements in the crashes of dot-com stocks. "Just as you nibble on that discarded scrap of IPO cabbage, the box comes crashing down around you. You'll make a tasty soup," wrote the authors, who compared the investor to a bunny and the shares to a trap. The analogy continued throughout the article but was used sparingly, occasionally peppered in with statistics and helpful hints for maintaining a grip in a volatile market.

In the above instance, the twist on words works because it isn't overdone and it grabs the reader. But don't worry if you can't come up with a clever lead. If you have one, use it. If not, try another approach.

One common mistake made by new writers is to bury the lead too far into the copy. Look at your writing and see if you have made this error. A good clue that you have done so is an overload of history and supporting information early in the article. Remember that the point of the lead is to leave the reader wanting to know more about the subject. Piling on too much information early in the piece will undermine your intent.

When you write a lead, try to use powerful verbs and vivid phrasing. That's not to say that you should wax poetic in the opening lines, but do critically examine the verbs you have chosen. Does "investigate" work better than "look at"? How about "ambush" instead of "surprise"? My thesaurus has served me well in crafting stronger sentences. Make sure that you have yours ready and waiting when you sit down to write.

If you are having trouble writing the lead, don't worry. Stressing about an assignment is a sure way to keep your computer screen blank. If the lead proves to be a stumbling block, try writing another part of the article first or brainstorming five or six sample openings. (See the inset on page 252 for example leads that can get you started.) Read other articles in the publication and analyze their opening paragraphs.

If you're still stymied, walk away from your work for a while. Some of my best ideas have come to me when I was focused on something other than my writing. Perhaps I was washing dishes or driving to the store, and the lead for the article popped into my head. Try changing your environment or directing your attention to another task. That first compelling sentence might come to mind when you least expect it.

Don't mislead the reader. Don't open a serious piece with a humorous lead, or vice versa. The tone of the lead should be similar to that of the article as a whole.

Don't worry about being clever. Just write enough to give readers a taste of the article to come, leaving them hungry to read more.

Writing a Winning Lead

While there is no formula for writing a great lead, there are a few common types that you can learn to identify and then create yourself. Use the following examples to get your creative juices flowing, but let your own voice shine through in everything you write. And be aware that although I've usually provided just the first sentence or two of each lead, your final opening paragraph should be composed of two or more sentences.

Anecdotal. "Money was tight in the Doe household. The electric bill hadn't been paid since June, the phone was about to be turned off, and the cupboards held little more than boxed macaroni. With a sick infant still needing constant care, Jane Doe had to make the difficult decision to return to work."

Declarative. "Every day, millions of mothers go to work while the rest of the world looks on in either judgment or envy."

Descriptive. "The apartment is small, bare, but clean. This isn't a woman living in squalor who has let the roaches invade and filth get a foothold."

Direct Quotation. "'I do the best I can, but it's never enough,' said Jane Doe, a single mother of five who is struggling to find a job that will cover the bills."

Factual. "One in three Americans covers for a co-worker who leaves work to care for a child, says a recent *USA Today* poll."

First Person. "I never intended to go on welfare. I've always been a member of the workforce, but one day I was forced to ask for state help."

Fragment. "Diapers. Doctor's bills. Hospital stays. Formula. Food. Jane Doe has exactly $79 a month to cover all of those expenses."

Hypothetical. "What if you had five children and a husband who had deserted you, and made one dollar too much to qualify for state aid?"

Ironic/Humorous. "Jane Doe can whip up a Chicken Cacciatore in her three-by-eight kitchen that would put Martha Stewart to shame. She does not have her own television show, but she does have a great knack for cooking and a winning personality. Move over, Martha, because there's a thrifty, sassy alternative waiting for your time slot."

Parable. "Once upon a time, there was an ant who had the forethought to put away food for the hard times ahead."

Question. "How can a single mother feed five children, pay the bills, and save for a future on $79 a month?"

Shocking. "At the end of the day, Jane Doe has enough change in her pocket for a cup of coffee, but not enough to feed her five children. Today, they will go to bed hungry."

Summary. "Sometimes, the decision to return to work has ramifications beyond finding good day care. Single mothers find themselves frustrated by low pay, horrible hours, and a lack of jobs. Thankfully, a new government program, to be launched this spring, will change the picture for thousands of women."

The Body

As its name implies, the body of the article is the main portion of the piece—the meat. It is there that you provide solid information, answering the reader's questions and illuminating the subject of your work.

If you used any other kind of lead besides a summary lead (see page 252), the first paragraph of the body should provide the essential points that the article will cover. This paragraph is referred to by many different terms, including the *billboard paragraph,* the *theme graph,* and the *nut graph.* When the reader reaches this paragraph—which we'll refer to as the nut graph—she has already seen the headline and read the lead. She now wants to know why she should read further.

This brings up an important point. Most people are interested in reading about issues only to the extent that these issues affect them. A retiree might be concerned about stock market fluctuations due to trouble in the technology industry only because of the market's impact on her monthly investment income. A young couple buying a home, however, might care only about the market's effect on interest rates. And someone working for a tech company might care only about keeping her job. Decide who your reader is and make the nut graph speak to her, showing her how the article is relevant to her life.

If you're having trouble with the nut graph, think about how you would tell the story to a friend. What's the most important fact you'd want to convey? This should you help you define your article.

Depending on the outlet for which you are writing, the nut graph may take one sentence, one paragraph, or a couple of paragraphs. A breezy, conversational story usually opens with an anecdotal lead and covers the "so what" in the first two or three paragraphs. A hard news story for a publication like *Newsweek* gets to the point in the opening sentence by combining the nut graph with either a summary or descriptive lead, depending on the writer. Newspapers are often short on space and anxious to get to the point of the article quickly, so their writers usually combine the "so what" of the nut graph with the opening paragraph.

The analysis you did of the publication before you sat down to write (see page 247) should come in handy now. If necessary, look at the publication again, pick out the nut graphs, and see how they're handled in various articles. If you're having trouble finding it, ask yourself the nut question: "So what?"

If you're still not sure about the nut graph, consider the following example. Let's say you've been assigned a piece on how the Internet

Don't use three or four words when one or two will do. At this point in time is too wordy. Opt for now. As a result of is less effective than a simple because.

is affecting library usage. The piece is designed for a trade journal read by librarians. In the body of the article, you might want to touch on several main points: whether statistics show a decrease or increase in circulation; which libraries have Internet access; how patrons are reacting to library access as opposed to home access; what new policies or programs libraries are instituting to attract more traffic. The nut graph would sum up your article by saying something like:

> Internet access is available at virtually every public library, but patrons aren't necessarily making use of it. The American Library Council saw circulation numbers drop in 1999, an alarming trend that gives credence to doubts about the need for library accessibility as more and more people stay home to research. One library is reversing this trend, however, with an innovative program.

What this paragraph does is first state the problem: Patrons aren't coming in to use the Internet after all the work put into making it accessible in public places. Then it summarizes the main points of the article: Circulation numbers are dropping; people aren't researching away from home as much; this is what the librarians feared would happen. And finally, it gives the "so what:" An innovative program at one library demonstrates ways in which librarians can get people out of their houses and back into the library.

Whatever information you put into your nut graph will need to be supported by facts in the subsequent paragraphs. So after the nut graph, begin substantiating your statements. Remember all that research you did? All those great interviews and quotes you gathered? Now is the time to work them in, but be careful not to overdo it. A quotation can be powerful, but keep in mind that long quotations can diminish the impact of the piece. For example, let's look at two different uses of the same quote. If you were interviewing a welfare mother, she might say the following:

> "I had no money to feed my children and had to stretch to make the electric bill and the telephone bill. They were threatening to evict us. I couldn't find a job that would pay enough to cover day care and rent and all the other bills. When John Smith, my caseworker, came to my house, it was like a miracle walked in the door."

As a paragraph on its own, that quote does explain the desperate situation faced by the welfare mother. However, with powerful writing on your part, you can make it much stronger, painting a more vivid picture of the woman's plight:

> The lights went out on Tuesday. The telephone was dead by Thursday. For dinner that night, all six of them split one can of chicken noodle soup and went to bed dreaming of the free school lunch the next day. Everyone except Jane Doe. She spent the night pacing the floor of her run-down apartment, worrying about the eviction notice in her hand and hoping for an answer to come knocking on her door. It did, on Friday morning, in the form of a caseworker from social services. "When John Smith . . . came to my house, it was like a miracle walked in the door," said Jane.

While the second paragraph is longer, it paints a far more vivid picture of what Jane was experiencing on the day John showed up. Instead of "telling" the reader, it "shows" her—an important tactic in good writing. I'm sure you could think of fifty different ways to approach that same paragraph, and that's fine. All writers should try to carve out their own approach, voice, and style so that each article becomes their own. Just make sure that the final words have the impact you intended.

Before you write the conclusion, check your article to see if all the sections hold together and if everything you've included is relevant to the piece. New writers, especially, frequently throw in every fact they've gathered, even if the information is extraneous to their article. (To learn how to avoid other common errors, see the inset on page 256.) Once you're sure that your article is on track, you'll be ready to craft your conclusion.

The Conclusion

You've done it. You've created a great article that proves the points you made in the opening. Now you have to write the conclusion. While this might seem like a time to skate through and write whatever pops into your head, it's not. The conclusion of an article is just as important as the lead. If it's done well, your reader will remember your article long after the page on which it's printed has begun to yellow.

You don't have to print every quote verbatim. You can cut or use part of a quote for more drama. You can also insert a word or two—placing the inserted material in square brackets—if the speaker dropped a preposition or qualifier when she spoke to you. Be careful not to lose the speaker's meaning, however. Distorting a quote's meaning is against the law.

Taking the Time to Get It Right

You've finished the body of your article, and you're ready to write your conclusion and add those little extras that will make your piece a real standout. But don't be too quick to move on to the final stages of the assignment. Especially if you're new to article writing, you'll want to check your piece for a number of very avoidable problems. Before writing your conclusion, ask—and honestly answer—the following questions.

☐ **Does all the information you've included really belong in this article?** Is every fact you've included timely, and is it relevant to the thesis of your piece? If not, be ruthless and take it out. This applies to all types of articles, from essays to feature stories.

☐ **Does the article flow smoothly and hold together?** Look at the sentences that bridge the paragraphs, and note if they provide smooth transitions. Have you used words like *meanwhile, however, nevertheless, for example, first, then,* and *in other words* to move the reader from one thought to the next? If not, your article may seem choppy and disjointed.

☐ **Did you use active verbs such as** *ran, made, find,* **and** *moving*? Active verbs can add to the impact of your words.

☐ **Did you use short, powerful quotes?** Weak or meandering quotations can lessen the impact of your piece and lose the interest of

the reader. (See page 254 for more information about using quotations.)

☐ **Did you adhere to the rules of grammar throughout the piece?** Keep in mind that *every* part of your article should be well written. And don't make the mistake of using odd punctuation or irregular grammar to make a point. While it's okay to occasionally give yourself poetic license, strong verbs and descriptive nouns are what make writing effective—not cutesiness or "creative" grammar.

☐ **Did you verify all your facts and double-check your quotations?** It's easy to transpose numbers, drop zeroes, and misspell names. Be sure to check your article against your notes. And if you're not sure of something, take the time to confirm a statistic or other fact.

☐ **Did you leave any questions unanswered?** Make sure that you delivered what you promised in the opening of the article.

As stated earlier, the best kind of article is circular, meaning that the conclusion returns the reader to the points you made in the opening sentence and delivers a whammy of an ending. Sometimes this isn't possible. In the days when I covered school board meetings, there were often times when nothing controversial happened, no big decisions were made, and thus, no news was created. My articles ended up being recaps of the minutes, and weren't exactly powerful pieces of writing because the subject didn't allow for anything unique. These articles incorporated a standard summary conclusion. In this kind of ending, the writer wraps up the main points made in the article in a couple of sentences.

However, when you are writing about a provocative topic, you can make your readers remember your words simply by writing a great conclusion. And if you have kept the reader's attention all along and she's read everything else you've written, you *owe* her a wonderful summation paragraph.

How can you create a memorable finale? First, go back to your lead paragraph. Read it once, read it twice. Now look through all of your notes and see if you have a powerful quote that would make an effective ending for the story. If that great quote has already been used in the body of the article, see if you can pull it out and put another quote in its place.

Now read over the rest of the article and list the points you've made. The conclusion is essentially a reflection of the whole piece and should quickly reiterate the main points. Let's return to our story on the welfare mother. The conclusion of that article might read as follows:

> After a month on the job, Jane's life is much more secure. The bills are paid, the children are no longer hungry, and the savings account she dreamed of is finally a reality. The intervention of John Smith, one man in a bureaucracy plagued by red tape, made all the difference in Jane's life. "For me, it's been like day and night. A month ago, the future seemed dark and hopeless. Now I see days bright with possibilities."

Again, you might write that entirely differently. You might want to end on a darker note, possibly with a statistic about how many people are still in Jane's boat. Or you might mention the impact of upcoming federal legislation on the welfare issue. Whatever you write, make sure it solidifies your message and makes the reader remember you.

Don't rush through the writing of the conclusion. If you spend time on this important component, your entire article will be better.

Writing a Good Sidebar

As discussed earlier in this chapter, most editors like sidebars—boxed information that provides helpful hints, resources, or a summary of the article's main points. So by mastering the art of sidebar writing, you can boost your income as you provide added value for the publication's readers.

Most sidebars are quite short, under 200 words. They use active verbs and usually feature bullets or short phrases as sub-headlines. For instance, if you wrote an article about building a house, you might want to include a sidebar on the most important qualities to look for in a builder. In that case, you would write five to seven short tips, as anything more than that usually loses the reader and runs longer than the publication desires. Try to stay away from long sentences. Instead, opt for quick, action verb-filled phrases like "Check references," "Visit other houses," etc.

Write a short paragraph, two or three sentences, to accompany each tip. If you are writing a simple list of resources, write a sentence explaining what each group does and what specific need each book addresses—just enough so that the reader understands why these sources are in the sidebar.

Sidebars can perform other functions as well. If you've written a technical piece that's filled with industry jargon, a sidebar can define those terms. Sidebars can also be used for comparison. If you've written a story on local educational programs, you could accompany that with a sidebar on national trends. You can also do the reverse—write the story about a national trend, and break out a paragraph or two highlighting the impact of that trend on one small pocket of the country. This would show the small picture in reference to the big one.

Some sidebars are designed for use as planning guides. An article on building a house can be accompanied by a time line of the different steps involved, or by one on the process of securing a mortgage. Always keep your reader in mind. An article on building a house for less than $50,000 wouldn't work with a sidebar on gold faucets.

You can also write up a list of trivia or fun facts, and let the editor either keep the sidebar intact or sprinkle the facts throughout the story. Children's magazines love to run little-known facts with their articles, so consider going the extra mile when you research and write such a piece.

Sidebars can also be used to highlight information covered in the article. In longer pieces, editors sometimes like to pull out the main points and put them in a sidebar. Again, the rules of short, quick, active sentences apply here.

A sidebar can perform many functions. It can provide helpful hints, list valuable resources, summarize the central points of the article, define technical terms, offer a planning guide, or present fun facts. In each case, this miniarticle adds value to the main piece.

Composing Your Source List

As explained earlier in the chapter, it is always a good idea to offer a source list to your editor to show that you are a careful, conscientious writer, and to make the fact-checking process easier. But even if your editor doesn't require a source list, it's smart to put one together. After you've written a number of articles, you'll appreciate being able to turn to source lists to find this expert or that information. Most writers re-use information in one shape or another in future articles. Files of accurate source lists will allow you to easily locate the original data.

Your source list should include the name, address, title, phone number, e-mail address, and any other pertinent information about each of your contacts, including, of course, your interview subjects. If the contact has written a book on the relevant subject, that, too, should be included. If possible, state the best times to contact the source.

Your source list should also include standard bibliographic data for each website, book, newspaper, or other publication from which you gleaned information for your article. Be aware that each source should be included on your list even if the information provided was ultimately presented in your own words, rather than in the form of a quote.

Organize the entries in your source list neatly and logically, either in alphabetical order or in the order in which the source material appears in the article. If you know in advance that a fact checker will be following up on your article, be sure to let your sources know this so that they won't be surprised by the phone call.

It's always a good idea to create a source list for every article you write—not just for the editor, but also for your own records. Later, if you decide to write another piece on a similar topic, a list of possible interview subjects, books, and other resources will already be available to jump-start your research.

MAILING THE ARTICLE IN

You've performed exhaustive research and composed a great article, complete with all the "extras" like source lists and sidebars. While you may be eager to send in your work and get it off your desk, it's just as important to get this part of the assignment right as it is to conduct a thorough interview and to properly structure your article. So instead of rushing, carefully review the contract or letter of acceptance, plus any notes you made during your conversation with the editor, to find out how she wants you to submit the finished piece. Then turn to page 160 of Chapter 7. There, you'll find complete details on submitting your article so that it reaches the editor without a glitch.

1 The **headline**, along with the **subhead** that appears after the colon, defines the article's focus.

2 **Byline.** The word "contributor" tells the reader this is a freelanced article, not a staff-written piece.

3 The **lead** starts with an anecdote that makes the business story more human and reader-friendly. It also shows the subject of the article—The Work Resource Center—in action.

4 The **nut graph** foreshadows what the program provides for workers, which is the "so what" of the story. Essentially, the article implies that if this woman can succeed, so can others, and The Work Resource Center can help make it happen. Note that in this article, the nut graph has been combined with the lead rather than starting off the body of the piece.

5 The **body** of the article starts here.

6 The subject is not a typical welfare recipient, an important point for this article.

7 Berger is the quintessential example of a success story for this program, which is why she was profiled.

8 This paragraph shows the success of both Berger and the program.

9 Her quote supports and proves the facts above.

10 Statistics "prove" a story better than any quote or anecdote.

11 This is the "what is it" line that explains, in one sentence, what the organization does.

12 Although this information about the program comes late in the article, the anecdote that led the article off did a good job of providing this information early on.

13 This paragraph fleshes out what was mentioned in the nut graph at the end of the lead paragraph.

1 **Lending a Helping Hand:**
Program Provides Resources
for Finding and Keeping Employment

2 By Shirley Kawa-Jump, *Courier* Contributor

3 Single mother Paula Berger hadn't been on welfare long when she sought the help of The Work Resource Center so she could get back on her feet and out into the work force. **4** Berger realized that she would be facing many challenges in finding a new job and needed to find resources that would help her pull all the elements— job searching, resume writing and daycare options—into one package.

5 **6** She had a degree in business administration, as well as one in fashion merchandising. However, the first opportunity for Berger that came along, through a WRC-hosted job fair, was a $6.50 per hour security job. **7** "It wasn't enough money, but for me, it was an opportunity," she said.

8 The job was in Kentucky, so Berger worked with WRC to find child-care arrangements. Not long after that first position, Berger interviewed with Tape Products Co. for a temporary position. In just over a year and a half, Berger has not only found a permanent position at that company, but moved all the way up to territory sales manager. She said the support of WRC, and in particular her retention specialist, Patricia Cook, have helped her find the perfect fit. **9** "I'm proof that if you hold on and persevere, life gets better," she said.

Karen Dudley, employee services representative for WRC, said success stories like Berger's are common at WRC. **10** The four-facility organization has an 82 percent retainment rate, with 70 percent of the program's participants moving upward in their chosen fields. More than 1,400 people are served by the program annually. **11** **12** WRC is a private, nonprofit organization, funded through a fee-for-services agreement with state and local agencies, as well as through contract work for area businesses, in addition to charitable contributions. "We are designed to help people move from welfare to work and then retain their employment," said Dudley.

13 WRC offers a wide range of services to job seekers, including technical training, stress and time management techniques, upward mobility training, interview counseling, resume assistance, and family support. Dudley said forming a support system for people trying to get off welfare is one of the most important components for long-term success. **14** "A lot of people find that when they are in the welfare system, they lose that support system and those resources," she said.

15 WRC provides continual support in a variety of ways, from use of the copier to follow-up counseling sessions for newly hired people. **16** In Ohio, able-bodied welfare recipients have a maximum of 36 months of eligibility before they must return to the work force. "We try to match people with the right job so they can have the flexibility they need to work with whatever disabilities or special challenges they might face," said Dudley.

17 For employers, WRC is a resource, not only for finding employees, particularly in entry-level positions, but also for counseling managers in issues facing people returning to the work force. Jude Reser, director of human resources for The Crowne Plaza Hotel, said the company has utilized WRC's services to understand challenges facing employees who may be having trouble with rehabilitation or who have domestic violence issues at home. **18** "We want to catch those problems before the employee misses too much work and slips into the cracks. That wouldn't be the best thing for the employee and it's not good for the company to lose a valuable employee."

She said some workers prefer to talk to WRC staffers about conflicts they are facing between their personal and professional lives. Reser said she is willing to work with WRC and the employee to retain a good worker. **19** "This is a family-friendly organization. If one family member, meaning an employee, is in trouble, then I want to help them. So I'll call WRC."

20 Rhonda Feagin, certified nursing assistant coordinator for Ivy Woods Health Care Center in Price Hill, said the facility has found a number of good employees through WRC. **21** Each week, the employees and management can sit down for an hour with a WRC staffer and discuss any issues or problems. **22** "We can talk and get it resolved right away. It helps everyone get along better," she said.

23 Dudley said WRC's mission is all about helping people, in whatever capacity they need that assistance. **24** In the future, the program would like to offer funding to help families take time out to go to the zoo or other family-type outings. "A lot of times, money doesn't stretch that far. We want to not only provide jobs for people, but also provide a way for them to enjoy their families," she said. **25**

14 *Again, the quote supports the facts.*

15 *This tells why the program is important.*

16 *This kind of detail is essential and shows the writer did the homework necessary to find the laws that affect this policy.*

17 *This paragraph demonstrates the benefit of the program to the reader audience—business people.*

18 *The following quote supports and further explains Reser's stance. It's also an example of the program in action from an employer's viewpoint.*

19 *This quote provides an employer's take on the program's benefits.*

20 *All feature and service articles, and especially those written for newspapers and other traditional media, interview at least three people to provide a thorough, unbiased viewpoint.*

21 *Rather than mirroring the earlier comments by Reser, this section discusses different benefits of the program.*

22 *Another employer success story. If the article were directed to employees, the focus would be different.*

23 *This is the **conclusion** of the article, summarizing the program's benefits and discussing future plans.*

24 *Most articles that discuss a specific program, business, or person, should mention future plans near the end of the piece.*

25 *This is a "feel good" ending that leaves the reader with a positive view of the program. It also echoes the headline, which described the program as a helping hand.*

If you run into problems during the researching or writing of an article, immediately contact your editor and explain the difficulty you've encountered. She will be able to guide you in finding appropriate information, suggest a different angle, or otherwise adjust your approach so that you can complete the assignment.

OVERCOMING OBSTACLES

When you are researching and writing an article, there are as many things that can go wrong as there are things that can go smoothly. Every experienced writer has had an assignment that didn't work out or that proved to be much more difficult than she expected. The solution is to be ready with a contingency plan, and to be open and honest with your editor throughout the entire article-writing process. Otherwise, you could end up with a mess on your hands, a contract breach, and a smear on your reputation. Editors understand that things can go wrong and are willing to work with you to fix the situation, if possible; but they can do so only if you communicate with them *before* the deadline.

Your Research Does Not Support Your Premise

Suppose that you pitched a piece to an editor about the benefits of one prescription drug over another. Then, as your research progressed, you found that the experts disagreed with your point of view. What would be the wisest course of action? Would it be best to continue along your original route, or would it be smarter to change paths by adopting a new premise—one supported by the evidence you gathered?

There are certainly different ways to handle this or any other dilemma you may encounter along the way. But before you decide which direction to move in, *always talk to your editor*. Warn her that your research is leading you down a different path. In some cases, the editor will scrap the article. In others, she will tell you to go ahead and write about whatever you find. Either way, it pays to be honest with your editor early on, rather than surprise her with something she did not expect. And who knows? Your new article may end up being more interesting than the one you originally proposed.

You Don't Understand the Subject

Sometimes, you may find yourself unable to understand the subject that you've tackled. Perhaps you failed to complete the research necessary to understand the topic, or perhaps the subject matter is simply over your head. You interview expert after expert, hoping that one of them will provide the explanation that you need. But they don't. And when you finally sit down to compose the article, you find a jumbled mess of notes that fails to form anything cohesive.

If this happens to you, stop, take a breath, and start over by returning to the initial focus of the article. Let's say you were assigned a story on managed health-care plans. Somewhere along the way, you got confused about how managed care works. The interviews you conducted were unfocused, and as a result, your information won't make much of an article.

Your first step should be to read over all of your notes, and write down what you *do* know about the topic. Then write yourself a list of questions designed to fill in the gaps. Very likely, you will be able to find answers to many of your questions in books and articles on managed health care, and through the Internet. Then, if any questions remain, review your list of sources, find the expert who seems best suited to answer those questions, and contact her for a second interview. It is far easier to admit you need more information than to struggle for hours to write an article on a subject that you don't quite understand.

When you are done, if you are still unsure if you "got it," consider asking one of your sources to read over certain sections of the article to check for accuracy before you submit the entire piece. This is an especially good strategy when your article has a technical, financial, or legal focus. However, tread cautiously. Point out to the person reading the article that she should be offering her opinion on the information, not using this as an opportunity to rewrite the piece with her particular slant.

Note that while clarifying a few quotes or a technical issue is okay, you should never allow an interview subject to see the finished article before publication, and you should never allow a subject to edit your article, and thereby give it a biased point of view. Unless you are writing a think piece, commentary, or personal essay, all articles should be impartial. In fact, some magazines, journals, and newspapers have a strict policy against letting a source read an article prior to publication because of the tendency of sources to rewrite and influence the writer's story. Check with your editor if you are unsure about the publication's stand on this. Then, if the publication has a policy against letting sources read articles before they go to print, call an expert who won't be featured in your article, and ask her to provide an unbiased opinion on the information as you presented it.

You're Going to Be Late

Punctuality is vital in the publishing world. Deadlines are often cut very close so that publications can provide their readers with up-to-date material.

With that said, let's consider the possibility that at some point, while working on some article, you will find yourself unable to meet your deadline. Perhaps the interview central to your article will fall through at the last minute. Perhaps your research will take longer than expected. Whatever the reason, *you must notify the editor as soon as possible.* If you don't tell the editor about your problem until the day of the deadline—or worse, until after the deadline has passed—you will seal your fate at that publication.

Some editors leave a little room between the assigned deadline and the *drop-dead deadline*—the absolute last day that something can be submitted and still make it into the issue. If you are positive you can get the piece in before that date, call and ask the editor for an extension. Sometimes, though, you may not be able to meet either the assigned deadline or the drop-dead deadline. In that case, by contacting your editor well in advance, you will enable her to either find another article to fill the space or assign another writer.

Never make an editor a promise that you can't keep. You will kill your career before it even gets started.

Editors are generally understanding people who know that things can go wrong during research and writing. However, they are not forgiving to writers who let them down time and time again. One late story—with notification—is okay. Several late stories in a row, and you'll never work for that editor again.

Your Editor Requests a Rewrite

Your first assignment with a publication can involve a great deal of rewriting as you and the editor work together to make your copy match what the publication envisioned. In some cases, the editor may not have clearly communicated her vision, so that the material you turned in didn't live up to what she had pictured. In other cases, the editor may change her mind and decide that the article would work better with a different slant or with different sources. Whatever the reason for the rewrite request, be aware that this does happen and should not be a cause for alarm on your part.

An editor may communicate the need for a rewrite in different ways. She may red pen the piece with changes and send it back to you, or she may explain the need for a rewrite over the phone or in a letter. However she expresses the need for changes, be sure that you have a clear understanding of what is expected. The last thing you want to do is turn in a second draft that isn't quite "there." Ask for clarification or offer to do a rewrite of one section first so that she can review it before you tackle the rest of the article.

Above all, don't take a rewrite request, no matter how major, as a personal attack on your writing. Don't let ego get in the way of doing your job. Remember that these are just words, not oxygen, and that deleting a few here and there or changing some won't be detrimental to your health.

That's not to say that you won't ever experience pangs of disappointment when an editor returns your piece with markings on it.

Five Ways to Make Your Editor Happy

As you write your first article, your second article, and hopefully even more articles, what can you do to make sure that your work pleases your editor and inspires her to offer you further assignments? Fortunately, there are plenty of ways to make a good impression and gradually build a solid reputation. Editors are always looking for professional writers, and most complain that there are far too few of them out there. By following five simple guidelines, you will convince your editor that you are a member of this rare breed of professionals.

1. Check It Twice. Then Check It Again. Go beyond proofreading and check your piece for worn-out clichés, confusing jargon, and unnecessary words. Most professional writers review their work several times, reading it both silently and aloud, to be sure the article is as good as possible.

2. Send It in Early. Turn a quality article in *before* the deadline and you're guaranteed to make the editor very happy. Turn it in late, and both you *and* your editor will look bad.

3. Be Flexible. When the editor changes her mind about the story's slant or asks you to do a different piece from the one you proposed, be open to these opportunities. Remember that she's looking for someone who can fill the publication's needs, whatever they may be.

4. Be There in a Pinch. I once received a substantial raise from an editor simply because I was there when she needed me. Another freelancer missed a deadline, I filled in, and my editor was grateful.

5. Learn From Your Mistakes. Editors expect you to make mistakes, but they don't expect you to make the same mistakes over and over again. Once is forgivable; twice is unprofessional.

Just look at it from a business standpoint and realize that it's the editor's job to ensure that every article fits the publication's needs to a T. Learn from any mistakes and apply the knowledge you gain to the next piece.

DOING THE FOLLOW-UP

Once you've landed an assignment and completed most or all of your work on it, you may be tempted to rest on your laurels. But if you're truly interested in building a freelance writing career, your brain should already be churning with ideas for future pieces, and you should recognize that the package or e-mail you use to submit the completed article is a prime opportunity to land additional assignments with that publication. Then, once the final article is out of your hands, you'll want to tie up all the loose ends—to secure a copy of the printed article and to submit your invoice. The following steps will help ensure that all loose ends are correctly tied up and that assignments will continue to stream in long after the present article has been read and filed away.

Pitch Another Idea

One of the best ways to generate a constant stream of work is to submit a query letter for a new article whenever you hand in a completed assignment. But don't rush the writing of the new query. Devote as much time and care to the crafting of this proposal as you did to the first one.

As soon as you receive your acceptance letter or contract from the publication, it's time to start brainstorming for new article ideas. As you work with the editor, learn as much as you can about the publication so that you can refine your ideas to meet the editor's needs. Then, when you hand in your assignment, include a query letter for another article. Spend as much time on this as you did on your original query because, despite that first assignment, you are still a new writer in that editor's eyes. In fact, you will be proving your worth as a contributor throughout your work on your first few pieces.

If you have a couple of article ideas, you can pitch both in your follow-up query letter, but be careful not to give either idea short shrift. Take the time to develop the pitch, including again any relevant quotes or statistics. By now you should know if your editor prefers outlines with a query letter. Prepare any additional materials, if needed, and include them.

If you are submitting your finished assignment by e-mail, don't put your query in the body of your e-mail. Since the article itself is attached or pasted into the body of your e-mail, your query could easily get lost in the shuffle. Instead, mention in your cover e-mail that you have another idea you would like the editor to consider, and state that you will be sending it along in a subsequent e-mail or postal mail. Keep in mind that unless you have an established, long-term relationship with an editor, it is always best to send follow-up correspondence by traditional mail, whether you're pitching subsequent ideas, thanking her for the opportunity to work at the publication, or requesting copies of your article. Editors usually don't like a lot of e-mail clogging up their inbox, and may get irritated with you if you send an unsolicited message.

In your opening paragraph, thank the editor for the first assignment. (See Sample Letter for the Published Writer Submitting a Follow-Up Letter and Query on page 214 of Chapter 9.) Many publications employ several different writers, and the signature on your query might not be sufficient to remind the editor of who you are. As always, keep the letter professional, courteous, and as concise as possible. This is not the time to talk about your family or your dog's illness. In fact, it may never be. Writing professionally is a business and should always be treated as such.

What if you didn't enjoy your experience working for that publication? This does happen, and happened once to me. In this case, just send a letter thanking the editor for the assignment. It's never a good idea to send a letter of complaint. As mentioned earlier, editors move from publication to publication, and you don't want to burn any bridges. Although it might be momentarily pleasurable to vent your frustrations, consistently professional conduct will yield more lasting rewards.

Ask for a Copy of the Article

As you learned in Chapter 9, it is vital to send copies of your published works along with your queries. These clips, as they're called, will support your statement that you have been published, and will demonstrate your skill as a writer. But don't assume that the editor will remember to send you a copy of your article. By the time your piece comes out, the editor will have moved on to another issue and will be consumed by a new deadline. Make it your responsibility to get a copy of the appropriate issue of the publication.

Don't forget to secure copies of all your published articles. Although the standard number of author copies provided by a publication is two, most editors will be willing to give you more if you need them.

To make sure that you remember to secure a copy of your article, go back to the Tracking Chart you made when you sent out your queries, and add a few new columns so that you can note when you sent the article in, when your payment is expected, and when the finished article is due to appear. Then, when the article comes out, either drop a short e-mail or call the editorial assistant and politely ask her to mail you the number of author copies promised in your contract—usually two. The first copy is for your files, and should remain intact. The second copy can be cut up and pasted onto a single sheet, and then photocopied for inclusion in your queries. This will allow you to mail out several clips without making your queries too bulky. It's a good idea, if you can fit it in, to include a copy of the publication's *banner*—the title and publication date that appear on the front cover—so that subsequent editors can see when and where your piece appeared.

Try to get copies of everything you publish, whether or not you think you will use the clips in the future. As you get further along in your career, you may choose to specialize (more on that in Chapter 12). Then, if you decide that do-it-yourself articles are your niche, that short piece you wrote on "How to Fix a Leaky Faucet" should be made part of your portfolio. Also, for tax purposes, it helps to have copies of your published articles so that, if it ever becomes necessary, you can prove that you are a professional writer.

Submit Your Invoice

Always be sure to send an invoice, even if the editor assures you that she will take care of payment. Besides simply being good business practice, this is the best way to ensure that you get your check.

The timing of the invoice is important. Wait until your article is done, meaning that all revisions have been completed and the editor has indicated she is happy with the final draft. If your article doesn't get used and your contract specifies a kill fee (see more on contracts in Chapter 11), then send an invoice for that amount. However, if the editor says that she doesn't have room in this issue, but is thinking of using your piece in a future issue, hold off on the kill fee invoice for a while. You'll receive a higher fee if the piece is actually used, so it's in your best interest to wait.

Always send your invoices by regular mail, with the editor's name on both the envelope and the invoice itself. It's all too easy for this important document to get misplaced if you send it by fax or e-mail. Traditional mail also offers proof that you sent your invoice on time, and is the best assurance that it will reach the right person.

Keep track of your invoices by making a notation on your Tracking Chart in the payment column. A quick note like "Sent Invoice # 206 on 9/22" is sufficient. If payment doesn't arrive on time, send a follow-up invoice and mark it as the second billing for that article.

You don't need fancy software or specialized paper for creating invoices. If you have accounting software for your writing business, invoice templates are usually included. However, most word-processing software also has a template for creating billing documents. This is usually adequate in the beginning, when your income from writing is minimal.

Make sure you specify the title of the article, the date the final draft was approved by the editor, and the expected publication date on your invoice. This will help the editorial and accounting departments keep track of your article and payment. Don't send the invoice in the same envelope as your follow-up letter. Always keep the financial and creative issues separate.

The best way to ensure that you get paid for your writing is to submit an invoice as soon as the final draft has been accepted by your editor. Don't skip this step even if the editor has assured you that she will take care of the payment.

CONCLUSION

After reading this chapter, you should have a good grip on the basics of interviewing and article construction. As your writing evolves, more of your personal style and voice will become part of every article you write. You may also find that you enjoy writing one type of article, or that you prefer to write on one particular subject. If you plan on taking your writing career past the occasional article in a magazine, turn to Chapter 12. There, you will find information on building a career as a full-time freelance writer.

CHAPTER 11

$\mathcal{T}$HE CONTRACT

Most writers find the opening of their first acceptance letter a heady experience. In the excitement over the sale, it's common to pay little attention to the contract that accompanies the longed-for letter. But even if your intention is to sell only a couple of articles, it's important to be aware of the rights and responsibilities conferred on you by the publishing agreement. And if you've decided to build your freelance article writing into a career, it's vital that you have a complete understanding of each and every term of your contract, and that you know which terms are negotiable and which are not.

This chapter will walk you through a standard contract, clearly explaining how each of its terms affects you, the writer. It then will look briefly at the negotiation process so that you understand which terms are up for negotiation by the new writer, which terms may usually be negotiated by the better established writer, and which terms are virtually set in stone.

THE CONTRACT

Most publications prefer to work with a contract. It protects the publication and, in most cases, it protects the writer, too. That's why it's important to avoid writing articles on the basis of only an oral agreement and a handshake. Without either a contract or a letter of agreement, which some publications use in place of a contract, you will

If a publication doesn't issue a contract or state the terms in a letter of agreement, feel free to draw up a contract of your own and ask the company to sign it. If the publisher refuses to do so, this is a fair indication that he isn't interested in protecting your rights—and that it might be wiser to find another home for your article.

have no recourse if the publisher neglects to pay you or otherwise treats you unfairly. When no formal agreement exists, the writer is usually the loser.

Don't be afraid of contracts or be put off by legal terminology. Most of the contracts offered to freelance writers are relatively short, are written in relatively straightforward language, and cover the same basic issues. The inset on page 280 presents a sample publishing agreement, and the clause-by-clause breakdown provided below clearly explains all of the terms you are likely to find in the contracts you are offered.

No matter the length of the contract or the type of article you are selling, *never* sign a contract without reading it first. Always know exactly what rights you are selling and what rights you are retaining. And never throw away a contract, because some publications may reprint your work years after it first appears. This has happened to me, and only by producing the original agreement, which showed that the publication did not purchase reprint rights, was I able to stop the magazine from using my work. Also remember that once you have signed the contract, you are legally bound to abide by its terms. That's why reading and understanding every element of the publishing agreement is so important.

Identifying the Parties

Contracts usually begin by identifying the parties involved. The author of the article—you, in other words—is referred to as the "writer," and the publishing company is referred to as the "publisher." Be aware that this line of the contract should contain your legal name, not your pseudonym or nickname. Note that from this point on, the contract will always refer to you as the writer and to the publishing company as the publisher rather than using your actual names.

Article Details

Often under the heading "Article Details," the contract spells out the writer's obligations regarding the delivery of the completed manuscript to the publisher, as well as his obligations regarding rewrites. A few of the publisher's obligations are also detailed in this section of the contract.

Be sure to read this section over and verify that every detail is consistent with what was originally proposed. Sometimes you'll find that the editor or publisher has made changes in the delivery time because of a deadline change. If you don't read your contract, you might miss this fact—and miss your deadline.

Article Description

The first portion of the "Article Details" section usually describes the article under contract. Generally, it begins by stating the subject of the proposed article—"Teaching Pet Care," "Personal Essay on Time Management," or "Grisham Novel Review," for instance—and refers to the article as the "Work" or the "said Work." Although it may sound silly, it's worthwhile to check this line to confirm that it's the subject you proposed. Mix-ups do occur.

The contract further describes the article by specifying the desired length of the piece in words. Again, make sure that this is what you agreed upon with the editor. If the article has yet to be written, you may find that the publisher has specified a range, such as 800 to 1,000 words. Be sure to turn in an article that fits these parameters.

This section of the contract also may specify any "additional materials" that must be submitted with the article. These additional materials are the extras that we discussed in Chapter 10, including sidebars and art. As explained in that chapter, in some cases, the publication creates any desired sidebars in-house, and also takes care of any graphics or photographs. In other cases, though, the author is responsible for providing these materials. By reviewing this section of the publishing agreement, you'll learn what the publication expects you to supply.

Make note of the all-important "details" specified in your contract—the deadline for article submission, the desired word count, and any additional materials that must be included, for instance. Sometimes, the specifications in your contract will differ from those in your original proposal.

Submission Details

Although the word "deadline" is not used in contracts, the agreement will, of course, provide the date by which the article must be delivered to the publisher. In addition, many contracts stipulate the desired format in which your work should be submitted—text file on disk, for instance. It is important to note the publisher's requirements in this regard so that your finished piece will be submitted by the deadline in the correct form. And if your contract does not specify the desired format, it is vital to ask your editor about this requirement.

Assume that you will have to perform one rewrite of your article without receiving any additional compensation. To produce an article that match's the publication's needs, a writer often has to work with the editor to refine or reshape the piece.

Revisions and Rewrites

Proposed articles often change as the research is completed, or as the editor reads over the piece and decides that a different direction is warranted. For this reason, the standard contract generally requires the writer to provide one revision of his article. Some publications offer additional money if you have to perform a major rewrite of your piece. This fee, which can range anywhere from 5 to 20 percent of the original article fee, is rare, though, so don't expect to see a rewrite fee specified in most contracts.

The Kill Fee

Contracts sometimes specify a *kill fee*—a fee that will be paid to you if the publisher changes his mind and decides not to use your article. Not all publications have the budget for kill fees, though, so don't expect to see one in contracts from smaller magazines, newspapers, and journals, or in contracts from e-zines.

Contracts that include kill fees further stipulate the circumstances under which such a fee will be paid. In the sample contract on page 280, for instance, the kill fee will be paid if the article fails to meet the publisher's requirements, if the writer cannot provide a rewrite of the article, or if the publisher changes editorial direction and no longer needs the article. Depending on the publication, kill fees generally range from 20 to 50 percent of the original article price.

If no kill fee is specified, there may still be a "Failure to Use" clause that stipulates what will happen to the article if the publisher doesn't use it within a specified period of time. Most publications put a six-month limit on their holding time of a piece, and will return all rights and materials to you if they decide not to publish it. While this is not as good as being paid for nonuse, it should be part of the contract. Otherwise, you will be left in limbo while the publisher sits on your material. Be aware that once you've signed a contract, you can't sell the article elsewhere without permission from the original publication. That's why it's vital for the contract to cover this contingency.

Other Details

Other issues are also usually covered in the "Article Details" section of the contract. First, some publications, though not all, will pay for your telephone or travel expenses. If they do, it will be stipulated in your agreement. Just be sure to keep a copy of your telephone bill and an accounting of any other covered expenses, as you will probably have to turn them in before being reimbursed.

Second, this portion of the contract may state the number of copies of the publication that the publisher will give you when your article appears. The standard number of author copies offered is two, but you can often get as many as ten without paying for them. Be aware that not all publications formally state the number of copies you will receive, but most will be willing to add such a clause to their contract if you ask, and virtually all will supply the copies upon request with or without a mention of it in your agreement.

Finally, because more and more publications now place author photos and biographies alongside articles, this section of the contract may stipulate that the publication will use your likeness and biographical data. Sometimes, the contract will specify that the author must provide these materials. National publications, however, often send out professional photographers to get the shot they want. If the contract makes no mention of who will provide the author photo and biographical information, assume that task is yours.

Payment Details

Under a heading such as "Payment Details," the contract provides all-important information about payment. Here you will learn the fee you will be paid for your work, and the date on which your payment will be issued in relation to either the publisher's receipt of the finished article or the publication of the piece. This section also specifies when expenses will be reimbursed and when kill fees will be paid, should this become necessary. This section of the contract may also state that you should submit an invoice—a fact that should be noted immediately on your Tracking Chart. (For information on submitting an invoice, see page 268 of Chapter 10.)

Be sure to carefully review the payment details stated in your contract, making certain that the stated fee is the amount you agreed on verbally. If it isn't, immediately contact the editor and resolve the issue. Then note the stated payment dates, ideally adding them to your Tracking Chart so that you can keep an eye on things and, if necessary, take steps to jog the publisher's memory later on.

Rights

Although rights are sometimes specified in the "Payment Details" section of the contract, they are of such importance that they merit their own discussion, and sometimes merit their own section in a contract. What are we referring to when we talk about rights? According to the current Copyright Act, the author is the owner of all rights of a literary work. This means that the author controls where a work is reproduced; how—and if—it is adapted to make a book, a movie, or anything else; how it is distributed; how it is performed; and how it is displayed in a Power Point presentation, in a slide show, or through any other means. The author may grant one, several, or all of his rights to the publisher, but *such a grant must be in writing*. Thus, the contract must spell out any rights that the author hands over to the publisher.

There are generally six different contract rights with which you should have some familiarity. One or more of the following may be stipulated in your agreement.

Five basic rights are protected under copyright law: reproduction, adaptation, distribution, performance, and display.

All Rights

When a contract purchases *all rights,* the term means exactly what it says—all rights to the article are being granted, forever, to the original publisher. That publisher can reprint your article as many times as he desires, can run it on his website, can make a movie of it, can do essentially anything he wants with the piece for that one initial fee.

This is the absolute worst deal to which a writer can agree. Avoid signing away all rights unless you are 110 percent sure that you will never have a use for that piece again.

If you are contemplating giving up all rights, ask yourself these questions:

■ How long is the piece? Is it short, or is it a longer piece, parts of which might form the basis for future articles?

■ Is the payment offered worth the work you put into the article considering that this will be your only compensation for the piece?

■ Is the publication reputable? Will having your work run in it repeatedly be good for your career?

■ Are you just starting your career, or can you use an established reputation to negotiate with the editor?

If you do give all rights to the publisher, this is a perfect opportunity to negotiate a higher payment. The publisher will be making money off your article forever. Try to get as big a slice of that pie as you can. (To read more about negotiations, see page 279.)

First Serial Rights

Also called *First North American Serial Rights,* these rights are the ones most commonly granted in a contract. First serial rights grant the publisher of a periodical (a *serial*) the exclusive right to print your article first. However, the publisher is allowed to print your work only that one time, and all other rights are retained by you. Once the first serial rights expire—generally thirty to ninety days after the piece appears—the copyright will revert to you and you will be able to resell the article elsewhere.

First North American Serial Rights is usually abbreviated as FNASR. Place this acronym on your finished article when you submit it to serve as a reminder of the specific rights purchased by the publication.

One-Time Rights

These are similar to first serial rights in that the publisher is granted the right to run your article once. However, unlike first serial rights, one-time rights are not exclusive, and thus give you the right to sell the piece elsewhere at the same time.

Obviously, this is not the best arrangement for the publisher. Exclusivity is of vital importance to most publications. *Redbook* does not want to run the same story that *Glamour* is carrying. While there are times when you will be able to sell one-time rights, you'll find that first serial rights are much more common.

Second Serial Rights

Also called *reprint rights,* second serial rights give the publisher the right to sell your article to another publication after your work has appeared in the first one. Sometimes the contract specifies the time during which the first publication can sell these rights—usually ninety days. After the stated termination date, the publisher must send any prospective buyers back to you. If no termination date is specified in the agreement, the publisher can keep selling the rights forever.

When at all possible, try to retain second serial rights. This will give you the ability to resell your article as a reprint, which is one of the biggest moneymakers for most writers. (See page 189 in Chapter 8 for more information on reprints.) If the publication does demand second serial rights, read the contract carefully and be sure that the serial rights clause states a termination date. If not, the contract is nearly as bad as one that grants the publisher all rights.

Electronic Rights

Never blithely agree to a contract without first reading and understanding all of its terms. It is vital to know exactly what rights you are signing away.

Electronic rights is a blanket term that encompasses all reprints of your material in an electronic form—on websites, in online magazines, in CD-ROMs, in databases, etc. Any of these existing technologies, as well as any emerging technologies, can be lumped into this category.

This is the most hotly debated clause in writers' contracts today, and one of the most confusing issues, as well. Some publications assume that they have electronic rights even though they include no such clause in their contracts. Some writers give away their electronic rights without fully understanding the impact of doing so. As a result of the confusion, a number of authors have sued over the unauthorized use of their work, and at least one publisher, Gruner & Jahr, has conceded that it has no right to reprint author material electronically if the contract does not grant the company such rights.

What might this clause mean to you? Let's suppose that you wrote a great article on finding a preschool for your child and you signed away the electronic rights. The publisher who bought the rights could now resell your piece to a CD-ROM publisher that was designing an interactive school selection program. Or the publisher could post your piece on its website, keeping it in the publication's archives and rerunning it on the Internet whenever it so desired. And in each of these cases, the publication would pocket all of the money.

If you have any say, don't sign away the electronic rights to your article. There are few limitations on this clause right now, and with the proliferation of e-zines hungry for content, you stand to lose a good deal of income by granting these rights to someone else.

Dramatic, Television, and Motion Picture Rights

When a contract grants a publisher dramatic, television, and motion picture rights, it means that the publisher will have the right to sell the story for dramatic adaptation. Few publication contracts include this clause simply because most nonfiction articles aren't going to make great movies or plays. However, if you are writing a human interest article that tells a touching true-life story, watch your contract. If you sign away dramatic rights and Hollywood wants to turn that article into a movie-of-the-week, you may miss out on a considerable jackpot.

Other Legalities

The section of the contract sometimes termed "Other Legalities" offers both you and the publisher certain protection.

You are offered protection by the clause that promises you the final, edited version of your article for consideration "while there is still reasonable time to make changes." Should you not approve of the changes made in your article by the editor, you can take your name off the byline and still receive the agreed-upon fee. I have done this a couple of times when I disagreed with the editor's version of my work.

This section of the contract offers the publisher protection by having you, the writer, guarantee that the article is accurate to the best of your knowledge, and does not contain any material that is libelous or defamatory. (See the inset on page 247 of Chapter 10 to learn more about libel.) Most contracts will also have you warrant that you are the sole author of the work, that the work does not infringe on anyone else's copyright or trademark, and you haven't sold it to anyone else at the same time.

This section of the contract, in effect, releases the publisher of all liability in the event of a lawsuit. Although some publications will provide and fund counsel for you should the article lead to litigation, most publications now place the entire burden of truth on the writer's shoulders. This is why it is so important for you to double-check all your facts and use only the most reliable sources in your research.

THE NEGOTIATIONS

Hopefully, you now understand most or all of the terms of your contract. Should you have any questions about the meaning of any portion of the agreement, by all means speak to your editor. He should be able to explain any confusing terms.

As you learned earlier in this chapter, your contract spells out many important issues, from your fee to your ability to resell the piece at a later time. Clearly, it's a good idea to get the most favorable contract possible, as your agreement may greatly affect the income you make as a result of this and future sales of the piece. With that said, it

A Sample Contract

If you have written a relatively short article—a personal essay, for instance—you may receive a contract that is shorter than the standard agreement. Most contracts, though, roughly offer the same basic terms. So although your contract may vary from the following in setup or format, the items it covers will probably be similar to those included below.

Contributor Rights Agreement

Date: 1/1/20––

Contract between: Lisa Frost (writer) and Stay at Home Mom (publisher).

Article Details:

The writer agrees to prepare an article on the subject of Home Office Security (the "Work") with a word length of 800 words. The writer will provide the following additional materials for said Work: sidebar of resources, photo of interview subject Carol Parsons, with compensation included in total fee. The Work will be delivered to the Publisher in e-mail text file format by the following date: January 31, 20––. The writer agrees to provide one revision of the Work.

A kill fee of 20% ($120) will be paid in the event that the final Work is unacceptable to the publisher. A kill fee will be paid under the following circumstances only: 1) The Work does not meet the requirements the publisher had in mind 2) The writer refuses to provide a rewrite of the Work 3) The publisher changes editorial direction and no longer needs the Work.

The publisher agrees to reimburse the writer for the following expenses with documentation: telephone calls.

Should a major rewrite be requested, the writer will receive, in addition to regular fee, the following compensation: $50.

Finally, the writer will be provided 3 (three) copies of the publication in which his/her Work appears.

Payment Details:

The publisher agrees to pay the writer $600 within 30 days of receipt of said Work, given that all agreed-upon requirements have been met. This fee purchases First North American Serial rights only. All other rights reserved by the writer. The publisher also agrees to reimburse the agreed-upon expenses within 30 days of submission of receipts. Kill fees will be paid within 30 days of notification, should this be necessary.

Other Legalities:

The publisher agrees to provide the writer the final, edited version for consideration while there is still reasonable time to make changes. The writer reserves the right to withdraw her name from the Work without affecting payment should a disagreement about the final draft occur.

The writer guarantees that the Work is accurate to the best of her knowledge and does not contain any material that could be construed as libelous or defamatory. In return, the publisher agrees to provide and fund counsel to the writer should any litigation result from above mentioned article.

Lisa Frost	*December 1, 20––*
Writer	Date
Karen Stone	November 15, 20––
Publisher	Date

should be recognized that if you're a *new* writer, you face a dilemma. On one hand, you're thrilled to sell your article and want to celebrate your sale and sign your contract no matter *what* it stipulates. On the other hand, you've worked hard to write your article and want to get the terms that you feel you deserve. What to do?

In the beginning, you may not be able to negotiate better terms. And that's fine. As a new writer, your primary goal is to gain experience and exposure. It isn't necessarily a bad thing to occasionally give up all rights or accept a little less money if you think that the sale will lead to bigger and better things down the road. But keep in mind that editors do expect some negotiation for certain terms. Most likely, you will neither surprise nor anger your editor by asking for a few changes. So even if you don't feel comfortable negotiating now, consider asking for better terms as your experience grows and your reputation builds. The following discussions will help you determine which terms are negotiable and worth fighting for, and which usually cannot be altered.

What's Negotiable

As mentioned above, you may not want to negotiate for better terms on your very first article. But as you get more assignments—and, thus, more bargaining power—you'll want to negotiate for the kinds of terms that will have the greatest impact on your income and your career.

At the start of your career, don't expect to have the bargaining power of an established writer. As your experience grows, you will be in a better position to negotiate for better contract terms.

The best place to start negotiating is with the rights clause. (See pages 276 to 279 for a brief explanation of each kind of rights.) As discussed earlier in the chapter, if at all possible, you should avoid granting the publisher all rights to your work. Especially if the article is a long one—say, 3,000 words—you will want to be able to use some of that work in other publications by breaking the article into smaller ones or re-using some of the research in a different piece. By giving away all rights, you will limit your own use of a piece that represents a good deal of work, not to mention a good many possible sales.

If your contract grants the publication all rights, chances are that your editor won't change the terms to grant one-time rights—although that certainly would be nice. However, you *can* ask the editor to insert the word "print" before the rights clause. In other words, instead of saying, "This fee purchases all rights," the contract would state, "This fee purchases all print rights." By limiting the publisher's rights to printed copies of your work, the wording would make it necessary for the publisher to offer a new contract if he wanted to use your article on the magazine's website, for instance. You would also then be free to sell the article to another publisher for website use only. This could provide you with a bit more income from that one piece. But even if your editor refuses to make this or any other change, be aware that most publications do become more willing to negotiate as time goes on and they become more familiar with you and your work. So don't be afraid to keep asking for better rights clauses. If nothing else, you may plant the seeds for change.

Whatever contract term you want changed, don't be afraid to ask. You'll never know if you can get a better contract deal unless you request the changes you want.

Another term that is open to negotiation is the one that stipulates the payment rate. Early in your career, you won't have the leverage needed to get additional money for your work. But this will change as the months pass. After working with the editors of two different publications for more than a year, I wrote a letter to each one explaining why I felt that I merited higher fees. For one of the magazines, for instance, I had landed several cover interviews with celebrities, including Lillian Vernon, Bob Vila, and Dave Thomas. In both cases, the editors agreed that my experience, work, and skills justified a boost in pay, and the subsequent contracts from both showed 25- to 30-percent higher pay rates.

In addition to negotiating an overall fee, consider asking for additional payments for extras like sidebars or photos. This material is sometimes provided by the publication's in-house staff. However, editors know that it can be less expensive to pay a freelancer a flat fee for these extras than it is to pay a salaried staffer. So don't hesitate to bargain for this additional amount if you can supply what is needed.

While most small and medium-sized publications will not pay a writer's traveling expenses, virtually all are willing to cover phone costs. So if you are writing a national piece that will require numerous interviews, be sure to ask for the payment of telephone expenses. Keep in mind, though, that the publication will require documentation—a copy of your phone bill, in other words.

Yet another term that you might want to negotiate is the kill fee. As explained earlier in the chapter, this is the fee that will be paid to you for a finished article that is "killed"—that is, not used. Circumstances do arise that push articles out of the loop, never to be used again, particularly if the writer is working on trendy pieces or current events articles. In addition, it is now becoming more common for magazines to overassign each issue in an attempt to have more material than they need. Editors do so with the full intent of killing two or three pieces a month. Therefore, although you might spend many hours researching and writing a project, the chance that your article will fail to get into print has increased over the last few years.

If you think you could easily resell the article elsewhere, then agreeing to the stated kill fee might be fine. If, however, the piece you are writing will work only at this one publication, try to negotiate full payment whether the article is used or not.

The number of author copies you receive is another area that can be negotiated. In fact, because copies of the publication cost the publisher very little, this is an especially easy item to negotiate even if you're a new writer. So if you want copies to hand out at the next family gathering, go ahead and ask for them.

As demonstrated by my story on page 282, in order to successfully negotiate a contract with a publisher, you do need to support your request. If you can demonstrate your value or the value of the proposed article, your editor will be more willing to give you what you want. If necessary, put your requests in writing so that your editor can discuss these negotiations with other members of the editorial staff or run them straight through to the publisher.

What's Not Negotiable

While most editors expect some negotiation of contract terms, they don't expect an all-out war. And certain contract items are usually not open for negotiation.

Liability and litigation clauses are pretty much standard from contract to contract, and are not changed for any writer, regardless of his background or experience. You will not be able to eliminate this clause from your contract.

The revisions clause is another portion of your contract that you won't be able to eliminate. Most editors won't make you spend months of your life revising an article. They won't have the time to oversee such a lengthy revision, and won't want you to waste your efforts on a piece that may never be right. However, just as you would expect to revamp a project if your boss was unhappy with the final results, you should expect to complete at least one revision on each article, and possibly two. This is considered standard procedure.

After you've been with a publication for a while, you can probably negotiate and change "payment on publication" to "payment on acceptance," meaning that you will get paid sooner for your work.

When You Need Legal Assistance

If you're like most freelance writers, you will be able to evaluate, negotiate, and meet the terms of most of the contracts you receive *without* legal assistance. Sometimes, though, it is necessary to call in a lawyer or a writers' group either to negotiate a better publishing agreement or to make sure that the terms of your contract are honored.

The National Writers Union website offers a listing of typical grievances that they have arbitrated for their members. These include nonpayment for work, negative gossip about a writer's work, and foreign sales being made without the author's knowledge. But the issues that may require legal assistance are wide ranging. During my own career, I once asked a lawyer for help in changing a contract clause that I found completely unacceptable. Still other times, I contacted attorneys when my work was stolen and reprinted by other publications. In all cases, just the word "attorney" was enough to make the publisher back down.

Whenever possible, you should, of course, attempt to solve any contract problems through discussions with your editor. However, if your requests fall on deaf ears, and if the issue is important enough to merit legal advice—if, for instance, you stand to lose a large fee or an important credit—do not hesitate to contact an attorney. Be aware, though, that only a lawyer who is well versed in publishing issues is likely to be of help to you. To find someone with the necessary expertise, contact either the National Writers Union (see page 321 of the Resource Directory) or your local journalism school for recommendations.

While calling in a lawyer is a last resort, if you choose this option, be prepared to stick to your guns and to walk away from a deal, if necessary. Not every publisher is reputable, not every contract is fair. By standing up for your rights and fighting for a just agreement, you will help not only your own career, but also the careers of all the writers who follow.

Publishers are unlikely to change a check run date to accommodate a new writer. For most writers, the payment date stipulated in the contract is virtually set in stone. However, an established freelancer who has been with the magazine for some time may be able to have his contract changed from "payment on publication" to "payment on acceptance." This means that the payment will be sent out earlier—possibly months earlier.

When to Withdraw

Sometimes the terms of a contract are terrible. You may be asked to write 4,000 words, relinquish all rights, and settle for less than a hundred dollars for your work. You may be asked to let the editor change your work in any way he wishes, without your having a chance to review the final version of the article. Or you may be asked to turn in the piece on speculation, with no guarantee of payment and no stated date by which the publication must either buy the piece or return it to you. I've even seen contracts for online sites that promise the writers payment only if they help direct enough traffic to the page to generate some advertising revenue—a condition that leaves payment, if any, vague and undefined. If this is the case, and if the publication is completely unwilling to negotiate, then you have a choice to make. You can accept the offer, or you can reject the contract and try to find another outlet for your piece.

This decision is entirely up to each individual writer, and must be made on a case-by-case basis. There is no checklist that can help you decide when you should take your writing elsewhere. A smart strategy is to weigh the amount of work you will be putting into the piece against the contract you've been handed. I once signed away all rights to a piece that I knew I'd never use again, and that took me perhaps twenty minutes to write. To me, my work was worth the $75 fee and the credit that was given to me by the magazine. At other times, though, I have stood my ground on the rights issue because I knew I could sell that piece again.

If you are just starting out, you won't have much bargaining power, and should weigh a number of factors before you decide to accept or reject a contract. Don't feel that you have to walk away from a deal because it fails to offer *everything* you want. Rather, judge if the publication offers *anything* that can be of use to you—clips, a prestigious byline, useful connections, or increased credibility, for instance— and determine if the deal would benefit you in the long run. Once you have a few clips under your belt or have gained more experience, you'll be able to request—and receive—the contracts you deserve.

If you decide to withdraw from a contract, be sure to do so in a professional manner. Editors move from publication to publication, and talk to one another about how particular writers behave. You don't want to leave a bad impression of yourself—even if the publication itself is behaving less than professionally. Once your decision has been made, let the editor know through either a letter or a phone call. Don't dawdle, because the editor needs time to fill the slot left by your withdrawal. As with any business dealing, if you behave

If it ever becomes necessary to withdraw from a contract, be sure to do so in a professional manner, and to advise the publication of your decision as soon as possible.

courteously and professionally, you will build a good reputation in the field, something money can't buy.

CONCLUSION

Your contract details your rights and responsibilities as the author of your article, and the publication's rights and responsibilities as the publisher of your work. If you've taken the time to read this chapter, you've discovered that in the vast majority of cases, you won't need an attorney to understand your contract or to negotiate better terms. However, if you intend to pursue a career in writing, you *will* need to carefully read each and every contract you sign, and to understand exactly what terms can (and should) be changed. By developing an understanding of this important area of the business, you can, over time, become your own best negotiator.

CHAPTER 12

BUILDING YOUR CAREER

If you have reached this chapter, you've probably had a few articles published. Perhaps you're an experienced freelancer who has been relatively successful over the last few years. You might be thinking of making the leap into full-time work, or you might want to move up to bigger-paying markets.

This chapter will help you decide how you will build your career in writing. It will consider the option of working full-time, and it will help you determine if you should specialize in one area or cover a broad range of categories. Plus, it will review the many other ways in which you can put your writing ability to use in order to maintain a steady income and gain valuable experience.

SHOULD YOU WRITE FULL-TIME?

Making the leap from part-time to full-time writer can be scary. Most full-time writers work out of their home office and put in more hours than a nine-to-five employee. Being a home worker requires a great deal of initiative and determination. While it looks wonderful from the outside, this kind of life can be lonely and uncertain. But for those who love writing and are willing to persevere, the rewards can be great.

Is This the Right Work for You?

Several factors should go into your decision to work full-time from home. The first of these have to do with your ability to work on your

Before making the decision to quit your regular job, remember that writing income is very unpredictable.

own and your desire to work as a writer. In other words, you must consider whether this is really the right type of work and the right type of work environment for you.

Be honest with yourself: Are you your own best boss? If left alone, few people would be motivated to go to the office and work a full day. The temptation to ignore work is doubled at home, where there are a hundred other things vying for your attention—the television, the laundry, the refrigerator, the yard work. There are days when it takes a great deal of effort to get into the office and be productive.

When you are working for yourself, you rarely get time off, even though it seems as if the opposite would be true. If your income is necessary to pay the bills, you work harder to maintain that level, maybe even to increase it a bit. Payment from writing work fluctuates from month to month. If one big article is delayed for three months, it can make a huge dent in your income level. You then end up working harder to fill the gap left by that one piece.

I rarely take a weekend off, and hardly ever take a vacation without my laptop. Part of what motivates me is a real economic need for my income. However, the primary force that drives me into my office every day and keeps me there long after everyone else has gone to bed is the love of working with words. If I didn't love this job, I couldn't do it. Period. So ask yourself if you truly love writing—if you love it more than any other job you could do. If you don't love what you do, it will be a million times harder to stay motivated during the lean times, to stay focused when the work is piled higher than you, and to keep yourself in that chair day after day. It always has to come back to a passion for taking words and crafting them into pieces that people will remember.

Have I scared you? I hope not—and yet, I hope I have. Writing full-time is not a business for the meek. All the rejection you encountered when this was a part-time endeavor becomes multiplied. The worry about having enough work to pay the bills is quadrupled. But if you love what you do, the reward is a hundredfold.

Can You Make It Financially?

To be a full-time professional writer, you have to love what you do. There will be days when it's hard to get one word out. If you don't love your job, it will make that first word a thousand times harder to find.

Next, look hard at your household's financial picture. If you are scraping by from month to month, and your current income is necessary to put food on the table, quitting your job to try full-time freelance writ-

Is a Freelance Career Right for You?

If you're having trouble figuring out how—and if—you want to develop your freelance writing career, take this quick quiz. The following analysis can help you understand your own strengths and weaknesses and make the best decisions for your specific situation. If you discover that you are weak in one area—organization, for instance—you can find someone to help you set up your office and files. If you recognize that you aren't knowledgeable about the business aspects of self-employment, you can contact organizations that will provide you with the guidance you need. And if you realize that a steady paycheck is more appealing than the prospect of self-employment, you can keep your regular job and enjoy writing as a part-time pursuit. To learn more, just ask yourself the following questions:

☐ What are my strengths and weaknesses?

☐ Am I organized? If not, can I change the way I do things so my work is better kept on track?

☐ Am I a procrastinator? If so, can I teach myself some anti-procrastination techniques?

☐ Is there one area in which I have a special interest, or am I happier writing about a variety of topics?

☐ Do I have the personality to write investigative journalism pieces, personal essays, think pieces, research articles, or lighter features?

☐ Am I willing to try my hand at a number of different article genres until I find what works best for me?

☐ Do I see writing as a regular part of my life, or just as a temporary endeavor?

☐ Could I write, and market myself as a writer, on a full-time basis?

☐ Do I know enough to run my own business? If not, am I willing to invest the time and effort to learn about running a business?

☐ Am I more comfortable with the regular paychecks, health insurance, pension plan, paid vacations, and other benefits that come with a regular job? Would I be better off trying my hand as a staff writer or making my writing a part-time enterprise?

☐ Do I have the courage to continually put my articles in the mail—to face the inevitable criticisms and rejections, as well as the challenges that come with acceptance?

☐ Do I have the persistence, dedication, and drive needed to make my dream come true?

ing simply isn't a good idea, and won't be a good idea until you have a lot of work lined up. There will be months—maybe a few, maybe many—when work is scarce or when paychecks are delayed for one reason or another. If you are to get through those tough times, you will need to have a backup plan as well as savings from which you can draw.

If you are serious about establishing yourself as a full-time writer, you must create a business card for yourself.

Keep it simple, but make sure that it includes all your contact information. You can add "Writer" to the title area, and you can even give your business a name, if you so desire. Above all, don't clutter the card up or make it look "cute" or otherwise unprofessional. This card is the last impression someone will have of you, and you want it to be a positive one.

Now, be realistic about how much work you can handle in a month. It's fine to look through *Writer's Market* and see the listings for 3,000-word articles that pay a dollar a word. You might think that all you need do is land two or three of these a month, and you'll be set. Unfortunately, few professional writers land that many big assignments. Just as important, if you were able to get these assignments, it is unlikely that you could *handle* two or three of them a month. A national assignment of that magnitude requires a great deal of time and effort to assemble.

For the sake of argument, let's say that you were lucky enough to land a big job. Remember that the bigger the article and the better-paying the market, the more work the editor expects you to put into the story. A 3,000-word article might require ten interviews and several resource sidebars. It might cover a touchy issue that a good many sources won't want to discuss with you. Either way, it probably wouldn't be a piece of cake, and would require a significant investment of your time—perhaps as much as six weeks—leaving you few hours to work on other assignments. So in that six-week period, you would earn only about $3,000. What would a year of such assignments amount to?

Now let's consider another seemingly plummy assignment. From the outside, you may think it would be a dream to work as a travel writer for *Travel & Leisure,* which pays about $5,000 for a feature article. What a blast—to get $5,000 per feature article for writing about your adventures around the world! But try to be realistic about this picture, too. Could you really up and leave your home, your family, and your life for weeks at a time? Would you enjoy vacations that are really working trips, not times to lie on the beach and drink margaritas? A good travel writer sees a destination through different eyes from those of the typical vacationer.

To determine if writing full-time is economically feasible for you, sit down and take a good look at your expenses. What kind of income must you bring in to cover all those bills, and still have money left over for savings? Now add maybe 30 to 40 percent. Why? If you work for yourself, you'll also be in charge of buying your own supplies, paying your own taxes, and covering your own health insurance. You may be lucky enough to have a spouse who provides benefits for the family. However, you should still set aside money for your own retirement, life insurance, and disability insurance.

I'm not trying to discourage you from becoming a full-time writer. I'm just trying to give you a true picture of what you can expect on the financial front. What works when you are part-time, and have a dependable income from another job, may not be as profitable when you are a full-time writer. A two-week delay in a check can be a big issue when writing is your only source of income. The phone company, unfortunately, doesn't ascribe to publishing's cycle of payment.

Are You Ready to Run Your Own Business?

It comes as a shock to some writers that working as a full-time free-lancer is about more than doing the work and trying to cover normal living expenses. It also involves running a business.

For many writers, the most challenging aspect of being on their own is the number of roles they must play. As a sole proprietor, you will have to do all your own invoicing and your own bookkeeping—unless you have a fortune to spend on an accountant who will do this for you. You'll also be in charge of doing your own filing, organizing, and cleaning. If you're like most writers, these are the chores you hate the most. Writers tend to be creative people who are uninterested in the minutiae of running a business. The writing is the fun part. Billing and taxes are a necessary evil.

When you run your own business, you also have to make careful selections of office supplies and equipment. While it might be tempting to run out and buy the fastest PC on the market, or to get that snazzy copy machine you saw at the office supply store, remind yourself that you won't need all that at the outset. Your income will be sporadic, work will come and go in waves, and high monthly expenditures for top-of-the-line office equipment will make it difficult if not impossible for you to make ends meet. Run your writing business like a business. Justify every expense before you make a purchase. Plan for the quarter, the year, the next five years. Running a business by the seat of your pants is not a good way to make money.

If you aren't comfortable with certain aspects of running your own business, you'll be glad to know that help is available. To start, consider contacting the United States Small Business Administration (SBA). One of the SBA's programs, SCORE, pairs retired entrepreneurs with those new to self-employment. This mentoring can be invaluable as you face the hurdles of being on your own. The SBA also

Don't overlook the importance of health insurance. Check with the Small Business Administration for information on programs that fit writers' budgets. In addition, contact those writers' organizations that offer group health insurance and disability insurance. (See the "Groups and Organizations" listings in the Resource Directory, beginning on page 319.)

Consult with an accountant to find out how much you should reserve throughout the year for taxes.

has a great deal of information on successfully operating a home business, and can point you in the right direction regarding any legal or financial requirements in your town.

Additional information about running a business can be found on the shelves of your local library and bookstore. *How to Start a Home-Based Writing Business* by Lucy V. Parker and Karen Ivory, for instance, covers all the basics of working at home—and everything is specifically geared for the writer. (See the Resource Directory on page 325 for further information.)

Finally, recognize that you probably have experts all around you. Your accountant can tell you much of what you need to know. A friend who has been down the home business route can offer advice from the trenches. And working writers in a local or online writers' group can answer many of your questions about everything from buying computer software to keeping records for your yearly taxes.

When Part-Time Is the Best Choice

Sometimes, as much as you might wish it were otherwise, writing full-time simply isn't the best option. Whether you need the regular income and benefits provided by a conventional job, or you have family obligations that make full-time writing an impossibility, there are many cases in which writing must be slotted in on a part-time basis.

If you can pursue your writing only part-time, you will have to be extra vigilant about making the time you need to research and write your queries and articles. You'll also have to work harder at motivating yourself, particularly if your regular job is physically draining. Make the most of the time you do have. Take work on the train, jot down notes during lunch breaks, and invest in a laptop or portable word processor so you can work while you are waiting for an appointment.

Scheduling interviews with sources can be especially difficult when you have a full-time job, as most potential interviewees will be working during the times that you are busy with your own job. Explain to your interview subjects that you work full-time, and ask if you can interview them early in the morning or at the end of the day. Another option is to conduct your interviews by e-mail or fax.

Not every freelance writer wants or can afford to work on her writing full-time. If you've chosen to make writing a part-time career

It takes a special kind of person to be a full-time at-home worker. Know yourself before making the leap into a full-time freelance career.

only, that's fine. It works for a lot of people. But if you want that career to flourish, realize that you may have to be a bit more imaginative and resourceful than the person who writes on a full-time basis.

SHOULD YOU SPECIALIZE?

One of the best ways to build a career in writing is to specialize in a single area. Sometimes a writer deliberately chooses an area of specialization, and sometimes this happens naturally as a writer gravitates toward an area that is especially interesting to her or that offers her a great deal of work. As my career progressed, for instance, I found that there was more demand for my writing in business magazines and trade journals. And by specializing in this area, I gained the experience I needed to move into copywriting, which now provides an additional source of income. In fact, specialization often opens many doors. After establishing themselves as experts in their fields, some writers have been offered book contracts and speaking engagements, and some have been asked to write syndicated newspaper columns. The benefits of choosing a specialty are many.

Specialization—a focus on a single type of article or a specific subject—can be a great means of building a career in writing. Just be sure that you enjoy the area you've chosen, and that the market's demand for articles on this topic can sustain you for years to come.

If you decide to specialize in a particular area, be sure that both the market's demand for articles on that subject and your own interest in the topic are sufficient to sustain you for years to come. Are there a number of publications covering that area? Is there a continued interest in the subject? While you might enjoy writing about feng shui, for instance, limiting yourself to a narrow topic such as this can restrict your marketability. So although you can certainly write the occasional article on feng shui, try to write on a range of decorating topics, as this is more likely to keep you busy. Also be sure that you enjoy the area you've chosen. If you get stuck in a slot that doesn't really interest you, it will make it all the more difficult to walk into your office every day.

Once you've chosen a specialty, start building up your clips by working for smaller publications. This will give you a file of work to show editors at higher-level markets so that you can gradually move up the ladder, getting bigger and better assignments.

Recognize that being a specialist in one area requires you to constantly keep abreast of that topic. Find out who the experts are and keep track of new research and trends. Subscribe to appropriate newsletters and magazines; scan the newspaper for information; and

Ten Freelancing Do's

If you want to be a successful full-time freelance writer, there are a number of things you can do to help your business thrive. Just as you prepared yourself for the submission process in Chapter 1, you'll now want to set yourself up for a rewarding full-time career. The following guidelines should help:

1. Be Sure You Have the Proper Office Equipment. While you don't need a lot of equipment to run your business, it is important to have a few basics. A good computer is a must. Although it doesn't have to be the fastest on the market, it should be able to handle current word processing programs. Couple this with full-time Internet access to help you in your research, and you'll have most of the technology in place. You'll definitely need a printer and a fax/modem in your computer. Another option is a multifunction printer, which can serve as a copier, scanner, fax, and printer. This device can be very useful and more cost-effective than buying those machines separately. And, of course, you'll need a telephone.

2. Build Up Your Resource Library. Writers interested in publishing only an occasional article can easily use library copies of resource books like *Writer's Market*. But once you decide to establish a career, you will need your own current copy of *Writer's Market* and, if you want to publish online, a book such as *Online Markets*

for Writers, as well. This is also a good time to consider purchasing the Internet version of *Writer's Market* because it will give you continuous updates on the changing world of article publishing. And don't overlook the need for a good dictionary and thesaurus—two books that are musts for every writer.

3. Subscribe to Writers' Magazines. Writers' magazines not only help keep you current in your industry, but also are chock full of information on writing techniques. The best ones are those that deal almost exclusively with freelancing: *Writer's Digest* and *ByLine*. (See Chapter 4 for more information.) Also consider signing up for online writers' e-zines like *Writing for Dollars, The Writing Parent,* and *The Write Moves.*

4. Treat Writing as a Full-Time Job. Having a successful freelance business means working regular hours every day. Create a To Do list and prioritize your activities, just as you would at any job. While this doesn't mean that you can't take an afternoon off and go to the mall, you

attend meetings, conventions, trade shows, or information sessions for people in that field. If you can show an editor that you are remaining current, you'll have a much better shot of convincing her to give you a chance. Editors don't want their publication to be the *last* to run vital information.

What if you find that your specialty is becoming more of a hindrance than a benefit? If you aren't being offered enough work in your should expect to invest as much time as you would if you worked for someone else—and sometimes more.

5. Never Forget That This Is a Business. Maintain good mileage records and keep all receipts from other business expenses. The IRS needs proof of your deductions, and it's up to you to provide the required receipts. Also set up files for your rejections, queries, ideas, and clips. As your business grows, so will the piles of paper that fill your office. Without a filing system, you'll be unable to find your desk, much less a copy of the interview you conducted last week.

6. Every Week, Try to Send Out at Least Three Queries. I keep between thirty and forty queries in circulation at any given time. Most writers who work full-time have a 40-percent sale rate—meaning that 40 percent of their queries result in sales—and maintain these same submission numbers to ensure a constant flow of work.

7. Turn Rejections Into New Queries— Immediately. When a rejection comes in, try to turn around the same idea or article that very day. A query that sits on your desk isn't making any money. You've already invested a great deal

of time in the piece. Now take a few minutes to tune it up and send it to a new home.

8. Make Use of Reprints. As mentioned earlier in the book, reprints are great income generators. For literally a few minutes of time, you can make as much as several hundred dollars—all from an article that has already been researched and written. Keep an eye on reprint markets so that you'll be ready to resell as soon as an article's copyright reverts to you. (See Chapter 8 for more about reprints.)

9. Turn in Pristine Work *on Time*. Nothing beats a good reputation. If your work is consistently good, editors will gladly reward you with continued assignments. You may even be made a contributing writer—a position that will keep a steady stream of income flowing your way.

10. Join Professional Organizations. Membership in professional organizations will not only give you a chance to commiserate with other writers, but also provide a great opportunity to network—which, of course, can help you find work. Fortunately, a wide variety of organizations are available for writers of all types. See the "Groups and Organizations" listing in the Resource Directory.

area, try branching out into related subjects. If you specialize in business financing, for instance, try to sell articles on consumer finances. Or, if you prefer, add a completely new and different area of expertise. Just be aware that you may need to start at the bottom again, particularly if you are moving into an area that is completely dissimilar to your first one. A specialist in retirement planning might have to prove her skill before landing a big assignment with a parenting magazine.

To be a specialist in one area, you must immerse yourself in that field. Read the journals, watch the documentaries, talk to the experts—do whatever you have to do to stay current.

Usually, though, a writer's work speaks for itself. Editors look for writers who demonstrate they can take an assignment, no matter what the topic; find comprehensive research; interview subjects; and write interesting, informative articles. If your clips are good, you should have little trouble convincing an editor to give you a shot in a new area.

Is specialization a requirement for success? Being a generalist has its benefits, too. By having the ability to write about a wide variety of topics, you are economy-proofing your business. If interest in technology articles wanes, you can concentrate more efforts in the home decorating area. General writers fare especially well at newspapers, which have a high demand for all kinds of articles, and at e-zines, which often have very wide focuses.

Some writers enjoy variety, and find it helps them maintain enthusiasm for their work. Although my main concentration is in business issues, I still write personal essays and parenting articles from time to time. It's fun to do something different once in a while.

MOVING UP THE LADDER

As your career progresses, you're probably going to want to break into bigger, better-paying publications. For some writers, this next step up can be frustrating. You may feel as if you're starting all over again—and in many ways, you are. However, by evaluating what you've been doing, you can make the changes necessary to get to the next level. It will take some work—and some honest self-evaluation—but the rewards can be great.

Review Your Query Packages

Perhaps you have enjoyed success at smaller publications, and have even received encouraging personal notes from editors at the larger markets. But you haven't made any sales at the higher-level publications. If this is your situation, the reason for your dilemma might be found in your queries. While your query packages may have worked well with small and even medium-sized markets, remember that top publications demand more from their writers—at all stages of the process. Your letters may need to be stronger, more fleshed out, and a clearer indication of the job you would do on the article itself. Your clips may need to be more relevant or impressive.

Begin your query analysis by studying your chosen markets, just as you did in Chapters 4 and 5. As before, visit the library and take out the last six months of issues of your target publications. But this time, look for the elements that set your queries apart from the printed material. Is the tone of your letters different from that of the articles? Are your clips written in a dissimilar style? Are your proposed ideas just a little off the mark from the topics that made it into print? Be honest. And if you're stumped, call in a friend—preferably a writer—to help you with this step.

Once you've finished comparing the queries to the publications, take another look at the letters themselves. Are your queries sufficiently developed? A top publication usually wants additional detail in the form of either an outline or a more complete letter that thoroughly explains your approach. Now, consider the experts you've mentioned in your letter and/or outline. Do they have sufficient credentials and recognition to merit a national quote? If not, consider contacting sources who would interest a broader audience.

If your clips aren't quite on a par with the material in the publication, this, too, might be an obstacle in your path. Consider either sending new clips, or, if you don't have anything stronger, spending more time with mid-sized publications to build your clips file. All you need are a few good assignments that are in keeping with the material in the top markets.

After you have modified your query package as needed, try persisting at one magazine at a time. Editors appreciate writers who continue to send in good ideas and increasingly better clips. Eventually, you will be rewarded with a sale. It may not be the big one you dreamed of, but even a small assignment can allow you to break into a big market and make a name for yourself.

Review Your Writing

Editors at top publications want writers who can handle all aspects of a complicated assignment, which is why they look for experienced freelancers with strong writing and research abilities. What is acceptable at smaller publications might not be what is required at a top magazine or newspaper.

Make an effort to be as unbiased as possible when trying to determine how your writing compares with material in the upper-level publications. Remember that the writers of these articles worked their way up, too, honing their skills along the way. It might be time to work on your own writing skills and learn some of the techniques the pros use to give their writing more life and make every word count.

If you suspect that your writing skills could benefit from further development, return to Chapter 7, and consider the suggestions for books, courses, workshops, and conferences. Many of these resources are designed to help intermediate and advanced writers reach the next level with their craft. Don't view this as starting over; rather, see it as refining your talent to meet market demands. I don't know of a single writer, myself included, who doesn't continue to attend classes for the purpose of enhancing her skills.

If you need help with article structure, read through Chapter 10, which walks you through the format of a typical article. This will be especially helpful if you are most experienced at writing essays and fillers, and now want to branch out into full-length research pieces.

New techniques and approaches can help even the best writer improve her skills. If nothing else, further education in your craft will give you the confidence you need to succeed.

Go in at the Bottom

To get into the upper-level publications, consider starting at the bottom with fillers and short articles. One fabulous short article can very quickly lead to longer assignments.

The best way to gain entry to a large publication is to start small with a short filler piece. Sometimes you need to prove yourself with a few great sentences before you're allowed to tackle the big story. Write up a few short articles specifically for the publications that hold the most appeal for you, and send them out on a regular basis. Don't stuff five ideas into one envelope and send it to the editor. Try one at a time, spaced a few days or a couple of weeks apart, so that each proposal gets the individual attention it deserves.

Don't feel you are wasting the skills you have accumulated thus far. Small pieces can pay well and are easy to fit into your schedule. And don't make the mistake of thinking you can dash off a 200-word filler on finding a good plumber in ten minutes. If you are aiming high—and even if you aren't—it's vital to craft each piece with care.

If you are a specialist in one area who is branching out into a completely unrelated type of writing, you'll need to work your way up again through these short articles. It won't take long, because excellent writing skills are valued in this industry. Editors know that a good writer will not only make their lives easier but also enhance the value of their publications. Thus, they are always willing to award assignments to writers who consistently demonstrate their skill and professionalism.

Overcome Your Fears

Fear is a real part of most writers' lives, and is sometimes the biggest barrier to success. You could undermine yourself without even realizing you are doing so simply because you are afraid of failure. You might worry that your skills haven't been sufficiently developed, that you won't be able to handle a huge assignment, that the pressure of "performing" for a big magazine will be too great. Why, you think, should you even *attempt* to reach those higher-level markets? Stop. All you are doing is making it harder on yourself.

My advice? Move beyond where you are today by ignoring your own self-doubt and concentrating on your achievements thus far. This will give you the confidence you need to reach just a little bit further next time—to accept an assignment that may seem just out of reach. This is similar to the runner who feels she has reached the end of her endurance level, yet takes twenty more steps before finally stopping. The next day, she runs forty more steps, then one hundred, until she reaches her goal.

Don't let fear put a roadblock in your path. All writers experience insecurity at some point in their careers. The key to success is to move ahead *despite* any fear of failure.

When I worked on the staff of a daily newspaper and decided to leave the paper to pursue a freelance career, my path was far from smooth. It had been so long since I'd had to approach an editor or pitch a story idea, I was pretty sure I'd forgotten how it was done. It took time, but I ultimately carved out a business by following the steps discussed in this chapter. And I never looked back. I now write the stories I want to write, when I want to write them. You can do this, too. If you are happy with your current writing career, that's great. By all means, stay there as long as you are happy. But if you're dreaming of more, don't hold yourself back. Believe in yourself and the rest will follow.

OTHER OPTIONS

Writing articles is a great job, but the pay is sporadic at best. Most freelancers who work full-time find that in any given year, they have many lean months, a few good months, and one or two fabulous months. This can make budgeting a headache.

Fortunately, there are a number of other ways in which you can put your writing abilities to use, and thereby maintain a steady income. As an added bonus, through your work in other arenas, you can often build up an area of specialization and enhance your researching and writing skills as well.

Writing Books

Not all article ideas make great books. Consider both the anticipated audience and the competition before choosing your topic.

If you already have an area of specialty and are regarded as an expert in your field, consider writing books as a way to increase your credibility and bank account. But be forewarned: Getting a book into print is just as hard, if not harder, than getting articles into publication. The competition is strong. Market needs fluctuate, influenced by different trends. Publishers consolidate, budgets change, and demand for certain subject areas ebbs and flows.

However, if you have published several articles about your particular topic, you have a great advantage. You can clearly show the publishing house that there is a market for the information you are writing and that you are an accomplished and—most important—a *publishable* writer. In fact, when composing your book proposal, be sure to include information about the articles you have written, along with where they have appeared, the circulation of those publications, and any reader or editor response you received. This will greatly increase the effectiveness of your query.

Writing books can be lucrative, although the wait between checks can be excruciating. Most publishers pay royalties only twice a year. (If you thought that budgeting on article income was difficult, imagine dealing with two paychecks a year!) However, while you're waiting for those checks to arrive, your books will provide you with a great deal of exposure both within your area of specialization and within the writing community, enhancing your image as an expert and as a writer.

Before you send a proposal out to a publisher, be sure to do some research to determine if your topic has enough meat to be a book. Remember that magazine articles are about narrow ideas, while books cover broader ideas. Therefore, while "Shortcuts to Great Sauces" might make a great article, it might not make much of a book— although *Shortcuts to Great Meals* could certainly work. When considering a topic, ask yourself the following questions:

- Who would read this book?

- Is there enough interest in this topic?

- Is there enough material to fill 400 pages?

- What other books are already out there on this topic, and how will this one be different?

- What will it take, in terms of time and effort, to write this book?

- Will this idea sell to a publisher?

If your answers indicate that there is, indeed, a ready market for your book, and that you have both the time and the resources needed to complete the manuscript, then go ahead and start working on your proposal. But be sure to do it right. Just as you need to craft a great query to sell your articles, you need to write a great proposal if you're going to make a positive impression on a book editor. Your library and bookstore carry a variety of books on getting books published. I recommend Rudy Shur's *How to Publish Your Nonfiction Book*, which is a complete guide to understanding the book market, choosing appropriate publishers, and writing a winning query.

Once you have a book in print, consider excerpting parts of it in articles if you have retained the rights to do so in your contract. This can be a great way to further supplement your income, and to capitalize on the research and writing you have already completed.

Joining a Newspaper Staff

One of the best jobs for building up experience while being paid is that of a staff reporter at a newspaper. Typically, you will cover a "beat," which is one area or industry. The work can be grueling, depending on the paper and the amount of activity in your area. Most papers need one or two stories from beat reporters on a daily basis. That requires a lot of legwork and writing. However, if you're looking for a quick education in writing, this is a great place to get it. The pay is not phenomenally great—$25,000 to $35,000 a year, typically— but you will learn a great deal.

One caution: If you are also thinking about freelancing, read your contract carefully. Some newspapers restrict their writers from covering anything for a publication that hits the same circulation area.

A job on the staff of a newspaper will give you a quick education in writing while providing a steady— albeit modest—paycheck.

Others are more lenient. Either way, whatever you write for the newspaper is usually the newspaper's, not your own. Under a *work for hire* contract—which is what most staff reporters sign—you give up all rights to your work. This is rarely negotiable because the newspaper wants the right to archive and re-run all the material it publishes.

Copywriting for Businesses and Agencies

Copywriting requires the ability to encapsulate corporate messages in short, quick pieces. Research the area before deciding if it's right for you.

Many companies need material written for their newsletters, their websites, and their brochures, and some even need simple thank-you letters composed for their clients. While some companies employ staff writers, others outsource virtually all of their copy needs, either to freelancers or to marketing and advertising agencies, who in turn employ freelancers. This can provide a great source of income for capable freelance writers.

Most of my work in this field came about as a direct result of an article I once wrote on a particular company. When I interviewed the owner of the business, he asked if I did other types of writing. I was able to pick up several jobs just by being at the right place at the right time with the right skills.

Copywriting offers dependable pay, generally on a monthly basis. It is not the most glamorous job, and your name rarely appears on anything you write since you are producing material for a client. However, in addition to the income, this type of work can provide valuable exposure to a particular business or field—a real boon if you're trying to build up an area of expertise. If you are interested in covering health issues, for instance, consider writing copy for a doctor's office or a physicians' practice group. You can learn a great deal of medical terminology, interact with experts in the field on a continual basis, find out what the people in that profession are reading or are interested in reading, and build up a relationship with potential sources—all while being paid.

If you do freelance work for a marketing or advertising agency, be prepared for hard deadlines and fast turnaround times. The creative team—which is comprised of an art director, graphic designer, and writer—usually has to respond instantly to client requests, providing ad copy, brochure copy, and other sales materials. The good news is there is a great deal of demand for freelance writers to fill in during the busy times.

If you develop a balance between your copywriting and your article writing, you can enjoy a steady income. My work is divided fifty-fifty between corporate writing and articles, giving me year-round pay and assignments. As a bonus, my copywriting jobs provide me with an insider's view of how industries work.

Be aware, though, that marketing and public relations copy is vastly different from traditional writing. In a marketing setting, your goal is to sell, not to provide unbiased information about a subject. Some writers have difficulty separating the two worlds and are happier writing articles, newsletters, and website copy.

Generally, freelance copywriting work is not advertised in the newspaper. Most companies will look for full-time writers this way, but not for outside writers. If you are interested in producing copy for a business, create a resumé that stresses your work in that area, and compile clips of your copywriting work. When you send the package off to the company, consider offering to write a few press releases or a brochure at a reduced price just to get some copywriting experience—and to give the company a further taste of your work.

The most important step in this process is follow-up. Marketing directors at businesses and agencies receive packages like this every day, but usually don't act on them until they have an immediate need for a writer. Then the one they choose is often the one on the top of the inbox pile. You can move past the inbox and into a freelance job simply by calling the marketing director a week or two after you send out your package and offering to meet with her in person to review your experience, as well as the company's needs. If she isn't interested, wait a month and call again. Companies' needs for copy wax and wane, so persistence can pay off.

Consider using copywriting experience to develop an area of specialty.

Writing Greeting Cards, Poetry, and More

Many magazine and newspaper freelancers enjoy doing all kinds of writing. If you can write touching verse or humorous one-liners, there are markets that will pay you for your work. These markets can also help you build up a reputation in the field, especially if your long-term goal is to sell a book of poetry or to be a humorous essay writer.

Americans buy nearly 8 billion greeting cards a year, and the copy on every single one of those cards is written by someone. Many of these companies buy at least 20 percent of their material from freelancers, and some use freelancers for *all* of their needs. In addition, hundreds of magazines and other publications use short poems and comical one-liners to fill their white space. These can supply quick income for the skilled writer.

As you might expect, you can't just write up a slew of poems and send them out to every company and publication that uses verse. Instead, you must study the different markets for cards, poetry, jokes, and other short material to understand where your particular voice and talents fit. If you are interested in writing verse for greeting cards, look up the companies in your resource books and contact them, requesting a copy of their submission guidelines. The requirements vary from company to company. Some want your ideas on 3-x-5 cards, some want you to sign a disclosure agreement before submitting any material, and some want you to create dummy cards. Find out what the company wants before you send in your submission.

Payment for greeting cards is usually a one-time fee that can range from a few dollars to as much as several hundred. Unfortunately, though, payment for poetry is little to nothing, and short humor pieces don't provide more than a few dollars each. But if you are trying to build up a reputation as a humorous essay writer, having a few one-liners published or a few cards with Hallmark's Shoebox line won't hurt.

CONCLUSION

Whether you choose to work full-time or part-time, there are many ways to foster the growth of a rewarding freelance writing career. But be patient, and remember that this cannot be done overnight. Establishing a career takes hundreds of little steps that build over the years, slowly increasing your reputation, your contacts, and your skills.

As you make decisions, approaching new markets and looking for additional ways to use your writing ability, always keep your goals uppermost in your mind. If your ultimate goal is to make it into the pages of *Time* magazine, for instance, getting a job as a staff reporter for a newspaper would be a smart career move, while writing for a greeting card company would not. By choosing your work carefully, you can build a career that not only thrives but is also deeply satisfying.

CONCLUSION

This book, *How to Publish Your Articles*, was designed to guide you in getting your articles into print. Now that you have reached the end of the book, you should have a thorough appreciation of the inner workings of the article publishing industry, and should understand the step-by-step system that can help you get both your ideas and your finished articles onto an editor's desk in professional form.

In these pages, you've also met other people who have been where you are, and have successfully navigated the waters of the publishing industry. They have made it, and you can, too. If you have the drive and talent to pursue your writing, then following the Square One System will get your work published. It's as simple as that. Nothing happens overnight, of course, but by taking one tiny step after another, you can reach your goal.

When you finally see your words in print, you will be amazed and proud. It's a feeling that can't quite be expressed in words. No matter what your reasons for writing, regardless of the topic you've covered, seeing your name attached to a piece of your writing in a magazine, journal, or newspaper will be a thrill. You will be a published writer. And once you've achieved that milestone, you will know that you can do it again and again.

Throughout the process of publishing, never lose the joy of creating in the midst of deadlines and query letters. Do a little dance when

Don't give up on your dream. Don't lose sight of where you want to be. Be persistent, remain focused, and you will get there.

your words appear in print. Raise a glass to celebrate every goal you reach, no matter how small.

I thought it would be apt to conclude the book with an echo of the beginning, and add a quote from author Richard Bach. As a side note, his novel *Jonathan Livingston Seagull* was one of the first I can remember reading when I was a young girl. I was truly impressed by the way Bach crafted those words, bringing such a simple story to life. His later books, some of which detailed his path to becoming a writer, inspired me to strive for my own dream. I have learned a lot from other writers over the years, but I remember him as one of the first to get me started on that journey.

His advice to writers is very direct and true: "You are never given a wish without also being given the power to make it come true. You may have to work for it, however." And that, I believe, sums up the essence of what becoming a published writer is all about.

$\mathcal{G}$LOSSARY

All words that appear in *italic type* are defined within the glossary.

abstract. A structured summary of an academic *dissertation*. An abstract encapsulates the purpose, methods, results, and conclusions of the dissertation.

academic journal. A publication designed to bring the latest in research, breakthroughs, and case studies to readers in a specific field. Unlike *trade journals,* which are intended primarily to help readers better run their business or perform their job, academic journals are created to advance the thinking in a particular area.

academic review. See *review.*

acquiring editor. The person at a publication who has the power to make article-buying decisions. The *editor* who performs this job may not have this actual title, but may instead have the title of *editor-in-chief, managing editor, section editor,* submissions editor, or executive editor.

advertising insert. A section inserted in a *newspaper* for advertising purposes. This insert may contain articles that relate to the theme of the insert; for example, you may find tips on lawn care in an insert for gardening supplies advertisements. It differs from other inserts in that its primary purpose is to advertise, and that many of the articles are provided by the advertisers. See also *community insert; specialty insert.*

advertising schedule. A publication's calendar that details when ads have to be placed for particular issues. This schedule often runs parallel to the *editorial calendar.*

all rights. A type of rights, granted in a contract, that gives the *publisher* legal permission to reproduce the article, or do anything else he wants with it, forever. The author of the article can never resell that particular piece to another publication.

alternative publication. A small *newspaper* or magazine that publishes cultural, political, and literary material.

angle. The defined approach taken in an article by a writer. Also called a slant, this is one facet of the larger *topic* on which the writer has chosen to focus.

AP style. The preferred writing style of the Associated Press. This is the predominant style used by *newspapers*. The details for this style—which covers the use of numerals versus spelled-out numbers, the rules that govern capitalization and abbreviation, etc.—are found in the *Associated Press Stylebook and Libel Manual*.

APA style. One of two main styles used in academic papers, the other being *MLA style*. APA style is established by the American Psychological Association. Information on this style can be found in the *Publication Manual of the American Psychological Association*.

archives. Stored copies of articles that have been run in the past by a publication. At a *newspaper*, this is commonly called the *morgue*.

art. The industry term for any graphics, photographs, or other images that might accompany an article.

ASCII format. Also known as text only, this format strips a file of all formatting—boldface, italics, etc.—and converts it to a single-spaced, plain document that can be read by most software programs.

assignment. An article that is given to a writer by an editor, with a specific *deadline*. Assignments usually result from *query letters* and are accompanied by a *contract* or a *letter of agreement*.

association newsletter. A *newsletter* produced by an association or organization, and designed to inform readers about upcoming events, new resources and services, and advances in their particular field or industry.

attachment. A file attached to an e-mail message. With the number of viruses floating around, most editors don't want attachments. They would prefer you to save your article as an *ASCII* (text only) file and paste it into the body of the e-mail message.

audience. The readers of a specific publication. These are the people you are directly trying to reach with your article.

audience profile. An analysis of the average reader of a targeted publication. Compiled using *demographics* and a market analysis, an audience profile helps the writer determine exactly which *angle* to take with the article.

author biography. A list of a writer's credits. Also called an author bio, most are a page in length and list only the writer's most relevant or prestigious publishing credits. See also *curriculum vitae*.

author copies. Copies of a publication that are given to the author of an article printed in that issue. See also *tearsheet*.

banner. The full title and publication date that appear on the front cover of a *newspaper*, magazine, or other *periodical*.

beat. A subject area or industry that is assigned to a newspaper *staff reporter*. For instance, the reporter can be assigned to report on all crime activity, on political happenings, or on specific news within one town or region.

billboard paragraph. The paragraph that sums up the general *angle* of an article, providing the essential points that the piece will cover. This is also referred to as the nut graph or theme graph.

body. The main portion of an article. This is where the writer provides solid information, answering the reader's questions and illuminating the subject. The body follows the *lead* and precedes the *conclusion.*

byline. The name of the author as printed at the top or end of an article.

case study. A *first-person* fictionalized or real account of a dilemma, and the method used to resolve it. This type of article is carried by *academic journals,* and often focuses on personal and interpersonal crises.

Chicago style. The style set by the University of Chicago. Most consumer publications use either Chicago style, detailed in *The Chicago Manual of Style,* or *AP Style* when making decisions regarding punctuation, spelling, abbreviation, and other elements of writing style.

circulation. The number of people who buy and/or receive a given publication. This can be either a *closed circulation* or an *open circulation.*

city magazine. A regional publication that profiles people, services, and events in one community. This can be as small as a chamber of commerce publication, and as large as a full *consumer magazine* that focuses on one state or city.

clips. Copies of published articles submitted by a writer to an *editor.* Usually, a writer includes two or three photocopied samples of work with a *submission package* or *query letter* to demonstrate his experience in a particular area of writing.

closed circulation. Readership that is limited to subscription or membership. This is the case with many *trade journals* and *academic journals.* See also *circulation; open circulation.*

common copyright. Copyright that is established by placing a *copyright notation* on a work, rather than formally registering the work with the United States Copyright Office.

community insert. A section inserted in a *newspaper* to provide information—including history, statistics, and/or profiles of prominent citizens—on one area, town, or community. See also *advertising insert; specialty insert.*

conclusion. The summary paragraph of an article. In general, this part of the article should echo the opening of the piece and wrap up the story.

conference paper. An academic article based on a conference presentation. Sometimes, conference papers, as well as *dissertations,* are published in collections that center on one *topic,* such as plant studies.

consumer magazine. A magazine available to the general public on newsstands or through subscription. Some consumer magazines address a broad *audience,* such as women, while others address a *niche* market, such as people interested in the history of a certain region.

consumer newsletter. A *newsletter* put out by a company and directed to its customer base. This publication is generally filled with helpful information, and may contain coupons or advertised specials.

contract. The formal written agreement between a writer and *publisher* that defines the rights and responsibilities of each party. The contract should spell out what rights the publication is buying, along with the *deadline* for the article; any *kill fee;* any extra material the editor wants the writer to provide, such as *art* or a *sidebar;* and other important terms.

contributing editor. An honorary *editor* who also provides articles for a publication. Contributing editors are usually given a position on the *masthead,* and are often recognized experts in a given field.

contributing writer. A *freelance writer* who is given regular writing assignments and a preferred status for assignments within a publication. Often, a contributing writer, who may also be called a *contributing editor,* is mentioned on the *masthead* of the publication.

copy. Actual lines of writing. This is the text in an article or other piece of writing.

copyeditor. The person at a publication who is in charge of correcting and proofreading articles. This *editor* makes changes in the *copy* and double-checks it for grammatical errors, spelling problems, and other possible mistakes.

copyright. The legal overall right granted to an author or *publisher* for ownership of a written work. Under this ownership comes a number of specific rights, including the exclusive rights to print, sell, distribute, or translate the work. See also *common copyright; copyright notation.*

copyright notation. A written notice on a work that spells out authorship. This usually consists of the copyright notation symbol, ©, followed by the author's name.

copywriting. Providing *copy* for corporations or marketing and advertising agencies. This can range from the writing of press releases to that of brochures and website material, depending on the needs of the client.

cover letter. A short letter written to an editor to spark his interest in an article. The cover letter is accompanied by a copy of the already-written article. If the article has not yet been written, the writer sends a *query letter* instead.

cultural commentary. A *first-person* consumer-oriented article that expresses the writer's opinion on a cultural issue or trend. These pieces can be fairly short or can run several hundred words in length.

curriculum. A sample course of study submitted as an article to an academic journal. The curriculum is usually accompanied by notes and commentary from the teachers and students.

curriculum vitae. A summary of an academic's educational and professional background. Usually, a vitae should be only a couple of pages in length and list only the writer's most relevant and prestigious credentials.

deadline. The date by which a given article has to be completed and submitted to the publication.

defamation. Damage of a person's reputation, character, or good name via something that is written *(libel)* or spoken *(slander).*

demographics. Statistics that profile specific characteristics of a human population, such as age, gender, income level, level of education, and region of the country.

dissertation. An academic paper written to prove a thesis. Dissertations are often presented at conferences and form the basis of *conference papers,* or are printed in *academic journals.* The summary of a dissertation is called an *abstract.*

dramatic, television, and motion picture rights. The right to sell an article or story for dramatic adaptation.

editor. The person at a publication who works with the writer, shaping the article and making it fit the publication. The editor also gives out *assignments,* sends out *contracts* or *letters of agreement,* and serves as the writer's main point of contact. See also *acquiring editor; copyeditor; editorial assistant; editor-in-chief; managing editor; section editor.*

editorial. A *first-person* consumer or academic article that expresses the writer's view of a topic. These pieces are usually less than 900 words in length and are sometimes called *op-eds* when they are written for *newspapers.*

editorial assistant. The person at a publication who helps an *editor* by making photocopies, filing, etc. The editorial assistant is the first to see *unsolicited* material and usually makes the first decision regarding the material's appropriateness for the publication.

editorial calendar. A publication's internal schedule in which the editors lay out their themes for the coming year's issues. These calendars are generally created at the end of the year. Writers can request a copy of the editorial calendar along with the *writer's guidelines,* or can find the calendar online. Often, the editorial calendar is the same as or runs parallel to the *advertising schedule.*

editorial lead time. The amount of time between an article's *deadline* and its publication date. This can vary from two to nine months, depending on the publication.

editor-in-chief. The person at a publication who oversees the editorial staff and ensures that all articles fit the publication's editorial focus. The editor-in-chief has the final say over everything that runs in the publication.

electronic rights. A blanket term that encompasses all *reprints* of an article in electronic form—on websites, in online magazines, in CD-ROMs, in databases, or in any emerging technologies.

emoticon. An e-mail shorthand symbol that uses standard punctuation marks to represent different thoughts and emotions. An example of an emoticon is a symbol that uses a colon and parentheses to represent a smiley face [:)]. Emoticons should be avoided in professional correspondence with *editors.*

e-query. An electronic *query package.*

e-submission. An electronic *submission package.*

evergreen. A story or article that is recycled year after year, and is usually run to coincide with certain seasons. Almost every consumer publication carries some type of evergreen, whether it is an annual story on weight loss or one on Christmas baking.

e-zine. An online magazine. Some of these have print counterparts, but predominantly, they are limited to web distribution.

fact checker. A staff member employed by a publication to check the facts in every article before it is printed. Fact checkers use the *source list* submitted by the writer to verify the quotes, statistics, and other information that appear in the article.

fair use. A provision in the *copyright* law that allows for limited copying of published works without permission. Because the law is subject to different interpretations, it is generally best to avoid quoting from copyrighted material.

feature article. An article that is presented as a special attraction in a magazine, *newspaper,* or journal. This piece is usually the cover article, meaning that there is a mention of it on the cover of the publication. It is similar to a *news story,* and is usually written in the *third person.* In an academic journal, a feature article is designed to provide in-depth, comprehensive information on breakthrough thinking and its application in the reader's world.

filler. A short article of 200 words or less that is designed to do exactly what its name implies—to fill a space. Depending on the publication, fillers can range from *news stories* that don't merit feature treatment to *humor pieces,* anecdotes, puzzles, jokes, and poems. These articles are usually written in *third person* and represent one of the best opportunities for a new writer to break into a publication.

First North American Serial Rights. See *first serial rights.*

first person. Writing that has the "I" viewpoint, meaning that the story is seen from the point of view of the writer. First-person writing is used often in *personal essays, humor pieces,* and other articles that describe the writer's direct experiences. This style builds a relationship with the reader, as if the writer were telling the story to a close friend.

first serial rights. The rights most commonly granted in a contract. Also called First North American Serial Rights (FNASR), these rights grant the *publisher* of a *periodical* (a serial) the exclusive right to print an article first. After these rights expire, the writer is free to resell the article to other publications.

FNASR. See *first serial rights.*

format. The manner in which a submitted article should be physically set up on the page. This information is often found in the *writer's guidelines,* and covers such parameters as margins, line spacing, and font.

freelance writer. Someone who writes for a publication without being on staff.

freelance writing. Writing sold to a publication by someone who is not on the publication's staff.

generalist. A writer who does not specialize in any one area, but rather writes on a wide range of *topics.*

header. The information printed at the "head" of a submitted article, running along the top of the page. The header should include the article's title or a keyword for the title, the writer's last name, and the page number.

headline. The title of an article. This short line should be kept to seven words or less, and use strong, active phrasing to encapsulate the piece and attract the attention of the reader. It is sometimes followed by a "subhead" that further explains the focus of the article.

homogeneous readership. A readership in which everyone shares common beliefs and interests. This is often found in *trade journals* and other publications that are distributed to readers who work within the same field, and may also be found in small local *newspapers.*

hook. The opening of an article or *query letter* that draws the reader in and interests him in the material.

horizontal trade. A *trade journal* that is directed toward people in the same type of job—human resource managers, for instance—though not necessarily in the same indusrty.

how-to article. A consumer-oriented article that provides step-by-step information on completing a physical or creative project—fixing a car, planting watermelons, or decorating a cake. Usually written in *second person,* these articles can range widely in *word count.*

how-to/application. An academic article that provides in-depth information on improving or remedying a particular situation. Usually written in *third person,* the how-to/application incorporates information from a number of sources and experts.

HTML. The language that most web pages are written in and coded with. The majority of *e-zines* take care of the coding for the writers.

human interest article. An article that touches the heart of readers. These are often stories of people overcoming tragedies, learning from setbacks, or caring for others.

humor piece. An article designed to entertain people and make them laugh. Most humor pieces are written in *first person* and run no longer than 1,000 words in length.

in-house. Within a specific publication's staff. Editors, for instance, may refer to their "in-house style," or specific articles may be written "in-house"—by the staff of the publication.

interview. A conversation conducted by a writer for the purpose of eliciting facts and statements from another individual. Interviews may be conducted in person, on the phone, by e-mail, by postal mail, or by fax.

interview/profile. A consumer-oriented article based on an *interview* with a celebrity or expert, and written either in a question-and-answer format or as a traditional *third-person* article, with quotes from the primary subject. These pieces can run anywhere from 200 to 2,000 words or more, depending on the publication. See also *profile/interview.*

invoice. A bill sent to a publication by the *freelance writer* of an article after the piece has been completed and approved. Writers should always submit an invoice so there is a paper trail for all business transactions.

issue number. A number that tells you how many editions of the publication have been published in the current year. It may appear on the cover or at the top of the table of contents, or, in magazines, may be included in the Statement of Ownership and Copyright, usually located in the back pages and combined with subscription and mailing information. See also *volume number.*

kill fee. A fee paid to the writer of an article if the *editor* changes his mind and decides not to use the piece. Not all publications have the budget for kill fees.

lead. The opening paragraph of an article. There are many different types of leads, but every lead should outline the story that follows and inspire the reader to read further.

lead time. See *editorial lead time.*

letter of agreement. The letter from the editor buying or accepting the submitted or proposed article. Sometimes, this letter is used in lieu of a *contract.* When that is the case, it is important to make sure that all the usual terms of the contract are spelled out in the letter.

libel. A written statement that damages a person's reputation, character, or good name. The statement can appear in a letter, in an article, or even in a posting on an e-mail list or bulletin board. See also *defamation; slander.*

lifestyle section. The section of a *newspaper* or other publication that deals with gardening, books, home interiors, food, and other topics that are not hard news.

link/hyperlink. The address phrase that lets you click and immediately be taken to a particular Internet address. It is often highlighted in a different color so that people realize it's a "live" link, meaning that it works.

magazine. See *academic journal; consumer magazine; trade journal.*

managing editor. The person at a publication who coordinates the different departments—such as the editorial department, art department, and typesetting department—to maintain a smooth production process and meet deadlines.

marketing newsletter. A *newsletter* sent by a company to potential and current clients. The sole purpose of this newsletter is to serve as a soft marketing piece—to show that the company is doing a good job.

mass-market magazine. A large *consumer magazine*—one with a circulation of more than half a million.

masthead. The list of staff members—including *editors,* designers, and more—usually printed in the beginning pages of a magazine or *newspaper.*

MLA style. One of two main styles used for formatting academic papers, the other being *APA style.* MLA style is the one preferred by the Modern Language Association. Information on this style can be found in the *MLA Style Manual and Guide to Scholarly Publishing.*

morgue. The industry term for a newspaper's *archives.* A morgue usually has print or microfiche copies of articles that reporters can use for background research.

multiple submission. The practice of submitting one article to more than one publication at the same time. This is also called a simultaneous submission.

news story. A consumer-oriented article that provides serious coverage of a topical subject. Written in *third person,* these articles generally run 200 to 1,500 words in length, and rely on at least three sources to provide unbiased coverage.

newsletter. A short collection of articles—usually four to eight pages in length—designed to provide quick information about a subject, giving readers an easy way to stay current on trends or literature. There are four main types of newsletters: association, consumer, marketing, and professional.

newspaper. A publication that is issued on a daily or weekly basis, and contains current news, editorials, features, and usually advertising.

niche. A well-defined area of interest or *audience* that is addressed by a publication. Often, *secondary magazines* hit niches by focusing on a specific industry, region, hobby, or profession.

non-refereed journal. An *academic journal* at which submitted articles are not formally reviewed by a board of experts before being accepted.

nut graph. See *billboard paragraph.*

off the record. Comments made by an interview subject that are not part of the formal *interview.* Comments made off the record should not be printed by a writer without permission from the interview subject.

one-time rights. Rights granted in a contract that allow the publication to print an article only once. This is the best deal for the writer but is not very common.

op-ed piece. A consumer-oriented *first-person* article that expresses the writer's opinion on a particular topic. Formally called an opinion-editorial, these articles usually run 400 to 600 words in length. Some op-eds offer a supporting viewpoint on an issue that was covered in an earlier article; others are written to inform readers about issues facing society or a particular neighborhood.

open circulation. Readership that is not limited to subscription or membership. In general, publications found on newsstands have an open circulation. See also *circulation; closed circulation.*

opinion-editorial. See *op-ed piece.*

outline. A written summary that details how a proposed article will be constructed. Sometimes submitted with a *query letter,* the outline gives the *editor* a thorough picture of the research that has thus far been gathered, the interview subjects that will be contacted, and the *angle* that the writer will take. Large-circulation publications often require outlines or detailed *query letters.*

outsider opinion piece. An academic article generally written in *first person* by someone outside the academic community. The purpose of such an article is to provide a unique perspective, highlighting techniques or information that may have worked in the nonacademic world.

overinterviewing. The practice of asking more questions during an *interview* than are needed for the current article. The purpose is to have enough material to create several *spin-off* articles.

payment on acceptance. A type of payment plan in which the writer is paid for his article when it is submitted to and approved by the editor.

payment on publication. A type of payment plan in which the writer isn't paid for his article until it appears in print. Because an article may not appear in print until months after its acceptance, this arrangement is not as beneficial to the writer as *payment on acceptance.*

peer-reviewed journal. See *refereed journal.*

periodical. A *newspaper,* magazine, journal, or other publication that comes out periodically—at regular intervals. This is sometimes referred to as a serial.

personal essay. A *first-person* consumer-oriented article on either a personal problem that the writer has faced and overcome, or a meaningful event. Sometimes referred to as a personal experience piece, these articles generally run 400 to 1,000 words in length.

personal experience piece. The academic counterpart of a *personal essay*. In this *first-person* account, the writer presents a problem that he has faced, and then explains the solution he used to solve it.

photo feature. An article that is light on writing and heavy on photos, with the text serving only to explain the graphics. In general, the photographer or a staff writer is assigned to write the text for a photo feature.

pitch. A letter or conversation in which a writer tries to persuade an editor to buy his article.

plagiarism. The act of copying another person's work and passing it off as your own.

press kit. A folder—provided by a company, organization, or association—that presents information on the group itself. Such kits usually include industry statistics and lists of potential interview subjects, as well as explanations of industry terms and trends.

print rights. A publisher's rights, granted by contract, to print an article on paper, but not to distribute it in an electronic manner or post it on a website or *e-zine*.

professional newsletter. A *newsletter* distributed by a trade association or group. These publications often contain industry information that is designed to keep readers current on new trends and technologies.

profile/interview. An academic article based on an *interview* of an individual, usually an expert with esteemed credentials. These articles can vary in length, and can be written in either a question-and-answer format or a narrative, depending on the publication. See also *interview/profile*.

proposal. See *query letter*.

publisher. The person at a publication who oversees the entire operation. At some publications, the publisher may also serve as *editor-in-chief*. Also, the business entity that edits, produces, markets, and otherwise makes available a printed and/or electronic publication.

query letter. A letter of inquiry sent to a publication by a *freelance writer* as a means of proposing an article idea to the publication. The query letter is designed both to sell the idea of the article and to convince the editor that the writer has the knowledge and skills necessary to complete the article. See also *cover letter*.

query package. A package sent to a publication by a *freelance writer* for the purpose of selling an article idea. The package generally includes a *query letter*; published *clips*, if any; and a self-addressed, stamped envelope; and may also include an *outline* of the article and an *author biography*. See also *submission package*.

refereed journal. An *academic journal* at which all submitted articles are rigorously examined by an editorial *review board* before being accepted.

reprint. An article that previously appeared in one publication, and is later printed in another publication.

reprint rights. See *second serial rights*.

research and trend report. An academic article that provides information on relevant trends, phenomena, companies, or individuals. Generally compiled by organizations, these reports can often be used as the foundation for other academic articles.

review. A consumer or academic article that provides a short critique of a book, movie, play, product, service, website, workshop, restaurant, or other item of interest to the publication's *audience*. Written in the *first person*, a review is designed to provide the writer's perspective on the review subject.

review board. A board of experts that reviews all articles submitted to a *refereed journal.*

round-up. A *third-person* consumer-oriented article that compiles responses from a variety of people on one subject, or in answer to a particular question. These articles generally run from 500 to 1,000 words in length. Sometimes, these articles are referred to as surveys and incorporate statistics, such as the percentage of respondents who gave one answer over another.

SASE. A self-addressed, stamped envelope. A SASE should be included in every *submission package* and *query package,* as it enables the editor to easily respond to the proposal.

SASP. A self-addressed, stamped postcard. These postcards can be sent to editors to request a response to a previously sent *submission package* or *query package.*

second person. Writing that has the "you" viewpoint by addressing the reader. This is common in *how-to articles*—pieces that provide advice or information.

second serial rights. The rights, granted in a *contract,* that permit the *publisher* to sell an article to a second publication after it has appeared in the first one. These rights are also referred to as reprint rights.

secondary magazine. A medium-sized *consumer magazine* that focuses on a specific *niche,* or area of interest, and therefore covers a secondary market. Secondary magazines usually fill the gaps left by large magazines, which address a wider range of readers.

section editor. An *editor* in charge of one section of a publication, such as health or books.

serial. See *periodical.*

service piece. A *third-person* consumer-oriented article that falls into the *how-to* category, but goes further than just explaining how to do something

by informing, educating, and advising the *audience* about an important issue or life skill like investing, working, or making a purchase. A service piece generally runs 500 words or more in length.

sidebar. A short piece that accompanies an article and provides helpful hints, resources, or a summary of the article's main points. These boxes of information are set apart from the main article and are usually less than 200 words in length.

simultaneous submission. See *multiple submission.*

slander. A spoken statement that damages a person's reputation, character, or good name. See also *defamation; libel.*

slant. See *angle.*

slush pile. The term used to describe the stack of *unsolicited* articles—articles that were not requested by an editor. Articles in the slush pile are usually read by an *editorial assistant.*

solicited. Requested. A solicited article has been requested by an *editor,* usually in response to a *query letter* sent by a *freelance writer.*

source list. The list of sources used by a writer in researching an article. The list should include contact information for all interview subjects, as well as bibliographic data for each website, book, journal, or other publication from which the writer gleaned information for the article. This list is often submitted to the publication's *fact checker* so that he can verify all information.

spam. Junk e-mail.

specialist. A writer who specializes in one particular area or industry. This could range from a writer who produces only *personal essays* to a writer who covers only breaking medical issues.

specialty insert. A section inserted in a *newspaper* for informational and advertising purposes. This insert generally has a theme and is supplemented by freelanced *tips articles* or, occasionally, reports written by business owners. Unlike an *advertising insert,* a specialty insert is more focused on content than ads. It may be produced to celebrate a special event, like a festival, or it may be designed to present articles on a related theme that the newspaper doesn't have room to print. See also *advertising insert; community insert.*

spin-off. An article that is based on another article, but has a slightly different focus or *angle.* For example, a 2,000-word article on investing could result in several spin-offs on mutual funds, IRA plans, and stock market advice.

staff reporter. A writer hired by a newspaper to cover a particular *beat.* In the early days of newspapers, this person was sometimes called a "stringer."

stringer. See *staff reporter.*

style sheet. A sheet that details the style and format preferred by a publication. Academic publications usually use either *MLA style* or *APA style.* Consumer and trade publications usually prefer either *AP style* or *Chicago style.*

submission guidelines. See *writer's guidelines.*

submission package. A package that is sent to a publication by a *freelance writer* for the purpose of selling an already-written article to the publication. The package generally includes a *cover letter;* a copy of the article; published *clips,* if any; and a self-addressed, stamped envelope; and may also include a *curriculum vitae.* See also *query package.*

survey. An academic article based on a question asked of experts in the field. Results are reported in statistical form, and to round out the survey, the article usually contains brief *interviews,* charts, opinion analyses, or short discussions of relevant research.

syllabus. An outline or summary of the main points of a lecture or course of study. These course examples are printed as articles in some *academic journals.*

syndicate. An agency that sells the same article simultaneously to different *newspaper* outlets. The article is then printed in numerous publications throughout the country. Most syndicate writers are established experts who have built up years of experience in their chosen area of focus.

tearsheet. An original copy of a printed article "torn" from the publication's pages. Most *editors* send writers complete copies of the publication, known as *author copies,* instead of tearsheets.

technical article. A *third-person* article, written for a *trade journal,* that covers issues which the typical layman's publication wouldn't examine in its articles. Technical articles vary in length, depending on the material being covered, and always use industry-specific language.

text only format. See *ASCII format.*

theme graph. See *billboard paragraph.*

theoretical essay. An academic article, written in *first person* or *third person,* and designed to help advance the discussion of different theories. Theoretical essays often present evidence that supports or refutes a specific viewpoint.

third person. The most distant of all writing forms. In this type of writing, "he," "she," and "they" are the pronouns used. Third-person writing is generally employed in objective articles such as *news stories* and *feature articles,* and is sometimes used in *interview/profile* pieces as well. It is appropriate when the writer is trying to present important information or show an unbiased front.

tips article. An article that provides readers with hints and advice in a quick, easy-to-read format. Specifically, these pieces tell the reader how to do something better or more economically. They are common in *consumer magazines.*

topic. The subject of an article. This should be narrowed and tightened until the writer develops a specific *angle* that will appeal to the readers of the target publication.

trade journal. A magazine or small newspaper published specifically for people in certain businesses or professions to increase career and business knowledge. Unlike an *academic journal,* a trade journal is designed to help readers better run their business or perform their job.

unsolicited. Not requested. An unsolicited article is sent by a *freelance writer* to a publication without being asked to do so. It then remains in a *slush pile* until someone—usually an *editorial assistant*—is able to review it and determine its suitability for the publication.

URL. The address of a website. URL stands for Uniform Resource Locator.

vertical trade. A *trade journal* that is directed toward everyone in one particular industry—veterinarians, for instance

volume number. A number that is legally required on all publications and tells you how many years the publication has been published. It may appear on the cover or at the top of the table of contents, or, in magazines, may be included in the Statement of Ownership and Copyright, usually located in the back pages and combined with

subscription and mailing information. See also *issue number.*

wire service. A service, such as Associated Press, that electronically distributes news and articles to *newspapers* and magazines around the country. For many publications, buying a story from a wire service costs a fraction of the price paid to a *freelance writer,* making wire service stories an economical choice.

word count. The number of words in the article, not including the *headline* or *byline.* Because space is such an important commodity in the article world, it is vital to provide the editor with an accurate word count that comes within a few words of the requested count.

work for hire. A contractual arrangement in which the employer or company for whom the writing is prepared is considered the author, and owns all of the rights to the work. Many *staff reporters* and copywriters sign such *contracts,* preventing them from reprinting any of the work they produce while employed with that company.

writer's guidelines. The set of rules for submitting articles to a particular publication. Sometimes referred to as submission guidelines, the guidelines supply specific information about formatting, grammar, and style, and also provide payment information and *contract* terms.

RESOURCE DIRECTORY

Many groups and organizations provide help for aspiring and established writers alike by offering opportunities for networking, and by making available a number of significant resources, including educational programs, job listings, and more. In addition, a wide range of books, periodicals, and websites can guide you to appropriate markets for your work; provide helpful guidelines for producing successful query packages, developing your writing skills, and negotiating contract terms; and explore other subjects that may be of interest to you. Keep in mind that although this directory includes essential writers' resources, it should be regarded as a jumping-off place. Your local bookstores, your library, and the ever-growing web of Internet sites are sure to provide you with other valuable sources of guidance, information, and inspiration.

GROUPS AND ORGANIZATIONS

American Medical Writers Association (AMWA)
40 West Gude Drive, Suite 101
Rockville, MD 20850-1192
Phone: 301–294–5303
Fax: 310–294–9006
Website: www.amwa.org

Founded in 1940, the AMWA is the major professional organization for writers of biomedical information. Continuing education through classes, conferences, and workshops is the main focus of the organization, which has twenty-one regional offices, including ones in Canada and Europe. AMWA's Core Curriculum program is considered one of the most extensive continuing education programs available to professionals in this field. An advanced curriculum is also available. The group offers chapter meetings, book and journalism competitions, networking resources, and job market listings. The AMWA website has an online job listing section, a freelance directory, and a bulletin board system available to members only. The relevant links section is available to members as well as the general public.

American Society of Journalists and Authors (ASJA)
1501 Broadway, Suite 302
New York, NY 10038
Phone: 212–997–0947
Fax: 212–768–7414
Website: www.asja.org

The ASJA is the leading organization for writers of nonfiction material. Membership is open to freelance writers who can show a sustainable history of publication in major print and Internet magazines, newspapers, books, or scripts. Members receive a monthly newsletter, access to jobs and projects through the ASJA Writer Referral Service, networking resources, and discount services, as well as offerings of various seminars and workshops. ASJA's website offers links to member websites, article alerts on issues pertinent to writers, information sheets on different aspects of freelance writing, and contract watch information. Although most of the information on the ASJA website is open to the public, there is also a members-only section.

Editorial Freelancers Association (EFA)
71 West 23rd Street, Suite 1910
New York, NY 10010
Phone: 212–929–5400
Fax: 212–929–5439
Website: www.the-efa.org

Founded in 1970, the EFA is the largest national organization for self-employed writers, researchers, editors, and other publishing industry professionals. The group strives to improve the capabilities of and rewards for those who work for themselves. EFA offers comprehensive health insurance, educational programs, legal and accounting services, a bimonthly newsletter, and networking. The EFA website contains a members-only job listing, bulletin board center, and e-mail listserv, as well as online courses and workshops available to both members and nonmembers.

National Association of Science Writers, Inc. (NASW)
PO Box 294
Greenlawn, NY 11740
Phone: 631–757–5664
Fax: 631–757–0069
Website: www.nasw.org

NASW was formally incorporated in 1955 to provide a forum for science writers who wish to improve the conditions that promote good science writing. Benefits include a quarterly newsletter that presents member news, job listings, and discussions of issues and controversies of the business. The group also offers regional meetings, seminars, and fellowships through its sister organization, the Council for the Advancement of Science Writing; and can provide group health and disability insurance and press cards. Online members are given space to create and maintain personal web pages; are allowed one e-mail address; and are welcome to join membership mailing lists, view job postings, and access the members-only section of the NASW website. The website also offers a freelance section with some articles available to the public, information on upcoming workshops, a science bookstore, and relevant links.

National Writers Union (NWU)

113 University Place, 6th Floor
New York, NY 10003
Phone: 212–254–0279
Fax: 212–254–0673
Website: www.nwu.org

The NWU is a trade union devoted to improving pay and working conditions for freelance writers. A proactive group, the union supports its members in the event of contract disputes and misappropriation of material, and offers grievance resolution services, contract advice, health and dental plans, educational programs and materials, job banks, networking, and more. The NWU website offers several divisions—including Books, Journalism, Business/Technology, Poetry and Fiction, and Cartoonist sections—each of which includes specialized articles and information. Much of the advice and articles presented on the site are available to the public, with the exception of the job bank program, which allows members only to search for job leads. The NWU Agent Database and other select information are also available to members only.

Newsletter & Electronic Publishers Association (NEPA)

1501 Wilson Boulevard, Suite 509
Arlington, VA 22209
Phone: 800–356–9302
Fax: 703–841–0629
Website: www.newsletters.org

NEPA is an international nonprofit group that serves newsletter and other specialized publishers with education, training, and networking. Member benefits include a subscription to the bimonthly *Hotline* newsletter, assistance with legal representation and counseling, discounted fees for conference and seminar attendance, full access to NEPA's website, and much more.

The Newspaper Guild

501 Third Street, NW, Suite 250
Washington, DC 20001
Phone: 202–434–7177
Message Center: 800–585–5TNG
Fax: 202–434–1472
Website: www.newsguild.org

A labor union for those working in any aspect of the media, The Newspaper Guild's purpose is to improve working conditions and ensure fair pay for its members while encouraging good journalistic practices. With more than 35,000 members in the United States, Canada, and Mexico, the guild is comprised of writers, designers, reporters, editorial assistants, photographers, editors, commercial artists, technicians—virtually anyone who works in a print media field. The guild offers a monthly newsletter, arbitration assistance, and other services.

The Society for Scholarly Publishing (SSP)

10200 West 44th Avenue, Suite 304
Wheat Ridge, CO 80033-2840
Phone: 303–422–3914
Fax: 303–422–8894
Website: www.sspnet.org

The SSP was founded in 1978 to unite all areas of scholarly publishing—commercial, academic, governmental, and societal—into one group that works "to facilitate learning, communication and the advancement of appropriate technologies." Members of SSP receive discounted attendance at the SSP Annual Meeting, various educational seminars held in a variety of locations, and coursework through the University of Chicago Publishing Program. SSP also offers e-mail alerts, a member directory, and various links and information through its website.

The Society for Technical Communication (STC)

901 North Stuart Street, Suite 904
Arlington, VA 22203-1822
Phone: 703–522–4114
Fax: 703–522–2075
Website: www.stc.org

The STC is a professional organization available to all those involved in technical communication, including writers, editors, publishers, illustrators, teachers, engineers, and scientists. Members are offered discounts on society publications, discounted attendance at the annual conference, group rate insurance plans, and subscriptions to the monthly magazine *Intercom* and the quarterly journal *Technical Communication.*

Society of American Business Editors and Writers (SABEW)

Missouri School of Journalism
76 Gannett Hall
Columbia, MO 65211-1200
Phone: 573–882–7862
Fax: 573–884–1372
Website: www.sabew.org

Membership in SABEW is restricted to those whose writing is made up primarily of business, financial, or economic subject matter. Members can participate in a variety of contests, an annual convention, conferences and workshops, a resumé bank, and networking; and receive a bimonthly newsletter. The SABEW website offers job openings, participation in discussion groups, conference and workshop information and registration forms, and article archives that are available to members and nonmembers alike.

Society of National Association Publications (SNAP)

1595 Spring Hill Road, Suite 330
Tysons Corner
Vienna, VA 22182

Phone: 703–506–3285
Fax: 703–506–3266
Website: www.snaponline.org

SNAP is a nonprofit organization designed to serve the needs of those who create association and society publications. Members receive a bimonthly magazine, *Association Publishing,* which covers all the ins and outs of the industry. The website offers a career center to assist both members and nonmembers in finding employees or employers, a research center, a calendar of events, and conference listings. If you are thinking about starting your own newsletter or magazine, this professional organization can help.

The Society of Professional Journalists (SPJ)

3909 North Meridian Street
Indianapolis, IN 46208
Phone: 317–927–8000
Fax: 317–920–4789
Website: www.spj.org

Founded in 1909 as Sigma Delta Chi, the SPJ was created to promote the free practice of journalism as well as high ethical standards for journalists. The organization offers a wide array of programs to assist its members in professional development, as well as monetary awards and fellowships for students. Members receive a subscription to *The Quill* magazine; access to an online directory of sources and resources; and discounts on a variety of products and services, including office supplies, insurance, and travel.

United States Copyright Office

Library of Congress
101 Independence Avenue, SE
Washington, DC 20559-6000
Phone: 202–707–9100 (for form or publications requests)
202–707–3000 (information line)
Website: www.lcweb.loc.gov/copyright/

Although your work is copyrighted with or without official documentation, if you are still worried that a publishing company might steal your work, the Copyright Office can provide you with legal protection by officially copyrighting your manuscript. You can order the necessary forms over the phone or download them from the website.

The United States Small Business Administration (SBA)

409 Third Street, SW
Washington, DC 20416
Phone: 800–827–5722
Website: www.sba.gov

The SBA was founded in 1953 to provide financial, technical, and management assistance to small business owners, thus helping owners start, run, and expand their businesses. The SBA website offers a wealth of information on every aspect of starting and operating a small business, as well as data on local SBA offices.

BOOKS

The Associated Press Stylebook and Libel Manual

Norm Goldstein, editor, The Associated Press, and Louis D. Boccardi. New York: Perseus Press, 1998.

This book provides useful facts and references for journalists, as well as information on usage, grammar, and spelling. With separate sections on writing in such specialized areas as sports and business, and guidelines for writing photo captions, proofreading text, and handling copyright and libel issues, this is a must-have for all writers.

The Chicago Manual of Style: The Essential Guide for Writers, Editors, and Publishers, 14th Edition

John Grossman. Chicago: University of Chicago Press, 1993.

The Chicago Manual of Style offers guidelines for writers, editors, publishers, copywriters, proofreaders, indexers, and everyone in between. Information is provided on all aspects of usage and style, from how to properly number the pages of a book to how to use a hyphen.

The Copyright Permission and Libel Handbook: A Step-By-Step Guide for Writers, Editors, and Publishers

Lloyd J. Jassin and Steven C. Schechter. New York: John Wiley & Sons, 1998.

Written by publishing attorneys, this guide explains copyright and libel law in straightforward, jargon-free language. The summary checklists and examples help you understand the complicated, sometimes tedious laws.

Editor and Publisher Syndicate Directory

New York: Editor and Publisher, updated annually.

Produced by *Editor and Publisher* magazine, this guide provides valuable information about newspaper syndicates, including contact personnel and executive and editor names, as well as a listing of syndicated authors and artists. Information is listed alphabetically by syndicate name and is also grouped by subject matter, with frequency of publication and size provided. This inexpensive guide is excellent when you want to find out who publishes what and where. The website for the magazine, www.editorandpublisher.com, provides ordering information.

The Elements of Style, 4th Edition

William Strunk and E.B. White. New York: Allyn & Bacon, 1999.

Long considered the classic book on grammar and style issues, *The Elements of Style* covers elementary rules of usage and elementary principles of composition; provides a look at commonly mis-used words and expressions; and presents tips on refining your writing style. This is a must for every writer.

Encyclopedia of Associations

Tara E. Sheets, editor. Detroit: The Gale Group, updated annually.

A guide to both national and international organizations in a wide variety of fields, this book is a useful research tool for nonfiction writers. The *Encyclopedia of Associations* can help you find contact people for interviews, research different industry newsletters, and locate groups that provide statistics on different industries. Due to the size and cost, this valuable resource must be used in your local library.

Every Writer's Guide to Copyright and Publishing Law

Ellen M. Kozak. New York: Henry Holt and Company, 1997.

This guide provides writers, editors, publishers, and others with simple explanations of copyright, fair use, contracts, work-for-hire, and more.

File . . . Don't Pile!: For People Who Write

Pat Dorff, Edith Fine, and Judith Josephson. New York: St. Martin's Press, 2000.

This book was designed specifically to help writers become organized and maintain clear and accurate records. Information is presented in a fun, easy-to-read format, offering a humorous approach to a common problem.

Gale Directory of Publications and Broadcast Media

Jeff Summer, editor. Detroit: The Gale Group, updated annually.

For writers hoping to submit freelance material to newspapers, this book is a good place to start. The *Gale Directory* provides listings of newspapers, ra-dio stations, and television stations nationwide, as well as a few trade journals and magazines.

Getting Permission: How to License & Clear Copyrighted Materials Online & Off

Richard Stim. Berkeley, CA: Nolo Press, 1999.

Written by an intellectual property lawyer, *Getting Permission* guides writers through the gray areas of copyright law. The author explains the law, discusses ambiguities such as public domain, and provides information on tracking copyright holders and writing permission letters. The book comes with a floppy disk that contains boilerplate forms ready to download and use.

Home-Based Business for Dummies

Paul Edwards, Sarah Edwards, and Peter Economy. Foster City, CA: Hungry Minds Inc, 2000.

Written for people just starting an at-home business, this book covers everything from selecting the right business to understanding self-employment taxes. If you need help establishing a business—and especially if you're looking for information on legal and financial aspects—*Home-Based Business* will prove invaluable.

How to Publish Your Nonfiction Book: A Complete Guide to Making the Right Publisher Say Yes

Rudy Shur. Garden City Park, NY: Square One Publishers, 2001.

Written by a book publisher with over two decades of experience, this book provides an insider's view of the book publishing world and a step-by-step system for getting your book into print. The author helps you define your book's category, audience, and marketplace; choose the best companies for your project; write a winning submission package; and send your proposal out in a way that optimizes your chance of success. If you want to increase your credibility and income by getting your book into print, this is a great place to start.

How to Publish Your Poetry: A Complete Guide to Finding the Right Publishers for Your Work

Helene Ciaravino. Garden City Park, NY: Square One Publishers, 2001.

This book is a comprehensive guide to breaking into the world of print poetry. The author provides a description of the poetry publishing world, walks you through the use of market resources, guides you in writing a persuasive submission package, and presents a proven system for sending your package out. This is an excellent resource for article writers who want to supplement their income or enhance their reputation by getting their poetry into print.

How to Start a Home-Based Writing Business, 3rd Edition

Lucy V. Parker and Karen Ivory. Old Saybrook, CT: Globe Pequot Press, 2000.

This book is a great match for anyone who wants to both write and pay their bills. The authors provide tips on buying necessary equipment, marketing your services, establishing a work schedule, setting fees, collecting payment, keeping records, paying taxes, and a wealth of other writing-related business tasks and issues.

Hudson's Subscription Newsletter Directory

Howard Penn Hudson, editor. Rhinebeck, NY: Newsletter Clearinghouse, updated annually.

This annual directory provides listings of all the subscription newsletters in the country. If you are thinking about starting your own newsletter, the directory will tell you what else is out there. If you have specialized in a given area, this book will guide you to newsletters related to your field. The directory is pricey, though, so look for it in your library rather than your bookstore.

The International Directory of Little Magazines & Small Presses

Len Fulton, editor. Paradise, CA: Dustbooks, updated annually.

An essential resource, particularly for beginning writers, this directory provides basic contact data as well as market information, payment rates, and more, for over 5,000 small presses and magazines.

Kirsch's Handbook of Publishing Law: For Authors, Publishers, Editors and Agents

Jonathan Kirsch. Los Angeles: Acrobat Books, 1994.

Written by an attorney, this manual covers legal issues relevant to writers, publishers, editors, and agents. All discussions are easy to understand, and are accompanied by examples and sample forms.

MLA Style Manual and Guide to Scholarly Publishing, 2nd Edition

Joseph Gibaldi and Herbert Lindenberger (Foreword). New York: Modern Language Association of America, 1998.

Designed for both scholars and aspiring scholars, the *MLA Style Manual* provides tips on preparing a prospectus and other academic documents, utilizing abbreviations, and providing proper citations. The book also offers information on publishing and legal issues, as well as the basics of writing and usage.

Newsletter Sourcebook, 2nd Edition

Mark Beach and Elaine Floyd. Cincinnati: Writer's Digest Books, 1998.

For those who want to start their own newsletter, this book provides examples of successful ones, as well as offering useful information on layout and design. The concepts covered can also be applied to creating online publications.

Online Markets for Writers

Anthony Tedesco and Paul Tedesco. New York: Henry Holt and Company, 2000.

This book is chock full of information on breaking

into online markets. The beginning provides tips on getting published online, while the balance presents an extensive list of potential markets. The top ten paying markets are highlighted, along with proven guidelines for breaking into them. Publisher information, editor contact data, payment terms, editorial needs, and areas of focus are covered within each market listing.

The Procrastinator's Handbook: Mastering the Art of Doing It Now
Rita Emmett. New York: Walker & Company, 2000.

This is a great book for writers who need help getting organized and moving toward their goals. Designed to help you combat your fears, learn how to stop putting things off, and become more productive, the book clearly explains procrastination and includes lists of tips and helpful hints.

Publication Manual of the American Psychological Association, 5th Edition
Washington, D.C.: American Psychological Association, 2001.

Designed for those who write for scholarly publications in the social science field, this valuable reference tool includes guidelines for preparing manuscripts in conformity with the APA style, discusses contemporary language usage, and examines the industry's publishing standards.

The Reader's Guide to Periodical Literature
New York: H.W. Wilson, updated annually.

Available in print, CD-ROM, and online versions, *The Reader's Guide* is an index of general interest English-language periodicals searchable by author and subject. The *Guide* is a helpful research tool whether you are seeking background information or trying to determine if a particular article approach has been used previously.

The Standard Periodical Directory
New York: Oxbridge Press, updated annually.

Available in both print and CD-ROM versions, *Standard* has a companion website that offers additional information and updates. This directory includes information on a variety of periodical publishers in the United States and Canada. The website—www.mediafinder.com—includes a free search feature as well as a fee-based service.

Starting and Running a Successful Newsletter or Magazine, 2nd Edition
Cheryl Woodard. Berkeley, CA: Nolo Press, 1998.

If you are interested in creating your own newsletter or magazine, this book will answer any questions you may have. Written by the co-founder of several successful magazines, it covers all aspects of the business, including finding funding, increasing sales and ad revenue, attracting topnotch talent, and more.

Ulrich's International Periodicals Directory
New Providence, NJ: R.R. Bowker, updated annually.

Published in five volumes, with a web update option, *Ulrich's* includes nearly 250,000 entries. Each edition contains contact information for publishers from 200 countries; information about online serials and CD-ROM serials; listings for 7,000 United States newspapers and 4,000 non-US papers, and more. Split into different media categories, *Ulrich's* information is comprehensive, but, unfortunately, is not always up-to-date. Therefore, be sure to check the contact information by other means when possible before sending out queries and submissions. The website, www.ulrichsweb.com, offers a fee-based search and indexing service.

The Writer's Handbook
Sylvia K. Burack, editor. Boston: The Writer, Inc., updated annually.

This book provides a number of media information listings as well as hundreds of pages of essays on writing in general. Although heavier on essays than on market information, *The Writer's Handbook* does provide a basic overview of each covered publication. Each entry contains the publisher's address and phone number, the editor's name and title, the type of market covered, the type of material bought from freelancers, and submission requests and payment guidelines. In the back is information on a wide variety of contests, organizations, art councils, awards, and conferences. Although the handbook provides a section on small markets, such as greeting cards, the majority of the book is dedicated to magazines.

Writer's Market

Kirsten C. Holm, editor. Cincinnati: Writer's Digest Books, updated annually.

The most thorough resource book available on this subject, *Writer's Market* contains hundreds of publication tips, essays on writing, and nearly 1,000 pages of information on publications open to freelanced material. Each market entry presents information on the publication's policy of working with freelancers, fees, and the sections open to freelanced material; complete contact information; a description of the material published; and details such as circulation, basic submission guidelines, and needs of the publication. The back includes information on additional resources, contests, awards, and other writing opportunities. The Internet Edition offers up-to-the-minute information and a searchable database. This book is invaluable to any writer who wants to publish in commercial, trade, technical, or professional outlets.

PERIODICALS

ByLine

PO Box 130596
Edmond, OK 73013-0001
Phone: 405–348–5591
Website: www.bylinemag.com

Devoted to the beginner, *ByLine* magazine offers monthly how-to articles on both the craft and business of writing in different genres. In addition, the magazine publishes short stories, poetry, personal essays, and other short works by novice and student writers, providing those new to the industry with an opportunity to see their work in print.

Editor & Publisher

770 Broadway
New York, NY 10003-9595
Phone: 888–313–5530 (subscriber services)
646–654–5270 (editorial office)
Website: www.editorandpublisher.com

Although not designed specifically for writers, this is the best magazine on the North American newspaper industry. *Editor & Publisher* can be invaluable for any writer interested in learning about publishing trends and gaining a better understanding of editors.

Poets & Writers

72 Spring Street
New York, NY 10012
Phone: 212–226–3586
Website: www.pw.org

Although this monthly magazine focuses mostly on creative writing, it does present a great deal of information on the craft that will help all writers. Plus, you'll learn about research, news, and trends in the industry; get updates on grants and conferences; and find interviews with top writers.

The Writer

Kalmbach Publishing Company
PO Box 1612
Waukesha, WI 53187-1612
Phone: 800–446–5489
Website: www.writermag.com

This monthly magazine provides an overview of the craft, articles on writing, and market information. Although the emphasis is on literary writing, all genres are discussed, and extensive contest and grant information is provided in every issue.

Writer's Digest

PO Box 2123
Harlan, IA 51593
Phone: 800–333–0133
Website: www.writersdigest.com

This monthly magazine, which addresses beginner and intermediate writers, presents information on every conceivable genre, market updates, and a wide variety of tips and contests. Overall, it is the most complete of the magazines on the market. Published by the same house that puts out *Writer's Market*, *Writer's Digest* includes monthly updates of the resource guide in its pages.

Writer's Journal

Val-Tech Media
PO Box 394
Perham, MN 56573-0394
Website: www.writersjournal.com

Published monthly, *Writer's Journal* offers an opportunity for writers to showcase their work by entering contests. Winning articles are published in each issue. In addition, *Writer's Journal* offers market-specific information and writing tips, as well as interviews with authors.

INTERNET SITES

Ask Jeeves

Website: www.ask.com

Somewhat like a search engine, Ask Jeeves provides information in the form of links and sources in response to any question that is typed into the search box.

Bartleby.com

Website: www.bartleby.com

This fabulous site enables you to use online reference books. Type in a word and find a dictionary, encyclopedia, or links to both *Bartlett's Familiar Quotations* and *Simpson's Contemporary Quotations*. Plus, an extensive section with links to classic reference manuals answers your questions on usage.

Contentious

Website: www.contentious.com

An e-zine for anyone who provides content online, Contentious offers tips and articles on issues such as the differences between online and offline writing, the types of work available online, and new editing rules brought to light by this new medium.

Dictionary.com

Website: www.dictionary.com

If you have a quick spelling, definition, or grammar question, this site probably has the answer. Offering writing resources such as grammar guides, dictionaries in several languages, a language discussion forum, a language translator, and a quick search option for both dictionary and thesaurus questions, Dictionary.com is a one-stop shop for all your language needs.

FedStats

Website: www.fedstats.gov

For anyone working on a project that requires statistical backup, this site is the place to go. FedStats offers statistics from over a hundred United States agencies, searchable by topic or agency, and broken into additional groups such as states.

Freelance Online

Website: www.freelanceonline.com

Calling itself "a directory of and resource center for freelancers in the field of communications," this site features a collection of resources targeted toward new writers, an "Open Forum" bulletin board where new or experienced writers can post questions and participate in discussions, and a directory of members.

Freelance Writing

Website: www.freelancewriting.com

Freelance Writing offers a comprehensive collection of writing links, articles, and newsletters, as well as a discussion forum, job bank, and directory of freelance writers. The site also contains a "fun room" that presents ways to combat writer's block, software demos, and a book raffle.

FreelanceSuccess.com

Website: www.freelancesuccess.com

This website offers numerous links, articles, and market resources specifically for freelance writers. FreelanceSuccess has a paid subscription newsletter and hosts online classes on a variety of topics directed to professional writers.

Glossary of Literary Terms and Handbook of Rhetorical Devices

Website: www.uky.edu/ArtsSciences/Classics/
    Harris/rhetform.html

A searchable listing of literary terms as well as a handbook of rhetorical devices, this site can be used as both a reference and a learning tool. The site even includes a challenging Self Test.

Guide to Grammar and Writing

Website: http://webster.commnet.edu/grammar/

This is an easy-to-navigate, thorough guide to aspects of grammar from sentence level to composition level. The site is searchable, with grammar quizzes and an "Ask Grammar" feature, and also provides links to other resources.

Ideal Online Library

Website: www.idealibrary.com

Ideal is a collection of electronic academic journals, reference works, and databases from various publishers, searchable by journal title or subject. Information is provided on a pay-per-view basis to individuals. Groups and institutions, including public libraries, can purchase access to certain journals.

Inscriptions

Website: www.inscriptionsmagazine.com

This subscription-based weekly e-zine features how-to articles; interviews with writers and editors; and listings of job opportunities and contests. Visitors to the site can view back issues of the publication by using the site's search function.

International Online Writers Association (IOWA)

Website: www.project-iowa.org

This nonprofit online writer's organization offers monthly real-time online workshops using Internet Relay Chat, weekly real-time online critiques for writers needing assistance with a specific project or aspect of writing, unscheduled "round robins" in chat rooms and on the website, and access to an online resource library. Membership in IOWA is free.

Internet News Bureau

Website: www.newsbureau.com

Designed for businesses and journalists, Internet News Bureau (INB) offers morning e-mails of relevant press releases to anyone who signs up for the service. Much like PR Web, INB provides writers with story leads and informs them of experts in a given field.

The Invisible Web

Website: www.invisibleweb.com

This directory of databases, archives, and search engines is unique in that it provides a more targeted, accurate search than most traditional search engines.

The IRS Small Business Corner

Website: www.irs.ustreas.gov/prod/bus_info/
    sm_bus/pre-start.html

This IRS site provides answers to questions about starting a small business. Necessary paperwork, forms, and tax requirements are all covered in a comprehensive, easy-to-understand format. The information can be helpful to a freelancer working from home, or to a writer looking for quick explanations of business terms and processes.

iVillage.com

Website: www.ivillage.com

This website features a number of wonderful boards in the Readers and Writers section dedicated to helping writers develop, write, and sell their work. There is a Writing Articles board, as well as others devoted to different genres.

Klocke Publishing Presents

Website: www.klockepresents.com

This site is a hub for a number of more specialized sites. The main site provides how-to articles on the craft and business of writing; links to the publisher's more specialized sites, such as The Writing Parent and The Writing Child; and links to a variety of other writing-related sites.

Laughing Bear

Website: www.laughingbear.com

This site provides information on starting and operating a small newspaper or literary magazine, and includes links to further resources. Laughing Bear also publishes a monthly newsletter.

LibWeb

Website: sunsite.berkeley.edu/Libweb/

This searchable database provides links to over 6,100 libraries worldwide, giving you access to a range of information and services.

Markets for Writers

Website: www.marketsforwriters.com

From the authors of *Online Markets for Writers*, Markets for Writers is a free resource for those interested in publishing online. The site offers information on hundreds of online publishers, including writers' guidelines, pay, and policies, as well as information on contracts, query letters, and adapting print work to fit the Internet marketplace.

National Academy Press

Website: www.nap.edu

This useful resource for science, technology, and health writers allows visitors to search by keyword or gain access to a selection of National Academy Press publications, all of which are available to read online, free of charge.

News Bytes

Website: www.newsbytes.com

Run by *The Washington Post*, News Bytes offers a rundown of headlines from across the globe, particularly business, technology, and political news. The site also offers press releases; a newsletter sign-up option; and "My Bytes," a service that provides updates of current happenings.

Newsletter Access

Website: www.newsletteraccess.com

This website provides a searchable directory of over 5,000 newsletters. If you are looking for specialized information on a given topic or for experts in that field, this index will help you locate the information you need.

Newswise

Website: www.newswise.com

Newswise maintains a comprehensive database of news releases from institutions engaged in scientific, medical, liberal arts, and business research. You can search, browse, or download any article or abstract, and you can locate experts to serve as interview subjects.

Old Farmer's Almanac

Website: www.almanac.com

Old Farmer's Almanac provides basic information on weather, gardening, cooking, and astrology, as well as household tips and other "down home" information. This is a great resource for sidebar material and interesting facts that can be sprinkled throughout an article.

PBS You

Website: www.pbsyou.org

PBS You is a lifelong learning program offered by the same people who produce shows such as *Sesame Street.* The site offers listings of educational programming available to adults, with scheduling information. PBS You also offers telecourses on writing and various topics of interest to writers, and provides help in honing writing skills and finding topic ideas.

Pitsco's Ask an Expert

Website: www.askanexpert.com

Like ProfNet Global, this site provides links and contact information for people seeking experts on any given topic. Ask an Expert is a more commercial, family-oriented site, though, offering help to anyone with a question they'd like answered.

PR Web

Website: www.prweb.com

This site offers recent press releases organized by industry. PR Web can locate current and upcoming events in a specific area of interest, and can also guide you to professionals or experts in a given field.

ProfNet Global

Website: www.profnet.com/reporters.html

A service of PR Newswire, ProfNet provides writers with access to expert sources. You can e-mail the staff with information on the type of expert you are seeking, or search through the site's database to locate an expert on your own. You can also subscribe to weekly tip sheets that provide news leads from experts in the field.

Pub List

Website: www.publist.com

Pub List offers links to and information on thousands of academic and commercial publications. It covers both national and international markets and offers a spotlight on one journal every time you visit the site.

Sharp Writer

Website: www.sharpwriter.com

This site is a comprehensive, easily searched collection of websites, books, and other resources on every aspect of writing from grammar to writer's block. Sharp Writer also provides its own online magazine, *The Informed Opinion,* with articles on different writers' issues and concerns.

ShawGuides, Inc: The Guide to Writers Conferences and Workshops

Website: www.writing.shawguides.com

This easy-to-use guide can help you find writers' conferences, workshops, seminars, and retreats that meet your personal and professional needs. Type in either your area of interest or the desired location, and ShawGuides will provide you with a list of upcoming activities and events.

Topica

Website: www.topica.com

Topica provides members with access to thousands of newsletters and discussion groups, allowing you to locate and communicate with others in the writing world and to find information of relevance to your work.

UniGuide Academic Guide to the Internet

Website: www.aldea.com/guides/ag/ attframes2.html

A resource created for the research and academic community, UniGuide provides listings of academic and educational sites in a variety of fields. Each site featured on UniGuide has been approved by a group of content experts to ensure educational value. Members of the site are encouraged to participate by commenting on the site offerings provided.

University of Alberta Guide to Proper Internet Citation

Website: www.library.ualberta.ca/guides/
  citation/index.cfm

This site provides guidelines for citing Internet and other electronic sources in the APA style, as well as links to other style guidelines.

Web Wire

Website: www.webwire.com

Web Wire provides free press releases, a means by which the media can request resources, and a free home page option that displays recent releases of interest to the Web Wire member. Use this site to learn about current events and trends in a given industry, and to locate resources for your work.

Wooden Horse Publishing

Website: www.woodenhorsepub.com

Created to assist writers in marketing and selling their work, Wooden Horse provides up-to-date information on the hot places where working non-fiction writers can submit work or queries, offers tips, and suggests proven learning tools.

Write Tools

Website: www.writetools.com

Write Tools is a compilation of links to sites, databases, and tools that can serve every imaginable need of the writer, editor, or fact checker.

Writer and Market

Website: writerandmarket.searchking.com

A database with well over 1,300 writing-related links, Writer and Market can help you locate magazines, e-zines, newspapers, workshops, reference sites, and more. Whether you want to get published, find an agent, or explore the option of self-publishing, this is the place to start your search.

Writer's Market

Website: www.writersmarket.com

Subscribers to the Writer's Market website are pro-

vided with the same listings of commercial and trade magazines, book publishers and agents, greeting-card markets, and script-writing markets as those who purchase the book. The site offers the added ease of a search function, the ability to bookmark markets for later review, personalized markets based on a subscriber's profile, and a wealth of market tips.

Writer's Resource Center

Website: www.poewar.com

Created to serve the needs of writers on the Internet, the Writer's Resource Center provides links to valuable sites, articles, and book reviews that are useful to freelancers. A job listing section is also included.

Writer's Toolbox

Website: www.writerstoolbox.com

Writer's Toolbox offers a collection of links to various online resources for writers of all genres. It also includes articles on the craft of writing, a bulletin board for posting questions, a chat room, and a mailing list.

Writers Write

Website: www.writerswrite.com

Writers Write was designed to provide aspiring writers with a comprehensive collection of information on online publishing. The site features a searchable database of online publishers, lists of conferences and workshops, job listings, and a message board and chat community where writers can ask questions and network.

YahooGroups

Website: www.yahoogroups.com

Like the Topica website, YahooGroups provides a database of online mailing lists on a variety of interests. Several groups are available for just about every writing genre. In addition, general interest groups can help writers locate information on topics of interest.

INDEX

All writers dream of seeing their books in print. While some succeed, the fact is that most don't. Why? Most writers simply don't know what publishers are looking for. Or they didn't—until now. Written by a publisher with over twenty-five years of experience, this book helps you avoid the common pitfalls that foil most writers, and maximize your chance of getting your nonfiction book into publication.

This book begins by helping you define your book's category, audience, and marketplace so that you know exactly where your book "fits in." Following this, you will be guided in choosing the best publishing companies for your book, and crafting a winning submissions package. Then the Square One System will tell you exactly how to submit your package so that you optimize success, while minimizing time, cost, and effort. A special section on contracts will turn legal mumbo-jumbo into plain English, allowing you to be a savvy player in the contract game. Most important, this book will help you avoid the errors that so often prevent writers from reaching their goal.

$16.95 • 252 pages • 7.5 x 9-inch quality paperback • 2-color • Reference/Writing • ISBN 0-7570-0000-2

Perhaps you began writing poetry as a means of private expression. Or maybe your verse was meant to share your feelings with that special someone. But now those goals have changed, and you want to get your poetry into print.

Written for the poet who wishes to enjoy greater success in the world of publishing, this book is a complete guide to breaking into the world of print poetry. The book begins by providing a window to the publishing world so that you can see the kinds of publications you should target. You will learn about great market resources for locating appropriate publishers, and you will learn the importance of defining your audience. Following this, the author helps you write a persuasive submissions package, and presents a proven step-by-step system for sending your package out—a system designed to maximize results. When the acceptance letters start rolling in, the author helps you select the publications that will allow you to meet your personal goals. You will even learn of the resources that can help you further develop your special gift.

$14.95 • 192 pages • 7.5 x 9-inch quality paperback • 2-color • Reference/Writing • ISBN 0-7570-0001-0

In today's topsy-turvy world of film production, getting a screenplay sold and produced is no easy task. To play the film game, you need to know the rules. *How to Sell Your Screenplay* not only lets you in on the rules, but also lets you in on the secrets of winning the game.

Written by two veteran screenwriters, *How to Sell Your Screenplay* was designed as a complete guide to getting your screenplay seen, read, and sold. The book begins by giving you an insider's understanding of how the business works. It then guides you in putting your script into the proper format so that you can make a professional first impression. Later chapters introduce you to the roles of the industry "players," including agents, lawyers, producers, and more; guide you in preparing a perfect pitch; provide you with the proven Square One System for query submission; and aid you in making the best deal possible. Throughout, tips from experts will show you how to swim with the sharks without getting eaten by them.

$17.95 • 320 pages • 7.5 x 9-inch quality paperback • 2-color • Reference/Writing • ISBN 0-7570-0002-9

For more information about our books, visit our website at www.squareonepublishers.com.